BLACK L

Bankruptcy & Related Law

Including BAPCPA

Steve H. Nickles
David G. Epstein

SECOND EDITION

THOMSON
✦
WEST

Bankruptcy
and Related Law:
Including BAPCPA

BLACK LETTER OUTLINES

Bankruptcy and Related Law:
Including BAPCPA

by Steve H. Nickles

C.C. Hope Chair in Law and Management
Wake Forest University Law School and
Babcock Graduate School of Management

David G. Epstein

Professor of Law
Dedman School of Law, Southern Methodist University

SECOND EDITION

THOMSON
—★—™
WEST

Mat #11573169

COPYRIGHT © 1989 WEST PUBLISHING CO.
© 2006 Thomson/West
   610 Opperman Drive
   P.O. Box 64526
   St. Paul, MN 55164–0526
   800–328–9352

ISBN–13: 978–0–314–06579–7
ISBN–10: 0–314–06579–2

 PRINTED ON 10% POST CONSUMER RECYCLED PAPER

Preface

This "Black Letter" is designed to help a law student recognize and understand the basic principles and issues of law covered in a law school course. It can be used both as a study aid when preparing for classes and as a review of the subject matter when studying for an examination.

Each "Black Letter" is written by experienced law school teachers who are recognized national authorities on the subject covered.

The law is succinctly stated by the authors of this "Black Letter." In addition, the exceptions to the rules are stated in the text. The rules and exceptions have purposely been condensed to facilitate quick and easy recollection. For an in-depth study of a point of law, citations to major student texts are given.

If the subject covered by this text is a code or code-related course, the code section or rule is set forth and discussed wherever applicable.

FORMAT

The format of this "Black Letter" is specially designed for review. (1) **Text.** First, it is recommended that the entire text be studied and, if deemed necessary, supplemented by the student texts cited. (2) **Capsule Summary.** The Capsule Summary is an abbreviated review of the subject matter which can be used both before and after studying the main body of the text. The headings in the Capsule Summary follow the main text of the "Black Letter." (3) **Table of Contents.** The Table of Contents is in outline form to help you organize the details of the subject and the Summary of Contents gives you a final overview of the materials. (4) **Practice Examination.** The Practice Examination in Appendix B gives you the opportunity to test yourself with the type of questions asked on an exam and compare your answer with a model answer.

In addition, a number of other features are included to help you understand the subject matter and prepare for examinations:

Perspective: In this feature, the authors discuss their approach to the topic, the approach used in preparing the materials, and any tips on studying for and writing examinations.

Analysis: This feature, at the beginning of each section, is designed to give a quick summary of a particular section to help you recall the subject matter and to help you determine which areas need the most extensive review.

Examples: This feature is designed to illustrate, through fact situations, the law just stated. This, we believe, should help you analytically approach a question on the examination.

Glossary: This feature is designed to refamiliarize you with the meaning of a particular legal term. We believe that the recognition of words of art used in an examination helps you to better analyze the question. In addition, when writing an examination you should know the precise definition of a word of art you intend to use.

We believe that the materials in this "Black Letter" will facilitate your study of a law school course and assure success in writing examinations not only for the course but for the bar examination. We wish you success.

THE PUBLISHER

Summary of Contents

■ I.   EXTRA JUDICIAL COLLECTION DEVICES

■ II.   JUDICIAL DEBT COLLECTION

■ V.   DEBTOR'S STATE LAW REMEDIES A/K/A COLLECTIVE CREDITOR ACTION

■ VIII.   STAY OF COLLECTION ACTIONS AND ACTS

■ IX.   PROPERTY OF THE ESTATE

■ XII.   POSTPETITION TRANSFERS

■ XV.   LEASES AND EXECUTORY CONTRACTS

■ XVI.   DISCHARGE

■ XVII.   CHAPTER 13 CASES

■ XVIII.   CHAPTER 11 CASES

■ XIX.   ALLOCATION OF JUDICIAL POWER OVER BANKRUPTCY MATTERS

APPENDICES

*

Table of Contents

■ V. DEBTOR'S STATE LAW REMEDIES A/K/A COLLECTIVE CREDITOR ACTION

■ VIII. STAY OF COLLECTION ACTIONS AND ACTS

■ X

EXEMPTIONS:

■ XI. AVOIDANCE OF PREBANKRUPTCY TRANSFERS

■ XII. POSTPETITION TRANSFERS

■ XIII. EFFECT OF BANKRUPTCY ON SECURED CLAIMS

◼ XIV

CLAIMS:

■ XVI

DISCHARGE:

■ XVII. CHAPTER 13 CASES

■ XVIII. CHAPTER 11 CASES

■ XIX. ALLOCATION OF JUDICIAL POWER OVER BANKRUPTCY MATTERS

APPENDICES

Capsule Summary

■ I. EXTRAJUDICIAL COLLECTION DEVICES

As long as the debtor is making payments when due, debtor-creditor law is of little practical significance. The debtor, of course, does not always make the required payments. Because of the delay and expense involved in litigation, the creditor is likely initially to employ extrajudicial tactics to obtain payment.

A. COMMON LAW THEORIES AND LIMITATIONS

Courts have sought to moderate the conduct of creditors by allowing debtors to recover for unreasonable collection activities under the following common law tort concepts: defamation, invasion of the right to privacy, and intentional infliction of mental anguish. Recoveries on these theories, however, are relatively rare. It is difficult to match the usual facts of debt collection with the elements of these torts.

B. FEDERAL FAIR DEBT COLLECTION RACTICES ACT (FDCPA)

A number of states statutorily regulate the collection of consumer debts. Congress has enacted the Fair Debt Collection Practices Act (FDCPA). The FDCPA only applies to the efforts of "debt collectors" to collect "consumer debts."

■ II. JUDICIAL DEBT COLLECTION

Ordinarily, the state will not get involved in forcefully taking a debtor's property until the creditor gets a judgment. It is through this process of the creditor reducing its claim to judgment that the state determines the validity and the amount of the debt. After judgment, the state in essence aligns itself with the creditor and takes the debtor's property—forcibly if necessary—and sells it to satisfy the creditor's judgment.

A. EXEMPT PROPERTY

"Exempt property" is important if, and only if, the debtor is an individual (i.e., a natural person). Today, all states constitutionally or statutorily restrict creditor recourse to certain property belonging to individuals.

1. PERSONAL PROPERTY

All states exempt certain personal property from creditor process.

2. REAL PROPERTY

Almost all states also have exemption laws designed to protect the family home, i.e., the "homestead," from the reach of certain classes of creditors.

3. PROCEDURE

The procedure for asserting rights under an exemption statute usually requires the debtor timely to assert exemptions.

4. LIMITS ON EXEMPTIONS

Exemptions are mainly limited to protecting a debtor's property against attachment, garnishment, judgment liens, and execution.

5. FEDERAL COURT

Creditors' process issued from a federal court generally is subject to exemptions provided by the law of the state where the court sits.

6. FEDERAL LAW

a. Federal Exemptions

There are also federal statutes that exempt property from the reach of creditors in either federal court or state court.

b. Restrictions on Garnishment

Title III of the Consumer Credit Protection Act provides a statutory minimum exemption of wages from garnishments.

B. PREJUDGMENT REMEDIES

In *very limited* circumstances, the state will impound property of the debtor during the pendency of the lawsuit.

1. ATTACHMENT

a. Origin and Purpose

Today, the writ of attachment seizes the debtor's property in order to secure the debt or claim of the creditor in the event that a judgment is obtained.

b. Limits on Attachment

Attachment is *not* available to every creditor in every collection action. Rather, the use of attachment is generally limited in several ways:

1) Kind of Action

2) Grounds Necessary

3) Bond Required

4) Due Process

c. Procedure for Attachment

In most states, a creditor seeking attachment must first file a complaint. The creditor then files an affidavit stating facts establishing the ground for attachment and posts any necessary bond. The writ of attachment is directed to the sheriff of a county in which property of the defendant is located.

d. Levy

The act of the sheriff in taking custody over the property of the defendant is commonly referred to as "levy".

e. Advantages of Attachment

A creditor with an attachment lien enjoys a number of advantages: (1) security; (2) priority; (3) jurisdiction; and (4) leverage.

f. Hazards of Attachment

There are at least three distinct hazards associated with attachment: (1) fees; (2) liability for wrongful attachment; and (3) bankruptcy of the debtor.

g. Terminating an Attachment

Failure to obtain a judgment will result in the attachment being dissolved. A debtor may also terminate the attachment and obtain the attached property by posting a "discharging" or "dissolution" bond or a "forthcoming" or "delivery" bond.

2. PREJUDGMENT GARNISHMENT

Garnishment (or, in most New England states, trustee process) is a collection remedy directed not at the defendant but rather at some third person, the garnishee, who owes a debt to the principal debtor, has property of the principal debtor, or has property in which the principal debtor has an interest.

3. REPLEVIN

Replevin (and "sequestration" and "claim and delivery") are proceedings to recover possession of any personal property and can only be maintained by one who has some property interest in and the immediate right to possession of the property sought to be recovered.

4. RECEIVERSHIP

A prejudgment receiver is a disinterested party, appointed by the court to administer, care for, collect and dispose of the property or the fruits of the property of another brought under the orders of the court by litigation. Reported cases in which a receiver has been appointed generally involve allegations of danger of loss, deterioration, or other impairment of the value of property that is the subject matter of the action or that will be necessary to satisfy any judgment in the action.

5. CONSTITUTIONAL DUE PROCESS LIMITATIONS ON PREJUDGMENT REMEDIES

While the relationship between the various cases is somewhat unclear, the following basic propositions seem clear from the major United States Supreme Court cases: Basically, prejudgment remedies are not unconstitutional per se; the use of prejudgment remedies is subject to due process limitations; due process requires notice and an opportunity for an adversary proceeding; and, in at least some, emergency-like situations, a pre-seizure ex parte hearing coupled with the opportunity for a prompt post seizure adversary proceeding will satisfy due process.

C. OBTAINING A JUDGMENT

Most collection actions result in a default judgment for the creditor.

D. POSTJUDGMENT COLLECTION CONCERNS

1. JUDGMENT LIENS

Rendition or docketing of a judgment operates as a general lien on all of the debtor's interests in real property located within the county or other jurisdiction of the court.

2. EXECUTION

Execution is the process whereby a judgment creditor can have the judgment debtor's property seized and sold in satisfaction of the judgment. In most states a writ of execution can reach both personalty and realty. The property seized pursuant to a writ of execution is to be sold by the sheriff to satisfy the creditor's judgment.

3. CHART COMPARING POST JUDGMENT ON THE DEBTOR'S REAL PROPERTY WITH POSTJUDGMENT LIENS ON THE DEBTOR'S PERSONAL PROPERTY

4. CREDITOR'S BILL

At early common law, the Court of Chancery developed an equitable counterpart to execution—the creditor's bill (sometimes referred to as creditor's suit). A creditor unable to satisfy its judgment completely through execution could file a bill in the Court of Chancery asking that court to compel the debtor to turn over his assets to be sold to satisfy the creditor's judgment.

5. SUPPLEMENTARY PROCEEDINGS

A supplementary proceeding is a summary, in personam action, administered by the court in which the judgment was obtained and governed by the provisions of the applicable state law. Most supplementary proceedings statutes provide for (1) discovery of assets through the right of examination of the debtor and others; (2) issuance of injunctions to prevent disposition of property; (3) discretionary power to appoint receivers; and (4) orders for the sale of property.

6. EXECUTION SALES

Property on which the sheriff levies execution is usually not turned over to the judgment creditor in satisfaction of its claim. Rather, the sheriff sells the property and, after paying the costs of the sale, gives the net proceeds to the creditor. Any surplus ordinarily goes to the debtor.

7. GARNISHMENT

Execution to enforce a judgment reaches only property that the debtor possesses and controls. To reach property of a debtor held by a third party (e.g., *D*'s bank account at *G* Bank) or to collect money owed to the debtor (e.g., *D*'s wages owed by her employer *G*), a creditor uses a post-judgment form of garnishment.

■ III. FRAUDULENT TRANSFERS

A. WHAT IS FRAUDULENT TRANSFER LAW?

1. STATUTE OF 13 ELIZABETH

The basis of the modern law of fraudulent conveyances is the Statute of 13 Elizabeth, enacted in 1570.

2. "BADGES OF FRAUD"

a. Early Common Law: *Twyne's Case*

The Statute of Elizabeth requires "intent to delay, hinder or defraud." Since proof of a particular intent is a difficult task, courts soon developed "badges of fraud," i.e., circumstances indicative of intent to defraud. The first such case was *Twyne's Case* (1601).

b. Acceptance by the States

In virtually every American jurisdiction, the Statute of 13 Elizabeth has been either recognized as part of the inherited common law or expressly adopted or enacted in more or less similar terms. The concept of "badges of fraud" has also been generally adopted, although what constitutes a "badge of fraud" varies from jurisdiction to jurisdiction.

c. Preference Is Not a Badge of Fraud

Preferring one creditor over others is generally *not* a badge of fraud.

3. MODERN UNIFORM LAWS

They are the Uniform Fraudulent Conveyance Act (UFCA) and the newer Uniform Fraudulent Transfer Act (UFTA). They are basically the same but have some important differences. Most states' laws include one or the other.

B. WHICH TRANSFERS ARE FRAUDULENT TRANSFERS?

1. ACTUAL FRAUD

The UFTA, like the Statute of Elizabeth and the UFCA, reaches transfers made with "an actual intent to hinder, delay or defraud any creditor of the debtor."

2. CONSTRUCTIVE FRAUD

More important, the UFTA, like the UFCA, reaches some transfers in which the debtor was completely free from fraudulent intent: transfers of the property of an insolvent or financially troubled debtor for which the debtor receives less than "reasonably equivalent value," section 5(a).

3. FRAUDULENT OBLIGATIONS ARE ALSO COVERED

Although the statute is entitled the Uniform Fraudulent *Transfer* Act, it applies also to obligations.

C. WHAT ARE THE CONSEQUENCES OF DETERMINING THAT A TRANSACTION IS A FRAUDULENT TRANSFER?

1. WHO HAS A REMEDY?

The UFTA confers remedies only on some creditors.

2. WHAT ARE THE REMEDIES?

a. Getting the Property That was Transferred by Voiding the Transfer

b. Getting Money Instead

3. AGAINST WHOM CAN A RECOVERY BE HAD?

As attorney for *C*, a creditor as to whom a transaction is a UFTA fraudulent transfer, you can look for recovery from *T*, the "transferee" of the fraudulent transfer or any subsequent transferee.

D. LOOKING BACK: FRAUDULENT TRANSFER AND GARNISHMENT

Garnishment law is important to a creditor when a third party owes money to the creditor's debtor or has property that belongs to the creditor's debtor. Fraudulent transfer law is important to a creditor when property that once belonged to the creditor's debtor now belongs to some third party.

E. LOOKING AHEAD: FRAUDULENT TRANSFER LAW AND BANKRUPTCY

Two separate provisions of the Bankruptcy Code, section 544(b) and section 548, empower the bankruptcy trustee to avoid a transaction entered into before the bankruptcy if the transaction is a fraudulent transfer.

■ IV. CREDITORS WITH SPECIAL RIGHTS

A. CONSENSUAL LIENS

1. ARTICLE 9 SECURITY INTERESTS

Consensual liens on personal property are governed by Article 9 of the Uniform Commercial Code.

a. Terminology of Article 9

Article 9 has a language all its own that can best be explained by example.

1) Creation and Attachment

The creation of a security interest requires a security agreement. It is also necessary that the secured party give value and that the debtor then have—or later acquire—rights in the collateral.

2) Perfection

To achieve maximum possible priority, it is necessary for the secured party to "perfect" its security interest.

3) Filing

Where filing is required to perfect, the document filed is called a "financing statement." It need contain only the names and addresses of the parties and indicate the collateral covered, section 9–502.

b. Organization of Article 9

Article 9 of the Code is divided into seven parts. Parts 1 through 5 are ordinarily covered in detail in courses in commercial law. Part 7 deals with the transition from the "old" Article 9 to the Revised Article 9. Part 6 deals with default and the rights of the debtor and creditor in default. Only Part 6 will be discussed at any length in this book.

c. Section 9–317

There is, however, one section in Part 3 of Article 9 that merits consideration in a debtor-creditor law primer. Section 9–317 provides that an unperfected security interest is "subordinate" to a judicial lien on the same property.

d. Part 6 of Article 9

The application of Part 6 of the Uniform Commercial Code is conditioned on default by the debtor.

1) Meaning of Default

The term "default" is not specifically defined in the Code. The circumstances which constitute default are a matter of agreement between the parties.

2) Rights Upon Default

When the debtor is in default, Part 6 of Article 9 gives the secured party the following general choices: (1) ignore its security interest, obtain a judgment on the debt, and proceed by execution and levy and execution sale; (2) when the collateral consists of rights to payment owed to the debtor by some third party such as accounts, collect the amounts due from that third party, i.e., the account debtor; and (3) repossess the collateral and either keep it in full satisfaction of the debt or resell it and apply the sales proceeds to reduce the debt.

2. MORTGAGES

There is no single uniform law governing real property security, and the rights of a mortgagee on default of the mortgagor vary considerably from state to state. The important rights are: redemption; strict foreclosure; and sale (judicial or pursuant to a power of sale).

B. LIENS BY OPERATION OF LAW

1. COMMON LAW LIENS

Some creditors are given additional rights by operation of law. Common law grants to certain creditors a possessory lien on property of their debtors. A common law possessory lien is the right to retain the property of another for some particular claim or charge upon the property so detained. For example:

1. Common law from very early times gave the innkeeper a lien on the goods of the guest brought by him into the inn.

2. Similarly, a common carrier has a lien for freight charges on all goods delivered by it.

3. And an artisan who, at the request of the owner, performs services on a chattel has a common law possessory lien on such chattels.

2. EQUITABLE LIENS

Equitable liens are based on one of two equitable maxims. First, as equity looks upon as done that which is agreed or intended to be done, an agreement that evidences an intention to create a consensual lien but fails to do so, creates an equitable lien. Second, equity regards as done that which ought to be done and so creates equitable liens to avoid unjust enrichment.

C. STATE STATUTORY LIENS

Other sources of additional rights for certain creditors are state and federal statutes. Legislation has enlarged many of the liens recognized at common law and many of those asserted in equity.

D. FEDERAL CLAIMS

The largest creditors are, of course, the various governmental entities. A governmental creditor may be either a general creditor or a lien creditor. When its claim is secured, the government has all the rights of a secured creditor; when its claim is not secured, it has all the rights of a general creditor.

Additionally, a number of states statutorily prefer governmental claims against delinquent debtors to those of private creditors. The federal government's claims are given preference over claims of other creditors primarily by two statutory provisions: the federal priority provision, 31 USCA § 3713, more commonly referred to by its Revised Statute designation, RS 3466; and the Federal Tax Lien Act, 26 USCA §§ 6321-23.

1. FEDERAL PRIORITY PROVISION

Section 3466 applies to every kind of debt owing to the federal government: tax and nontax. The statute generally provides that a claim of the United States Government shall be paid first when a person indebted to the Government is insolvent. The statute does not apply, however, in a bankruptcy case.

2. FEDERAL TAX LIEN

Sections 6320 to 6344 of the Internal Revenue Code (title 26) provide for the creation and enforcement of a tax lien.

a. When Does the Federal Tax Lien Arise?

Section 6321 sets out three requirements for the creation of a federal tax lien: (1) IRS' assessment of the tax liability; (2) IRS' demand for payment of this tax liability; and (3) the taxpayer's failure to pay.

b. What Property is Covered By a Federal Tax Lien?

Section 6321 describes the property covered by a federal tax lien: "All property and rights to property, whether real or personal, belonging to such person." "All" in this context truly means all.

c. How Can the Tax Lien Be Enforced?

The United States can enforce its federal tax lien by levying on (taking) and selling property of the taxpayer.

d. What Are the Rights of a Third Party Who Buys Property From the Taxpayer After the Tax Lien Arises?

The facts creating such a buyer versus IRS priority contest will fit into one of the three patterns:

√ The sale by the taxpayer occurred before creation of the tax lien, i.e. before tax assessment;

√ The sale by the taxpayer occurred after creation of the tax lien but before filing of the federal tax lien;

√ The sale by the taxpayer occurred after creation and filing of the federal tax lien.

e. What Are the Rights of the Taxpayer's Other Creditors?

A person who is not paying his federal taxes is probably not paying his nongovernmental creditors and probably lacks sufficient assets to pay all claims against him. Which claims have priority is determined by the doctrine of choateness and also by the federal statute that allows most creditors to win over an unfilled tax lien and allows some creditors to win even if the tax lien is filed.

3. CIRCUITY OF PRIORITY PROBLEMS

Both section 3466 and the federal tax lien, by imposing a second priority system on the state priority system, cause circuity of priority (circular priority) problems. The Supreme Court has adopted adopted a two-step analysis to resolve this dilemma. The federal law of priorities was first applied. An amount equal to the interests that take prior to the federal claim under federal law was set aside to be paid out first. State law was then used to divide the amount so set aside.

4. OTHER FEDERAL CLAIMS

Most people indebted to the federal government are not insolvent, and most claims of the federal government are not federal tax claims. Accordingly, most federal claims are governed by neither the federal priority provision nor the Federal Tax Lien Act. The controlling law is other federal law that may incorporate state law.

E. SETOFF

The "right of setoff" (also called "offset") allows entities that owe each other money to apply their mutual debts against each other, thereby avoiding the absurdity of making *A* pay *B* when *B* owes *A*. Citizens Bank of Maryland v. Strumpf (1995).

F. RECOUPMENT

In a setoff, the mutual debts can arise from different transactions. The doctrine of recoupment allowing netting debts that arise out of a single integrated transaction so that it would be inequitable for the debtor to enjoy the benefits of that transaction without also meeting its obligations.

■ V. DEBTOR'S STATE LAW REMEDIES A/K/A COLLECTIVE CREDITOR ACTION

A. ASSIGNMENTS FOR THE BENEFIT OF CREDITORS

An assignment for the benefit of creditors is the state law counterpart of bankruptcy law's Chapter 7. More specifically, an assignment for the benefit of creditors is a voluntary transfer of assets by the debtor to another person in trust to liquidate the assets and distribute the proceeds to the creditors of the debt-transferred.

B. WORKOUTS A/K/A COMPOSITION AND EXTENSION

Today, the term "workout" is used to describe a negotiated, nonbankruptcy modification of debts. A workout is the state law counterpart of bankruptcy law's Chapter 11. Legally, a workout is a contract. Indeed, you probably studied "workouts" in your first year contracts course except that your contracts teacher used the less "trendy" phrase compositions and extensions. An agreement can be both a composition and an extension: an agreement to take less over a longer period of time.

■ VI. BANKRUPTCY: AN OVERVIEW

A. DIFFERENCES BETWEEN BANKRUPTCY AND STATE LAW

Initially, four basic differences between bankruptcy and state debtor-creditor law should be noted.

1. First, bankruptcy law is federal law.

2. Second, bankruptcy compels collective creditor collection action and emphasizes equality of treatment, rather than a race of diligence.

3. Third, the prospects for debtor relief are much greater in bankruptcy.

4. Fourth, the vocabulary of bankruptcy law is different from the vocabulary of state collection law.

B. THE LAW OF BANKRUPTCY

Article I of the Constitution empowers Congress to "establish uniform laws on the subject of Bankruptcies throughout the United States." For most of the 20th century, bankruptcy law was the Bankruptcy Act of 1898, commonly referred to as the "Bankruptcy Act." It was replaced in 1978 by a law commonly referred to as the "Bankruptcy Reform Act of 1978" or "Bankruptcy Code." The Bankruptcy Code has been regularly amended; the most comprehensive bankruptcy amendments were enacted in 1984.

1. The Bankruptcy Code

The Bankruptcy Code is Title 11 of the United States Code.

2. Bankruptcy Rules of Procedure and Forms

It is also necessary to deal with the Bankruptcy Rules. Pursuant to the authority of 28 USCA § 2075, the United States Supreme Court promulgated Bankruptcy Rules.

3. Role of State Law

In large part, bankruptcy law, or the law applied in bankruptcy, is also state law because courts applying the federal bankruptcy law look to state law to determine questions such as (1) what are the property rights of the debtor and (2) what are the claims of the creditors to that property.

C. FORMS OF BANKRUPTCY RELIEF

There are two general forms of bankruptcy relief: (1) liquidation and (2) rehabilitation or reorganization. The Bankruptcy Code provides for these two petition under Chapter 7 or Chapter 11 automatically "stays," i.e., restrains, creditors from taking further action against the debtor, the property of the debtor, or the property of the estate to collect their claims or enforce their liens, section 362.

A. TIME STAY ARISES

The automatic stay is triggered by the filing of a bankruptcy petition. It dates from the time of the filing, not from the time that a creditor receives notice of or learns of the bankruptcy.

B. SCOPE OF THE STAY

1. SECTION 362

Paragraph (a) of section 362 defines the scope of the automatic stay by listing all of the acts and actions that are stayed by the commencement of a bankruptcy case. It is comprehensive and includes virtually all creditor collection activity against the debtor.

2. SECTION 1301

When a Chapter 13 case is filed, section 362 applies and also section 1301. By reason of section 1301, the filing of a Chapter 13 petition automatically stays collection action against guarantors and other co-debtors with respect to consumer debts.

3. SECTION 105

Section 105 grants to bankruptcy courts the power to issue orders "necessary or appropriate to carry out the provisions of this title." Courts have used this section 105 power to stay or restrain creditor action against third parties.

C. TERMINATION OF THE STAY

Paragraph (c) of section 362 describes two situations in which the automatic stay terminates automatically.

1. WITH RESPECT TO PARTICULAR PROPERTY

Section 362(c)(1) provides that the automatic stay ends as to particular property when the property ceases to be property of the estate.

2. OTHERWISE AND GENERALLY

Section 362(c)(2) provides that the automatic stay ends when the bankruptcy case is closed or dismissed or the debtor receives a discharge.

3. FREQUENT FILINGS

The stay is sometimes automatically terminated because the debtor has earlier filed another bankruptcy case.

D. RELIEF FROM THE STAY

A bankruptcy court may grant relief from the automatic stay on request of a "party in interest," section 362(d). The relief will not always take the form of termination of the stay. Section 362(d) provides for "relief" "such as by terminating, annulling, modifying, or conditioning such stay." The Rules provide that the "request" in section 362 takes the form of a motion, Rules 4001(a), 9014. The facts of the reported cases make clear that the "party in interest" in section 362 is usually a creditor, usually a secured creditor.

What does a creditor have to allege in its motion and establish in its proof in order to obtain relief from the stay? The grounds for relief from stay are set out in section 362(d).

1. SECTION 362(d)(1)

The most general statutory ground for relief from the stay is "for cause," section 362(d)(1).

2. SECTION 362(d)(2)

Under section 362(d)(2) a lien creditor can obtain relief from the stay if the debtor does not have any equity in the encumbered property, AND the encumbered property is not necessary to an effective reorganization.

3. SECTION 362(d)(3)

Section 362(d)(3) is available only to a creditor with a lien on "single asset real estate," a phrase defined in section 101. That definition looks not only to the nature of the real estate but also to the nature of the debtor and the amount of "secured debts." Under section 362(d)(3), a creditor with a lien on single asset real estate has a right to relief from stay unless the debtor, within 90 days after the order for relief, has either (A) filed a reorganization plan or (B) started monthly payments. If the debtor selects alternative A, the plan must be one that has "reasonable possibility of being confirmed within a reasonable time."

4. RELATIONSHIP OF SECTION 362(d) SUBSECTIONS

Note that section 362(d)(1), section 362(d)(2), and section 362(d)(3) are connected by the conjunction "or." A creditor is entitled to relief from the stay if it is able to establish grounds for relief under either section 362(d)(1), section 362(d)(2), or section 362(d)(3).

5. BURDEN OF PROOF IN SECTION 362(d) LITIGATION

Section 362(g) allocates the burden of proof in stay litigation. The creditor or other party requesting the relief has the burden on the issue of whether the debtor has an equity in the property. The debtor or bankruptcy trustee has the burden on all other issues.

E. CONSEQUENCES OF VIOLATING THE STAY

Actions that violate the stay are void, i.e., they have no legal effect. Also, a person who violates the stay can be liable for damages.

F. REVIEW QUESTIONS

■ IX. PROPERTY OF THE ESTATE

A. WHY IS PROPERTY OF THE ESTATE AN IMPORTANT CONCEPT?

"Property of the estate" is one of the most important, most basic bankruptcy concepts. The filing of any bankruptcy petition automatically creates an "estate," and that estate includes the assets of the debtor as of the time of the bankruptcy filing, section 541(a).

B. WHAT DOES PROPERTY OF THE ESTATE INCLUDE?

Section 541 is the primary section to turn to in answering the question "what does property of the estate include?" With only minor exceptions, property of the estate includes all property of the debtor as of the time of the filing of the bankruptcy petition.

■ X. EXEMPTIONS

A. WHAT PROPERTY IS EXEMPT?

Under the Bankruptcy Code, all pre-bankruptcy property in which the debtor has an interest becomes property of the estate, but an individual debtor is permitted to exempt certain property from property of the estate.

1. DEBTOR'S CHOICE

In bankruptcy, an individual debtor may assert the exemptions to which she is entitled under state laws and under federal laws other than title 11, section 522(b)(2). Or, in rare cases, she can alternatively assert exemptions provided by the Bankruptcy Code.

2. CHOICE OF LAW

When a debtor asserts state-law exemptions, which is the usual case, the Bankruptcy Code provides rules for deciding which state's law is the source of the exemptions.

3. WAIVERS OF EXEMPTIONS

Whether an individual debtor elects to claim under nonbankruptcy exemption law or under section 522(d), waivers of exemption are not enforceable, section 522(e).

4. TIMELY OBJECTING TO EXEMPTIONS

Objecting to a debtor's claim of exemptions is permitted, but an untimely objection is ineffective even if the applicable law does not allow an exemption the debtor has claimed.

5. PRE–PETITION CONVERSIONS OF PROPERTY—BANKRUPTCY ESTATE "PLANNING"

Case and statutory law limit a debtor converting non-exempt property to exempt property on the eve of and in anticipation of bankruptcy.

B. WHAT IS THE SIGNIFICANCE IN BANKRUPTCY OF EXEMPT PROPERTY?

1. GENERAL

Generally, an individual debtor is able to retain his or her exempt property. Exempt property is not distributed to creditors in the bankruptcy case and is protected from the claims of *most* prepetition creditors after the bankruptcy case.

2. SECTION 522(f)

Some liens on exempt property that are valid outside of bankruptcy can be invalidated because of bankruptcy. The general invalidation provisions, discussed infra in Chapter XI, are applicable to liens on exempt property. And section 522(f) empowers the debtor to avoid judicial liens that impair exemptions and to avoid security interests that are both nonpurchase money and nonpossessory on certain household goods, tools of the trade, and health aids.

3. SECTION 722

Possessory security interests in exempt personal property, purchase money security interests in exempt personal property, and any security interests on exempt personal property not covered by section 522(f) may be extinguished through "redemption." Section 722 authorizes an individual debtor to redeem or extinguish a lien on exempt personal property by paying the lienor the value of the property encumbered ("the amount of the allowed secured claim.").

C. REVIEW QUESTIONS

■ XI. AVOIDANCE OF PREBANKRUPTCY TRANSFERS

In the absence of bankruptcy, some transfers of a debtor's property can be invalidated under state laws, such as state fraudulent conveyance laws. The Bankruptcy Code incorporates these state laws in section 544(b) so that a transfer of a debtor's property that can be invalidated under state law in the absence of bankruptcy can be invalidated under section 544(b) in the event of bankruptcy.

Chapter 5 of the Bankruptcy Code also contains several other "avoidance" provisions. Accordingly, some payments, sales, exchanges, judicial liens, security interests and other transfers that are valid under state law can be avoided in bankruptcy.

A. BASIC ISSUES

1. TRANSFER MEANS VOLUNTARY AND INVOLUNTARY

The Bankruptcy Code's avoidance provisions reach both "voluntary" transfers such as a debtor's making a gift to a relative or granting a mortgage to a creditor and "involuntary" transfers such as a creditor's garnishing the debtor's bank account or subjecting the debtor's real property to a judgment lien.

2. WHEN AVOIDANCE IS AN ISSUE

In working with these avoidance provisions, law students and lawyers are called on to answer two basic questions: (1) what are the consequences of avoiding a transfer and (2) which transfers can be avoided.

3. PROCEDURE

Avoidance in bankruptcy of a prebankruptcy transfer requires litigation and raises all of the usual litigation questions.

B. WHAT ARE THE CONSEQUENCES OF AVOIDING A TRANFER?

1. RECOVERING TRANSFERRED INTEREST FOR THE ESTATE

When the bankruptcy trustee avoids an absolute transfer of property, that property then becomes property of the estate. In the case of a lien that is avoided, the creditor loses the lien and her claim is unsecured.

2. RECOVERING VALUE

The consequences of avoidance are not limited to recovery of the property transferred, are not limited to the person to whom the transfer was made. Under section 550, the court can order the recovery of the "value of the property" transferred, rather than the property. And, under section 550, the recovery can be sought not only from the initial transferee but either later transferees or a person who benefited from the transfer.

C. PREFERENCES

Bankruptcy law—section 547—condemns certain preferences. Section 547(b) sets out the elements of an avoidable preference; the bankruptcy trustee may void any transfer *of property of the debtor* if he or she can establish:

(1) The transfer was "to or for the benefit of a creditor"; and

(2) The transfer was made for or on account of an "antecedent debt," i.e., a debt owed prior to the time of the transfer; and

(3) The debtor was insolvent at the time of the transfer; and

(4) The transfer was made within 90 days before the date of the filing of the bankruptcy petition, or, was made between 90 days and 1 year before the date of the filing of the petition to an "insider" (which is defined in section 101 and includes relatives of an individual debtor and directors of a corporate debtor); and

(5) The transfer has the effect of increasing the amount that the transferee would receive in a Chapter 7 case.

Section 547(b) sets out the elements of a voidable preference. Section 547(c) excepts certain prepetition transfers from the operation of section 547(b). If a transfer comes within one of section 547(c)'s exceptions, the bankruptcy trustee will not be able to invalidate the transfer even though the trustee can establish all of the requirements of section 547(b).

D. SETOFFS

State law generally, universally provides for setoff, which is the cancellation of cross demands between two parties. Subject to certain exceptions, setoffs allowed under state law are generally protected and generally allowed in bankruptcy under section 553, but they are also subject to the automatic stay of section 362.

E. FRAUDULENT TRANSFERS AND OBLIGATIONS

1. SECTION 548

The Bankruptcy Code, like nonbankruptcy law, invalidates transfers that are fraudulently made and obligations that are fraudulently incurred. Indeed, the Bankruptcy Code fraudulent conveyance provisions are very much like the nonbankruptcy fraudulent conveyance statutes considered supra. Section 548 is based on the Uniform Fraudulent Conveyances Act and permits avoiding transfers that were made within one year before the bankruptcy and that are either actually or constructively fraudulent.

2. SECTION 544(b)

Section 548 is not, however, the only provision in the Bankruptcy Code that invalidates fraudulent conveyances. The trustee may also use section 544(b) to invalidate fraudulent conveyances. Section 544(b) does not specifically provide for the invalidation of fraudulent conveyances. Rather it empowers the bankruptcy trustee to avoid any prebankruptcy transfer that is "voidable under applicable law by a creditor holding an unsecured claim that is allowable." Section 544(b) effectively incorporates state and non-bankruptcy, federal fraudulent conveyance law into the Bankruptcy Code.

3. CHART COMPARING OF SECTIONS 548 AND 544(b)

F. TRANSFERS NOT RECORDED OR OTHERWISE PERFECTED

State law requires recordation or other public notice of a number of transfers. Real estate recording statutes require the recording of deeds and real property mortgages. And, Article 9 of the Uniform Commercial Code calls for public notice (perfection) of most security interests in personal property.

A bankruptcy trustee may avoid certain prepetition transfers that are not recorded or perfected. The Bankruptcy Code does not have its own public notice requirements. It does not simply invalidate all transfers not recorded at a certain time. Rather, the Bankruptcy Code makes use of the notoriety requirements of state law to avoid, under sections 544, 545, 547 and 548, prebankruptcy transfers that were not perfected under state law.

G. TRANSFERS NOT TIMELY RECORDED OR OTHERWISE PERFECTED

State law usually does not care if perfecting a lien is delayed as long as perfection happens before somebody else gets a claim to the property. In bankruptcy, however, delay itself can result in avoidance of a lien even though perfection occurs before bankruptcy. The bases are sections 547(e) and 548(d).

1. SECTION 547(e)

Although it is easy to see the reason for invalidating liens that are not timely perfected, it is difficult to understand why section 547 should be the mechanism for invalidating such liens. The easy way to invalidate such secret liens would be to add a section to the Bankruptcy Code to the effect that any lien that can be recorded or otherwise perfected under state law must be recorded within 10 (30?) days after it is obtained in order to be valid in bankruptcy. While that is the "easy way," it is not the way of the Bankruptcy Code.

Basically, the Bankruptcy Code's method for attacking delayed perfection is to "deem" that for purposes of applying the requirements of section 547(b), which defines a preference, the date of transfers not timely recorded is the date of perfection, not the actual date of transfer.

2. SECTION 548(d)

Section 548(d) is similar to section 547(e). Section 547(e) fixes the time when a transfer is deemed made for purposes of the preference invalidation provisions of section 547. Section 548(d) fixes the time when a transfer is deemed made for purposes of the fraudulent conveyance invalidation provisions of section 548: when the transfer is so far perfected that no subsequent bona fide purchaser of the property from the debtor can acquire rights in the property superior to those of the transferee. The purpose of section 548(d) is to prevent a fraudulent conveyance from escaping invalidation by being kept secret for over a year.

3. SECTION 544(b) [Not]

The most important thing for you to know about the application of section 544(b) to transfers that were not timely recorded is that section 544(b)'s application is *not* important. Section 544(b) will not allow avoidance even if the transfer is not recorded for a long time and just before bankruptcy.

H. LANDLORDS' LIENS

Sections 545(3) and 545(4) are the easiest invalidation provisions to read, understand and apply: "The trustee may avoid the fixing of a statutory lien on the property of the debtor to the extent that such lien . . . is for rent. . . ."

I. DISGUISED PRIORITIES

Section 507 of the Bankruptcy Code is a priority provision; it sets out the order in which the various unsecured claims against the debtor are to be satisfied. It displaces any state priority statutes. Section 545 protects this federal priority scheme from disruption by state priority provisions that are "disguised" as statutory liens. Section 545 reaches spurious statutory liens which are in reality merely priorities.

J. SELLER'S RECLAMATION AND RETURN RIGHTS

1. RIGHTS GRANTED BY STATE LAW

When a buyer fails to pay for goods it accepts, the seller has a legal right to recover the contract price, UCC § 2–709. This legal right to be paid is of limited practical significance if the buyer is insolvent. Accordingly, the Uniform Commercial Code grants certain unpaid sellers a right to recover the goods. Section 2–702 of the Uniform Commercial Code empowers a seller under limited circumstances to reclaim (recover) the goods if the transaction was a credit sale *and* the buyer, who had represented solvency, was insolvent when the goods were received.

2. EFFECT OF BANKRUPTCY LAW ON STATE–LAW RIGHTS

What is the effect of the bankruptcy of the buyer on the seller's right of reclamation? Section 546(c) is the principal provision dealing with this question. Section 546 does not create a right of reclamation. Instead, it sets out the effect of bankruptcy on a right of reclamation created under nonbankruptcy law. Section 546(c) has four requirements. If a seller has complied with these four requirements, the bankruptcy trustee *cannot* invalidate the seller's right of reclamation under section 544(a), section 545, section 547, or section 549.

3. EFFECT OF DEBTOR'S TRANSFER OF RIGHTS IN GOODS

If the debtor has disposed of the goods prior to the seller's reclamation demand, then there is nothing to reclaim: under nonbankruptcy law, the reclamation remedy is limited to the goods that the seller delivered. Similarly, if the debtor has granted another creditor a security interest that covers its entire inventory, there is nothing to reclaim: under nonbankruptcy law, a security interest has priority over a right of reclamation.

4. PRIORITY CLAIM

Even an unpaid seller who is unable to reclaim is entitled to a priority claim.

5. BANKRUPTCY RIGHT OF RETURN

A 1994 amendment to section 546(h) adds a very limited right of return of goods to an unpaid seller for credit in Chapter 11 cases.

K. REVIEW QUESTIONS

■ XII. POSTBANKRUPTCY TRANSFERS

A. WHEN DO POSTBANKRUPTCY TRANSFERS HAPPEN?

Postbankruptcy transfers of property of the estate present problems primarily in Chapter 7 cases. Only in Chapter 7 cases does the right of possession of property of the estate pass to the trustee; only in Chapter 7 cases are the proceeds from the trustee's liquidation of property of the estate what is distributed to creditors. In Chapter 11 and Chapter 13 cases, the debtor continues to possess property of the estate postpetition and creditors are paid under a plan that is generally based on the debtor's future earnings. And, in Chapter 11 and Chapter 13 cases, most postpetition transfers of property of the estate are permitted by section 363. Accordingly, section 549 is much more important to Chapter 7 cases than to Chapter 11 cases or Chapter 13 cases.

B. HOW DOES A POSTBANKRUPTCY TRANSFER HAPPEN?

For most purposes, the date of the filing of the bankruptcy petition is the critical date in a Chapter 7 case. Subject to limited exceptions, only the property of the debtor as of the date of the filing of the petition becomes property of the estate. Generally, property acquired by the debtor after the bankruptcy petition has been filed remains property of the debtor. During the hiatus between the filing of the bankruptcy petition and the bankruptcy trustee's taking possession of the property of the estate, the debtor will usually have possession and control of the property of the estate. At times, the debtor will, after the filing of the petition, transfer property of the estate to some third party.

C. HOW DOES SECTION 549 AFFECT POSTBANKRUPTCY TRANSFERS OF PROPERTY OF THE ESTATE BY THE DEBTOR?

A purported transfer of estate by the debtor is generally ineffective. The debtor has no rights in the rights that she can convey. The property belongs to the estate. Section 549 protects transferees, however, in certain circumstances. Generally, section 549 protects the *transferee* if: (1) The transfer was authorized by the Bankruptcy Code or by the bankruptcy court; or (2) the transfer was after an involuntary petition for postbankruptcy consideration; or (3) the transfer was a real property transfer that was recorded before the bankruptcy was noted in the real property records.

D. HOW DOES SECTION 542 AFFECT POSTBANKRUPTCY TRANSFERS OF PROPERTY OF THE ESTATE BY THIRD PARTIES?

Some postpetition transfers of property of the estate are made by persons holding property of the debtor, not the debtor. Under section 542(c), a third party who in good faith transfers property of the estate after the filing of the petition is protected from the bankruptcy trustee if the third party had "neither notice nor actual knowledge of the commencement of the case." Even though section 542(c) protects the person who transfers property of the estate postpetition, section 549 empowers the trustee to recover the property from the transferee.

E. REVIEW QUESTIONS

■ XIII. EFFECT OF BANKRUPTCY ON SECURED CLAIMS

A. WHAT IS A SECURED CLAIM?

The Bankruptcy Code deals with "claims," not creditors. Accordingly, under the Bankruptcy Code there will be creditors with secured claims, not secured creditors. A creditor has a secured claim if it holds a lien on or has a right of setoff against "property of the estate." The claim is secured only to the extent of the value of "such creditor's interest in the estate's interest in such property," section 506(a). "Such creditor's interest" becomes important if more than one creditor has a lien on the same property. The phrase "estate's interest" becomes important if the debtor is a co-owner or has an otherwise limited interest in the encumbered property.

B. INVALIDATION OF LIENS

Some liens that are valid outside of bankruptcy can be invalidated in a bankruptcy case. Section 522(f) considered supra, empowers the debtor to invalidate certain liens on certain exempt property. Sections 544, 545, 547, 548 and 549, considered supra, empower the bankruptcy trustee to invalidate certain transfers that create liens. Note the effect of lien invalidation. All that is eliminated is the lien. The creditor's claim remains. Lien invalidation converts a secured claim into an unsecured claim.

C. WHAT CAN HAPPEN TO SECURED CLAIMS DURING BANKRUPTCY?

Most liens cannot be avoided under sections 522(f), 544, 545, 547, 548 or 549. What effect does bankruptcy have on a creditor that holds a valid in bankruptcy lien?

1. DELAY IN REALIZING ON COLLATERAL

The automatic stay of section 362 prevents a creditor from enforcing its lien against property of the estate or property of the debtor.

2. DEBTOR'S USE, LEASE OR SALE OF COLLATERAL

Not only does the Bankruptcy Code bar the secured creditor from recovering its collateral, the Bankruptcy Code also empowers the debtor to continue using the collateral.

3. NONACCRUAL OF INTEREST

The amount of a claim is fixed by the amount that is owed at the date of the filing of the petition. Interest that has not accrued ("matured") as of the date of the filing of the petition is not allowable as part of C's claim in the bankruptcy case, section 502(b)(2).The rule that the creditor does not earn interest after the bankruptcy petition is filed also applies to secured creditors with one exception. Section 506(b) provides for postpetition interest for over-secured creditors. If, and only if, the amount that is owed on a secured claim is less than the value of the collateral securing the claim, "to the holder of such claim, interest on such claim."

4. LOSS OF PRIORITY

Section 364(d) empowers the bankruptcy court to approve the debtor's granting a postpetition creditor a lien on encumbered property that has priority over all prepetition liens.

5. LIMITATIONS ON FLOATING LIENS

In commercial credit transactions, security agreements usually provide that the collateral includes property that the debtor later acquires. Such after-acquired property clauses are expressly permitted by section 9–204 of the UCC; such after-acquired property clauses are expressly cut off in bankruptcy by section 552(a), except for proceeds and other specified forms of earnings from and product of prepetition collateral.

6. RETURN OF REPOSSESSED PROPERTY

Section 542(a) compels the holder of a secured claim that has taken possession of its collateral prior to bankruptcy to return it to the debtor when she files a bankruptcy petition.

7. EFFECT OF DISCHARGE ON SECURED CLAIMS

A bankruptcy discharge simply relieves the debtor from any further personal liability for the debts covered by the discharge. A bankruptcy discharge does not wipe out the debts: the ability of creditors to look to other parties such as guarantors and insurers is unaffected. And, a bankruptcy discharge does not wipe out liens: the ability of secured creditors to look to their collateral is unaffected.

D. SATISFACTION OF SECURED CLAIMS

1. RECOVERY OF COLLATERAL

If the holder of a secured claim recovers its collateral, the secured claim is extinguished.

2. PAYMENT OF AMOUNT EQUAL TO THE VALUE OF THE COLLATERAL IN CHAPTER 7 AND CHAPTER 11 CASES

If the holder of a secured claim does not recover its collateral, it should receive a payment equal to the value of the collateral.

a. Chapter 7

In a Chapter 7 case, this payment can come from the trustee's sale of the collateral, or this payment can come from the debtor.

b. Chapters 11 and 13

What the holder of a secured claim receives in a Chapter 11 case or a Chapter 13 case depends on the provisions of the plan. A Chapter 11 plan or a Chapter 13 plan can modify the rights of the holder of any secured claim other than a claim secured "only by a security interest in real property that is the debtor's principal residence," sections 1123(b)(5), 1322(b)(2). As a general rule, however, unless the secured creditor agrees otherwise, the plan must provides for distributions to the holder of a secured claim that have a present value at least equal to the value of the collateral.

3. PAYMENT OF THE DEBT IN FULL IN CHAPTER 13 CASES AND CHAPTER 11 CASES WITH INDIVIDUAL DEBTORS

Statutory and practical reasons sometime require a debtor to pay the secured debt fully even though the collateral is worth less than the debt.

E. POSTPONEMENT OF TAX LIENS IN CHAPTER 7 CASES

1. If No Valid Tax Lien, Then Section 507(c)(7)

If the government has not obtained a tax lien prior to bankruptcy or if the tax lien has been avoided in bankruptcy, the tax claim will be an unsecured claim. Such an unsecured claim is governed by section 507(a)(7), not section 724.

2. IF VALID LIEN IN CHAPTER 7, THEN SECTION 724

Section 724 only applies if (1) Chapter 7 bankruptcy and (2) claim for taxes secured by a valid in bankruptcy tax lien. Section 724(b) postpones the payment of such a tax claim until the complete payment of all claims entitled to priority under section 507(a)(1)-(6). The priority provisions of section 507 are considered in Chapter XIV.

F. REVIEW QUESTIONS

■ XIV. CLAIMS

A. WHY IS "CLAIM" AN IMPORTANT BANKRUPTCY CONCEPT?

The word "claim" appears throughout the Bankruptcy Code, throughout a bankruptcy case. For example: the automatic stay that is triggered by the filing of an involuntary or voluntary petition bars actions by holders of claims to collect on their claims from the debtor or property of the estate; a discharge bars further efforts by holders of claims to collect their claims from the debtor; and distributions in a Chapter 7 case are made to holders of claims.

B. WHAT IS A CLAIM? (AND, WHO CARES?)

The term "claim" is defined in section 101: "right to payment, whether or not such right is reduced to judgment, liquidated, unliquidated, fixed, contingent, matured, unmatured, disputed, undisputed, legal, equitable or unsecured." Both legislative history and case law describe the definition as an effort to be as comprehensive and inclusive as possible.

C. WHAT IS AN UNSECURED CLAIM?

A claim is unsecured if the creditor has not obtained a consensual, judicial, or statutory lien or if the value of the property subject to the lien is less than the amount of the creditors claim. Consider the following examples of unsecured claims:

D. COLLECTION OF UNSECURED CLAIMS FROM THE DEBTOR

The section 362 stay coupled with the section 727 discharge makes it necessary for most holders of unsecured claims to look to the "property of the estate" for the satisfaction of their claims.

E. WHAT PROPERTY IS DISTRIBUTED TO HOLDERS OF UNSECURED CLAIMS?

1. WHAT PROPERTY IS DISTRIBUTED TO HOLDERS OF UNSECURED CLAIMS IN CHAPTER 7 CASES?

The bankruptcy trustee has a statutory duty to sell the "property of the estate," section 704(1). The net proceeds received from the liquidation of the "property of the estate" are to be distributed to the holders of unsecured or general claims. Net means that some proceeds—lots of proceeds—are typically excluded, which means that the great majority of Chapter 7 cases are "no asset" cases, at least in the sense that there are no assets available to pay unsecured claims.

2. WHAT PROPERTY IS DISTRIBUTED TO HOLDERS OF UNSECURED CLAIMS IN CHAPTER 12, CHAPTER 13, AND INDIVIDUAL CHAPTER 11 CASES?

In Chapter 12 cases and Chapter 13 cases, the plan controls the payment to holders of unsecured claims; but the debtor must commit all "disposable income" to the repayment plan.

3. WHAT PROPERTY IS DISTRIBUTED TO HOLDERS OF UNSECURED CLAIMS IN OTHER CHAPTER 11 CASES?

In Chapter 11 cases, like Chapter 12 and 13 cases, the plan controls the payment to holders of unsecured claims. Chapter 11's treatment of holders of unsecured claims, however, is significantly different from Chapter 12 or 13's. The formulation, acceptance, and confirmation of Chapter 11 plans are considered later.

F. WHICH HOLDERS OF UNSECURED CLAIMS ARE ELIGIBLE TO PARTICIPATE IN THE BANKRUPTCY DISTRIBUTION?

1. PROOF OF CLAIM

The debtor will file a list of creditors, section 521. The court will then send notice of the bankruptcy case to the listed creditors, section 342. The creditors that wish to participate in the distribution of the proceeds of the liquidation of the "property of the estate" must file a proof of claim, sections 501, 726. In Chapter 11 cases, a creditor is required to file a proof of claim only if its claim is scheduled as disputed, contingent, or unliquidated, section 1111(a); Rule 3003(b)(1).

2. ALLOWANCE

In a Chapter 7 case, the proceeds of the liquidation of the property of the estate are distributed only to unsecured creditors whose claims are "allowed," section 726. If a proof of claim has been filed, the claim is deemed allowed "unless a party in interest objects," section 502(a).

G. WHAT IS THE ORDER OF DISTRIBUTION?

There are a number of statements in reported cases, law review articles, and legal texts praising the theme of equality of distribution to creditors in bankruptcy proceedings. Such statements must be using the term "equality" in the *Animal Farm* sense; in bankruptcy, some creditors are clearly "more equal" than others. In a bankruptcy case, certain allowed unsecured claims are entitled to priority in distribution over other unsecured claims. Section 507(a) sets out the levels of priorities.

1. TREATMENT OF PRIORITY CLAIMS IN 7

Section 726 establishes the rules for distribution in a Chapter 7 case to the holders of unsecured claims. Basically, the distribution is to be as follows:

1. Priorities under section 507 (section 507 is considered below)

2. Allowed unsecured claims which were either timely filed or tardily filed by a creditor who did not know of the bankruptcy

3. Allowed unsecured claims which were tardily filed by creditors with notice or actual knowledge of the bankruptcy

4. Fines and punitive damages

5. Postpetition interest on prepetition claims.

Each claim of each of the five categories must be paid in full before any claim in the next category receives any distribution. Each claim within a particular category shares pro rata if the proceeds from the liquidation of the property of the estate is insufficient to satisfy all claims in that category.

2. TREATMENT OF PRIORITY CLAIMS IN 11, 12, 13

Chapter 11, Chapter 12 and Chapter 13 require the plan to provide for payment in full of all priority claims, although the payments of claims within certain priority classes may be stretched over a period of time, sections 1129(a)(9), 1222(a)(2), 1322(a)(2).

3. SECTION 507 TREATMENT OF PRIORITIES

The task of distributing the proceeds from the sale of the property of the estate is complicated by the fact that claims do not come neatly labeled "claims entitled to priority under section 507." Instead, it is necessary to recognize which claims are entitled to priority under section 507. Priority claims, listed in order of their priority inter se, are these:

1. Administrative Expenses

2. Ordinary–Course Claims in Involuntary Cases

3. Wage Claims

4. Employee Benefit Plans

5. Certain claims of farmers and fishermen

6. Consumer Deposits

7. Domestic Obligations

8. Tax Claims

9. Claims against depository institutions with respect to commitments of regulatory agencies to maintain the institution's capital.

4. SECTION 510 TREATMENT OF SUBORDINATION

Section 507, the priority provision, has the effect of moving certain, specified claims to the head of the line. Section 510, the subordination provision, has the effect of moving some claims further back in the line. Section 510 requires subordination in two instances: (1) Where there is a subordination agreement that would be enforceable under nonbankruptcy law, section 510(a); and (2) when a seller or purchaser of equity securities seeks damages or rescission, section 510(b).

5. CLASSIFICATION OF CLAIMS

In a Chapter 7 case, the debtor has no control over how the property of the estate is to be distributed. Section 726 prescribes the scheme of distribution to unsecured creditors in a Chapter 7 case. All allowed, unsecured nonpriority claims are treated alike: a pro rata distribution will be made to the holders of such claims after all priority claims are paid in full, section 726(a)(2). However, in a Chapter 11 case, a Chapter 12 case or a Chapter 13 case, a debtor's plan can affect how the property of the estate is to be distributed. The plan can treat some unsecured claims differently than others: it can classify claims and provide for different treatment for each class, sections 1123(a)(1), 1222(b)(1), 1322(b)(1).

H. REVIEW QUESTIONS

■ XV. LEASES AND EXECUTORY CONTRACTS

A. OVERVIEW

1. HYBRID NATURE OF LEASE AND EXECUTORY CONTRACT

Generally, the Bankruptcy Code's provisions dealing with the debtor's assets are separate from the Bankruptcy Code's provisions dealing with the debtor's obligations and the estate's obligations: property of the estate in section 541, allowable claims and administrative expenses in sections 502 and 503. A lease or executory contract involves potentially both property of the estate and a claim against the debtor or the estate.

2. BANKRUPTCY PROVISIONS

The principal provisions of the Bankruptcy Code dealing with leases and executory contracts are sections 365, 1110, 1113, and 1114. The core provision is section 365.

3. DIFFERENT WAYS OF TREATING LEASE OR EXECUTORY CONTRACT

The bankruptcy treatment of a lease or executory contract can take one of three possible forms: rejection; assumption; and assignment.

4. DEBTOR LIMITED IN CHANGING LEASE OR EXECUTORY CONTRACT

Leases and unexpired contracts can be treated in different ways under the Bankruptcy Code, but a debtor does not have a legal right to modify or change the terms of an unexpired lease or an executory contract.

5. SUMMARY

To review, look primarily to section 365 to determine the effect of bankruptcy on a debtor's leases and executory contracts. Under section 365, a bankruptcy trustee can either: reject a lease or executory contract; assume a lease or executory contract; or assign a lease or executory contract.

B. EFFECT OF REJECTION, ASSUMPTION, ASSIGNMENT

1. IF LEASE REJECTED

If the lease is rejected, the debtor has no further right to use the building for his barbershop. If the lease is rejected, the debtor has no further personal liability on the lease. The rejection of the lease is, of course, a breach of the lease, section 365(g). The lessor will have an allowable unsecured claim against the bankrupt estate for back rent and future rentals, section 502(g), 502(a)(6).

2. IF LEASE ASSUMED

If the lease is assumed, the leasehold continues to be an asset of the estate. The debtor can continue to operate his barbershop in the building. Assumption covers the burdens of the lease as well as the benefits. By assuming the lease, the trustee or debtor in possession is obligating the estate to make all payments under the lease. This obligation is a first priority administrative expense.

3. IF LEASE ASSIGNED

What if the trustee or debtor in possession sells the lease to Aunt Bea Taylor who wants to open an adult bookstore in the building? Such an assignment "relieves the trustee and the estate from any liability for any breach of such contract or lease occurring after such assignment," section 365(k). After the assignment, the lessor can look only to Aunt Bea for the payment of the post-assignment obligations under the lease.

C. PROCEDURE FOR REJECTION OR ASSUMPTION

Section 365(a) contemplates court approval of rejection or assumption. Rule 6006 provides that the assumption or rejection is a contested matter governed by Rule 9014. Neither the Code nor the Rules indicate what standard the court should apply in determining whether to grant or withhold its approval. Most, but not all, cases seem to give great deference to the "business judgment" of the debtor in possession or trustee in approving a motion to reject an unexpired lease or executory contract. Because assumption of an unexpired lease or executory contract creates an administrative priority obligation that must be paid before other unsecured claims, courts give greater weight to creditors' objections to motions to assume.

D. THE GAP PERIOD

There is going to be some gap period between the filing of a bankruptcy petition and action on a contract or lease. Section 365 does not expressly deal with the performance obligations of the nondebtor party to a lease or executory during this gap period. Most courts seem simply to assume that the nondebtor party is so obligated. If L is leasing a building or machinery to D, L's performance (providing the building or machinery) continues after D's bankruptcy filing. Section 365(d)(3) expressly deals with the performance obligations of the debtor party to a nonresidential real property lease: it requires a debtor/lessee to "timely perform" all obligations under a nonresidential real property lease.

E. LIMITATIONS ON THE EFFECT OF REJECTION OF A LEASE OR EXECUTORY CONTRACT

Nothing in section 365 limits the availability of rejection. Section 365 does, however, set out four situations in which the effect of rejection is limited. Most significantly, section 365(h) limits the effect of rejection of a lease of real property when the debtor is the landlord. A trustee for a debtor who owns rental real property may not use section 365 to evict tenants. Even, if the trustee decides to reject the debtor/lessor's leases, the tenant has a right to remain in possession.

Chapter 11 also limits the rejection of collective bargaining contracts in Chapter 11 cases, section 1113; and section 1114 limits the rejection of employee benefits contracts in Chapter 11 cases.

F. LIMITATIONS ON ASSUMPTION AND ASSIGNMENT

1. CONTRACT LIMITATIONS

Contract clauses that prohibit or limit the assumption and assignment of leases and executory contracts will not be effective in bankruptcy, section 365(e), (f).

2. PROCEEDS OF ASSIGNMENT OF LEASE

What happens to the "substantial sums" that the trustee receives when he sells the "nonassignable lease"? Recall that the debtor's interest in the lease was section 541(a)(1) property of the estate and that proceeds from the sale of property of the estate are property of the estate, section 541(a)(6). Accordingly, it would seem that the answer to this question is that the "substantial sums" from the sale of the "nonassignable lease" would, like the rest of the property of the estate, be available for distribution to unsecured creditors in a Chapter 7 case and be available for the debtor's plan performance in a Chapter 11 or 13 case. The result may be different if we change the real property lease to a cable franchise contract and second add, a security interest in the contract.

3. LEASES AND EXECUTORY CONTRACTS THAT CANNOT BE ASSUMED OR ASSUMED AND ASSIGNED

There are some leases and executory contracts that cannot be assumed and assigned, including a lease terminated before bankruptcy; a loan commitment or other financing arrangement cannot be assumed; and contracts that are not assignable under "applicable law". "Applicable law" can be the common law of contracts.

4. REQUIREMENTS FOR ASSUMPTION AND ASSIGNMENT

Section 365(b) sets out the requirements for assumption of a lease or executory contract.

G. DEFINITION OF EXECUTORY CONTRACT

Most courts agree that an executory contract for purposes of bankruptcy is one that is so far unperformed on both sides that the failure of either party to complete her performance would be a material breach excusing further performance from the other party. See Countryman, *Executory Contracts In Bankruptcy*, 57 Minn.L.Rev. 439 (1973); 58 Minn.L.Rev. 479 (1974).

H. REVIEW QUESTIONS

■ XVI. DISCHARGE

A. WHICH DEBTORS RECEIVE A DISCHARGE?

1. CHAPTER 7

In counseling a beleaguered debtor about Chapter 7, it is very important to ascertain her eligibility for discharge—to determine whether any of the grounds for withholding discharge can be established by the bankruptcy trustee or a creditor. If the debtor is denied a discharge, she loses two ways. The debtor will leave the bankruptcy case without her section 541 property yet owing the same debts that she owed at the time of the filing of the bankruptcy case less any distribution that creditors received from the trustee.

a. Substantive Grounds for Withholding a Chapter 7 Discharge

The grounds for withholding a discharge, i.e., objections to discharge, are set out in section 727(a). These ten grounds are exclusive. Unless the bankruptcy trustee or a creditor is able to establish one of these ten objections, the debtor in a Chapter 7 case will receive a bankruptcy discharge.

b. Procedure for Objecting to a Chapter 7 Discharge

Objections to discharge are initiated by complaints, filed with the bankruptcy court. Rule 4004 sets the time for filing complaints objecting to discharge. Any such complaint must be filed within 60 days of the first date set for the meeting of creditors.

2. CHAPTER 11 CASES: BUSINESS ENTITY DEBTORS

a. Confirmation Operates as Discharge

In Chapter 11, the confirmation of the plan operates as a discharge, section 1141(d).

b. Grounds for Denying

The grounds for denying a discharge in a Chapter 11 case are different from the grounds for denying a discharge in a Chapter 7 case.

c. Applying Section 1141(d)(3)

Some examples show when a Chapter 11 discharge may be denied.

3. CHAPTER 13

a. Discharge Depends

In Chapter 13 cases, unlike Chapter 11 cases, the confirmation of the plan does not effect a discharge. In Chapter 13, the question of whether a debtor will receive a discharge cannot be resolved until the debtor either completes her payments under the plan or completes her efforts to make payments under the plan, section 1328.

b. Reasons for Denying Discharge

Section 1328(a) makes mandatory the discharge of a debtor who has completed all of the payments required by his Chapter 13 plan. Section 1328(b) gives the court discretion to grant a "hardship" discharge to a debtor who has failed to make all of the payments required by his Chapter 13 plan. Section 1328(b) lists three factors that the court should consider in exercising this discretion. Section 727 is not included in the list; section 727 is not applicable in Chapter 13 cases.

B. WHICH OBLIGATIONS ARE AFFECTED BY A BANKRUPTCY DISCHARGE?

Even when the debtor receives a discharge, she is not necessarily freed from all of her obligations. Certain obligations are not affected by a discharge. In determining whether a discharge affects an obligation, it is especially important to remember that section 523 excepts certain debts from the operation of a discharge. Section 523 applies in all Chapter 7 cases, in Chapter 11 cases involving individual debtors, and in Chapter 13 cases in which the debtor receives a section 1328(b) "hardship discharge," section 727(b), 1141(d)(2), and 1328(c).

1. CHAPTER 7

Section 523(a) sets out 19 exceptions to discharge. Some exceptions are based on the nature of the debt. Other exceptions are based on the conduct of the debtor in connection with the debt. The exceptions include certain obligations having to do with:

- Taxes

- Fraudulent Obligations

- Unscheduled Debts

- Fraud as Fiduciary

- Domestic Obligations

- Willful and Malicious Injury—Section 523(a)(6)

- Fines Owed Government

- Student Loans

2. CHAPTER 11

Second, every Chapter 7 discharge is subject to the exceptions to discharge of section 523. In Chapter 11, section 523 only applies if the debtor is an individual, section 1141(d)(2). Section 523 does not apply if the Chapter 11 debtor is a corporation or a partnership.

3. CHAPTER 13

In Chapter 13 cases, the discharge affects all debts provided for by the plan except

- Claims for alimony and child support as set out in section 523(a)(5);

- Educational loans as set out in section 523(a)(8);

- Drunk driving liabilities as set out in section 523(a)(9),

- Criminal fines and restitution obligations, and

- Certain long term obligations such as a house mortgage on which the payments extend beyond the term of the plan, section 1328(a).

4. PROCEDURE FOR ASSERTING AN EXCEPTION TO DISCHARGE

Section 523(c) directs that exceptions to discharge based on section 523(a)(2), (4), (6) or (15) must be asserted in bankruptcy court. Unless the creditor's motion is timely made, the debt is discharged. When a creditor is relying on any other part of section 523(a), there is no requirement that the exception to discharge be asserted in the bankruptcy court during the bankruptcy case.

C. EFFECT OF A DISCHARGE

A discharge protects the debtor from any further personal liability on discharged debts. Section 524(a) provides that a discharge voids a judgment on discharged debts and enjoins any legal "action" to collect such a debt from the debtor or property of the debtor. A discharge also bars extrajudicial collection "acts" such as dunning letters or telephone calls to collect discharged debts.

D. REAFFIRMATION

1. WHAT IS A REAFFIRMATION AGREEMENT?

A reaffirmation agreement is an agreement between a debtor and one of her creditors that the debtor will pay a debt she incurred before her bankruptcy filing that, but for the reaffirmation agreement, would have been dischargeable in the bankruptcy case. Under contract law, such an agreement is legally enforceable even though there is no bargained-for exchange, i.e., no consideration.

2. WHY MAKE SUCH AN AGREEMENT?

Why would a debtor make such an agreement? Some answers are: to keep encumbered property; to protect co-debtors; to avoid litigation about discharge; and to preserve a relationship with that creditor.

3. BANKRUPTCY LAW ISSUES

Most of the bankruptcy law issues relating to reaffirmation relate to concern that a creditor might pressure a debtor into reaffirming its debt.

E. PROTECTION FROM DISCRIMINATORY TREATMENT

Section 525 provides very limited protection for the debtor against discriminatory treatment, especially by government, based on the debtor having filed bankruptcy.

F. REVIEW QUESTIONS

■ XVII. CHAPTER 13 CASES

A. COMMENCEMENT OF THE CASE

A debtor may file for Chapter 13 relief if she: is *an individual, and h*as a "regular income," and has fixed unsecured debts of less than $290,525 and fixed secured debts of less than $871,550, section 109(e).

B. CO–DEBTOR STAY

The filing of a Chapter 13 petition triggers the automatic stay of section 362 that protects the debtor. In a Chapter 13 case, section 1301 also restrains a creditor from attempting to collect a debt from the co-debtor of a Chapter 13 debtor.

C. TRUSTEES

There will be a trustee appointed in every Chapter 13 case, section 1302(a). In almost all districts, the United States trustee appoints a standing trustee who serves as trustee in every Chapter 13 case, section 1302(d).

D. PREPARATION OF THE CHAPTER 13 PLAN

Only a debtor may file a Chapter 13 plan, section 1321. The court may dismiss a Chapter 13 case or convert it to Chapter 7 for "failure to file a plan *timely* under section 1321 of this title," section 1307(c)(3). The Code leaves the question of the meaning of "timely"—how many days the debtor has to file such a plan—to the Rules. It's within 15 days after filing the petition, Bankruptcy Rule 3015. The two most important plan preparation questions are: (1) How much does the debtor have to pay under the plan? And (2) How much do the various creditors get paid under the plan? To answer these questions, look primarily to sections 1322 and 1325.

E. CONFIRMATION OF THE CHAPTER 13 PLAN

In formulating a Chapter 13 plan, a lawyer or law student should look not only at section 1322 which deals with the contents of the plan but also section 1325 which covers confirmation of a plan. In Chapter 13, creditors do not vote on the plan. Chapter 13 requires only court approval. The standards for judicial confirmation of a Chapter 13 plan are set out in section 1325. Section 1325(a)(1) requires that the plan satisfy the provisions of Chapter 13 and other applicable bankruptcy law requirements.

F. CRAMDOWN (OR CRAM DOWN) OF SECURED CLAIMS IN CHAPTER 13

Secured claim plan confirmation issues arise only if the plan proposes that (i) the debtor retain the encumbered property and (ii) the secured claim be modified and (iii) the holder of the secured claim does not accept the plan. These issues are called cram down issues (or cram down issues). In order to cram down a Chapter 13 modification of a secured claim, the bankruptcy court must apply section 1325(a)(5)(B). The main requirement is that the plan must provide for the holder of a secured claim retain the lien securing such claim; and the value, as of the effective date of the plan, of property to be distributed under the plan on account of such claim is not less than the allowed amount of such claim.

G. TREATMENT OF HOME MORTGAGES IN CHAPTER 13 PLANS

Most home mortgages are protected from the cram down, protected from modification by a Chapter 13 plan. Section 1322(b) excepts claims "secured only by a security interest in real property that is the debtor's principal residence" from plan modification.

H. PREFERRING SOME CLAIMS

1. BY CLASSIFYING CLAIMS

A Chapter 13 debt can use claim classification to pay one or more of her creditors in full even though she does not have sufficient disposable income to pay all of her creditors in full. Under section 1322(b)(1), a Chapter 13 plan can divide unsecured claims into more than one class and treat the various classes differently. The primary limitation on this discrimination in the plan treatment of unsecured claims is that the classification may not "discriminate unfairly." The key word is, of course, "unfairly": any classification discriminates—what is required is that the discrimination not be unfair.

2. BY PAYING LONG–DEBT TERMS BEYOND THE PLAN

A Chapter 13 debtor can also use section 1322(b)(5) to make preferential plan payments on long-term debts. Section 1322(b)(5) only applies if the last payment on the debt is due after the last plan payment. With respect to such debts, a Chapter 13 debtor can simply make payments according to the contractual terms.

I. DISCHARGE

After completion of the payments provided for in the Chapter 13 plan, the debtor receives a discharge, section 1328(a). A section 1328(a) discharge is *not* subject to all of the exceptions from discharge set out in section 523.

J. DISMISSAL AND CONVERSION

Most Chapter 13 cases do *not* end in a discharge. Most bankruptcy cases filed as Chapter 13 cases are either dismissed or converted to Chapter 7 cases.

K. COMPARISON OF CHAPTERS 7 AND 13

Only a debtor may file a Chapter 13 petition. Each debtor who files a Chapter 13 petition could instead have filed a Chapter 7 petition. Before filing, the debtor's attorney should carefully compare Chapters 7 and 13.

L. COMPARISON OF CHAPTERS 11 AND 13

Any debtor who files a Chapter 13 petition could instead have filed a Chapter 11 petition. Accordingly, before filing, the debtor's attorney should carefully compare Chapters 11 and 13.

M. REVIEW QUESTIONS

■ XVIII. CHAPTER 11 CASES

Chapter 11 is about money. More specifically, Chapter 11 is generally about deciding who gets the difference between the liquidation value of a business and its going concern value. We know that in a Chapter 7 case, property of the estate is sold by the trustees and the net proceeds of the sale are distributed to creditors. In essence, in Chapter 7 cases, creditors' recovery is measured by the liquidation value. And, we know from the overview in Chapter VI, supra, that Chapter 11 contemplates that a debtor keep its assets, continue its business and pay creditors from future business operations. The question in Chapter 11 is how much creditors get paid—or, to restate, how much of the difference between liquidation value and going concern value goes to creditors.

A. COMMENCEMENT OF THE CASE

A case under Chapter 11 is commenced by the filing of a petition. The petition may be filed by either the debtor or creditors. Insolvency is not a condition precedent to a voluntary Chapter 11 petition. With two exceptions, any "person" that is eligible to file a voluntary bankruptcy petition under Chapter 7 is also eligible to file a petition under Chapter 11. The first exception is stockbrokers and commodity brokers: they are eligible for Chapter 7, but not Chapter 11. The second exception is railroads: railroads are eligible for Chapter 11, but not Chapter 7. If the Chapter 11 petition has been filed by an eligible debtor, no formal adjudication is necessary. The filing of the petition operates as an "order for relief," section 301. The requirements for an involuntary, i.e., creditor-initiated, Chapter 11 case are the same as the requirements for an involuntary Chapter 7 case, section 303. These requirements are discussed supra in Chapter VII.

B. OPERATION OF THE BUSINESS

Successful rehabilitation of a business under Chapter 11 generally requires the continued operation of the business. No court order is necessary in order to operate the debtor's business after the filing of a Chapter 11 petition. Section 1108 provides: "Unless the court . . . orders otherwise, the trustee may operate the debtor's business."

C. PREPARATION OF THE CHAPTER 11 PLAN

1. WHO PREPARES AND FILES

A Chapter 11 plan may be filed at the same time as the petition or any time thereof. Section 1121 answers the question who can file a Chapter 11 plan. Section 1121 gives a Chapter 11 debtor a period of exclusivity in which only it can file a plan. Section 1121(b) grants the debtor exclusivity for the first 120 days of the case. If the debtor files its plan within that 120 day period, no other plan may be filed during the first 180 days of the case while the debtor tries to obtain creditor acceptance of its plan, section 1121(c)(3).

2. CONTENTS OF THE PLAN

Section 1123 is entitled "Contents of Plan." Subparagraph (a) sets out the mandatory provisions of a Chapter 11 plan ("shall"); subparagraph (b) of section 1123 indicates the permissive provisions of a Chapter 11 plan ("may").

3. FUNDING FOR THE PLAN

Possible sources of such funding include: (1) new borrowing from creditors; (2) new equity capital from investors; and sales of assets.

4. CLASSIFICATION OF CLAIMS

Section 1123(a)(1) requires that the claims be classified, and section 1123(a)(4) requires the "same treatment" for all claims within a class. Section 1122 governs classification of claims in Chapter 11 plans.

D. ACCEPTANCE OF THE PLAN

Chapter 11 contemplates a consensual restructuring of the debtor's financial obligations. While Chapter 11 does not require that every holder of a claim approve the plan (and indeed allows the cramming down of a plan opposed by most holders of claims), it does require that creditors receive adequate information about a plan and have an opportunity to vote on the plan.

E. CONFIRMATION OF THE PLAN

Approval of a Chapter 11 plan involves not only creditor acceptance but also court confirmation. A bankruptcy judge has the power to confirm a Chapter 11 plan that has not received the needed majorities; a bankruptcy judge has the power not to confirm a Chapter 11 plan that has been accepted by all holders of claims and interests.

1. STANDARDS FOR CONFIRMATION

a. Plans Accepted by Every Class

Section 1129(a) sets out 13 confirmation requirements for plans accepted by every class. Subject to the limited exception of sections 1129(c) and 1129(d), a plan that has been accepted by every class of claims and every class of interests must be confirmed by the bankruptcy court if the 13 enumerated requirements of section 1129(a) are satisfied. Section 1129(b) does not apply to plans that have been accepted by every class of claims and every class of interests.

b. Plans Accepted by Less Than Every Class

Plans accepted by less than every class can be confirmed only if the additional requirements of section 1129(b) are satisfied. This is commonly called a cram down. Section 1129(b) requires that: (1) at least one impaired class of claims has accepted the plan; (2) the plan does not discriminate unfairly; and (3) the plan is fair and equitable.

2. EFFECT OF CONFIRMATION

After confirmation of a Chapter 11 plan, the debtor's performance obligations are governed by the terms of the plan. The provisions of a confirmed Chapter 11 plan bind not only the debtor but also the debtor's creditors and shareholders "whether or not such creditor, equity security holder, or general partner has accepted the plan," section 1141(a). Subject to limitations noted below, confirmation of a Chapter 11 plan operates as a discharge, section 1141(d). The following hypothetical illustrates the possible application of section 1141(a) and section 1141(d).

F. SPECIAL FORMS OF CHAPTER 11 CASES

1. PREPACKAGED

A prepackaged plan is a bankruptcy plan of reorganization which has been negotiated and accepted by the requisite number of creditors prior to the commencement of the bankruptcy case.

2. SMALL BUSINESS CASES

The 1994 bankruptcy legislation adds a definition of "small business" to section 101. A small business must (i) be engaged in commercial or business activities other than real estate and (ii) have liquidated, noncontingent debts of no more than $2 million. In Chapter 11 cases in which the debtor meets the "small business" definition, the court can dispense with the requirement of a creditors' committee on request of any party in interest. All other special Chapter 11 rules for small businesses apply only if the debtor elects.

3. SINGLE ASSET REAL ESTATE CASES

The 1994 amendments also added a definition of "single asset real estate" to section 101 and a new ground for relief from stay for single asset real estate debtor cases in section 362(d). Even though there is no statutory basis for treating Chapter 11 cases involving a real estate debtor different from other Chapter 11 cases, a distinct body of Chapter 11 single asset real estate case law has developed.

4. INDIVIDUAL CHAPTER 11 CASES

A Chapter 11 case in which the debtor is an individual is, in most respects, similar to a Chapter 13 case.

G. REVIEW QUESTIONS

■ XIX. ALLOCATION OF JUDICIAL POWER OVER BANKRUPTCY MATTERS

In the main, the substantive law of bankruptcy is in title 11 of the United States Code. Questions of judicial power over bankruptcy-related matters are, in the main, answered in title 28 of the United States Code.

A. HISTORY

Congress in 1978 decided to create a bankruptcy court with pervasive jurisdiction. Apparently for political reasons, Congress also decided that this bankruptcy court should *not* be an Article III court.

The 1978 grant of pervasive jurisdiction to a non-Article III bankruptcy court was successfully challenged in the *Marathon* case. Northern Pipeline, a Chapter 11 debtor, filed a breach of contract lawsuit against Marathon Pipeline in bankruptcy court. There was no question as to whether the bankruptcy court had jurisdiction over this lawsuit under 28 USCA 1471(c). Marathon Pipeline did, however, question whether section 1471(c) conferred Article III judicial power on non-Article III courts in violation of the separation of powers doctrine and filed a motion to dismiss. A divided Supreme Court sustained Marathon's challenge in Northern Pipeline Constr. Co. v. Marathon Pipeline Co. (1982).

After *Marathon*, Congress was urged to solve the constitutional dilemma by establishing bankruptcy courts as Article III courts. Congress rejected this solution. Instead, Congress in 1984 made the bankruptcy court a part of the federal district court, conferred jurisdiction in bankruptcy on the district court, and allocated judicial power in bankruptcy matters between the federal district judge and the bankruptcy judge. In the two-year gap between the 1982 Marathon decision and the 1984 legislation, the allocation of judicial power over bankruptcy was governed by an Emergency Rule adopted by all district courts.

B. OPERATION OF PRESENT LAW

In understanding the present law allocating judicial powers over bankruptcy matters, it is necessary to understand three separate sections in title 28: (1) 151, (2) 1334 and (3) 157.

1. BANKRUPTCY COURT AS PART OF THE DISTRICT COURT, SECTION 151

Section 151 refers to a bankruptcy judge and a bankruptcy court as a "unit" of the district court. It is important to keep this reference in mind when reading other sections in title 28 dealing with the allocation of judicial power in bankruptcy matters. When the term "district court" appears in section 1334 or section 157, it could be referring to the United States district judge and/or the bankruptcy judge. After all, the bankruptcy judge is a part of the district court—a "unit" of the district court.

2. GRANTS OF JURISDICTION TO THE DISTRICT COURT, SECTION 1334(a) and 1334(b)

a. Cases

Section 1334(a) vests original and exclusive jurisdiction in the district court over all cases arising under the Bankruptcy Code. "Case" is a term of art used in both the Bankruptcy Code and the Bankruptcy Rules. "Case" refers to the entire Chapter 7, 9, 11, 12 or 13—not just some controversy that arises in connection with it.

b. Proceedings

The term "case" is to be distinguished from the term "proceeding." A specific dispute that arises during the pendency of a case is referred to as a "proceeding." Section 1334(b) provides that the district courts have original but not exclusive jurisdiction over all civil proceedings, "arising under title 11, or arising in or related to cases under title 11."

"Proceedings" include "contested matters," motions brought in the main bankruptcy case and "adversary proceedings," lawsuits. Section 1334(b) grants the district court original but not exclusive jurisdiction over three types of "civil proceedings":

3. ROLE OF THE BANKRUPTCY COURT, SECTION 157

Clearly, section 1334 confers jurisdiction over bankruptcy matters to the district court. It is equally clear that most federal district judges have neither the time nor the inclination to exercise this jurisdiction. Accordingly, section 157 empowers the district judge to refer bankruptcy matters to the bankruptcy judge.

4. ABSTENTION UNDER SECTION 1334(c)

Abstention under section 1334(c) moves litigation from bankruptcy court to a state court. Section 1334(c)(1) provides for permissive abstention. If the district court believes that abstention would be "in the interest of justice" or "in the interest of comity with State courts or respect for State law," it has the option of abstaining. Section 1334(c)(2) provides for mandatory abstention in certain circumstances.

C. JURY TRIALS

There are two questions about jury trials in bankruptcy proceedings. First, when is there a right to a jury trial. Second, can the bankruptcy judge conduct the jury trial.

1. When Is There a Right?

The Supreme Court addressed this question (sort of) in Granfinanciera, S.A. v. Nordberg (1989), which found a right to jury trial in fraudulent conveyance litigation where (1) the trustee is seeking a money judgment and (2) the transferee has not filed a proof of claim. In so ruling, the Court compared "the statutory action to 18th-century actions brought in the courts of England prior to the merger of the courts of law and equity" and concluded that "actions to recover preferential or fraudulent transfers were often brought at law in late 18th-century England."

2. When Can a Bankruptcy Judge Hold a Jury Trial?

Section 157(e) answers the second question of whether a bankruptcy judge can hold a jury trial. Actually, the federal district judge and the parties to the proceeding answer the question of who holds the jury trial. Under section 157(e), the bankruptcy judge can conduct the jury trial only if she has been "specially designated" by the district judge and "all of the parties" consent.

D. REVIEW QUESTIONS

*

Perspective

■ *WHAT THIS BOOK IS ABOUT—A PREVIEW*

This is a book about debtors and creditors and about loans, credit extended for the purchase of property or service, taxes, a lease, a judgment, a tort claim for damages, or any other payment obligation. This book (and your law school course in bankruptcy or debtor–creditor law) are not about how or why the obligation was created. This book (and your course) are about what a debtor or creditor can do under state law, under federal law other than the Bankruptcy Code; and under the Bankruptcy Code when a debtor is unable or unwilling to pay that obligation.

This book begins when a debtor–creditor relationship breaks down, not when a debtor–creditor relationship begins. More specifically, this book begins with state law and federal law other than the Bankruptcy Code. It begins with the rights of an individual debtor and the remedies of consumer or commercial creditors under state and nonbankruptcy law when the debtor is unable or unwilling to pay. The longer, second part of the book deals with federal bankruptcy law, that is, with the bankruptcy law rights of an individual debtor or a business debtor to avoid or modify payment obligations and the effect of bankruptcy law on creditors' state-law and federal, nonbankruptcy remedies.

This book covers both individuals and businesses: both consumer debt and business debt. And, both bankruptcy law and nonbankruptcy law treat individual debtors different from and (generally) more favorably than business debtors.

This book is not just about debtors versus creditors but also about creditors versus creditors. A debtor who fails to pay one of its creditors generally fails to pay other creditors. And such a debtor may have the resources to pay some but not all of its debts. Then the real battle is among creditors over the debtor's assets, the value of which is less than the total of all of the debts. In such a battle among creditors, the outcome depends on nonbankruptcy concepts such as (1) priorities, (2) liens, and (3) priority among liens; and the outcome depends on the effects of bankruptcy law on these concepts.

■ LIENS AND PRIORITIES

Just as the law distinguishes among debtors, it also treats some creditors different from and more favorably than other creditors. There are at least three identifiable categories of creditors: (1) creditors with a "lien," (2) creditors with a "priority," and (3) creditors with neither a lien nor a priority. While each of these three classes of creditors has the same basic interest—prompt and complete payment of all debts—the law affords each class distinctive rights and remedies.

A "lien" is a property interest, i.e., a charge, on the debtor's rights in property that must be satisfied before the property or its proceeds is available for satisfaction of the claims of general creditors. A lien thus affects not only the lienor and the debtor but other creditors as well because it withdraws some of the debtor's resources that would otherwise be available for distribution to other creditors.

The lienor, i.e., a creditor with a lien, may resort to the encumbered property for the purpose of collecting its claim, yielding only to certain creditors with competing liens. To illustrate, assume that D has property worth $1,000 and owes A $300, B $400 and C $500. Assume further that D's property includes a 1996 Kia worth $400 on which B has a lien. In the event that D defaulted on his debts, B would have first right to the Kia or the proceeds from the sale thereof. If, however, D's Kia was worth only $300, B's claim for the other $100 would be treated no differently from the claims of A and C. A creditor is a lien creditor only to the extent of the value of its collateral.

A lien may be created by agreement, common law, statute, or judicial proceeding. Consensual liens on personalty are governed by Article 9 of the Uniform Commercial Code and are commonly referred to as security interests. Consensual liens on realty are generally called mortgages. The creation and perfection of consensual liens is treated in the commercial law course in most law schools and is beyond the scope of this BlackLetter. Judicial liens result from prejudgment collection efforts such as attachment or garnishment, from the judgment itself or recordation thereof, and from postjudgment efforts to enforce the judgment such as execution and garnishment. Common law and statutory liens are more difficult to describe and more difficult to identify but include landlords' liens, mechanics' liens, and tax liens.

Not all devices that are called liens are liens, however. Some are merely "priorities." Unfortunately, the word "priority" has two different meanings in debtor-creditor law:

    a.   rights of a lien creditor vis-à-vis another creditor with a lien on the same property, as this example illustrates:

- On January 10, S lends D $10,000 and obtains and perfects a security interest in D's equipment;

- On February 2, X lends D $20,000 and obtains and perfects a security interest in D's equipment;

- On March 3, D defaults on both loans. The equipment is only worth $8,000. Both S and X are lien creditors. The property subject to the two liens is not sufficient to satisfy both liens. It is necessary to determine which lien has PRIORITY.

    b.   rights of a creditor without a lien in an insolvency proceeding who gets certain, preferential treatment behind creditors with liens but ahead of creditors without liens.

The major distinction between liens and priorities is drawn on the basis of when the interest arises. A priority does not arise until distribution of a debtor's assets on insolvency. Liens normally arise before and are enforceable without regard to insolvency of the debtor. There are other differences, as this chart shows:

Liens	Priorities
1. Consensual, judicial or statutory	1. Almost always created by statute
2. Interest in particular property of the debtor	2. Satisfied from the general assets of the debtor
3. In a distribution governed by state law, lien creditors are paid first from the property subject to the lien. Some lien creditors have "priority" over other lien creditors.	3. Priorities generally affect only the rights of one general creditor (or group of general creditors) vis-à-vis other general creditors. Accordingly, in a distribution governed by state law, creditors with a priority usually are paid after lien creditors and before general creditors without any priority.
4. In a distribution governed by the Bankruptcy Code, liens that meet certain statutory standards are paid first.	4. All state-created priorities are invalid in a bankruptcy case. Bankruptcy law contains its own priority provision, section 507.

SOURCES OF DEBTOR–CREDITOR LAW

This BlackLetter considers both bankruptcy and nonbankruptcy debtor-creditor law. The nonbankruptcy part of debtor-creditor law is primarily state collection law. Much of the state law is codification of early English common law doctrine. To a large extent, the states' laws share a common design. They agree on the kind of rights available to individual debtors and the kinds of remedies available to creditors, but they disagree widely on the details. This book focuses on the general design of rights and remedies that are common throughout the country and considers some of the significant state collection law questions that arise throughout the country. When, later in practice, you encounter these questions, you will find that each state has one or more "how to" texts for lawyers that fill in the needed details.

Bankruptcy law is federal law. The Constitution in article 1, section 8, clause 4 empowers Congress to establish "uniform laws on the subject of Bankruptcies throughout the United States." Congress has acted pursuant to this grant of power, and states are therefore preempted from enacting bankruptcy laws. Bankruptcy laws can be found in Title 11 of the United States Code.

The present bankruptcy statute, generally referred to as the Bankruptcy Code, was enacted in 1978. It replaced the Bankruptcy Act of 1898.

The Bankruptcy Code has been regularly amended since 1978. The most significant amendments were enacted in 1984 and 2005. This book covers the Bankruptcy Code, as amended.

I

Extra Judicial Collection Devices

■ *ANALYSIS*

A. **Common Law Limitations**
1. Defamation
2. Invasion of Privacy
3. Public Disclosure of Private Facts
4. Wrongful Intrusion on Solitude
5. Emotional Distress

B. **Federal Fair Debt Collection Practices Act (FDCPA)**
1. Scope
2. Limits on Debt Collectors
3. Remedies

C. **Review Questions**

As long as the debtor is making payments when due, debtor-creditor law is of little practical significance. The debtor, of course, does not always make the required payments. The ready availability of consumer credit often leads to over-extension in debt and, subsequently, default. The creditor can proceed to collect the debt by using either extrajudicial or judicial methods. Because of the delay and expense involved in litigation, the creditor is likely initially to employ extrajudicial tactics to obtain payment.

The extrajudicial collection method most generally used is the dunning letter. This letter, containing a request for payment, can be either cordial or hostile depending on the policy of the creditor and the length of time that the debt is outstanding. Debtors seldom respond to a polite request for payment. Consequently, creditors seek other methods to recover the money due and owing, including telephone calls, personal visits, threats of lawsuit, and communications with an individual debtor's employer or neighbors or a business debtor's customers or suppliers. Occasionally the creditor or its agent becomes overzealous, particularly when the debtor is weak and vulnerable.

A. Common Law Theories and Limitations

Courts have sought to moderate the conduct of creditors by allowing debtors to recover for unreasonable collection activities under the following common law tort concepts: defamation, invasion of the right to privacy, and intentional infliction of mental anguish. Recoveries on these theories, however, are relatively rare. It is difficult to match the usual facts of debt collection with the elements of these torts.

1. Defamation

Defamation is aimed at publication of false material. Truth is thus a defense and, in most jurisdictions, is an absolute defense. A statement truthfully disclosing that a debt is due, owing, and unpaid is not actionable. A statement that falsely imputes a general unwillingness to pay debts or unworthiness to obtain credit may be the basis of a defamation action.

Another defense to defamation is privilege. A communication will be privileged if it pertains to a matter in which the recipient of the communication has a legitimate interest. Informing an employer that his employee has not paid his debts is a common collection tactic to induce payment through indirect pressure on the employee. Employers want to avoid the bother and costs of wage garnishment. Courts are divided as to whether employers have a sufficient interest to cause the communication to be privileged.

2. Invasion of Privacy

Debtors have also sued on invasion of privacy grounds for injuries resulting from creditors' communications with employers, though generally with little success.

3. Public Disclosure of Private Facts

Public disclosure of private facts is one form of invasion of the right to privacy. However, as a general rule, reasonable oral or written communications to an employer have not been viewed as a sufficient disclosure of private facts; as with defamation, the communication is privileged based on the employer's interest in his employee's debts.

Some courts have granted recovery where the creditor has done more than inform the employer that a debt is overdue: for example, contacting the employer on numerous occasions. Additionally, there are cases finding an invasion of privacy by communications such as calls to the debtor's neighbors, publication of the debtor's name and amount of debt in a newspaper, and posting a notice of the indebtedness at the creditor's place of business.

4. Wrongful Intrusion on Solitude

A second form of violation of the right to privacy is a wrongful intrusion on the solitude of the debtor. Obviously, every creditor contact, every intrusion, is not actionable. The creditor has the right to contact the debtor, that is, has the right to try and collect the debt. The problem is one of balancing the respective interests. Only unreasonable intrusions are actionable. In determining reasonableness, courts generally consider factors such as the content, nature, number, and time of communications.

5. Emotional Distress

Where a creditor's contacts with the debtor are "extreme and outrageous" and result in emotional distress, the debtor may be able to recover on a theory of intentional infliction of mental distress. First, the court must find that the creditor intended to inflict mental distress. Second, the court must find that the creditor's actions were extreme and outrageous—beyond all bounds of decency. Another difficulty attending this cause of action is the requirement that the emotional stress be severe. The normal strain caused by contact with a collection agency is not sufficient. The debtor has to establish serious mental stress. Most courts also have been hesitant to impose liability for mental distress alone and have insisted on some form of physical injury.

B. Federal Fair Debt Collection Practices Act (FDCPA)

A number of states statutorily regulate the collection of consumer debts. Congress has enacted the Fair Debt Collection Practices Act (FDCPA), which is 15 U.S.C.A. §§ 1692–1692o.

1. Scope

The FDCPA does not apply to all debt collection efforts. It does not apply to the collection of commercial debts—only consumer debts as those terms are defined in FDCPA. And, the FDCPA does not apply to all efforts to collect consumer debts. The FDCPA applies only to the efforts of "debt collectors" to collect consumer debts.

a. Meaning of Consumer Debt

A consumer debt for purposes of this law is any obligation or alleged obligation of a natural person to pay money arising out of a transaction in which the money, property, insurance, or services which are the subject of the transaction are primarily for personal, family, or household purposes. 15 U.S.C.A. § 803(3), (5).

b. Meaning of "Debt Collector"

The FDCPA definition of "debt collector" includes persons who regularly collect debts owing to someone else. 15 U.S.C.A. § 803(6). Accordingly, the FDCPA applies to a lawyer who regularly endeavors to collect "consumer debts" owing to her clients. The FDCPA does not, however, apply to the lender or creditor that is attempting to collect its own debts.

2. Limits on Debt Collectors

a. Contacting Third Parties

In connection with the collection of any debt, a "debt collector" may not contact any person other than the debtor, the debtor's lawyer, a consumer reporting agency, the creditor, the creditor's lawyer, and the debtor collector's lawyer, except to find information to locate the debtor. 15 U.S.C.A. § 805(b). And, when talking with other people to find the debtor, the debt collector must follow certain, strict guidelines, id. § 804; and the debt collector cannot talk to other people even for the purpose of locating the debtor after the debtor collector knows that the debtor is represented by a lawyer. Id. § 804(6).

b. Contacting the Debtor

FDCPA does not expressly limit the number of times, or the means by which, a "debt collector" may contact a debtor in attempting to collect a debt, but it governs such contacts. The contact must not be at a time or place "which should be known to be inconvenient" and must assume that the convenient time for communicating with a debtor after 8 o'clock a.m. and before 9 o'clock p.m. The collector cannot contact the debtor at the debtor's place of employment if the collector knows or has reason to know that the employer prohibits the consumer from receiving such communication. And, there can be no contact with the debtor if the debt collector knows the debtor is represented by an attorney with respect to the debt and has knowledge of, or can readily ascertain, such attorney's name and address. 15 U.S.C.A. § 805(a). All "debt collector" contact with the debtor must cease when the debt collector learns that the debtor is represented by an attorney, receives a written refusal to pay, or receives a written communication from the debtor requesting that such contacts end. Id. § 805(c).

c. Verifying the Debt

Once the debtor has been located and contacted, the "debt collector" must give the debtor the opportunity to require verification of the debt. No later than five days after first communicating with the debtor, the "debt collector" must send the debtor a written notice setting out the amount of the debt, the name of the creditor, the debtor's right to dispute the accuracy or existence of the debt, and the debt collector's duty to obtain verification of the debt if it is disputed by the debtor within thirty days. 15 U.S.C.A. § 809.

d. Unfair Conduct

In addition to the above rules limiting contacts by "debt collectors," FDCPA also generally forbids any conduct by "debt collectors" which is abusive, deceptive, misleading, or unfair and contains "laundry lists" of illustrative practices which are specifically forbidden. 15 U.S.C.A. §§ 807 & 808.

3. Remedies

A "debt collector" who violates the FDCPA is civilly liable for damages, including attorney's fees. 15 U.S.C.A. § 813. A violation of FDCPA is also considered an unfair or deceptive act or practice, in violation of the Federal Trade Commission Act. The Federal Trade Commission may thus seek a variety of remedies against a "debt collector" that violates the FDCPA.

C. Review Questions

1. Debtor owes Creditor money. Creditor sends Debtor's employer a very polite letter explaining the debt and asking the employer to encourage Debtor to pay it. Debtor want sues Creditor under the common law for defamation and public disclosure of private facts. On which theory is Debtor likely to prevail?

2. Debtor owes Creditor money. Creditor sends Debtor's employer a very polite letter explaining the debt and asking the employer to encourage Debtor to

pay it. Debtor want sues Creditor for damages under the Fair Debt Collection Practices Act. Is Debtor likely to win or lose?

3. Who is a debt collector subject to the FDCPA?

4. What debts does FDCPA cover?

5. How may a debt collector contact the debtor?

6. Can a debtor stop a debt collector from contacting her?

7. May a debt collector contact anyone else about the debt the debtor owes?

8. Debtor owes Creditor money. Creditor hires Debt Collector to collect the debt. Collector sends Debtor's employer a very polite letter explaining the debt and asking the employer to encourage Debtor to pay it. Debtor want sues Collector for damages under the Fair Debt Collection Practices Act. Is Debtor likely to win or lose?

9. What must the debt collector tell a debtor about the debt?

10. May a debt collector continue to contact the debtor if the debtor believes she does not owe money?

II

Judicial Debt Collection

■ *ANALYSIS*

    With Postjudgment Liens on the Debtor's Personal Property
  4. Creditor's Bill
  5. Supplementary Proceedings
  6. Execution Sales
  7. Garnishment
E. Review Questions

A creditor wants to collect as much as possible, as soon as possible, at the lowest possible collection cost. If the creditor's letters and calls and other extrajudicial collection efforts do not result in "voluntary" payment by the debtor, the creditor will look for some way to seize and sell the debtor's property and use the proceeds from the sale to reduce the amount of the debt.

In general, a creditor's state law remedies are ways to get the debtor's property away from her for the purpose of selling the property and applying the net sale proceeds to the debt. To maintain order, the state alone is authorized to use force in this process.

Ordinarily, the state will not get involved in forcefully taking a debtor's property until the creditor gets a judgment. It is through this process of the creditor reducing its claim to judgment that the state determines the validity and the amount of the debt. After judgment, the state in essence aligns itself with the creditor and takes the debtor's property—forcibly if necessary—and sells it to satisfy the creditor's judgment.

This process of seizure and sale of the debtor's property to satisfy a judgment is generally known as execution. The execution process is the base judicial collection remedy of all creditors and is the only judicial collection remedy of creditors without a consensual or statutory lien.

A. Exempt Property

"Exempt property" is important if, and only if, the debtor is an individual (i.e., a natural person). Today, all states constitutionally or statutorily restrict creditor recourse to certain property belonging to individuals. Property designated in these exemption provisions can *not* be reached by creditors through judicial collection efforts. A three-pronged purpose is commonly attributed to exemption statutes: protection of the debtor, protection of the family of the debtor, and protection of society. By allowing the debtor to retain certain property free from appropriation by creditors, exemption statutes extend to a debtor an opportunity for self-support so that he will not become a burden upon the public.

In looking at exemption statutes, a lawyer or law student should look for the answers to three different questions:

1. What property can a debtor claim as exempt?

2. What does a debtor have to do to claim the exemptions?

3. What creditors are not affected by a claim that property is exempt?

The exemption statutes of the different states answer these questions differently. There are two notable characteristics of state exemption statutes: (1) obsolescence and (2) extreme variety. Nevertheless, certain generalizations are possible.

1. Personal Property

All states exempt certain personal property from creditor process. In some jurisdictions, the exempt property is identified by type (e.g., the family bible, the family rifle); in others, by value (e.g., personal property of a value of $5,000); in still others, by both type and value (e.g., an automobile with a value of not more than $1,500). In most states, some specific provision is made for the exemption of life insurance (both the proceeds of the policy and the cash surrender value thereof) and wages.

2. Real Property

Almost all states also have exemption laws designed to protect the family home, i.e., the "homestead," from the reach of certain classes of creditors. Homestead laws only protect real property interests of the debtor and so are of no aid to the urban apartment dweller. Moreover, not all real property interests of the debtor may be the subject of a homestead claim. Common statutory limitations include the requirements that the debtor have a family, that the property be occupied and used as a residence (an almost universal limitation), that the owner have a specified (usually present, possessory) interest in the property, and (in a few states) that there be a formal declaration that the property is a homestead.

3. Procedure

The procedure for asserting rights under an exemption statute also varies from state to state. The burden usually is on the debtor to claim the exemption, and usually the statute sets a time limit on assertion of an exemption. Where the statute is of a "value" type—e.g., personal property of a value of $5,000—the statute generally provides for the appointment of appraisers who value property selected as exempt by the debtor. Where the statute specifies items of property that are exempt, courts are often confronted with the problem of applying a 19th century statute to 20th century property, e.g., whether a television set is a "musical instrument" or whether an automobile is a salesman's "tool of trade."

4. Limits on Exemptions

The protection afforded by an exemption statute is not absolute. The federal tax lien reaches and may be satisfied from exempt property. A number of states make similar exceptions for state taxes, claims for alimony and child support, materialmen and mechanics' liens.

By statute in most states and case law in other states, mortgages and security interests are generally not affected by an exemption statute. Thus, the bank that finances the purchase of a home or car will be able to seize and sell the property notwithstanding the fact that the property is covered by an exemption statute. Or, if *D* gives *C* a second lien on her car to secure a Christmas loan, *C* can, on *D*'s default, foreclose on *D*'s car.

On the other hand, an executory agreement to waive the benefit of an exemption has generally been held to be invalid as against public policy, notwithstanding some obvious similarities between such a waiver and a nonpurchase money mortgage.

5. Federal Court

Exemptions are mainly state law, even in federal court. Creditors' process issued from a federal court generally is subject to exemptions provided by the law of the state where the court sits.

6. Federal Law

a. Federal Exemptions

There are also federal statutes that exempt property from the reach of creditors in either federal court or state court. Most of the federal provisions relate to the benefits of federal social legislation such as money paid under social security and veterans' benefits.

b. Restrictions on Garnishment

Title III of the Consumer Credit Protection Act provides a statutory minimum exemption of wages from garnishments. Title III is not really an exemption provision. It does not exempt all or part of the debtor's wages. It merely protects the wages from garnishment. Once the wages have been paid to the debtor, creditors can look to the money to satisfy their claims.

1) Amount

Under Title III, creditors may garnish in the aggregate only 25% of a person's weekly "disposable earnings" or the amount by which his "deposable earnings" exceed thirty times the minimum hourly wage, whichever is less.

2) Loss of Employment

Title III of the Consumer Credit Protection Act also affords protection to a debtor from being fired because of garnishment. The Act prohibits the discharge of any employee by reason of the fact that his earnings have been subjected to garnishment "for any one indebtedness." Thus if D is indebted to C, and C garnishes D's wages several times in an attempt to satisfy his claim, D's employer cannot discharge him because of these garnishments: there is only "one indebtedness."

On the other hand, if D is indebted to both C and E and both garnish D's wages, D's employer can discharge him because of the garnishments: there is more than "one indebtedness."

The prohibition against firing is probably of limited practical significance in light of the difficulty of establishing the reason for dismissal and the absence of any express private remedy for wrongful discharge. The Act provides for enforcement by the Secretary of Labor. Courts are divided as to whether to imply a private right of action.

3) Relation to State Law

Title III does not preempt state statutes "prohibiting garnishments or providing for more limited garnishments than are allowed under [Title III]." Where state restrictions are stronger, it will be state law which regulates. Title III also makes provision for state law to apply in lieu of the wage garnishment provisions of Title III where the Secretary of Labor determines that the laws of that state provide restrictions on garnishment which are "substantially similar" to those provided in the Act.

B. Prejudgment Remedies

A creditor trying to collect a claim through the judicial process is not always able to obtain a judgment immediately. Litigation (even collection litigation) is costly and time-consuming. While the collection lawsuit is pending, the debtor may dispose of his assets or other creditors may seize the debtor's property to satisfy their claims. In *very limited* circumstances, the state will impound property of the debtor during the pendency of the lawsuit.

1. Attachment

a. Origin and Purpose

At early common law, attachment was a form of process to compel the defendant to appear and answer in a lawsuit if he failed to appear in response to the summons or original writ. The writ commanded the sheriff to attach (grab and hold) the property of the defendant to compel his appearance. If he appeared, the property was returned to him; if he failed to appear, the property was forfeited.

In the 17th century, the nature of attachment changed from a means of compelling the defendant's appearance to a prejudgment (provisional) collection remedy: attached property was no longer released upon the appearance of the defendant but remained attached until after judgment and collection of same. No longer is the main objective of attachment to coerce the defendant debtor to appear by seizure of his property. Today, the writ of attachment seizes the debtor's property in order to secure the debt or claim of the creditor in the event that a judgment is obtained.

Today, attachment is purely statutory. The statutes vary considerably as to when attachment is available.

Federal courts follow the local rules relating to attachment. Fed.Civ.Proc. Rule 64.

b. Limits on Attachment

Attachment is *not* available to every creditor in every collection action. Rather, the use of attachment is generally limited in several ways:

1) Kind of Action

The statutes providing for attachment commonly spell out specific kinds of actions that may be the basis for the issuance of an attachment. Attachment statutes in many states distinguish between claims *ex contractu* and claims *ex delicto*, sometimes establishing different requirements with respect to attachment for each type of claim, and sometimes providing for attachment only upon claims *ex contractu*.

2) Grounds Necessary

Attachment is usually available only on a showing of special statutory grounds. In general the statutory grounds deal with one of three situations:

- Where the plaintiff is unable to obtain personal service upon a defendant because the defendant is absent from the state, concealing himself, or a nonresident;

- Where the nature of the plaintiff's underlying claim entitles it to special treatment such as a claim based on fraud or a claim for "the necessaries of life";

- Where the defendant has assigned, disposed of, or secreted, or is about to assign, dispose of, or secrete property with the intent to defraud creditors.

3) Bond Required

A bond is commonly required. The usual condition of the bond is that the plaintiff shall pay all costs that may be awarded to the defendant and all damages that defendant may sustain by reason of the attachment, if the order of attachment is dissolved or if the plaintiff fails to obtain judgment against the defendant.

4) Due Process

As a result of Supreme Court decisions in *Sniadach v. Family Finance Corp.*, *Fuentes v. Shevin*, *Mitchell v. W.T. Grant Co.*, *North Georgia Finishing, Inc. v. Di–Chem, Inc.*, and *Connecticut v. Doehr* (all of which are discussed later in this Black Letter), states now require that the debtor be provided notice and an opportunity for a hearing or other sufficient due process before the debtor's property may be attached.

c. Procedure for Attachment

Attachment procedure varies considerably from state to state. In most states, a creditor seeking attachment must first file a complaint. The creditor then files an affidavit stating facts establishing the ground for attachment and posts any necessary bond.

Originally, the clerk of the court in which the action is pending was authorized to issue writs of attachment ex parte. Since *Sniadach* and its progeny, most states require the opportunity for some form of hearing before a judge.

The writ of attachment is directed to the sheriff of a county in which property of the defendant is located. The order instructs the sheriff to attach and safely keep all nonexempt property of the defendant within the sheriff's county, or so much thereof as is sufficient to satisfy the plaintiff's demand together with costs and expenses. It also directs the sheriff to make a written return to the clerk of the court in which the action is pending showing all property attached and the date of seizure.

d. Levy

The act of the sheriff in taking custody over the property of the defendant is commonly referred to as "levy". What "levy" requires depends on the nature of the property. Levy on real property generally involves some act giving notice to the defendant of the lien and some act giving public notice that the debtor's realty is encumbered, such as filing in the real estate record system.

A levy of attachment upon tangible personal property generally requires a seizure or taking possession or control of the property. If the chattels are capable of manual delivery, most jurisdictions require the sheriff to take the chattels into his actual custody by either removing them or appointing an independent keeper. Where the property to be attached is of a bulky or cumbersome nature and removal would be very difficult and expensive, levy does not require removal or seizure.

Levy on property creates a lien thereon. In most states this lien of attachment dates from the time of the levy, although in some states the date of the lien relates back to the date of the issuance of the writ.

e. Advantages of Attachment

A creditor with an attachment lien enjoys a number of advantages:

1) Security

While a collection action is pending, a debtor may try to dispose of his assets. An attachment lien is effective against subsequent purchasers from the debtor.

Example: *D* is in default on its loan obligations to *C*. *C* files a lawsuit and obtains an attachment lien on *D*'s collection of Franklin Mint coins by having the sheriff seize the coins pursuant to a writ of attachment. While *C*'s lawsuit against *D* is pending, *D* sells the coins to *B*. *C* then obtains its judgment against *D*. *C* will be able to sell the Franklin Mint coins to satisfy its judgment. *C's* attachment lien is effective against *B*, a subsequent purchaser from the debtor, *D*. To obtain its attachment lien, *C* had to levy on, i.e., seize, the Franklin Mint coins. *D's* lack of possession put third parties such as *B* on notice of possible creditor's claims.

2) Priority

Often, a debtor lacks sufficient assets to pay all of his creditors. In such instances, state law does *not* provide for pro rata distributions. Rather, state law provides a series of priority rules. Most of the rules are "first-in-time" rules: the earlier the creditor obtains its lien, the greater its priority. For example, a creditor with an attachment lien takes priority over a creditor who subsequently obtains a judgment lien on the same property.

Example: *D* owes *A* $10,000 and *B* $20,000. *D* is in default on both debts, and *D's* only significant nonexempt asset is Greenacre. *A* sues *D* and obtains an attachment lien on Greenacre. Subsequently, *B* sues *D*, obtains a $20,000 judgment against *D*, and obtains a judgment lien on Greenacre. Then, *A* obtains a $10,000 judgment against *D*. If a sale of Greenacre only yields $17,000, *A* will receive $10,000 of the sale proceeds and *B* will receive the remaining $7,000.

3) Jurisdiction

The priority and security afforded by the lien are not the only advantages to a creditor of obtaining a writ of attachment. Attachment can also be used as a basis for jurisdiction. State courts can take jurisdiction over nonresidents who have property in the state if that property is brought within the court's jurisdiction by attachment and if substituted service (such as service by publication) is made. Such jurisdiction, called "quasi-in-rem" jurisdiction is generally less valuable to plaintiffs than personal jurisdiction: a judgment quasi-in-rem binds only the parties to the action and not the entire world, and it imposes no personal liability on the defendant, the award being limited to the property seized.

The importance of quasi-in-rem jurisdiction—and hence of attachment as a jurisdictional mechanism—has declined over the years. There are two principle reasons:

1. Long-arm statutes have increased the availability of in personam jurisdiction.

2. Shaffer v. Heitner (1977), decreased the availability of quasi-in-rem jurisdiction. Prior to *Shaffer*, presence of property in a state was itself sufficient basis for quasi-in-rem jurisdiction of the courts of that state. In *Shaffer*, however, the Court held that the "minimum contacts" standard of International Shoe Co. v. Washington (1945), governs not only *in personam* jurisdiction but also *in rem* jurisdiction.

4) Leverage

A very important practical advantage of attachment is the leverage that it gives the plaintiff. By directing the sheriff to levy on property essential to the defendant/debtor, the creditor greatly strengthens its bargaining position. Deprivation of property used daily or essential to a business may induce the debtor to pay even if the claim is of questionable validity.

f. Hazards of Attachment

There are at least three distinct hazards associated with attachment:

1) Fees

As indicated above, a bond is generally required of the creditor. And, the sheriff will usually require an indemnity bond before levying on property to protect him from liability should he attach the wrong property and incur liability for conversion. The sheriff is also entitled to reimbursement of expenses incurred in levying on the property and in preserving the attached property. Last, but not least, an attaching creditor must pay its attorney for the legal work involved in obtaining an attachment lien.

2) Liability for Wrongful Attachment

Attachment of personal property deprives the debtor of the use of the property for the duration of the litigation. Attachment of real property makes it difficult if not impossible for the debtor to sell the property for the duration of the litigation. If the debt collection action ends in a judgment for the debtor, the debtor can recover any actual damages she has suffered as a result of the attachment. Additionally, if the creditor attached the debtor's property maliciously and without probable cause, the debtor can recover punitive damages.

Tort liability has even been imposed on a creditor who prevails in the debt collection action. If the creditor has directed the sheriff as to which property to seize, the creditor is liable to the debtor if excessive property is seized, and is liable to third parties if their property is wrongfully seized.

3) Bankruptcy of the Debtor

Attachment benefits a single creditor at the expense of the debtor and other creditors. A debtor deprived by attachment of the use of important property may decide to file a bankruptcy petition. Moreover, attachment may motivate the debtor's other creditors to initiate involuntary bankruptcy proceedings. Under section 547 of the Bankruptcy Code, an attachment lien obtained within 90 days of the filing of the bankruptcy petition is invalid if the debtor was insolvent when the lien was obtained.

g. Terminating an Attachment

Failure to obtain a judgment will result in the attachment being dissolved.

A debtor may also terminate the attachment and obtain the attached property by posting a "discharging" or "dissolution" bond; these bonds are conditioned that the defendant in the attachment suit will perform whatever judgment will be entered against him and that, in the event of his default thereof, the surety will pay the amount of the judgment.

A second class of bond available in most jurisdictions are "forthcoming" or "delivery" bonds. These are conditioned that if judgment in the attachment suit is rendered against the defendant, the property shall be forthcoming to satisfy such judgment, otherwise the surety will be liable to the extent of the value of the property. Such bonds release the property only from the custody of the levying officer; they do not release the attached property from the lien of attachment.

2. Prejudgment Garnishment

Garnishment (or, in most New England states, trustee process) is a collection remedy directed not at the defendant but rather at some third person, the garnishee, who owes a debt to the principal debtor, has property of the principal debtor, or has property in which the principal debtor has an interest.

a. How It Works

Prejudgment garnishment is a warning or notice to the garnishee that the plaintiff/creditor claims the right to have such debt or property applied in satisfaction of his claim, and that the garnishee should hold such property until the creditor's suit has been tried and any judgment satisfied.

Example: C brought an action against D to collect a debt that was due and owing, and C learned that G held property of D, C might garnish this property. If C is successful in her action against D, C's judgment could be satisfied by the property of D held by G, and, if G no longer had such property, C could recover from G personally.

The most common examples of garnishees are the employer of the principal debtor and the bank in which the principal debtor has a savings or checking account.

b.   Relation to Attachment

Prejudgment garnishment is frequently referred to as a form of attachment. The two remedies are similar in many respects. In a number of states, garnishment is not an independent remedy but rather is a proceeding ancillary to attachment. In other states, however, garnishment is an independent action available for grounds other than those required for the issuance of an attachment and subject to different provisions for bond. In all states, there are some differences between attachment and garnishment. The following chart compares attachment and garnishment.

Attachment	Garnishment
1. Statutory	1. Statutory
2. Federal courts follow state rules as to availability	2. Federal courts follow state rules as to availability.
3. Device for obtaining quasi-in-rem jurisdiction over a nonresident.	3. Device for obtaining quasi-in-rem jurisdiction over a nonresident.
4. Directed to property in the possession of the principal debtor.	4. Directed to property of the debtor held by the garnishee.

5. Prejudgment remedy	5. Both a prejudgment and a postjudgment remedy
6. Seizure of the property pending judgment	6. Property left in the care and custody of the garnishee
7. Lien on attached property, generally dating from time of levy	7. In a few states, no lien; generally held to create a lien that dates from the service of process on the garnishee.

3. Replevin

a. Nature of the Remedy

At early common law, a landlord could enforce its rights to rent by the self-help remedy of distraint, i.e., seizing the personal property of the tenant. If the tenant disputed the landlord's claim of unpaid rent, he could, upon giving the sheriff security, obtain a writ of replevin directing the sheriff to recover possession of the seized personal property, pending litigation of the tenant's rent liability.

In this country, replevin has developed into a more general remedy. Today, replevin (and "sequestration" and "claim and delivery") are proceedings to recover possession of any personal property. At the commencement of the action, the sheriff seizes, i.e., replevies the property and turns it over to the plaintiff, pending outcome of the litigation over possession. If the defendant wishes to regain possession of the goods replevied, he may give a delivery or forthcoming bond.

b. Limited Availability

Replevin may not be used by all creditors. Replevin can only be maintained by one who has some property interest in and the immediate right to possession of the property sought to be recovered. Unpaid unsecured creditors do *not* have a right to possession of their debtors' property. Unpaid secured creditors *do* have a right to possession of the property encumbered by their liens.

Example: Assume that Pizza Inc. owes *U* $100,000 and *S* $200,000. *U* is an unsecured creditor. *S* has a security interest in Pizza Inc.'s ovens. Pizza Inc. defaults on both debts. The remedy of replevin is not available to *U*; *S* can *possibly replevy* the pizza ovens. Either *U* or *S possibly* can *attach* the pizza ovens and/or other property of Pizza Inc.

Compared to Attachment

The following chart compares attachment and replevin.

Attachment	Replevin
1. Statutory	1. Statutory
2. Federal courts follow state rules as to availability, Fed.Civ.Proc. Rule 64	2. Federal courts follow state rules as to availability, Fed.Civ.Proc. Rule 64
3. Any nonexempt property in the possession of the debtor	3. Limited to personal property which the creditor has a lien on and/or the right to possess
4. Prejudgment remedy	4. Both a prejudgment remedy and a form of action
5. Seizure of the property by sheriff who retains custody thereof pending judgment	5. Seizure of property by sheriff who turns property over to plaintiff pending judgment
6. Lien on attached property, generally dating from the time of levy	6. Generally, thought to create a lien that dates from the time of seizure

4. Receivership

a. Nature of the Remedy

Receivership, like garnishment, is both a prejudgment and a postjudgment collection remedy. A prejudgment receiver is a disinterested party, appointed by the court to administer, care for, collect and dispose of the property or the fruits of the property of another brought under the orders of the court by litigation.

b. When Receiver Appointed

The power to appoint a receiver is inherent in a court of equity. The appointment of a receiver is to a considerable extent a matter resting in the discretion of the court to which the application is made. Courts are very reluctant to appoint receivers prior to judgment, i.e., receivers *pendente lite*. There is a wealth of dictum to the effect that the appointment of a receiver is a harsh remedy and is to be used sparingly—only when the securing of ultimate justice seems to require it. And, since receivership is an equitable remedy, a court will not appoint a receiver when there is an adequate legal remedy such as attachment. Reported cases in which a receiver *pendente lite* has been appointed generally involve allegations of danger of loss, deterioration, or other impairment of the value of property that is the subject matter of the action or that will be necessary to satisfy any judgment in the action.

In 1844 New York adopted a civil code uniting the practice of law and equity; the Field Code provided in what cases a receiver should be appointed. Numerous other jurisdictions have followed New York's lead. Most such provisions are little more than a codification of the rules of equity except with regard to corporations. Many states have provisions for the appointment of receivers of corporations both before and after dissolution.

c. Powers of Receiver

The receiver has only such powers as are specifically conferred upon him by the court or by the statute under which he was appointed. Absent a statutory provision to the contrary, the appointment of a receiver works a change in possession of, but not title to, the property over which the receiver is appointed; statutes governing the appointment of a receiver prior to judgment generally contain no provision to the contrary. The powers of receivers *pendente lite* are generally quite limited. The receiver is usually required to take possession of the property as soon as possible after the order appointing him has been entered. The order may contemplate the mere holding of the property for the purpose of preserving it or it may direct some active duties such as the continuance of a business, collecting rents and profits, or the sale of property.

d. Effect on Other Creditors

1) No New Lien

The preceding paragraphs indicate one of the primary reasons that a creditor petitions for the appointment of a receiver *pendente lite* is preservation of property of the defendant/debtor pending determination of the creditor's claim. Receivership is similar to provisional remedies already discussed in that it is also used as leverage to obtain a favorable settlement. Receivership, however, differs from attachment and garnishment in that no advantage *vis-à-vis* other creditors accrues to the creditor who secures the appointment of a receiver. The petitioning creditor does not gain a lien on the property over which the receiver is appointed. And, since the appointment of a receiver *pendente lite* generally does not affect title to the property, existing liens on the property remain valid, and creditors can continue to obtain liens on property held by a receiver *pendente lite*.

Example: *C* sues *D*; prior to judgment *C* obtains the appointment of a receiver to hold and manage Greenacre Farms, a tract of land owned by *D* in Orange County. Prior to *C*'s obtaining a judgment, *E* obtains a judgment against *D*. *E* dockets this judgment in the county in which Greenacre Farms is located. Under the applicable state law, the docketing of a judgment creates a lien on all real property held by the judgment debtor in the county of docketing. This judgment lien would reach Greenacre Farms.

2) Other Creditors Stayed

The appointment of a receiver does in a limited way affect the rights of other creditors. While the appointment does not divest existing liens or prevent the creation of new liens, lien creditors cannot enforce their claims and thus disturb the receiver's possession without the permission of the court. Consent of the court that appointed the receiver is also generally regarded as necessary in order to garnish property held by a receiver.

5. Constitutional Due Process Limitations on Prejudgment Remedies

a. The Cases

Commencing in the late 1960's, prejudgment remedies came under attack in and by the courts.

1) *Sniadach*

In Sniadach v. Family Finance Corp. (1969), the Court held that the Wisconsin statute providing for prejudgment garnishment of wages was unconstitutional. Justice Douglas' opinion emphasizes the hardship that results from wage garnishment and suggests that due process requires notice and hearing prior to the issuance of a writ, except in "extraordinary situations."

2) *Fuentes*

Fuentes v. Shevin (1972) expands the due process limitations first recognized in *Sniadach* to property other than wages, to prejudgment remedies other than garnishment. *Fuentes* involved replevin of consumer goods. The Court held the Florida and Pennsylvania replevin statutes unconstitutional; the opinion suggests that except in "extraordinary situations," notice and hearing must precede the seizure.

3) *Mitchell*

In Mitchell v. W. T. Grant Co. (1974), the Court held that a Louisiana statute permitting a judge to issue, without prior notice and hearing, a writ of sequestration based on a vendor's lien adequately balanced the property interests of the creditor and the debtor and satisfied due process. The opinion distinguishes this Louisiana statute from the Florida and Pennsylvania replevin provisions involved in *Fuentes*. The Louisiana statute requires the creditor to allege specific facts supporting its claim, rather than the conclusory allegations of right that were sufficient under the Florida and Pennsylvania provisions. In *Mitchell*, the application for prejudgment relief was made to a judge, not a clerk. And, the Louisiana statute at issue in *Mitchell* gives the debtor the right to an immediate post seizure hearing.

The majority opinion in *Mitchell* generated confusion (even among the Justices of the Supreme Court) as to whether *Fuentes* had been overruled. The *Mitchell* decision has also created uncertainty as to whether (1) *Mitchell* applies to all prejudgment remedies or is limited to prejudgment remedies such as sequestration that are available only to creditors with an interest in the property to be seized, and (2) whether *all* of the safeguards present in the Louisiana statute are necessary in the absence of a pre-seizure adversary hearing.

4) *North Georgia*

North Georgia Finishing, Inc. v. Di–Chem, Inc. (1975) relies on *Fuentes* in finding the Georgia prejudgment garnishment statute in violation of procedural due process. The *North Georgia* opinion also relies on *Mitchell* even though the creditor in *North Georgia* had no property interest in the bank account it was trying to garnish. "The Georgia garnishment statute has *none* of the saving characteristics of the Louisiana statute." The Georgia garnishment statute did not require specific factual allegations of entitlement, judicial participation, or provide the opportunity for a prompt post seizure hearing.

5) *Doehr*

Connecticut v. Doehr (1991) briefly reviewed the above four cases in holding that Connecticut's statute providing for prejudgment attachment of real estate did not satisfy the Due Process Clause. In so holding, the Court rejected the view of some lower courts that attachment of real estate did not trigger due process protection because the nonpossessory restrictions on alienation did not constitute a significant taking for due process purposes.

b.   A Synthesis of the Cases

While the relationship between the various cases is somewhat unclear, the following basic propositions seem clear:

- Prejudgment remedies are not unconstitutional per se.

- The use of prejudgment remedies is subject to due process limitations.

- Due process requires notice and an opportunity for an adversary proceeding.

- In at least some, emergency-like situations, a pre-seizure ex parte hearing coupled with the opportunity for a prompt post seizure adversary proceeding will satisfy due process.

C.   Obtaining a Judgment

A creditor, of course, wants to obtain the judgment as quickly and as inexpensively as possible. A default judgment is thus preferable to a judgment resulting from prolonged litigation. Most collection actions result in a default judgment for the creditor.

D.   Postjudgment Collection Concerns

1.   Judgment Liens

A debtor who is not paying one of her of creditors is typically not paying other creditors. Such a debtor may have sufficient property to satisfy some but not all creditors' claims against her. Accordingly, creditors are concerned with obtaining and maintaining priority over other creditors. In the debt-collection game, like the Wake Forest–UNC basketball game, you want to be at the head of the line.

Creditors' priority with respect to a debtor's real property is greatly affected by judgment liens. If the debtor's assets include Greenacre, the unsecured creditor who is the first to obtain a judgment lien on Greenacre will be the unsecured creditor paid first from the proceeds of the sale of Greenacre. (As we will see later, however, a secured creditor who properly recorded its mortgage before the judgment lien was docketed will have priority over the creditor with the judgment lien.)

WARNING! Do not confuse the term "judgment lien" with the term "judicial lien." Judicial lien describes any lien obtained through use of a court-related action. A judgment lien is one form of a judicial lien. Attachment liens, garnishment liens, and execution liens are other common examples of judicial liens.)

a. Source of Law

The law governing judgment liens is mostly state law. It is mostly state statutory law. The state statutes vary with respect to (i) the mechanics of obtaining a judgment lien, (ii) the scope of the lien, and (iii) the means of enforcing the lien.

b. Mechanics of Obtaining a Judgment Lien

1) Same State

What does a creditor with a state court judgment against D in State 1 have to do to obtain a judgment lien on D's property in State 1?

Some states statutorily provide that the rendition of a judgment itself creates a lien. No additional judgment creditor action is required to create a judgment lien. Other states have statutes that provide that a judgment lien arises only after "docketing" the judgment in a county in which the debtor has property. (Docketing is usually accomplished by the county clerk's making an entry of the judgment under the last name of the judgment debtor in the appropriate docket book.)

Typically, even in states where rendition alone creates the lien, a judgment rendered by a state court in County X, cannot create a lien on property in County Y until the judgment is docketed in County Y.

2) Federal Court

What if a creditor has obtained a *federal* court judgment against D in State 1? How does it obtain a judgment lien on D's property in State

1? Federal law, 28 U.S.C.A. § 1962, deals with enforcement of federal court judgments. It defers to the statutes of the state in which the federal court is situated. Docketing and the other similar steps that are necessary under state law to create a judgment lien apply to federal court judgments if the state statute so provides. State statutes, however, cannot impose conditions or requirements on federal court judgments that are more stringent than those applicable to state court judgments.

3) Different States

What if a creditor has obtained a state court judgment against D in State 1 and D owns land in State 2? Article VI, Section 1 of the Constitution of the United States requires each state to give full faith and credit to the judgments of other states. Nonetheless, unless State 2 is one of the states that has adopted the Uniform Enforcement of Foreign Judgments Act, D will have to (i) bring an action in State 2 based on the debt created by the judgment in State 2, (ii) obtain a new judgment in State 2, and (iii) docket that State 2 judgment in the manner provided for in State 2. Under the Uniform Act, the creditor will simply file its State 1 judgment with the appropriate Clerk of Court in State 2 and will then be able to docket its State 1 judgment in State 2. Almost all states have now adopted the Uniform Enforcement of Foreign Judgments Act.

c. Scope of the Judgment Lien

When a creditor has a judgment lien, what property is subject to the lien?

1) Real Property

The judgment lien operates as a general lien on all of the debtor's property subject thereto, not as a specific lien upon particular property. In almost all states that recognize the judgment lien, it is limited to real property—not a specific piece of real property, but all real property of the debtor or, in states that require docketing, all real property of the debtor in counties in which the judgment has been docketed. What constitutes "real property" for judgment lien purposes varies somewhat from state to state.

2) After–Acquired Property

In most jurisdictions in which a judgment gives rise to a lien, the lien reaches property obtained subsequently thereto.

There is, however, a conflict of authority as to the relative priority of judgment liens on after-acquired property.

Example: In January, *A* obtains a judgment against *D* and dockets his judgment in Orange County; in May, *B* obtains a judgment against *D* and she also dockets her judgment in Orange County. It is not, however, until November that *D* owns any real property in Orange County. Does *A*'s judgment lien on the real property acquired by *D* in November have priority over *B*'s judgment lien on the same property?

Some courts would answer in the affirmative: priority is governed by the order of docketing. A great majority of courts, however, would respond in the negative: while priority of judgment liens is generally determined by date of docketing, judgments attach simultaneously to after-acquired property, and thus the liens are of equal standing.

d. Enforcement of Judgment Lien

A judgment, or even a judgment lien, is not the final step in the collection process. As was stated by Justice Story in Conard v. Atlantic Ins. Co. (1828), a judgment lien "only creates a right to levy on the . . . [property of the judgment debtor], to the exclusion of other adverse interests subsequent to the judgment; and when the levy is actually made on the same, the title of the creditor for this purpose relates back to the time of his judgment so as to cut out intermediate encumbrances. . . . If the debtor should sell the estate, he [the judgment creditor] has no right to follow the proceeds of the sale. . . . The only remedy of the judgment creditor is against the thing itself by making that a specific title which was before a general lien."

Example: C obtains a judgment against D and dockets the judgment in Orange County in the manner statutorily prescribed. D subsequently transfers Orange County real property that she owns—real property that is subject to C's judgment lien—to T for $10,000. C's judgment lien gives it no rights as to the $10,000; the lien only reaches the real property now owned by T, and C's remedy is to enforce the lien as to such property.

The jurisdictions vary considerably with respect to the proper method of enforcement of judgment liens. In some jurisdictions, foreclosure proceedings is the only method; in other states, levy and sale under a writ of execution is required; and some states permit a choice between foreclosure actions and a writ of execution.

e. Duration of Judgment Lien

Jurisdictions also vary considerably with respect to time limits for enforcement of judgment liens. At common law, a judgment lien was presumed paid and became dormant so as not to support an execution if the judgment creditor failed to take out a writ of execution within a year and a day. A judgment lien that became dormant could be revived at any time by proceeding *scire facias*.

Today, most states statutorily limit the duration of judgment liens (or the enforcement of such liens). Ten-year periods are common.

On the other hand, most statutes provide for "revival" or "renewal." There are two basic differences between "revival" of a judgment lien and "renewal" of a judgment lien:

- Revival is by scire facias or judicial decree; renewal is by civil action on the prior judgment.

- Revival continues the judgment and judgment lien; renewal creates a new judgment and a new judgment lien. This is significant when there are intervening conveyances or encumbrances.

Example: Assume for example that *C* obtains a judgment against *D* and a judgment lien on Greenacre, *D*'s property, in 2005. In 2006, *X* obtains a judgment lien on Greenacre. If *C* later revives its judgment, it will still have priority over *X*. If *C* later renews its judgment, it will not have priority over *X*.

2. Execution

By way of review, what is the practical significance of a judgment lien? Does it give a creditor an interest in the debtor's chattels? In his real property? If so, what is the interest? Can the creditor lawfully seize the property? Can the creditor cause the property to be sold in satisfaction of his claim?

a. Nature of the Remedy

The generally negative answers to the above questions reveal the need for some further creditor remedy. Statutes provide for a single writ of execution by which a judgment creditor can have the judgment debtor's property seized and sold in satisfaction of the judgment. In most states a writ of execution can reach both personalty and realty; in a very few states a writ of execution does not reach realty; in still others, the judgment creditor is statutorily required to look first to the personal property of the debtor.

b. Lien

Execution creates a lien on the property seized by the sheriff. Most states date the execution lien from the time of levy. In a few states, the execution lien relates back to the date of issuance of the writ by the clerk or delivery of the writ to the sheriff.

These minority rules create problems as to the rights of third parties who obtain liens on or purchase property of the debtor after the writ has been issued but before the property has been levied on by the sheriff.

Example: Assume that C obtains a writ of execution against D on January 10 and delivers the writ to the sheriff. On January 11, B, a bona fide purchaser, buys a boat from D, the judgment debtor. On January 12, the sheriff levies on the boat. Under the minority rules, C's execution lien predates B's purchase.

Most jurisdictions that date execution liens from issuance or delivery of the writ statutorily protect "gap purchasers" such as B.

c. Procedure

As execution is statutory, the exact procedure varies somewhat from state to state.

1) Issuance

A writ of execution is issued by the clerk of the court in which the judgment was rendered. Issuance of the writ is a ministerial act and involves neither a hearing nor discretion on the part of the clerk. The writ is directed to the sheriff or some other statutorily authorized official; it orders the official to seize property of the debtor, sell it, and apply the proceeds in satisfaction of the judgment.

2) Levy

The act of seizing property is often referred to as *levy*. Levy is ordinarily effected by the sheriff's taking physical possession of the property. When that form of levy is impractical or impossible, constructive possession is taken by somehow giving public notice that the property is *in custodia legis*, as by recording a notice of seizure in the appropriate county records.

The writ specifies a "return date"; by that date, the sheriff or other official must return the writ to the issuing clerk with an endorsement stating the property seized and sold or the impossibility of finding leviable assets. The latter form of return is often referred to as return *nulla bona*. If the return is *nulla bona*, a second (*alias*) and further (*pluries*) writs may issue.

The *return date* is determined by reference to enacted law prescribing the number of days within which a sheriff must act in enforcing a writ of execution. As a general rule, the writ expires on its return date, and the sheriff loses authority to take further steps to enforce it if he has not by that time effected a levy. In such a case, the creditor must initiate the process anew by causing the issuance of another or *alias* writ of execution. If the writ expires after levy but prior to sale, the sheriff in most states is empowered to sell whatever property he has seized so long as he acts within a further period of time established by statute.

In many statutes, the judgment debtor is given the opportunity to select the property to be levied on by the sheriff. The execution statutes in most states direct that, when the sheriff makes the selection, he must exhaust the debtor's personal property before taking real estate. In practice, the creditor often locates executable property and points the sheriff to it.

3) Sale

The property seized pursuant to a writ of execution is to be sold by the sheriff to satisfy the creditor's judgment.

Delays in holding an execution sale may result in the loss of the execution lien. There are statutory limitations on the life-span of an execution lien. Additionally, a creditor will lose its execution lien if the lien becomes "dormant."

The classic statement of the judicial doctrine of dormancy is Excelsior Needle Co. v. Globe Cycle Works (1900):

> "The law is quite clear that the object of the execution is to enforce the judgment, and not to convert it into a security upon

the property, and still allow the judgment debtor to prosecute his business regardless of the lien of the execution. As was said in Freeman Executions, § 206: "In other words, it is not the mere issuing or delivery of the writ which creates a lien, but an issuing and delivery for the purpose of execution. The execution of a writ for the purpose of making or keeping it effective as a lien cannot stop with a mere levy upon the property. If the officer is instructed by the plaintiff not to sell till further orders, the lien of the execution and levy becomes subordinate to that of any subsequent writ placed in the officers' hands for service. . . . The law, therefore, seems to be settled that any direction by the execution creditor to the sheriff which suspends the lien or delays the enforcement of the levy renders the execution dormant against subsequent creditors or bona fide purchasers. However veiled may be the direction, however much it may be founded on a humane desire to protect the debtor, if it is tantamount to a mandate or instruction to the sheriff to withhold the execution of his process, during the interim that he accedes to this demand the levy ceases to be effective."

3. **Chart Comparing of Postjudgment Liens on the Debtor's Real Property With Postjudgment Liens on the Debtor's Personal Property**

	Real Property	Personal Property
1. type lien	judgment lien or execution lien	execution lien
2. property encumbered	all real property in county	specific item(s)
3. duration	statutory	case law
	Under most statutes, judgment liens do not become dormant for at least 5 years.	Under most cases, execution liens become dormant within a few months.
4. method of obtaining	docketing	levying

4. Creditor's Bill

a. Nature of the Remedy

At early common law, writs of execution were issued by courts of law and so were confined to those estates and interests of the debtor recognized at law. The creditor could not reach the debtor's equitable interests such as beneficial interests in property held in trust or the debtor's intangible property such as choses in action.

To provide a remedy for reaching such property, the Court of Chancery developed an equitable counterpart to execution—the creditor's bill (sometimes referred to as creditor's suit). A creditor unable to satisfy its judgment completely through execution could file a bill in the Court of Chancery asking that court to compel the debtor to turn over his equitable assets to be sold to satisfy the creditor's judgment.

b. Reach of the Remedy and Lien

By use of a creditor's bill, a judgment creditor can reach any nonexempt property interest of the debtor that is alienable or assignable under state law. While, as with other judicially created liens, there is some division in the case law as to the time the lien arises, "[t]he general rule is that the filing of a judgment creditor's bill and the service of process creates a lien in equity on the judgment debtor's equitable assets." Metcalf v. Barker (1902).

c. Possible Uses

The flexibility of equitable procedure allows the creditor's bill to be used in a variety of ways. A creditor's bill can be used as a liquidation device, i.e., a substitute for bankruptcy. A judgment creditor can file a bill not only for himself but also on behalf of such other judgment creditors as may choose to join the action. Under this general creditors' bill, the petitioning creditor does not obtain priority over other participating creditors; rather the court makes a *pro rata* distribution to all such creditors. Despite equity's preference for equality, a creditor may file a bill on his behalf alone and thus obtain priority over other creditors. Such judgment creditor's bills are far more common than the general creditors' bill described above. Usually the judgment creditor's bill includes a prayer for discovery of all of the debtor's property; the debtor and third parties holding property of the debtor are then examined in court to locate the assets. A common step after discovery is the issuance of an injunction to prevent the debtor from disposing of or encumbering the property. Sometimes a receiver is appointed for collecting money due to the debtor or taking charge of property requiring management.

d. Limitations

The creditor's bill has not only the advantages but also the limitations of an equitable remedy. For example, the notion that jurisdiction in equity will not be entertained where there is an adequate remedy at law requires exhaustion of legal remedies. There is some confusion as to what constitutes exhaustion of legal remedies in this context. There is uniformity of opinion that, subject to limited exceptions, a judgment must be obtained before a party is entitled to institute a suit by creditor's bill.

The difficulty arises in determining exactly how far a plaintiff must proceed after he has obtained a judgment. Most authorities indicate that a creditor must have: (1) a judgment, (2) execution issued and (3) return unsatisfied before obtaining a creditor's bill. Other courts merely require judgment and the issuance of execution.

The question of which rule is preferable would seem to be academic today in federal court and in states that have adopted rules of procedure modeled after the Federal Rules. Rule 2 abolishes the distinction between law and equity; Rule 18(a) authorizes joinder of legal and equitable claims; Rule 18(b) states that "whenever a claim is one heretofore cognizable only after another claim has been prosecuted to a conclusion, the two claims may be joined in a single action."

5. Supplementary Proceedings

a. History

Several statutory developments have limited the need for and use of the creditor's bill. In most states, the writ of execution has been extended to equitable interests in property and intangible property. Garnishment is now available in many states for the collection of judgments from property of the debtor held by third parties. And, a number of states have enacted an additional remedy: as part of his procedural reform in the middle of the nineteenth century, Field created a new remedy—proceedings supplementary to execution (also called supplemental proceedings)—designed to achieve the purposes of a creditor's bill by a more simple and summary process; a number of states followed New York's example. As the name of the remedy implies, supplementary proceedings could be used only after execution had been issued and returned unsatisfied. Subsequently, in a number of jurisdictions the title of the procedure was changed to proceedings supplementary to judgment, and the requirement of return of execution unsatisfied was eliminated.

b. How Used

While a creditor's bill is an independent, quasi-in-rem action, governed by equitable rules, and a supplementary proceeding is a summary, in personam action, administered by the court in which the judgment was obtained and governed by the provisions of the applicable state law, the reach of supplementary proceedings is very similar to that of the creditor's bill. Most supplementary proceedings statutes provide for (1) discovery of assets through the right of examination of the debtor and others; (2) issuance of injunctions to prevent disposition of property; (3) discretionary power to appoint receivers; and (4) orders for the sale of property.

In a few states, the supplementary proceedings provisions expressly abolish the creditor's bill. Absent any such express provision, the existence of supplementary proceedings in other states neither abolishes creditor's bills by implication nor limits the availability of creditor's bills. Supplementary proceedings need not be tried first and found wanting before a creditor's bill action can be brought. This is in accordance with the well-established equitable principle that where new power is conferred upon the law courts by statutory legislation, the former jurisdiction of equity is unaffected unless the statute contains negative words or other language expressly taking away the pre-existing equity jurisdiction, or unless the whole scope of the statute, by its reasonable construction and its operation, shows a clear legislative intent to abolish that jurisdiction.

c. Not Used Where Property Transferred

While supplementary proceedings usually afford a more expeditious remedy than the creditor's bill, there is at least one situation in which the creditor's bill is still used: recovery of property of the debtor that has been transferred to some third party in fraud of creditors. [The concept and elements of a transfer in fraud of creditors are considered infra.] As noted above, supplementary proceedings are summary in nature without the usual requirements as to pleadings or jury trial. Thus supplementary proceedings generally cannot be employed where a third party asserts an interest in the property. A few states have amended supplementary proceedings statutes so that the court can adjudicate rights and interests in the debt or property which is the subject of the proceeding.

6. Execution Sales

a. Role of Execution Sales

While obtaining a lien, through execution or otherwise, is important to a creditor for reasons previously stated, it is not tantamount to satisfaction of the claim. Property on which the sheriff levies execution is usually not turned over to the judgment creditor in satisfaction of its claim. Rather, the sheriff sells the property and, after paying the costs of the sale, gives the net proceeds to the creditor. Any surplus ordinarily goes to the debtor.

b. Type of Sale

Usually, the execution sale is by *public auction*. The sheriff's conduct of the sale is thoroughly regulated in most states by detailed statutes prescribing when the sale shall take place, how the sale will be advertised, and how and where it will be conducted.

c. Insuring Fair Sale

Most states also have statutory provisions designed to prevent the sale of property at execution sales for unfair prices.

1) Appraisal Statutes

One such statutory device is appraisal statutes. Such statutes generally provide (1) that an appraisal of the subject property must be made before the sale and (2) either that an execution sale must bring not less than a stated percentage of the appraised value or a stated percentage of the appraised value must be credited on the debt.

2) Redemption

Another statutory device providing some protection against inadequate bidding is redemption. Generally, the right of redemption is limited to the repurchase by the execution debtor, within a stated time and at a stated price, of real property sold at execution. Some states permit redemption of personal property; some states have extended the right of redemption to junior lienors of the debtor.

3) Judicial Review

An execution sale differs from a foreclosure sale in that the writ does not designate any specific property to be sold and the court gives no directions and imposes no conditions with respect to an execution sale, as it may do in its order for a judicial sale of specific property. While most statutes do not provide for judicial confirmation of an execution sale, the court from which the execution issued may, for sufficient cause shown, vacate a sale. Courts usually state that mere inadequacy of price is not sufficient to vacate an execution sale. There are cases to the contrary; additionally, a number of decisions have stated that where the price is inadequate, slight additional circumstances justify setting aside the sale.

d. Priority of Purchasers at Sale

1) General Rule: Caveat *Emptor*

One reason for the generally low prices realized at execution sales is the limited protection afforded purchasers at such sales. *Caveat emptor* is the answer customarily given to the unhappy execution purchaser who learns that there are other existing liens prior to that of the judgment creditor or that the judgment debtor had defective title to the property sold by the sheriff. The execution purchaser acquires only such interest as the execution debtor has and generally cannot recover for defects in title. Execution sales are made without implied warranties, either on the part of the sheriff or the execution creditor or debtor.

Most courts likewise hold that the doctrine of *caveat emptor* is applicable even where the levy and sale is made on property to which the judgment debtor has no title: a majority of the cases have denied recovery in actions by the purchaser against the sheriff or the judgment creditor for the price paid at the execution sale, where the debtor had no title to the property so sold. The purchaser's only remedy in such cases is usually by way of subrogation to the creditor's claim against the debtor.

2) Exceptions for Void Sale

The doctrine of *caveat emptor* is generally not applicable where the sale is rendered void because of irregularities in procedure; while the execution purchaser is not entitled to assume that he will obtain good title, he is entitled to assume that he will obtain such interest as the execution debtor has. Thus, where the sale is set aside, the execution purchaser has been given a variety of remedies: recovery from the person benefited by the sale price, subrogation to the plaintiff's rights under the judgment including any judgment lien, a lien on the property for all amounts paid, and injunctions to protect possession of the property until reimbursement. The execution purchaser, may, however, be required to account to the execution debtor for rents and profits from the use of the property.

7. Garnishment

a. Role of the Remedy

Execution reaches only property that the debtor possesses and controls. To reach property of a debtor held by a third party (e.g., D's bank account at G Bank) or to collect money owed to the debtor (e.g., D's wages owed by her employer G), a creditor uses garnishment.

b. Parties to the Proceeding

An understanding of postjudgment garnishment requires an understanding of three vocabulary terms: (1) garnishor, (2) principal debtor and (3) garnishee.

Example: C, a judgment creditor of D, wants to collect from D's bank account in G bank. C, the judgment creditor, would be the garnishor. D, the judgment debtor, would be the principal debtor. G, the third party that holds property or owes money to the principal debtor, would be the garnishee.

c. Procedure

Postjudgment garnishment begins with the garnishor's filing an affidavit stating that there is a judgment, that the judgment is wholly or partially unsatisfied and that the garnishee holds property of the judgment debtor. The court then issues a writ of garnishment that is served upon the garnishee and the principal debtor with a copy of the writ.

The garnishee is required to answer within a stated time. Failure to answer may result in a default judgment or contempt proceedings. In its answer, the garnishee must set out what, if any, funds, property, or earnings of the principal debtor it holds. Along with this disclosure, the garnishee may set up any defense to the garnishment action that it might have. The garnishee may make any defense which it might make if sued by the principal debtor. For example, the garnishee might assert that it has already paid over the funds or turned over the property to the principal debtor before it was served with the notice of garnishment. And, in most states, the garnishee may set off any of its claims against the principal debtor.

If the garnishee's answer is controverted by the garnishor, the controverted issue is tried as other civil cases. If the answer is not controverted, the answer is taken as true. If the answer admits indebtedness to the principal debtor, the court will render judgment against the garnishee for the admitted amount. Similarly, any property of the principal debtor acknowledged to be held by the garnishee will be ordered turned over to the court for sale to satisfy the creditor's judgment.

The garnishee is protected by statute in some states, case law in others, from double liability. Payment by the garnishee to the judgment creditor of the amount owed by the garnishee to the principal debtor liberates the garnishee *vis-à-vis* the principal debtor. On the other hand, a judgment in the garnishment proceeding limiting or negating the garnishee's liability to the principal debtor is generally held not to bar an action by the principal debtor for the debt.

To illustrate:

- C brings an action against D and obtains a judgment for $500. C, believing that G is indebted to D in the amount of $500, garnishes G. G acknowledges the $500 debt to D and pays this sum to C. D could not subsequently maintain an action against G to collect the $500.

- Same facts as #1 except that G denies any liability to D and prevails in the garnishment proceeding. D would not be bound by the judgment in favor of G from bringing an action against G to collect the debt.

- Same facts as #1 except that G acknowledges a debt of only $300 and pays that amount to C. D could maintain an action against G to collect any amounts owed by G in excess of $300 so that if the court in the second proceeding found that G did owe D $500, D could collect $200.

d. Lien

The service of the summons creates a lien. The garnishment lien in effect "impounds" property of the judgment debtor held by the garnishee and monies owed to the principal debtor by the garnishee. If after the service of a writ of garnishment and the creation of a garnishment lien, the garnishee returns the property of the principal debtor to the principal debtor (or some other party) or pays the principal debtor (or some other party) the money the garnishee owes to the principal debtor, the garnishee is at risk of having to make an equal payment to the garnishor.

Example: Assume that C obtains a $10,000 judgment against D. A writ of garnishment is served on G Bank where D has $6,000 in his bank account. If after the service of the writ of garnishment, G Bank permits D to withdraw the $6,000 from his bank account, G Bank can be held liable to C for the $6,000.

There is a division in the authorities as to the property subject to the garnishment lien. In some states, the lien reaches only property of the principal debtor and debts owed to the principal debtor as of the time of service of the summons. In others, the lien also reaches property of the principal debtor which comes into the possession of the garnishee and debts of the garnishee which accrue in the interim between service on the garnishee and answer by the garnishee; and, in a few states, the date of determination of the garnishment proceeding is the relevant date, if the garnishee's answer is controverted.

D. Review Questions

1. T or F   Executory waivers of personal property exemptions and homestead rights generally are enforceable.

2. T or F   A debtor voluntarily can encumber exempt personal property and her homestead, and the mortgage or other security interest she creates can be enforced against the property by the secured creditor upon the debtor's default in paying the secured debt.

3. Why might a debtor attempt to protect her wages under a state law exempting income rather than under Title III of the federal Consumer Credit Protection Act which restricts the amount of wages a creditor can garnish?

4. D owns a house in the city, where she regularly resides with her children, and also a one-acre plot of land in the country where she plans to build a vacation home for her and the kids. Can D exempt the country property from the claims of her creditors by designating it as her homestead?

5. Could D in Question 7 claim the city house as her homestead if she had no dependents?

6. T or F The plaintiff can attach property of the defendant in any case in which a judgment for money damages is sought.

7. Identify the usual procedural prerequisities to the issuance of a writ of attachment.

8. Does the sheriff sell attached property immediately after it is seized, or does the sale usually take place only after the attaching creditor obtains a judgment in the main action against the defendant?

9. T or F Success in a replevin action depends on the plaintiff establishing that she is the owner of the disputed property.

10. T or F The replevin remedy is ordinarily available to a plaintiff in an action for the recovery of goods and chattels only in extraordinary cases, such as when the defendant is threatening to dispose of or remove the property.

11. In the case *Sniadach v. Family Finance Corp.,* the Supreme Court held that notice and hearing must precede the garnishment of a debtor's wages. Five years later, in *Mitchell v. W.T. Grant Co.,* the Court held that prior notice and hearing were not required upon the attachment of a debtor's goods as long as the debtor had an opportunity to respond soon after the seizure. Did *Mitchell* overrule *Sniadach?*

12. When does a judgment lien arise?

13. C gets a judgment against D in County Y and dockets the judgment there. Does the lien of C's judgment reach D's lake property in County X?

14. Who issues a writ of execution?

15. What property of a debtor can be seized and sold through execution process?

16. T or F Property seized under a writ of execution is turned over to the judgment creditor.

17. What kind of a return does a sheriff make when she has been unable to locate property of the debtor to seize and sell under a writ of execution?

18. When does the lien of execution arise?

19. T or F Execution to enforce judgments rendered by federal district courts is governed by state enforcement procedures.

20. How is garnishment begun?

21. What is the consequence of a garnishee failing to answer a garnishment summons?

22. What is the consequence of a garnishee paying accrued wages to a judgment debtor after service of garnishment summons aimed at the debtor's wages?

*

III

Fraudulent Transfers

■ *ANALYSIS*

A. **What Is Fraudulent Transfer Law?**
   1. Statute of 13 Elizabeth
   2. "Badges of Fraud"
   3. Modern Uniform Laws
B. **Which Transfers Are Fraudulent Transfers?**
   1. Actual Fraud
   2. Constructive Fraud
   3. Fraudulent Obligations Are Also Covered
C. **What Are the Consequences of Determining That a Transaction Is a Fraudulent Transfer?**
   1. Who Has a Remedy?
   2. What Are the Remedies?
   3. Against Whom Can a Recovery Be Had?
D. **Looking Back: Fraudulent Transfer and Garnishment**
E. **Looking Ahead: Fraudulent Transfer Law and Bankruptcy**
F. **Review Questions**

D owes *C* $100,000. *D* owns Greenacre which is worth $100,000. *D* gives Greenacre to *X* with the understanding that *X* will later return Greenacre. Or, *D* sells Greenacre to *X* for $1 with the understanding that *D* can continue to use Greenacre as if she owned it. Or, D gives Greenacre to her children as a gift.

Without knowing anything about fraudulent transfer law, you know that:

- *D* probably cannot get away with any of these transactions, and

- It is probably not a good thing for a transaction to be regarded as a "fraudulent transfer."

You just need to know three more things about fraudulent transfer law:

- What is fraudulent transfer law?

- What transfers are fraudulent transfers?

- What are the practical consequences of the determination that a transaction is a fraudulent transfer under fraudulent transfer law?

A. What Is Fraudulent Transfer Law?

1. Statute of 13 Elizabeth

The basis of the modern law of fraudulent conveyances is the Statute of 13 Elizabeth, enacted in 1570. It provides that "covinous and fraudulent feoffments, gifts, grants, alienations, conveyances, bonds, suits, judgments and executions, as well of lands and of tenements as of goods and chattels, . . . devised and contrived of malice, fraud, covin, collusion or guile, to the end, purpose and intent, to delay, hinder or defraud creditors and others . . . shall be utterly void, frustrate and of no effect. . . . "

The law of fraudulent conveyances soon became something other than the language of the Statute. The Statute of Elizabeth says that fraudulent conveyances are "void," but void only as to persons "hindered, delayed or defrauded." In other words, a fraudulent conveyance is valid as between the grantor and the grantee; in other words, a fraudulent conveyance is not void but rather is voidable by certain creditors of the grantor. The language of the Statute also indicates that it is a penal statute with the remedy being the delivery of half the fraudulently transferred property to the crown and the other half to the defrauded creditor. Courts, however, since *Mannocke's Case* (1572), have taken the position that the judgment creditor need not rely on the remedy provided in the statute but can ignore the transfer and proceed directly on the property.

2. "Badges of Fraud"

a. Early Common Law: *Twyne's Case*

Note also that the Statute of Elizabeth requires "intent to delay, hinder or defraud." Since proof of a particular intent is a difficult task, courts soon developed "badges of fraud," i.e., circumstances indicative of intent to defraud. The first such case was *Twyne's Case* (1601). There *P* was indebted to *T* for 400 pounds and to *C* for 200 pounds. *C* sued *P* and, while the action was pending, *P* secretly conveyed to *T* by deed of gift all of his chattels (worth 300 pounds) in satisfaction of *T*'s claim. *P*, however, remained in possession of some of his property—some sheep— and treated them as his own. *C* obtained a judgment against *P*, but when the sheriff sought to levy on the sheep, friends of *P* prevented him from doing so, asserting that the sheep belonged to *T*. Thereupon *C* sued *T* to set aside the conveyance from *P* to *T* as a fraudulent conveyance.

The court held that the transfer was fraudulent, noting the following "badges of fraud":

1. The conveyance is general, i.e., of all *P*'s (the debtor's) assets;

2. The debtor continues in possession and deals with the property as his own;

3. The conveyance is made while a suit against the debtor is pending;

4. The transaction is secret; and

5. *T* (the transferee) takes the property in trust for the debtor.

b. Acceptance by the States
In virtually every American jurisdiction, the Statute of 13 Elizabeth has been either recognized as part of the inherited common law or expressly adopted or enacted in more or less similar terms. The concept of "badges of fraud" has also been generally adopted, although what constitutes a "badge of fraud" varies from jurisdiction to jurisdiction. Among the most commonly recognized "badges of fraud" are those mentioned in *Twyne's Case*; intra-family transfers; voluntary transfers, i.e., transfers of property without consideration; and transfers of all or a substantial amount of property immediately prior to anticipated litigation. Not only do states differ as to what facts give rise to a "badge of fraud," there is also no uniformity as to what weight is to be given to a particular "badge": whether it is conclusive of fraud, prima facie evidence of fraud, or merely admissible evidence of fraud.

c. Preference Is Not a Badge of Fraud
The "badge of fraud rule" that is most uniformly recognized is that, with some limited exceptions (as when an insider is preferred), preferring one

creditor over others is *not* a badge of fraud. It is not a badge of fraud for debtor, *D*, to pay creditor, *X*, in full and pay nothing to other creditors, *Y* and *Z*. Obviously, *D*'s payment to *X* hinders and delays the other creditors. If, however, *Y* or *Z* were permitted to set aside the payment to *X*, there would merely be a substitution of one preference for another. "Fraudulent conveyance law is intended to ensure only that some deserving creditor receives the debtor's reachable assets. Allocation of assets among creditors is determined by bankruptcy statutes." Note, *Good Faith and Fraudulent Conveyances*, 97 HARV.L.REV. 495, 522 (1983).

3. Modern Uniform Laws

a. UFCA

Because of the "confusion and uncertainties of the existing law," the National Conference of Commissioners on Uniform State Laws proposed the Uniform Fraudulent Conveyances Act (UFCA) in 1919. In the UFCA, the Commissioners sought to shift the focus from the debtor's intent to objective factors. At one time, twenty-four states had adopted the UFCA.

b. UFTA

In 1984, the National Conference of Commissioners on Uniform State Laws proposed a new fraudulent conveyance law, the Uniform Fraudulent Transfer Act, UFTA. Most states have now adopted the UFTA.

In your consideration of the UFTA, focus on sections 1, 2 and 3 which are definitional; sections 4 and 5 which answer the question which transfers are fraudulent transfers; and sections 7 and 8 which answer the question what are the consequences of determining that a transaction is a fraudulent transfer.

B. Which Transfers Are Fraudulent Transfers?

1. Actual Fraud

The UFTA, like the Statute of Elizabeth and the UFCA, reaches transfers made with "an actual intent to hinder, delay or defraud any creditor of the debtor." Section 4(a)(1). And, the UFTA in section 4(b) identifies a number of possible "badges of fraud" [although it does not use that phrase] that are relevant in determining whether there was any such "actual intent to hinder, delay or defraud." These eleven factors are meant to be a nonexclusive list "among other factors."

2. Constructive Fraud

More important, the UFTA, like the UFCA, reaches some transfers in which the debtor was completely free from fraudulent intent: transfers of the property of an insolvent or financially troubled debtor for which the debtor receives less than "reasonably equivalent value," section 5(a); see also section 4(a)(2). Accordingly, if D sells Greenacre and it can be shown that (i) D was insolvent at the time of the sale and (ii) the amount D received was less than the "reasonably equivalent value" of Greenacre, the transfer is a section 5(a) fraudulent transfer, regardless of D's intent.

a. Insolvency

Insolvency depends on a comparison of the debtor's debts and assets. Under section 2(a) if the amount of the debts is greater than the fair valuation of the assets, the debtor is insolvent—regardless of whether it is currently paying its debts. While nonpayment of debts creates a presumption of insolvency pursuant to section 2(b), that presumption can be rebutted by showing that the fair valuation of the assets is greater than the amount of the debts.

Note that "exempt property" is excluded from the term "asset." In states with "liberal" exemption statutes, most of an individual's property will be exempt. In such states, most individuals will be "insolvent" for UFTA purposes.

b. Reasonable Equivalent Value

All transfers by an insolvent debtor are not fraudulent transfers. Section 5 looks at both whether the debtor was insolvent and whether the debtor received "reasonably equivalent value." While the phrase "reasonably equivalent value" is not statutorily defined, the term "value" is. Section 3 definition of value includes "antecedent" debt. Accordingly, repayment of a debt is not a fraudulent transfer under section 5(a).

Example: D owes X \$10,000 and Y \$20,000 and Z \$30,000. D uses her last \$20,000 to pay Y. This debt repayment was not a section 5(a) fraudulent transfer.

"Reasonably equivalent value" under the UFTA is different from "consideration" under common law contracts. A mere peppercorn is not enough. The UFTA inquires into the adequacy of consideration; it is in essence a comparative value standard.

c. Liens

Mortgages, Article 9 security interests, and other liens are included in the definition of "transfer" in section 1. "Transfer" is one of a number of important definitions in section 1. On the other hand, mortgages and security interests are always given for value and exist only to the extent was given. So, attacking a lien as constructively fraudulent is doomed to fail whenever the debtor received the value that supports the lien.

Note, however, that the reasonably equivalent value must be received by the debtor/transferor. If, for example, D grants C a mortgage on Greenacre to secure a $100,000 loan that C makes to T and it can be shown that D was insolvent at the time of the mortgage, the mortgage is a section 5 fraudulent transfer. C may well have provided "reasonably equivalent value" but that value went to T, not the debtor/transferor D.

d. Preferring an Insider

Paying an antecedent debt to one creditor without paying debts to other creditors is a preference. Preferences, however, are not constructively fraudulent, even if the debtor is or thereby becomes insolvent, because there is reasonably equivalent value in paying an antecedent debt.

However, with two additional facts, this debt repayment might be a section 5(b) fraudulent transfer. If Y was a relative of D or other "insider" as that term is defined in section 1 and if Y had reasonable cause to believe that D was insolvent, then and only then will a debt repayment be a fraudulent conveyance.

3. Fraudulent Obligations Are Also Covered

Although the statute is entitled the Uniform Fraudulent *Transfer* Act, it applies also to obligations. Accordingly, if D, while insolvent, guaranteed a $100,000 loan from C to X, that guarantee would be fraudulent under section 5(a) since it was an obligation incurred while the debtor was insolvent without D the debtor's receiving reasonably equivalent value. C may have provided reasonably equivalent value, but it did not provide reasonably equivalent value to D, who incurred the obligation.

C. What Are the Consequences of Determining That a Transaction Is a Fraudulent Transfer?

Answering questions about the practical consequences of a determination that a transaction is a fraudulent transfer requires answering three more basic questions:

1. Who has a remedy?

2. What are the remedies?

3. Against whom can a remedy be had?

1. Who Has a Remedy?

The UFTA confers remedies only on creditors. The title of section 7 of the UFTA is "Remedies of *Creditors*" (emphasis added). Both UFTA section 7(a) and UFTA section 7(b) provide "a creditor . . . may."

a. Not the Debtor

The debtor/transferor does not have any remedy under either the UFTA or under case law, even where the transferee has promised to re-convey. Various reasons have been given for this rule: pari delicto, unclean hands, discouraging fraudulent conveyances.

Example: Assume that *D* transfers Greenacre to *X* who promises to reconvey. If the Greenacre transaction is a fraudulent transfer under the UFTA, creditors of *D* have remedies under the UFTA. *D* does not. Only *D*'s creditors have remedies under the UFTA.

b. Only Some Creditors

And, under the UFTA, not every creditor of the debtor/transferor has remedies with respect to every fraudulent transfer. Compare the titles of UFTA section 4 ("Transfers Fraudulent As to Present and Future Creditors") and section 5 ("Transfers Fraudulent As to Present Creditors"). As is suggested by the titles of the sections and stated by the text in the sections, a transaction that is a "fraudulent transfer" under section 5 ("without receiving a reasonably equivalent value") results in remedies only for present creditors.

The definitions of UFTA section 1 do not include the phrase "present creditor." UFTA section 5 explains that a "present creditor" is a "creditor whose claim arose before the transfer was made."

Example: On January 15, *D* borrows $100,000 from *P*. On March 3, *D* transfers Greenacre to *T*. On April 5, *D* borrows $200,000 from *F*. *P* is a present creditor. *P* thus has UFTA remedies if the April 5 transaction meets the requirements of either UFTA section 4 or section 5. *F* is a future creditor. *F* has remedies under the UFTA only if the April 5 transactions meets the requirements of UFTA section 4.

2. What Are the Remedies?

Once it has been determined that a transaction is a fraudulent transfer under the UFTA, look to sections 7 and 8 for the remedies. More specifically, look to UFTA section 7 when the creditor's objective is recovery of the property transferred.

a. Getting the Property That was Transferred by Voiding the Transfer

Compare UFTA section 7(a) with section 7(b). Section 7(a) is much more important than 7(b). Section 7(a) is available to all creditors as to whom the transfer is fraudulent. Section 7(a) contemplates that the court will enter an order avoiding the transfer to the extent necessary to satisfy the creditor's claim.

Notice that UFTA section 7(b) is available only to a creditor that already has a judgment against the debtor/transferor. Section 7(b) contemplates that the court will order a writ of execution without first avoiding the transfer. At first blush, UFTA section 7(b) might seem more cost efficient than section 7(a): a creditor who already has a judgment against the debtor/transferor can avoid the costs of establishing that the transfer was a fraudulent transfer under the UFTA. Blush again and consider the following hypothetical and rhetorical questions.

Example: Assume that *C* has a judgment against *D*. *D* has transferred equipment to *T*. *C* believes that the transfer was a fraudulent transfer. *C* decides to proceed under section 7(b) without first obtaining a court ruling that the transfer of equipment was a fraudulent transfer. How willing will a sheriff be to levy on property held by *T* when the only piece of paper that the sheriff has is a writ of execution issued to enforce a judgment against *D*? How willing will a buyer be to buy the equipment at a sheriff's sale if *T* is at the sale claiming that the equipment belongs to her? What is *C*'s liability exposure for conversation if *T* sues *C* and the court concludes that the *D-T* equipment transaction was not a fraudulent transfer?

b. Getting Money Instead

As *C* or attorney for *C*, you might want money instead of the property transferred by *D-T*. Then you will be looking to UFTA section 8(b) and (c) rather than UFTA section 7(a) and (b), and you will be looking to recover the lesser of the amount of *C*'s claim and the "value of the asset at the time of transfer."

3. Against Whom Can a Recovery Be Had?

And, as attorney for *C*, a creditor as to whom a transaction is a UFTA fraudulent transfer, you can look for recovery from *T*, the "transferee" of the fraudulent transfer or any subsequent transferee. Section 8(d) protects any such "good faith transferee to the extent of the value given to the debtor for the transfer."

If you really want to impress your teacher, try this question on her: "What is the significance of the use of the phrase 'good faith transferee' in UFTA section 8(b) but not UFTA section 8(a)? Does that mean that UFTA section 8(d)'s protection of 'good faith transferee' only applies to subsequent transferees?" And then tell her that you find this question especially troublesome because you know that UFTA section 8 is based on section 550 of the Bankruptcy Act and section 550 does not make a "good faith transferee" distinction between immediate and mediate transferees. Do that and she will never call on you again.

D. Looking Back: Fraudulent Transfer and Garnishment

When are you going to do "garnishment law" and when are you going to do "fraudulent transfer law"? Garnishment law is important to a creditor when a third party owes money to the creditor's debtor or has property that belongs to the creditor's debtor.

> Example: *C* is a creditor of *D*. *D* has money in *G* Bank. *G* Bank does not deny that the money is *D*'s. *C* can reach that money by garnishment.

Fraudulent transfer law is important to a creditor when property that once belonged to the creditor's debtor now belongs to some third party.

> Example: *C* is a creditor of *D*. *D* has transferred Greenacre to *F*. Greenacre is now *F*'s, not *D*'s. *C* can no longer look to Greenacre as a source of satisfying its claim against *D* unless the Greenacre transaction was a fraudulent transfer.

E. Looking Ahead: Fraudulent Transfer Law and Bankruptcy

We will consider fraudulent transfer law again in the bankruptcy part of the book. Two separate provisions of the Bankruptcy Code, sections 544(b) and 548, empower the bankruptcy trustee to avoid a transaction entered into before the bankruptcy if the transaction is a fraudulent transfer. Additionally, a prebankruptcy transaction made with the intent to hinder, delay or defraud creditors may prevent an individual from obtaining a discharge in his or her Chapter 7 bankruptcy case. Section 727(a)(2).

F. Review Questions

1. For the purpose of making it more difficult for creditors to reach her assets, D traded 10,000 shares of IBM stock to R in exchange for real estate of equal value. At all times D was solvent. Is the exchange a fraudulent conveyance as against A to whom D owed a debt at the time of the exchange? As against B to whom D became indebted after the exchange?

2. Are the answers to Question 1 different if D made the exchange solely for legitimate business reasons while insolvent?

3. Solely for legitimate business reasons, D exchanged stock for real estate worth about half the value of the stock. Is the conveyance of the stock fraudulent as against any of D's creditors?

4. D traded 10,000 shares of IBM stock to her brother in exchange for real estate worth only about half the value of the stock. At all times D was solvent. Is the conveyance of the stock fraudulent?

5. While insolvent, D borrowed $100,000 from B and secured the loan with a mortgage on previously unencumbered real estate worth $200,000. Does this secured transaction amount to a fraudulent conveyance as against any of D's creditors?

6. D defaulted on the loan referred to in Question 5, and B thus foreclosed the mortgage at a regularly conducted forced sale as permitted by the terms of the mortgage and by law. The real estate, which had appreciated in value, sold for $90,000, which equaled the balance due on the loan. D, of course, was insolvent. Is the mortgage foreclosure a fraudulent conveyance as against any of D's creditors?

7. D's assets totaled $250,000. Her principal creditors were A and B, each of whom she owed $150,000. D liquidated, paid A in full, and distributed most of the balance of the proceeds to creditors owed small amounts of money. Can B attack the payment to A as a fraudulent conveyance?

8. Is the answer to Question 7 different if A is D's brother?

9. For the purpose of preventing her creditors from reaching her assets, D sold 10,000 shares of IBM stock and purchased with the proceeds a large home

where she resided with her family. The stock could have been reached by creditors through execution process; the home cannot be reached through execution or other process because it is exempt from the claims of creditors. Is the sale of the stock a fraudulent conveyance?

10. What remedies are generally available to protected creditors for curing a fraudulent conveyance?

11. Even if the conveyance of the stock in Question 1 was actually fraudulent, can R sustain the conveyance and prevent A or B from setting it aside by showing that she, R, was a totally innocent purchaser? Is the answer the same if the real estate which R traded was worth only half the value of the stock?

12. Suppose that R was not an innocent purchaser for fair consideration in Question 11. Can creditor A or B recover damages from R rather than set aside the conveyance of the stock?

*

IV

Creditors With Special Rights

■ *ANALYSIS*

A. Consensual Liens

The preceding chapter focused on rights available to all creditors—rights afforded by the judicial process. Some creditors have rights in addition to those already discussed. Agreement of the parties is one source of such rights. The debtor and the creditor may agree that the creditor is to have a lien on certain real or personal property of the debtor.

Obtaining a consensual lien does not destroy or limit the creditor's rights. A lien creditor may proceed against the debtor personally, may utilize the various creditors' remedies discussed in the preceding chapters. Additionally, such a creditor has special rights in the property subject to its lien. The special rights include a right of foreclosure (the right to proceed against the security and apply it to the payment of the debt) and the right of priority (i.e., the right to take the security free from the claims of general creditors and later secured creditors).

1.   Article 9 Security Interests

Consensual liens on personal property are governed by Article 9 of the Uniform Commercial Code. (All our references are to the Official Text & Comments of Article 9 as revised in 2001).

a.   Terminology of Article 9

Article 9 has a language all its own that can best be explained by example.

Example: Assume that *D* wants to borrow $25,000 from *S* to buy a new sport utility vehicle (SUV). *S* is only willing to make the loan if the SUV will be security; *D* agrees. In "Code talk:"

• *D* is the debtor [D is also the "obligor," but we leave the Article 9 distinction between "debtor" and "obligor" to the Article 9 class.];

• *S* is the secured party;

• The SUV is the collateral;

• *S's* interest in the SUV is a security interest;

• The agreement creating the security interest is a security agreement. See section 9–102.

Since *S* is loaning *D* the $25,000 to acquire the collateral, *S's* security interest is a purchase money security interest. See section 9–103. Similarly, if *D* had financed a car with the seller, and the seller had obtained a security interest in the car, the security interest would be a "purchase money security interest."

1) Creation and Attachment

The creation of a security interest requires more than a security agreement. It is also necessary that the secured party give value and that the debtor then have—or later acquire—rights in the collateral. When these three requirements are satisfied, including that the debtor has rights in collateral, the security interest is said to have "attached."

2) Perfection

To achieve maximum possible priority, it is necessary for the secured party to "perfect" its security interest. Depending on the kind of collateral involved, a security interest may be perfected when it attaches (e.g., a purchase money security interest in consumer goods other than motor vehicles or fixtures, section 9–309); or it may be accomplished by a transfer of possession from the debtor to the secured party (e.g., negotiable documents, section 9–313); or perfection may be accomplished by filing, which is the usual case, section 9–310.

3) Filing

Where filing is required, the document filed is called a "financing statement." It need contain only the names and addresses of the parties and indicate the collateral covered, section 9–502.

b. Organization of Article 9

Article 9 of the Code is divided into seven parts. Parts 1 through 5 are ordinarily covered in detail in courses in commercial law. Part 7 deals with the transition from the "old" Article 9 to the Revised Article 9. Part 6 deals with default and the rights of the debtor and creditor in default. Only Part 6 will be discussed at any length in this book.

c. Section 9–317

There is, however, one section in Part 3 of Article 9 that merits consideration in a debtor-creditor law primer. Section 9–317 provides that an unperfected security interest is "subordinate" to a judicial lien on the same property. In other words, section 9–317 contemplates a situation where a judicial lien arises in the gap between the creation and perfection of a security interest: if D gave S a security interest in its equipment on October 7, and S perfected this security interest on December 21, any creditor who obtained an attachment or execution lien on the truck between October 7 and December 21 would have priority over S.

Section 9–317 is also important for what it does not say. It does not govern priority as between a secured creditor and a creditor with a statutory lien or between two secured creditors. It does not expressly state that a creditor with an unperfected security interest has priority over general creditors although that is certainly implied. Moreover, section 9–317 is silent as to the relative priority when the judicial lien arises before the security interest attaches. In such cases, it would seem that the first in time rule should apply regardless of whether the security interest is perfected immediately.

d. Part 6 of Article 9

The application of Part 6 of the Uniform Commercial Code is conditioned on default by the debtor.

1) Meaning of Default

The term "default" is not specifically defined in the Code. The circumstances which constitute default are a matter of agreement between the parties. Because the secured party usually has superior bargaining power, the security agreement will usually define default as broadly as possible. Common events of default include a missed or late payment, any impairment of the collateral such as failure to insure, impairment of the personal obligation such as bankruptcy of the debtor, and any feeling of insecurity that the prospect for payment is uncertain. In the absence of any definition of "default" in the security agreement, default occurs only on a failure to pay.

2) Rights Upon Default

When the debtor is in default, Part 6 of Article 9 gives the secured party the following general choices:

1. Ignore its security interest, obtain a judgment on the debt, and proceed by execution and levy and execution sale;

2. When the collateral consists of rights to payment owed to the debtor by some third party such as accounts, collect the amounts due from that third party, i.e., the account debtor;

3. Repossess the collateral and either keep it in full satisfaction of the debt or resell it and apply the sales proceeds to reduce the debt.

a) Ignore the Security Interest

In effect, the secured party ignores its security interest, ignores Article 9, and pursues its remedies under other law. This other law is covered in the preceding chapters of this book.

b) Notify Account Debtors

The second choice is covered by sections 9–607 and 9–608 of the UCC. In essence, section 9–607 authorizes the secured party, "if so agreed, and in any event after default," to notify the account debtor to make payments to her instead of to the debtor. Security agreements covering accounts commonly provide that the secured party can, without any event of default, notify account debtors to make payments directly to it, which arrangement is know as "notification lending."

Example: Assume, for example, that D Law Firm (D) owes S $100,000 and S has a security interest in D's accounts, i.e., amounts owed to D by D's various clients. D defaults. S can then instruct the clients, the account debtors, to make their payments to S. If the payments from the account debtors are not sufficient to satisfy the debtor's liability to the secured party, then the secured party can collect the deficiency from the debtor, section 9–608. So if S collects only $40,000 from D's clients, S can collect the other $60,000 from D.

c) Repossess and Sell the Collateral

The third choice is governed by a lot of different Code sections and by law school courses in secured credit. The first step is getting possession of the collateral, i.e., repossession.

i) Self–Help Repossession

Section 9–609 of the Code authorizes a secured party to take possession of the collateral upon default of the debtor and to do so without judicial process if this can be done "without breach of the peace." "Breach of the peace" is another phrase that is not defined in the Code. Most cases in which there has been a finding of breach of peace involve either self-help repossession by unauthorized entry into the debtor's house or self-help repossession after protests by the debtor or one acting on his behalf. Reported cases are divided as to whether repossession through trickery violates section 9–609's "breach of the peace" standard.

ii) Replevin

If self-help repossession cannot be accomplished without a "breach of the peace," the secured party can use judicial process. This "action" is variously referred to as replevin, claim and delivery, and sequestration. Regardless of the label, the remedy is essentially the same: the sheriff seizes the collateral pursuant to a court order. And, regardless of the label, there are constitutional requirements of notice and hearing. The state is issuing the writ; the state is seizing the property. State action! Due process requirements of notice and hearing must be satisfied. Almost every state has amended its replevin, claim and delivery, or sequestration procedures to provide for some kind of probable cause hearing before the writ is issued by the court and the collateral is seized by the sheriff.

iii) Redemption

In theory, the debtor has a right to redeem repossessed collateral. Section 9–623 provides that a debtor may redeem by "tendering fulfillment of *all obligations* secured by the collateral" as well as the expenses reasonably incurred by the secured party in retaking, holding and preparing the collateral for disposition. Most security agreements contain language accelerating the entire balance due on default. Thus, a debtor who was unable to pay a single installment will have to come up with the entire balance plus expenses in order to redeem.

In short, a debtor seldom redeems repossessed property.

iv) Strict Foreclosure

In the likely event that the debtor does not redeem, the secured party in some situations may simply retain the collateral in complete or partial satisfaction of the debt. Sections 9–620, 9–621, and 9–622 govern the secured party's keeping the collateral, i.e., "strict foreclosure."

The three keys to understanding these provisions are

1. There are special rules for "consumer goods" in section 9–620(e) and (f);

2. For other goods, the secured party can keep the goods in full satisfaction of the debt if (i) it so notifies the debtor and (ii) the debtor does not make a timely objection; and

3. Again, for goods other than consumer goods, a secured party can keep the goods in partial satisfaction of its debt if (i) it so notifies the debtor and (ii) the debtor actually agrees.

v) Sale

While collateral retention by the secured party is more common than collateral redemption by the debtor, it is not all that common. In many instances, the secured party will not want to keep the collateral. And, in many of the instances in which the secured party wants to keep the collateral, the debtor objects.

Accordingly, the secured party's resale of the collateral is far more common. The sale must be preceded by notification that complies with section 9–611 to 9–614. Section 9–610 requires that "every aspect" of the sale be "commercially reasonable." Look to section 9–627 to determine what is "commercially reasonable." While the sale can be "private" or "public," the secured party's ability to buy the collateral at a private sale is limited by section 9–610(c).

vi) Suing for Deficiency and Being Sued for Damages

If the net proceeds of the sale are not sufficient to satisfy the claim of the secured party, it has the right to proceed against the "obligor" to collect the deficiency under general state collection law, section 9–615. If the sale fails to comply completely with the requirements of Part 6 of Article 9, the secured party may, under section 9–626, lose its right to proceed against the obligor for any deficiency and may be liable to the debtor or obligor for damages under section 9–625.

2. Mortgages

There is no single uniform law governing real property security, and the rights of a mortgagee on default of the mortgagor vary considerably from state to state. There are, however, a number of similarities between Article 9 of the Uniform Commercial Code and the law of mortgages in most jurisdictions.

a. Redemption

The mortgagor's equitable redemption rights are similar to the debtor's redemption rights under section 9–623. The redeeming party must pay the entire debt; the right to redeem is terminated by the sale of the property or by strict foreclosure. In about one-half of the states, however, statutes augment the mortgagor's redemption rights. These statutes extend the period of redemption beyond foreclosure; the additional period varies from several months to several years. This statutory redemption differs from equitable redemption with regard to the sum payable to effect redemption: the basic factor is the sale price (plus interest at specified rate and other costs), not the debt secured by the mortgage.

b. Strict Foreclosure

In only a few states does the mortgagee have both the options that are available to a secured party under Article 9 of the Uniform Commercial Code: retention or resale. Retention of the mortgaged property, i.e., strict foreclosure, is available in certain circumstances in nineteen states, but is commonly used in only three states. In other states, foreclosure results in a sale of the property.

c. Sale

There are two types of foreclosure sales generally used in the United States: judicial sale and sale pursuant to a power of sale.

1) Judicial Sale

Judicial sale is more commonly used. The mechanics of such a sale are mostly a matter of local law. The legislation ordinarily provides for notice of a hearing, a hearing, judicial determination of default, notice of sale, sale, confirmation of sale, possible redemption (statutory) and entry of a judgment for any deficiency.

Until court confirmation, the judicial sale is not enforceable by the buyer. There are legal rules limiting the court's discretion in confirming the sale. Absent a statutory provision to the contrary, mere inadequacy of price without more does not justify a refusal to confirm—the inadequacy must be so gross as to shock the conscience. Nevertheless, in cases involving confirmation of the sale, adequacy of the price seems the primary concern. Moreover, in a number of states, there are "statutory provisions to the contrary." For example, in several states an appraisal in advance of the sale is required, and the sale is not confirmed unless the sales price is at least a certain percentage of the appraisal.

2) Private Sale

Because of the delays and expenses incident to foreclosure by judicial sale, mortgagees included provisions in the mortgage permitting sale without any judicial proceeding in case of default. This approach to foreclosure has only limited recognition in the United States. Several states legislatively exclude this extrajudicial procedure, and in only eighteen states is foreclosure under a power of sale the prevailing practice.

The conduct of the sale under a power of sale is determined by the provisions of the instrument creating it and by any statutory regulations governing its exercise. In the majority of jurisdictions using this type of procedure, the sale must be public, and preceded by notice (usually advertisement) specifying the amount of debt due, description of the property, date and location of sale and such other matters as either the mortgage or the applicable statute may provide. The critical attitude of the courts toward powers of sales makes them quick to grant relief against even slight irregularities. This willingness to overturn sales results in uncertainty of title and is probably the chief reason for the power of sale's failure to gain greater acceptance.

B. Liens by Operation of Law

1. Common Law Liens

Some creditors are given additional rights by operation of law. Common law grants to certain creditors a possessory lien on property of their debtors. A common law possessory lien is the right to retain the property of another for some particular claim or charge upon the property so detained. For example:

1. Common law from very early times gave the innkeeper a lien on the goods of the guest brought by him into the inn.

2. Similarly, a common carrier has a lien for freight charges on all goods delivered by it.

3. And an artisan who, at the request of the owner, performs services on a chattel has a common law possessory lien on such chattels.

a. Specific Versus General

A common law possessory lien is either specific or general. The former attaches to specific property as security for some demand which the creditor has with respect to that property. A general lien is one that the holder thereof is entitled to enforce as security for all the obligations which exist in his favor against the owner of the property. Specific liens have been favored by the courts. General liens exist only when (1) contracted for, (2) conferred by statute, or (3) so common and well-established that the parties to the transaction must be taken to have made their contracts in relation to such custom and usage. The burden of establishing the general lien is on the party claiming it, and courts have been reluctant to find the burden sustained. In certain callings, however, such as those of attorney, banker, factor, and innkeeper, the general lien is well-established.

b. Enforcement by Possession

A common law possessory lien is merely a device to coerce the debtor into payment of his debts by the retention of his property from him until he pays. In general, there is no remedy for enforcing the lien; the lienor has no right to sell the subject matter of the lien to satisfy his claim unless such right is expressly conferred by statute or agreement of the parties.

c. Effect of Loss of Possession

Although possession is essential to the creation of liens under common law and the lien is in essence a right to retain the goods until certain debts are paid, a change of possession does not necessarily destroy the lien. When the lien holder has parted with possession, it is a question for the jury whether he has so far voluntarily parted with possession as to warrant the conclusion that he has waived the lien. For example, if the owner of the property obtains possession thereof without the knowledge or consent of the lienor, the latter is not divested of his lien. A lienor who has voluntarily and unconditionally surrendered possession of the property cannot thereafter assert a lien on the property. Even if such a lienor subsequently regains possession of the property his lien is not restored.

Example: *C* makes *D* a dress and unconditionally delivers the dress to *D* before *D* pays the $100 charge. Subsequently, *D* returns the dress to *C* to have the hem lowered. *C* only has a lien on the dress for the hemming work.

2.   Equitable Liens

Equitable liens do not depend on the possession of the debtor's property by a creditor. Rather, the basis for an equitable lien is one of two equitable maxims.

First, as equity looks upon as done that which is agreed or intended to be done, an agreement that evidences an intention to create a consensual lien but fails to do so, creates an equitable lien.

Example: A mortgage which, through some informality or defect in terms or mode of execution, is not valid as a mortgage, will nevertheless generally create an equitable lien on the property described. Similarly, an agreement to give a mortgage creates an equitable lien.

Second, equity regards as done that which ought to be done and so creates equitable liens to avoid unjust enrichment.

Example: *B* enters into a contract to buy Greenacre from *S* for $10,000. *B* makes a partial payment of $2,000. *S* is unable to comply with the covenants of the contract as to the title she is to convey. Under these facts, *B* would have an equitable lien on Greenacre to secure the repayment of the $2,000, notwithstanding the absence of any agreement to this effect. A buyer under an executory contract for the sale of land has an equitable lien on the land for purchase money advanced, where the contract fails due to the fault of the seller.

Equitable liens also differ from common law liens in terms of rights available to the lienor. A holder of an equitable lien can enforce his lien by having the subject property sold to satisfy his claim.

C.   State Statutory Liens

Other sources of additional rights for certain creditors are state and federal statutes. Legislation has enlarged many of the liens recognized at common law and many of those asserted in equity. And, statutes have in many instances gone beyond the liens previously recognized in law or equity and created a number of additional liens. It is not feasible within the scope of this Black Letter to do more than indicate this source of liens and mention some of the more common statutory liens:

√   Employees' liens on the employer's personalty to secure payment of back wages;

√   Landlord's lien on tenant's property (codification of a common law possessory lien);

√   Materialmen's and mechanics' liens on land and the improvements thereon to secure the compensation of persons who, under contract with the owner or his agent, contributed labor or materials to the improvement of said land; and

√   Tax liens.

D.   Federal Claims

The largest creditors are, of course, the various governmental entities. A governmental creditor may be either a general creditor or a lien creditor. When its claim is secured, the government has all the rights of a secured creditor; when its claim is not secured, it has all the rights of a general creditor.

Additionally, a number of states statutorily prefer governmental claims against delinquent debtors to those of private creditors. The federal government's claims are given preference over claims of other creditors primarily by two statutory provisions: the federal priority provision, 31 USCA § 3713, more commonly referred to by its Revised Statute designation, RS 3466; and the Federal Tax Lien Act, 26 USCA §§ 6321–23.

1.   Federal Priority Provision

Section 3466 applies to every kind of debt owing to the federal government: tax and nontax. The statute provides:

(a)(1)   A claim of the United States Government shall be paid first when–

    (A) a person indebted to the Government is insolvent and–

        (i) the debtor without enough property to pay all debts makes a voluntary assignment of property;

        (ii) property of the debtor, if absent, is attached; or

        (iii) an act of bankruptcy is committed; or

NOTE: The phrase "act of bankruptcy" is an anachronism. The Bankruptcy Act of 1898 provided for "acts of bankruptcy" and made the occurrence of an act of bankruptcy a condition precedent to creditors' filing an involuntary bankruptcy petition against their debtor. While the Bankruptcy Code retains the possibility of an involuntary bankruptcy, it eliminated the concept of "acts of bankruptcy."

(B) the estate of the deceased debtor, in the custody of the executor or administrator, is not enough to pay all debts of the debtor.

(2) This subsection does not apply in a case under title 11.

This statutory language is misleading in two important respects: (1) how often the statute applies and (2) how the statute applies.

a.   When It Applies

The statute does not apply very often. Because of the limited meaning given to the word "insolvent," the statute only applies if (1) either (a) the debtor is insolvent *and* has made an assignment for the benefit of creditors or (b) the debtor is insolvent *and* has died and (2) no one has filed a bankruptcy petition.

b.   How It Applies

When the statute is applied, the claim of the federal government is not always "paid first." Section 3466 gives the federal claim first priority in "property of the debtor."

Remember the nature of a lien and the nature of a priority. A lien is a transfer of a present property interest. A lien holder has an interest in the encumbered property from the time that the lien comes into existence. If debtor, *D*, owned Blackacre and sold it to *X* before the triggering events of 3466 occur, the federal government could not claim priority in Blackacre over *X*. Blackacre was not "property of the debtor."

1)   Affect on Liens

Similarly, if *D* owned Greenacre and *Y* obtained a lien on Greenacre before the occurrence of the 3466 triggering events, the government should not have priority over *Y*'s lien. *Y*'s lien interest is a present property interest, is property of *Y*, not "property of the debtor."

2) Choatenes

However, only liens that are *specific and perfected* before the debtor becomes insolvent in the section 3466 sense take priority over federal claims. There is, however, considerable confusion as to when a lien is sufficiently specific and perfected or, to use the terminology the courts employ in section 3466 litigation, when the lien is "choate."

Probably the most comprehensive (and comprehensible) Court consideration of the choateness doctrine is in Illinois ex rel. Gordon v. Campbell (1946). In *Campbell,* the Court said that "the lien must be definite . . . in at least three respects . . . : (1) the identity of the lienor; . . . (2) the amount of the lien . . . and (3) the property to which it attaches." The lien there involved was a state statutory lien for unemployment contributions. The Court found the lien "not sufficiently specific or perfected" to take priority over a federal claim under section 3466. The statutory language—"all the personal property . . . used . . . in business"—was too vague and comprehensive. Thus, it would seem that judgment liens [which reach all of the debtor's real property in the county] and any statutory liens reaching all property of the debtor would similarly fall unless some specific property is seized by the lienor before the federal priority arises.

2. Federal Tax Lien

Sections 6320 to 6344 of the Internal Revenue Code (title 26) provide for the creation and enforcement of a tax lien. A lawyer or law student should look to these provisions for answers to the following questions:

1. When does a federal tax lien arise?

2. What property is covered by a federal tax lien?

3. How can the tax lien be enforced?

4. What are the rights of a third party who buys property from the taxpayer after a federal tax lien arises?

5. What are the rights of the taxpayer's other creditors after a tax lien arises?

a. When Does the Federal Tax Lien Arise?

Section 6321 sets out three requirements for the creation of a federal tax lien:

✓   IRS' assessment of the tax liability;

✓   IRS' demand for payment of this tax liability;

✓   The taxpayer's failure to pay.

The next section, section 6322, provides that a tax lien dates from the time of assessment. It is thus necessary to know when assessment occurs. Although assessment is only the first of three requirements for creating a tax lien, section 6322 makes the date of assessment important to the taxpayer, buyers from the taxpayer, and creditors of the taxpayer.

1) Time of Assessment

The date of assessment depends on whether the taxpayer acknowledged the liability in his return. When a person files a return acknowledging unpaid taxes, assessment simply involves noting the liability on a list in the office of the district director of the IRS, section 6203. If, for example, D sends the IRS a check for $3,000 along with her return that shows her tax liability is $7,000, assessment of the $4,000 liability would occur almost immediately after the return is received.

If the tax liability is not acknowledged on the return, considerably more time will elapse between the filing the return and assessment. If the tax liability is understated on the return, the deficiency must be discovered through an audit of the return. The taxpayer then must be notified and given the opportunity to respond to the finding of a deficiency. The actual assessment of the tax deficiency cannot be made until the taxpayer either acquiesces in the adjustment of his tax liability or exhausts his opportunities for administrative review.

2) Notice

Section 6303 requires that, after assessment, as soon as practicable," the taxpayer be given notice, stating the amount of the tax liability and demanding payment. The notice form that the IRS uses gives the taxpayer ten days to make payment.

3) Relation Back

Remember that while creation of the lien requires (1) assessment, (2) demand, and (3) failure to pay, the lien relates back to the time of the assessment. Remember also that the creation of the lien does not require recordation or other public notice of the lien.

4) No Filing Required as Against the Debtor

A valid tax lien arises without the federal government filing notice thereof in a public recordation system. It is quite possible that a taxpayer will not know that a tax lien has been imposed upon its property, that buyers from the taxpayer will not know, that other creditors of the taxpayer will not know. An unfiled federal tax lien is valid against the taxpayer and most third parties.

b. What Property is Covered by a Federal Tax Lien?

Section 6321 describes the property covered by a federal tax lien: "All property and rights to property, whether real or personal, belonging to such person." "All" in this context truly means all.

1) After–Acquired Property

The federal tax lien reaches not only all the property that the debtor has an interest in as of the time of assessment but also all property interests later acquired. If the taxes are assessed in June and the taxpayer acquires Greenacre in August, the tax lien would encumber Greenacre. Greenacre would be subject to the tax lien even if Greenacre was the debtor's homestead and exempt under state exemption laws.

2) Exempt Property

The tax lien reaches that part of the taxpayer's property that would otherwise be protected by state law from the reach of creditors. The Internal Revenue Code contains its own, nominal exemption provisions in section 6334.

c. How Can the Tax Lien be Enforced?

1) Levy and Sale

The United States can enforce its federal tax lien by levying on (taking) and selling property of the taxpayer.

2) Notice and Right to Hearing

As a result of Congressional action in 1997 and 1998, taxpayers enjoy new protection from the enforcement of federal tax liens.

For example, under new section 6330, no levy of the taxpayer's property may occur before the IRS notifies the taxpayer in writing of the right to a hearing. At the hearing, the taxpayer may raise any relevant issue, including "offers of collection alternatives, which may include the posting of a bond, the substitution of other assets, an installment agreement, or an offer-in-compromise." The hearing officer must take into consideration "whether any proposed collection action balances the need for the efficient collection of taxes with the legitimate concern of the person that any collection action be no more intrusive than necessary." Section 6330(c)(3).

d. What Are the Rights of a Third Party Who Buys Property From the Taxpayer After the Tax Lien Arises?

What is the impact of a federal tax lien on a buyer from the taxpayer? For example, X claims that she is entitled to Greenacre because she bought it from D for $10,000. The IRS claims that it is entitled to Greenacre because D owes $10,000 in back taxes and the IRS has a tax lien.

The facts creating such a buyer versus IRS priority contest will fit into one of the three patterns:

√ The sale by the taxpayer occurred before creation of the tax lien, i.e. before tax assessment;

√ The sale by the taxpayer occurred after creation of the tax lien but before filing of the federal tax lien;

√ The sale by the taxpayer occurred after creation and filing of the federal tax lien.

1) Sale Before Assessment

Clearly, the buyer prevails in the first situation. Section 6321 provides for a tax lien on property of the taxpayer. If X buys Greenacre from the taxpayer before tax assessment, then Greenacre is not "property . . . belonging to such person" at the time the lien arises.

2) Sale Before Filing

It is equally clear that buyers prevail in the second situation. Section 6323 is in part a recording statute; subsection (f) of section 6323 provides for recording the federal tax lien in the state record systems. Section 6323(a) protects "purchasers" from unrecorded tax liens; an unfiled federal tax lien is not valid as against a "purchaser." If X paid "adequate and full consideration," he is a "purchaser," as defined in section 6323(f)(6). If X paid or became legally obligated to pay adequate and full consideration before the federal tax lien was filed, he takes Greenacre free from the federal tax lien. *X* would be protected by section 6323(a) even if he knew of the unfiled federal tax lien.

3) Sale After Filing

Some buyers prevail even over filed federal tax liens. Under section 6323(b) certain third parties take free from a federal tax lien that was filed prior to the sale. For example, section 6323(b)(3) protects purchasers of personal property at retail. If *B* buys living room furniture from *D* Furniture Store Inc. the government cannot look to this furniture to satisfy its tax claim against *D* Furniture Store Inc. even though the government filed its federal tax lien.

A filed federal tax lien is, however, effective against most subsequent buyers from the taxpayer. If *X* buys Greenacre from *D* after the IRS files its federal tax lien, the IRS will have priority over *X*.

e. What Are the Rights of the Taxpayer's Other Creditors?

A person who is not paying his federal taxes is probably not paying his nongovernmental creditors and probably lacks sufficient assets to pay all claims against him. Which claims have priority? Remember, under section 6322, the tax lien dates from the time that the taxes were assessed. What if private creditors obtained liens on the debtor's property before the time that the taxes were assessed? Will all such earlier in time liens have priority or will earlier in time liens take priority over the IRS' tax lien only if they are "choate"?

1) Choate Liens Win

Case law indicates that (1) a private creditor will have priority over the IRS if the private creditor's lien was choate before the federal taxes were assessed, and (2) the choateness standard in federal tax lien act cases is different from the choateness standard in federal priority cases.

United States v. Security Trust & Sav. Bank (1950) was the first case to apply the "choate lien doctrine" to a priority problem under the Federal Tax Lien Act. *Security Trust* involved the relative priority of a federal tax lien and an attachment lien. Since an attachment lien is subject to contingencies that might terminate its enforceability, the lien was deemed inchoate and therefore ineffective against the subsequently arising federal tax lien.

Security Trust relied on section 3466 choateness cases as precedent. Subsequent federal tax lien cases have followed this practice. Nevertheless, the federal tax lien standard of "choateness" seems less stringent than that of the federal priority provisions. As noted previously, the Supreme Court has yet to find a competing lien choate in a case arising under section 3466. There are several Supreme Court federal tax lien cases in which the competing lien was held to be choate.

In Crest Finance Co. v. United States (1961), the Supreme Court accepted the government's concession that the competing lien was choate. The lien there involved was an assignment of accounts; the accounts were earned and due prior to the time that the federal tax lien attached.

In both United States v. City of New Britain (1954) and United States v. Vermont (1964), prior statutory liens on personal property were held choate. The liens involved in these tax lien cases are difficult to distinguish from the liens held *inchoate* in federal priority cases such as United States v. Gilbert Associates, Inc. (1953). In neither *New Britain* nor *Vermont* was the taxpayer divested of title or possession. The Court in *Vermont* distinguished *Gilbert* saying "different standards apply where the United States' claim is based on a tax lien arising under §§ 6321 and 6322."

2) Unfiled Tax Liens Lose

Section 6323(a) of the Federal Tax Lien Act provides that a private creditor will have priority over the IRS if it obtains a security interest, a mechanics lien, or a judgment lien before the federal tax lien is filed.

(a) Security Interest

Like a lot of statutes, the Federal Tax Lien Act uses words differently than you or we ordinarily use them. For example, section 6323(a) gives a "holder of a security interest" priority over an unfiled federal tax lien. Section 6323(h) defines "security interest" so as to limit the protection of section 6323(a) to creditors with *perfected* security interests.

Under section 6323(h), "security interest" includes consensual liens on both personal property or real property. The security interest is deemed to exist only after it is valid under local law against a "judgment lien." This was obviously intended to limit section 6323(a)'s protection to perfected security interests and recorded mortgages.

This use of the term "judgment lien" was unfortunate. Under the laws of most states, a judgment lien does not reach personal property, and therefore even an unperfected UCC security interest would be superior to a judgment lien and thus superior to an unfiled federal tax lien. Such a result would be inconsistent with prior law. There is no indication that Congress intended to change the law and accord priority to unperfected security interests. Instead, it is more likely that Congress did not understand the difference between "judgment lien" and "judicial lien." Most courts read the term "judgment lien" in section 6323(h) as including other types of judicial liens so that only perfected security interests qualify for the protection of section 6323(a).

(b) Lien Creditor

Section 6323(a) also provides that a "judgment lien creditor" takes priority over an unfiled federal tax lien. There is no statutory definition of a "judgment lien creditor." The term is, however, defined in Treasury Regulation section 301.6323(h)–1(g) in a way that includes all postjudgment *judicial* liens—execution liens as well as judgment liens.

Remember that a "judgment lien" is a particular kind of judicial lien. Under the laws of most states, a judgment lien is obtained by docketing a judgment in the real property record system, and the lien only reaches real property. Thus, a judgment creditor who obtains a judgment lien on real property by docketing its judgment takes priority over an unfiled federal tax lien. Also, a judgment creditor who obtained an execution lien on personal property by causing the issuance of a writ of execution and the levy on the debtor's property likewise takes priority over an unfiled federal tax lien.

(c) Relation to Choateness

The Federal Tax Lien Act nowhere mentions the choateness doctrine. To what extent does section 6323(a) displace the choateness doctrine? Most authorities suggest that if a creditor comes under section 6323(a), it does not also have to satisfy the choateness requirement. There are, however, cases to the contrary.

(d) Examples

The following examples illustrate the application of section 6323(a):

Example: On January 10, a federal tax lien arises. February 2, *E* obtains a judgment against the taxpayer, obtains a writ of execution, and causes the sheriff to levy on personal property of the taxpayer. March 3, IRS files its federal tax lien in accordance with section 6323(f). *E*'s execution lien would have priority (assuming that the term "judgment lien creditor" in section 6323(a) is given the meaning suggested in the Treasury Regulation.)

Example: On March 3, a federal tax lien arises. April 4, *J* obtains a judgment against the taxpayer and dockets its judgment in a county in which the taxpayer owns real property. May 5, IRS files its federal tax lien in accordance with section 6323(f). *J*'s judgment lien would have priority (assuming that a creditor who satisfies the requirements of section 6323(a) does not also have to satisfy a choateness test.)

Example: January 10, a federal tax lien arises. February 2, *S* makes a secured loan to the taxpayer and perfects its security interest. March 3, IRS files its federal tax lien in accordance with section 6323(f). *S*'s security interest would have priority.

Example: April 4, a federal tax lien arises. May 5, *X* makes a secured loan to the taxpayer but neglects to file a financing statement or otherwise perfect its lien. June 6, IRS files its federal tax lien in accordance with section 6323(f). IRS would have priority. *X* did not obtain a security interest AS DEFINED IN THE FEDERAL TAX LIEN ACT prior to federal tax lien filing.

3. Circuity of Priority Problems

Both section 3466 and the federal tax lien, by imposing a second priority system on the state priority system, cause circuity of priority (circular priority) problems. Circuity of priority can be best explained by illustration.

Example: Assume that *D* owns property worth $700 and owes *A* $600, owes *B* $400 and owes the federal government $500. Both *A* and *B* have liens on *D*'s property. *A* obtained her lien first and under the common law rule of "first in time, first in right" has priority over *B* under state law. As noted in the previous sections, both the federal priority provision and the Federal Tax Lien Act distinguish between choate and inchoate liens for priority purposes. Thus, if *B*'s lien is choate but *A*'s is not, and either section 3466 or the Federal Tax Lien Act is applicable, the federal claim would be superior to *A*'s claim, but junior to *B*'s. In summary, *A* "beats" *B* under state law; *B* "beats" U.S. under federal law. U.S. beats *A* under federal law. It is like the children's game of paper, scissors and rock.

How should the $700 be distributed? If *B* is paid before *A*, state law is ignored. If *A* is paid before *B*, it would seem that federal law is being ignored since under federal law *B*, but not *A*, is to be paid before the U.S.

The Supreme Court in United States v. City of New Britain (1954), adopted a two-step analysis to resolve this dilemma. The federal law of priorities was first applied. An amount equal to the interests that take prior to the federal claim under federal law was set aside to be paid out first. State law was then used to divide the amount so set aside.

Example: In the immediately preceding example, only *B*'s lien is prior to the federal government so $400, the amount of *B*'s claim, would be set aside. As *A* has first priority under state law, the $400 would be paid to *A*; the remaining $300 would be paid to the federal government. If the value of *D*'s property had been $1000, *A* would receive the first $400, the government would then receive $500 and the remaining $100 would be paid to *A*.

This seems to be a logical way of resolving the circuity problem, consistent with both federal and state law. The concern of the federal law is what amount is paid prior to the federal claim, not who is paid prior.

4. Other Federal Claims

Most people indebted to the federal government are not insolvent, and most claims of the federal government are not federal tax claims. Accordingly, most federal claims are governed by neither the federal priority provision nor the Federal Tax Lien Act. Assume, for example, that the SBA guarantees a secured loan to O.K. Supermarkets. The inventory that secures the SBA guaranteed loan is also collateral for an earlier in time loan by Kimbell Foods. If O.K. is unable to pay both debts and its inventory is not enough to pay both, whose lien has priority: SBA or Kimbell Foods?

Obviously, the Federal Tax Lien Act does not apply. And the federal priority provision does not apply since O.K. is not "insolvent" as defined under section 3466. What law controls a federal claim in a nontax, "noninsolvent" creditor conflict?

The Supreme Court in United States v. Kimbell Foods, Inc. (1979), held that:

- Federal law determines the priority of liens stemming from federal lending programs;

- Whether federal law incorporates state priority rules or fashions a separate federal rule such as the choateness rule is a matter of judicial policy;

- A federal rule such as the choateness doctrine is not necessary to protect the governmental interests underlying SBA and FHA programs;

- Accordingly, state priority rules and not the federal choateness rule control.

The holding in *Kimbell* is expressly limited to federal claims arising from SBA and FHA loans. The Court carefully leaves open the possibility that in some credit transactions protection of governmental interests may require some special federal rule such as the choateness doctrine.

E. Setoff

The "right of setoff" (also called "offset") allows entities that owe each other money to apply their mutual debts against each other, thereby avoiding the absurdity of making *A* pay *B* when *B* owes *A*. Citizens Bank of Maryland v. Strumpf (1995).

Example: *S* from time to time sold goods on credit to *B*. *B* owes *S* $20,000 for December deliveries, and *S* owes *B* $30,000 for damages caused by defects in the October and November deliveries. *S* could exercise its

4. T continued to generate additional accounts. Does S's security interest of the tax lien have priority as to accounts that arise on May 5? On June 6?

13. Would the answers to Question 7 be different if S's collateral was equipment rather than accounts?

14. On January 1, S loans D $10,000 and takes a security interest in T's accounts. The security agreement has a future-advances clause. S properly perfects her security interest on February 2. A federal tax lien arises against T on March 3 and notice of the lien is filed on April 4. On May 5, S makes an additional loan of $5000 to T so that the total of the secured debt is $15,000. What is the extent of S's priority over the federal tax lien?

15. Would the answer to Question 9 be different if S's collateral was equipment rather than accounts?

V

Debtor's State Law Remedies a/k/a Collective Creditor Action

■ *ANALYSIS*

3. Why Creditors Reluctant to Participate
4. Effect on Non–Participating Creditors
5. Preferring Some Creditors
6. Compared to Bankruptcy
7. Compared to Assignment for Benefit of Creditors

C. **Review Questions**

The remedies previously considered are all similar in that (1) all benefit the specific creditor that invokes the remedy and (2) all are creditor-initiated. This chapter will consider a couple of state debtor-creditor remedies—compositions/extensions and assignments for the benefit of creditors—that (1) benefit multiple creditors and (2) are at least in theory debtor-initiated. The qualifying words "in theory" are used because people just don't wake up in the morning, and, for the lack of anything else interesting to do, make an assignment for the benefit of creditors or enter into a composition and extension agreement. While these two remedies are debtor-initiated, they are creditor induced.

A. Assignments for the Benefit of Creditors

1. Nature of the Remedy

An assignment for the benefit of creditors is the state law counterpart of bankruptcy law's Chapter 7. More specifically, an assignment for the benefit of creditors is a voluntary transfer of assets by the debtor to another person in trust to liquidate the assets and distribute the proceeds to the creditors of the debt-transferred.

Example: *D* makes an assignment for the benefit of creditors to *A*. *C*, *D*'s creditor, will not be able to attach or execute on the property transferred. Legal title to the property is now in *A*. *A* is not indebted to *C*.

2. Assignee's Role

In the absence of special statutes, assignments for the benefit of creditors are regulated according to trust law. The assignee is accountable to creditors as a trustee is accountable to his beneficiaries. The assignee may be removed and may be personally surcharged for any breach of fiduciary duties.

3. Assignee's Duties

The assignee's duties and responsibilities are those of any trustee. She derives power and authority from the assignment, and, absent any statutory provision, she must be guided by the terms of the assignment. Under the common law, the primary duty of the assignee is to liquidate the assets and distribute the proceeds to creditors as expeditiously as possible. Even where an express power of sale is not contained in the instrument of assignment, the assignee has the power and the obligation to sell the debtor's property to convert it to cash to be distributed to creditors.

4. Relation to Fraudulent Conveyance Law

a. Assignment for Creditors Not Fraudulent Per Se

Consent of creditors is not a condition precedent to the making of an assignment for the benefit of creditors. The right to make an assignment is regarded as an incident of ownership. The primary common law limitation on use of an assignment for the benefit of creditors is the law of fraudulent transfers. As an assignment for the benefit of creditors places the debtor's property out of the reach of his creditors—legal title passes to the assignee so that creditors of the assignor can no longer levy on the property—it would seem that creditors would be able to void an assignment for the benefit of creditors under a fraudulent transfer statute. However, common law early took the position that creditors could not attack an assignment as a fraudulent conveyance if it was truly for their benefit.

b. Effect of Reserving Some Interest

An assignment for the benefit of creditors which reserves to the assignor any interest, benefit, or advantage out of the property conveyed to the injury of creditors is a fraudulent transfer. For example, an assignment is made voidable by the reservation to the assignor of control of the assigned property such as the power to revoke the assignment or to declare the uses to which the property shall be subject. Similarly, provisions in the assignment which require the assignee to delay liquidation render the assignment voidable as a fraudulent conveyance.

c. Partial Assignment

Some jurisdictions consider a partial assignment for the benefit of creditors, i.e., an assignment of less than all of the debtor's property, a fraudulent conveyance. The rationale for this position is that creditors are "hindered" and "delayed" if they are referred to the assignee for satisfaction and then have to come back to the debtor. Some states regard any assignment for the benefit of creditors by a solvent debtor as a fraudulent conveyance: since an immediate sale of the property of a solvent debtor would, theoretically at least, provide funds for the payment of all debts in full, the only result of an assignment by a solvent debtor is to hinder and delay creditors.

5. No Discharge

A common law assignment for the benefit of the creditors does not discharge the debtor from any deficiencies arising or resulting from the fact that the assigned property is liquidated for less than the amount required to pay creditors in full. [If creditors voluntarily discharge or release the assignor under such circumstances that a composition agreement can be found, the release or discharge will be effective; composition agreements are considered later in this chapter.] This lack of discharge is obviously a major disadvantage of assignments to the debtor and a major reason that assignments for the benefit of creditors are used almost exclusively by corporate debtors.

6. Preferential Payments

As the common law permits preferences, a common law assignment for the benefit of creditors which provides for preferential payments to designated creditors is not a fraudulent conveyance. Most courts, however, have held that debtors cannot use preferences to obtain discharges from creditors; assignments that condition preferential treatment on release of the unpaid portion of any claim are generally voided as fraudulent conveyances. To appreciate the reason for this rule, it is necessary to remember that the assignment places the debtor's property beyond the reach of his creditors. If the debtor could first transfer her property so that no creditor could reach it and then offer more of that property to creditors willing to "agree" to a discharge, creditors would have a powerful incentive to "agree."

7. Statutory Regulation

Today, assignments for the benefit of creditors are regulated by statute in most states. Some of these state statutes are mandatory; others merely directory. A state statute that is mandatory in its terms must be complied with in order that the assignment be valid. On the other hand, where the state statute is merely directory, the debtor may make a common law assignment or a statutory assignment. If the former is chosen, common law rules apply; if the latter is used, the statute must be complied with.

a. Recording

The state statutes customarily require recording of the assignment, filing schedules of assets and liabilities, giving notice to the creditors and bonding of the assignee, and subject the assignee to court supervision.

b. Prohibiting Preferences

Virtually all state statutes prohibit the granting of a preference—all creditors except those with liens or statutorily created priorities are to be treated equally. Some statutes, however, expressly provide for the very relief sought by a preferential assignment at common law, i.e., a discharge. Such provisions are, at best, of questionable validity. Article 1, section 8, clause 4 of the Constitution empowers Congress to establish "uniform laws on the subject of Bankruptcies throughout the United States." The exercise by Congress of this power suspends the power of states to enact bankruptcy laws. States may regulate the debtor-creditor relationship, but this regulation may not be a bankruptcy law. In determining whether a state statute is invalid as a bankruptcy law, the Supreme Court has seemed to place primary importance on the presence or absence of discharge provisions. See, e.g., Johnson v. Star (1933); International Shoe Co. v. Pinkus (1929).

c. Avoiding Powers

A number of state assignment statutes authorize the assignee to set aside prior fraudulent conveyances, and some empower the assignee to void preassignment preferences by the assignor-debtor. Even in these states, however, a bankruptcy trustee has an additional bundle of important rights which are unavailable to an assignee—rights granted by sections 544–549 of the Bankruptcy Code.

8. Relation to Bankruptcy

When the debtor has made substantial preferences or fraudulent conveyances or allowed liens, voidable in bankruptcy to attach to his property, creditors may decide that an assignment for the benefit of creditors does not adequately protect their rights. If so, the creditors may be able to force the debtor into bankruptcy. A general assignment for the benefit of creditors is a basis for ordering relief against the debtor in a creditor-commenced bankruptcy. See Bankruptcy Code section 303(h)(2). Section 543 empowers the bankruptcy court to require an assignee whose administration is superseded by bankruptcy to turn over the debtor's estate to the bankruptcy trustee, and to make an accounting.

An assignment for the benefit of creditors has certain advantages over bankruptcy to creditors. Its flexibility and informality save time and expense, and frequently result in better liquidation prices. Generally, the costs of administration of an assignment will be lower than those of a bankruptcy case. Thus, in the absence of fraudulent conveyances, preferences, or liens voidable in bankruptcy, the dividends to creditors from an efficiently administered assignment will probably be larger than those received from the administration of the same property in bankruptcy.

B. Workouts A/K/A Composition and Extension

1. Nature of the Remedy

Today, the term "workout" is used to describe a negotiated, nonbankruptcy modification of debts. A workout is the state law counterpart of bankruptcy law's Chapter 11.

Legally, a workout is a contract. Indeed, you probably studied "workouts" in your first year contracts course except that your contracts teacher used the less "trendy" phrase compositions and extensions.

- A composition is a contract between a debtor and two or more creditors in which the creditors agree to take a specified partial payment in full satisfaction of their claims.

- An extension is a contract between the debtor and two or more creditors in which the creditors agree to extend the time for the payment of their claims against the debtor.

An agreement can be both a composition and an extension: an agreement to take less over a longer period of time.

2. Governed by Contract Law

The same rules of law govern compositions and extensions. Both are governed more by principles of contract law than by state debtor-creditor rules. Compositions and extensions encompass all of the essential elements of a simple contract, and the absence of any of these elements renders the agreement invalid. Thus, there must be consideration.

The doctrine of Foakes v. Beer (1884), that part payment in money of a liquidated debt constitutes no consideration for a release of the unpaid balance would seem to invalidate composition agreements. Courts, however, have been able to find consideration in the agreement of creditors each with the other to scale down his claim and accept a lesser sum. Thus, a composition agreement requires the participation of at least two creditors.

3. Why Creditors Reluctant to Participate

The main disadvantage of a workout is that it is voluntary. A workout "works" only if creditors agree. And, there are two primary legal reasons that creditors are reluctant to enter into workout agreements.

1. First, creditors generally are unwilling to make concessions unless all other creditors make similar concessions. In a workout, unlike bankruptcy, the majority of creditors are unable to cram down concessions on dissenting creditors.

2. Second, a workout or composition does not prevent the debtor from later seeking bankruptcy protection. Creditors are reluctant to make significant concessions knowing the debtor might later effect further reductions through a bankruptcy filing.

4. Effect on Non–Participating Creditors

While more than one creditor must participate in a composition agreement, there is no requirement that all creditors agree. Creditors who do not agree to the composition are not affected by it.

Example: D is indebted to W, X, Y and Z. D proposes to pay each creditor 10% of its claim each month for the next six months, in full satisfaction of all liability. W, X and Y agree to this composition/extension. Z does not. As a nonassenting creditor, Z is unaffected by the agreement between W, X and Y. Z will not receive the monthly payments as provided in the agreement, but Z will be free to attempt to collect the full amount of its claim from D through extrajudicial or judicial means. If W, X and Y are aware that Z is not taking part in the composition/extension, Z's collection of 100% of its claim from D will not affect the composition/extension agreement.

5. Preferring Some Creditors

Similarly, all is well where the other creditors know that one or more of the creditors are being paid more or are being benefited in a way different from the rest. As noted previously, the common law does not condemn preferences; but the law is zealous in seeing that no creditor receives any secret consideration pursuant to a composition and extension agreement. Accordingly, where a creditor is given a secret preference, the other creditors have the right to void the agreement. The creditor with the preference can neither enforce nor void the agreement, and the debtor has a right to recover preferential payments from him. This last "rule" is almost always explained by the presumption of duress: the debtor is presumed to be vulnerable to creditor pressure because of the creditor's *de facto* power to refuse to enter into the composition and therefore to force the debtor to file a bankruptcy petition.

6. Compared to Bankruptcy

There are a number of reasons that a debtor might prefer a composition to bankruptcy. By making a composition with his creditors, the debtor avoids the stigma that attaches to bankruptcy while he achieves the same result—discharge from all or a substantial portion of his debts. The composition discharge is even broader in scope than that of bankruptcy. A composition releases a surety while a discharge in bankruptcy does not. See Bankruptcy Code section 524(e). A debt discharged by a composition is not revived by a new promise to pay it unless that new promise is supported by new consideration; a promise to pay a debt discharged in bankruptcy need not be supported by consideration in order to be enforceable. Cf. section 524(c). Further a composition does not bar future bankruptcy discharge—a Chapter 7 bankruptcy discharge bars another Chapter 7 discharge for six years. See section 727(a)(8).

a. Why Workout Rather Than Chapter 11

The reasons that a debtor might choose to use a workout rather than Chapter 11 are usually business reasons. Workouts are generally quicker than Chapter 11 cases. Workouts are generally less public than Chapter 11. Attorney's fees in a workout are usually lower than attorney's fees in a Chapter 11 case.

b. Why Chapter 11 Rather Than Workout

The reasons that a debtor chooses to use Chapter 11 rather than a workout are usually legal reasons. The mere filing of a Chapter 11 petition automatically stays all creditors from proceeding against the debtor or its assets. There is no workout counterpart of this automatic stay. One or more creditors can undertake judicial collection actions against the debtor during the pendency of the workout negotiations. And, the confirmation of a Chapter 11 plan binds all creditors, even dissenting creditors. Again, there is no workout counterpart.

7. Compared to Assignment for Benefit of Creditors

The following chart compares assignments for the benefit of creditors and compositions:

Assignment for the Benefit of Creditors	Composition
1. Common law; statutory	1. Contractual
2. Affects all general creditors	2. Only affects creditors who enter into the composition
3. Only debts voluntarily released by creditors discharged	3. Discharges all creditors who enter into composition
4. In most jurisdictions, all nonexempt property is delivered to a third person for sale with distribution of proceeds to creditors	4. Debtor retains property except as provided in the agreement
5. Basically liquidation device	5. Basically debtor rehabilitation device
6. General assignment for benefit of creditors basis for involuntary bankruptcy under section 303(h)(2)	6. Not a basis for an involuntary bankruptcy proceeding

C. Review Questions

1. What is an assignment for the benefit of creditors?

2. T or F   An assignment for the benefit of creditors requires the creditors' consent?

3. T or F   A creditor who participates in the distribution of a debtor's assignment for the benefit of creditors is barred from suing from a deficiency if the distribution the creditor receives from the liquidation of assets is less than the debt owed her.

4. An assignment for the benefit is governed by state law but somewhat resembles what kind of bankruptcy proceeding?

5. What is a composition agreement?

6. How is an extension agreement different?

7. What is a workout?

8. T or F   A composition agreement (or "workout") is legally effective only if all of the debtor's creditors agree and participate.

9. T or F   A creditor who participates in a composition agreement is barred from suing from a deficiency if the payment the creditor receives under the terms of the composition agreement is less than the original amount of the debt owed her.

10. A composition agreement is governed by state contract law but somewhat resembles what kind of bankruptcy proceeding?

VI

Bankruptcy: An Overview

■ *ANALYSIS*

A. **Differences Between Bankruptcy and State Law**
B. **The Law of Bankruptcy**
   1.   The Bankruptcy Code
   2.   Bankruptcy Rules of Procedure and Forms
   3.   Role of State Law
C. **Forms of Bankruptcy Relief**
   1.   Liquidation
   2.   Reorganization
D. **Bankruptcy Courts and Bankruptcy Judges**
   1.   Under the Bankruptcy Act of 1898
   2.   Under the Present Law
E. **Trustees**
   1.   Chapter 7 Cases
   2.   Chapter 13 Cases
   3.   Chapter 11 Cases
F. **United States Trustees**
G. **Review Questions**

The remainder of the Black Letter focuses on bankruptcy.

This book will introduce you to bankruptcy one concept at a time: stays, then property of the estate, then exempt property, then . . . . That is the easiest way to gain an initial understanding of bankruptcy law. As one of the great bankruptcy teachers, Steve Riesenfeld, observed, "Bankruptcy law is a series of lumps. Do not make mashed potatoes out of it."

The book will also explore some of the connections or relationships of these various concepts. For example, a determination that a doctor's malpractice insurance is property of the estate when she files for bankruptcy can affect the application of the automatic stay to creditors' efforts to collect under that insurance. The various bankruptcy concepts are connected or related. To paraphrase the noted writer Erica Jong, the law of bankruptcy is a "zipless web."

Judge Grant expressed the same thought much more eloquently in In re Depew (1989): "The Bankruptcy Code is not a fragmented and disconnected collection of miscellaneous rules. It is a complex tapestry of ideas. The colors and patterns that are woven into its fabric combine to compliment and reinforce each other. In order to create a single unifying theme—the equitable treatment of creditors and financial relief for over-burdened debtors. In doing so, the tensions between these seemingly inconsistent objectives have been balanced and harmonized. Consequently, title 11's various provisions should not be viewed in isolation. Instead, the interpretation should reflect the interplay between all of its different parts, so that the Bankruptcy Code can operate as a coherent whole. The meaning given to any one portion must be consistent with the remaining provisions of the Bankruptcy Code."

A. Differences Between Bankruptcy and State Law

Initially, four basic differences between bankruptcy and state debtor-creditor law should be noted.

- First, bankruptcy law is federal law.

- Second, state law focuses on individual action by a particular creditor and puts a premium on prompt action by a creditor. The first creditor to attach the debtor's property, the first creditor to execute on the property, etc. is the one most likely to be paid. Bankruptcy, on the other hand, compels collective creditor collection action and emphasizes equality of treatment, rather than a race of diligence. While bankruptcy law does not require equal treatment for all creditors, all creditors within a single class are treated the same. After the commencement of a bankruptcy case, a creditor cannot improve its position vis-à-vis other creditors by seizing the assets of the debtor. Similarly, the debtor's ability to make preferential transfers to creditors before bankruptcy is considerably limited.

- Third, the prospects for debtor relief are much greater in bankruptcy. For individual debtors, this bankruptcy relief may take the form of relief from further personal liability for debts because of a discharge. While no debtor is guaranteed a discharge, most individual debtors do receive a discharge. One of the primary purposes of the bankruptcy act is to "relieve the honest debtor from the weight of oppressive indebtedness and permit him to start afresh . . . . " Local Loan Co. v. Hunt (1934). For business debtors, this bankruptcy relief may take the form of a restructuring of debts by reason of a confirmed Chapter 11 plan.

- Fourth, the vocabulary of bankruptcy law is different from the vocabulary of state collection law. The Bankruptcy Code uses technical terms such as "automatic stay" and "impairment" that are not a part of state law. And, the Bankruptcy Code uses terms such as "debtor" and "redemption" that are a part of state law differently than state law. Accordingly, it is very important that you consistently and persistently check for the statutory definitions of terms used in the Bankruptcy Code.

B. The Law of Bankruptcy

Article I of the Constitution empowers Congress to "establish uniform laws on the subject of Bankruptcies throughout the United States." For most of the 20th century, bankruptcy law was the Bankruptcy Act of 1898, commonly referred to as the "Bankruptcy Act." It was replaced in 1978 by a law commonly referred to as the "Bankruptcy Reform Act of 1978" or "Bankruptcy Code." The Bankruptcy Code has been regularly amended; the most comprehensive bankruptcy amendments were enacted in 1984 and 2005.

1. The Bankruptcy Code

The Bankruptcy Code divides the substantive law of bankruptcy into the following chapters:

Chapter 1	General Provisions, Definitions and Rules of Construction
Chapter 3	Case Administration
Chapter 5	Creditors, the Debtor, and the Estate
Chapter 7	Liquidation
Chapter 9	Adjustment of the Debts of a Municipality
Chapter 11	Reorganization

The provisions in Chapters 1, 3 and 5 apply in every bankruptcy case, unless otherwise specified. Accordingly, if you are working on a problem in a Chapter 11 case, it will be necessary to deal with the provisions of Chapters 1, 3, 5 and 11.

2. Bankruptcy Rules of Procedure and Forms

It is also necessary to deal with the Bankruptcy Rules. Pursuant to the authority of 28 USCA § 2075, the United States Supreme Court promulgated Bankruptcy Rules. These rules, not the Federal Rules of Civil Procedure, "govern procedure in United States Bankruptcy Courts," Rule 1001. The Bankruptcy Rules are divided into ten parts. Each part governs a different stage of the bankruptcy process. For example, Part 1 of the Rules, Rule 1002 through Rule 1019 deals with issues related to commencement of cases. Rule 9009 refers to and sanctions Official Forms prescribed by the Judicial Conference of the United States.

3. Role of State Law

Bankruptcy law is also in large part state law. We are not here suggesting that there are state bankruptcy laws. Since Article I of the Constitution empowers Congress to enact uniform laws of bankruptcy and Congress has enacted such laws, principles of federal supremacy preclude state legislatures from enacting bankruptcy laws. Rather, bankruptcy law is in large part state law because courts applying the federal bankruptcy law look to state law to determine questions such as (1) what are the property rights of the debtor and (2) what are the claims of the creditors to that property. As the Supreme Court stated in Butner v. United States (1979):

"Congress has generally left the determination of property rights in the assets of a bankrupt's estate to state law. Property interests are created and defined by state law. Unless some federal interest requires a different result, there is no reason why such interests should be analyzed differently simply because an interested party is involved in a bankruptcy proceeding."

Increasingly, law professors and judges are questioning the extent to which judges should look to state law in applying provisions of the Bankruptcy

Code. In law review articles, reported decisions and law school classrooms, questions are being asked about the relationship between bankruptcy law and state law, about the extent to which the Bankruptcy Code does and should change state law.

Example: *D* enters into an employment contract with *C* Company that contains a covenant not to compete that completely complies with state law. Under state law, *D* cannot avoid her obligations under the covenant not to compete by breaching the contract; under state law, *C* Company can obtain injunctive relief to prevent *D* from competing. Should the result be different in bankruptcy? Should the Bankruptcy Code provisions on executory contracts and discharge and the bankruptcy policy of a fresh start enable *D* to avoid her obligations under the covenant not compete?

C. Forms of Bankruptcy Relief

There are two general forms of bankruptcy relief: (1) liquidation and (2) rehabilitation or reorganization. The Bankruptcy Code provides for these two forms of relief in five separate kinds of bankruptcy cases:

- Chapter 7 cases,

- Chapter 9 cases,

- Chapter 11 cases,

- Chapter 12 cases, and

- Chapter 13 cases.

This book does not deal with Chapters 9 and 12. Chapter 9 cases involve governmental entities as debtors, and it is infrequently used. Chapter 12 is limited to family farmer bankruptcy. This Black Letter will deal with the three basic forms of bankruptcy relief: Chapter 7, Chapter 11 and Chapter 13.

1. Liquidation

Chapter 7 is entitled "liquidation." The title is descriptive. In a Chapter 7 case, the trustee collects the nonexempt property of the debtor, converts that property to cash, and distributes the cash to the creditors. The debtor gives up all of the nonexempt property she owns at the time of the filing of the bankruptcy petition in the hope of obtaining a discharge. A discharge releases the debtor from any further personal liability for her prebankruptcy debts.

Example: *B* owes *C* $2,000. *B* files a Chapter 7 petition. *C* only receives $300 from the liquidation of *B*'s assets. If *B* receives a bankruptcy discharge, *C* will be precluded from pursuing *B* for the remaining $1,700.

As the preceding paragraph implies, every Chapter 7 case under the bankruptcy laws does not result in a discharge. Section 727(a) lists a number of grounds for withholding a discharge. And, even if the debtor is able to obtain a discharge, she will not necessarily be freed from all creditors' claims. Section 523 sets out exceptions to discharge.

The vast majority of bankruptcy cases are Chapter 7 cases. The term "bankruptcy" is often used to describe liquidation proceedings under the bankruptcy laws. References to "bankruptcy" in this Black Letter should generally be regarded as references to liquidation cases.

2. Reorganization

Chapters 11 and 13 generally deal with debtor rehabilitation or reorganization of the debtor's financial affairs, not liquidation of the debtor's assets. In a Chapter 11 or 13 case creditors usually look to future earnings of the debtor, not the property of the debtor at the time of the initiation of the bankruptcy proceeding, to satisfy their claims. The debtor retains its assets and makes payments to creditors, usually from postpetition earnings, pursuant to a court approved plan.

Chapter 11, like Chapter 7, is available to all forms of debtors—individuals, partnerships and corporations (though individuals infrequently use Chapter 11 because the process is so complex and costly). Chapter 13 can be used only by individuals with a "regular income" (as defined in section 101(30)) who have unsecured debts of less than $307,675 and secured debts of less than $922,975. [These numbers, and other numbers under the Bankruptcy Code, are adjusted periodically pursuant to section 104.]

D. Bankruptcy Courts and Bankruptcy Judges

1. Under the Bankruptcy Act of 1898

The Bankruptcy Act of 1898 provided for "bankruptcy referees." Originally, the judicial role of bankruptcy referees was relatively minor. The referee was primarily an administrator and supervisor of bankruptcy cases, not a judicial officer. Amendments to the Bankruptcy Act of 1898 made the bankruptcy referee more of a judicial officer. In 1973, the Bankruptcy Rules changed the title of the office from "bankruptcy referee" to "bankruptcy judge."

The 1898 Act used the term "courts of bankruptcy." A court of bankruptcy could be either the court of a federal district judge or the court of a bankruptcy judge. Any federal district court could be a "court of bankruptcy." Any judicial power conferred by the Bankruptcy Act of 1898 on the "court" could be exercised by either a federal district judge or a bankruptcy judge; any judicial power conferred by the Bankruptcy Act of 1898 on the "judge" could be exercised only by the federal district judge.

2. Under the Present Law

Congress deals with the bankruptcy court system separately from the substantive law of bankruptcy. The substantive law of bankruptcy is now in title 11 of the United States Code; the law relating to bankruptcy judges is in title 28.

a. Bankruptcy Court Part of District Court

Title 28 nowhere uses the term "bankruptcy referee." Section 152 of title 28 provides for "bankruptcy judges" to be appointed by the United States courts of appeals. Section 151 of title 28 states that these bankruptcy judges "shall constitute a unit of the district court to be known as the bankruptcy court." Under title 28, the bankruptcy court is not really a separate court; rather, it is a part of the district court.

Accordingly, the grant of jurisdiction over bankruptcy matters is to the district court, 28 USCA § 1334. The federal district judges then refer bankruptcy matters to the bankruptcy judges pursuant to 28 USCA 157.

b. Grant of Jurisdiction Under § 1334

It is important to understand the differences between 28 USCA § 1334 and 28 USCA 157. Section 1334 grants jurisdiction over bankruptcy cases and proceedings. All grants of jurisdiction are to the district court. Neither the phrase "bankruptcy court" nor the phrase "bankruptcy judge" appears in section 1334. Remember, however, that the bankruptcy judge is a unit of the district court under section 151. Thus, a grant of jurisdiction to the "district court" does not preclude the bankruptcy judge from playing a role in bankruptcy litigation.

The allocation of judicial power and responsibility over bankruptcy matters is one of the most controversial and complex areas of bankruptcy law and practice. We believe that you will find it easier to deal with the bankruptcy jurisdiction issues after you have gained a greater understanding of the substantive law of bankruptcy. Accordingly, bankruptcy jurisdiction issues will not be dealt with until later in this book.

c. Role of Bankruptcy Judge Under § 157

Section 157 spells out the role that the bankruptcy judge is to play in bankruptcy litigation. Section 157 is entitled "Procedures" and deals with referral of matters from the "district court" to the bankruptcy judge. Section 157 is not a jurisdictional provision; it does not grant jurisdiction to the bankruptcy judges. In summary, section 1334 speaks to what district courts can do and is jurisdictional. Section 157 deals with what the bankruptcy judges can do and is procedural.

E. Trustees

In every Chapter 7 case, every Chapter 12 case, every Chapter 13 case and some Chapter 11 cases, there will be not only a bankruptcy judge but also a bankruptcy trustee. Generally, the bankruptcy trustee will be a private citizen, not an employee of the federal government.

A bankruptcy trustee is an active trustee. According to section 323 of the Bankruptcy Code, the bankruptcy trustee is "the representative of the estate." The filing of a bankruptcy petition is said to create an estate consisting generally of the property of the debtor as of the time of the bankruptcy filing. Section 541. This estate is treated as a separate legal entity, distinct from the debtor. The bankruptcy trustee is the person who sues on behalf of or may be sued on behalf of the estate.

1. Chapter 7 Cases

The powers and duties of a bankruptcy trustee vary from chapter to chapter. Recall that Chapter 7 bankruptcy is liquidation in nature. The duties of a bankruptcy trustee in a Chapter 7 case include:

1. Collecting the "property of the estate," i.e., debtor's property as of the time of the filing of the bankruptcy petition;

2. Challenging certain prebankruptcy and postbankruptcy transfers of the property of the estate;

3. Selling the property of the estate;

4. Objecting to creditors' claims that are improper; and

5. In appropriate cases, objecting to the debtor's discharge. Section 704.

Remember that there will be a bankruptcy trustee in every Chapter 7 case. And, in most Chapter 7 cases, most of the work is done by the Chapter 7 trustee.

There will also be a trustee in every Chapter 13 case, and in most Chapter 13 cases the trustee does most of the work. But, the person who works as a Chapter 13 trustee is different from the person who works as a Chapter 7 trustee, and the work that she does is different.

A Chapter 7 trustee is selected to serve as trustee in a particular Chapter 7 case. While a person often serves as trustee in more than one Chapter 7 case at a time, her work as a trustee is dependent on her being appointed or elected to serve as trustee in that case, sections 701 and 701. By contrast, one or more individuals are selected by the United States Trustee to serve as trustee for all of the Chapter 13 cases in his or her district—to be the "standing Chapter 13 trustee."

2. Chapter 13 Cases

The duties of a Chapter 13 trustee also differ significantly from the duties of a Chapter 7 trustee. Section 1302 sets out the duties of a Chapter 13, and there seems to a considerable overlap between section 1302 and section 702 which sets out the duties of a Chapter 7 trustee.

The major differences between the work of a Chapter 13 trustee and the work of a Chapter 7 trustee mirror the major difference between Chapter 13 and Chapter 7: payments pursuant to a court approved plan as compared with payments pursuant to liquidation. Accordingly, a Chapter 13 trustee does not collect and liquidate the debtor's property. Instead, the Chapter 13 trustee reviews and, where appropriate, contests the debtor's plan of repayment, and, after court approval of the Chapter 13 plan of repayment, serves as disbursing agent for the payments to creditors under the plan.

3. Chapter 11 Cases

While there is a bankruptcy trustee in every Chapter 7 case and every Chapter 13 case, there is rarely a bankruptcy trustee in a Chapter 11 case. In Chapter 11, a bankruptcy trustee will be appointed only if the bankruptcy judge decides, after notice and hearing, that there is "cause," the "appointment is in the interest of creditors, any equity security holders, and other interests of the estate," or there are grounds to convert or dismiss the case. Section 1104(a).

Remember also that Chapter 11, like Chapter 13, contemplates rehabilitation, not liquidation, and that Chapter 11, unlike Chapter 13, is available to corporations and partnerships as well as individuals. The typical Chapter 11 case involves a business that continues to operate after the bankruptcy petition is filed. If a bankruptcy trustee is named in such a case, he or she will take over the operation of the business. As noted above, generally there will not be a trustee in a Chapter 11 case. The debtor will usually remain in control of the business after the filing of a Chapter 11 petition; such a debtor is referred to as a "debtor in possession."

F. United States Trustees

There was no such thing as a United States trustee until the 1978 bankruptcy legislation. During the debate on bankruptcy legislation, considerable concern was expressed over the bankruptcy judges' involvement in the administration of bankruptcy cases. While both the House and the Senate seemed to agree that the bankruptcy judge should not perform administrative functions, there was disagreement over who should. The compromise was an experimental United States trustee program involving parts of certain states and the District of Columbia. Congress has since expanded the United States Trustee program virtually nationwide.

The Executive Office of the United States Trustee (EOUST) is located in Washington, D.C. There are 20 something regional operations covering all federal judicial districts, except Alabama and North Carolina where a bankruptcy administrator essentially performs the same duties.

The United States Trustee is a government official, appointed by the Attorney General. Essentially, the United States trustee performs appointing and other administrative tasks that the bankruptcy judge would otherwise have to perform.

To illustrate, the United States trustee, not the bankruptcy judge, selects and supervises the bankruptcy trustees. Although the United States trustee can act as trustee in a Chapter 7 case or a Chapter 13 case (but not a Chapter 11 case), section 307, he or she is not intended as a substitute for private bankruptcy trustees. The United States trustee is more of a substitute for the bankruptcy judge with respect to supervisory and administrative matters.

G. Review Questions

1. T or F   Bankruptcy law is federal law.

2. T or F   A whole lot of the law applied in bankruptcy cases is state law.

3. How do you reconcile the (correct) answers to Questions 1 and 2?

4. What are the two general forms of bankruptcy relief?

5. What chapter of the Bankruptcy Code deals with liquidation?

6. What chapters of the Bankruptcy Code deal with reorganization of persons other than governmental entities and family farmers?

7. What is the difference between bankruptcy liquidation and bankruptcy reorganization?

8. Jurisdiction of bankruptcy is vested where?

9. What is the technical relationship between a federal district court and the bankruptcy court for the district?

10. When (in what kinds of cases) is a trustee always appointed in bankruptcy, and when is the appointment of a trustee discretionary?

*

VII

Commencement, Conversion, and Dismissal of a Bankruptcy Case

■ *ANALYSIS*

A bankruptcy case begins with the filing of a petition with the bankruptcy court. Section 301(a). Generally, the debtor files the petition. Such debtor-initiated cases are often referred to as "voluntary." Creditors have a limited right to initiate "involuntary" bankruptcy cases against the debtor under Chapters 7 and 11. Section 303.

A. Voluntary Cases

Section 301 deals with the commencement of voluntary cases under Chapter 7, 9, 11, 12 or 13. It provides that a bankruptcy petition may be filed by any "entity that may be a debtor under such chapter." Section 109 sets out who is eligible to be a debtor under each chapter.

1. Who Can File

a. By Chapter

1) Chapter 7

Section 109(b) contains two limitations on the availability of Chapter 7 (liquidation) relief to a debtor:

1. The debtor must be a "person." "Person" is defined in section 101(41) as including individuals, partnerships, and corporations. A sole proprietorship would not be a "person." The individual who is the proprietor is the person who is the debtor.

2. The debtor may not be a railroad, insurance company, or banking institution. Railroads are eligible for bankruptcy relief only under Subchapter IV of Chapter 11. Insurance companies and banking institutions are excluded from relief under the Bankruptcy Code because their liquidations are governed by other state and federal regulatory laws.

2) Chapter 11

With a couple of small exceptions, any person who is eligible to file a petition under Chapter 7 is also eligible to file a petition under Chapter 11, section 109(d).

3) Chapter 13

There are three significant limitations in section 109(e) on the availability of Chapter 13:

1. The debtor must be an individual. A Chapter 13 petition may not be filed by a corporation or a partnership.

2. The individual must have "income sufficiently stable and regular to enable such individual to make payments under a (Chapter 13 plan)," sections 101, 109(e). This includes not only wage earners, but also self-employed individuals, and individuals on welfare, pensions, or investment income.

3. The debtor must have "noncontingent, liquidated" unsecured debts totaling less than $307,675 and "noncontingent, liquidated" secured debts of less than $922,975. These amounts are adjusted from time to time pursuant to section 104 to reflect changes in the Consumer Price Index.

a) Debts Excluded from the Debt Limit

Note that not all debts are included in the debt limit. Debts that are contingent or unliquidated are ignored. Note also that all debts are not counted the same. The test is not a single limit but rather a limit on unsecured debts and a limit on secured debts.

b) Partly Secured Debts

Consider the application of these limits to partly secured debt. What if *D* owes *C* $1,000,000 and that debt is secured by property worth $800,000?

Most courts would find that *C*'s debt does not disqualify *D* from 13—that *D*'s obligation to *C* is a secured debt of $800,000 and an unsecured debt of $200,000. The statutory basis for such a finding is section 506 of the Bankruptcy Code which provides that a claim is secured only to the extent of the value of the collateral for the debt.

As this example illustrates, a single transaction outside of bankruptcy can create both a secured claim and an unsecured claim in bankruptcy. If *D* borrows $800,000 from *C* in a single transaction with a single set of documents, *C* will have both a secured claim and an unsecured claim if the collateral for the $800,000 loan has a value of less than $800,000.

b. Global Limitation on Individuals in Any Chapter

Within 180 days before filing bankruptcy, any "individual" must have received consumer credit counseling from an approved agency. No individual may be a debtor under "this title" (i.e., the entire Bankruptcy Code) unless he or she received this counseling. Section 109(h).

c. Other Filing Issues

1) Insolvency Not Required

While too much debt makes a debtor ineligible for Chapter 13, too much assets does not make a debtor ineligible for Chapter 7, 11 or 13. Please note that insolvency is not a condition precedent to any form of voluntary bankruptcy action. A debtor may file a petition under Chapter 7, 9, 11, 12 or 13 even though solvent.

2) Joint Filing

A husband and a wife may file a single joint petition for voluntary relief under any chapter that is available to *each* spouse. Section 302. If a husband and a wife jointly file under Chapter 13, their aggregate debts are subject to dollar limits.

3) Frequent Filing

As the preceding pages examining paragraphs (b), (d), and (e) of section 109 indicate, there are debtors that are eligible for some chapters of bankruptcy relief but not eligible for others. Additionally, there are individual debtors who are not eligible for relief under any chapter: section 109(g) adds what could be roughly called a "frequent filing" limitation. Under section 109(g), an individual debtor is not eligible to be a debtor under 7, 11 or 13, if he or she was a debtor in a bankruptcy case within the last 180 days that was:

(i) Dismissed by the court for failure of the debtor to abide by court orders or appear before the court, or

(ii) Dismissed on motion of the debtor following the filing of a request for relief from the automatic stay. Note that section 109(f) does not bar an individual who has completed a Chapter 7, 11, or 13 case from immediately filing for bankruptcy again.

4) Filing Fee

A debtor who files a bankruptcy petition must pay a filing fee. The court may dismiss the bankruptcy case for nonpayment of fees. No provision is made for *in forma pauperis* bankruptcy.

5) Commencement

A voluntary bankruptcy case is commenced when an eligible debtor files a petition. Section 301(a). No formal adjudication is necessary. The filing operates as an "order for relief," section 301(b).

B. Involuntary Cases

An involuntary case is a bankruptcy filing by creditors of a debtor to force the debtor into bankruptcy. Section 303 deals with bankruptcy petitions filed by creditors.

1. Limitations on Involuntary Petitions

Section 303 contains a number of significant limitations on involuntary petitions:

1. Creditors may file involuntary petitions under Chapter 7 or 11 but not Chapter 9, 12 or 13.

2. Certain debtors are protected from involuntary petitions. Insurance companies, banking institutions, farmers, and charitable corporations may not be subjected to involuntary petitions.

3. The petition must be filed by the requisite number of creditors. Generally, three creditors with unsecured claims totaling at least $12,300 must join in the petition. (Again the dollar amount is adjusted from time to time pursuant to section 104 to reflect changes in the Consumer Price Index.) If, however, the debtor has less than twelve unsecured creditors, a single creditor with an unsecured claim of $12,300 is sufficient.

2. Effect of Filing an Involuntary Petition

While the filing of an involuntary petition effects a commencement of the case, it does not operate as an adjudication, as an order for relief. The debtor has the right to file an answer. If the debtor does not timely answer the petition, "the court shall order relief," section 303(h). If the debtor does timely answer the petition, the court "shall order relief against the debtor" only if one of the two grounds for involuntary relief are established.

3. Grounds for Relief

a. Debtor Not Paying Debts

The first basis for involuntary relief is that the debtor is generally not paying debts as they come due. This is sometimes referred to as "equitable insolvency"; it is different from the definition of insolvency in section 101.

b. Receiver or the Like Having Taken Possession of Debtor's Property

The alternative basis for involuntary relief is that within 120 days before the petition was filed, a general receiver, assignee, or custodian took possession of substantially all of the debtor's property or was appointed to take charge of substantially all of the debtor's property. The appointment of a receiver in a mortgage foreclosure action to the possession of Greenacre, less than substantially all of the debtor's property, would not be a basis for involuntary relief.

4. What Happens During the Gap Period Between Filing and Order of Relief

Usually there will be an interval of at least several weeks between the filing of an involuntary petition and the order of relief against the debtor.

a. Court May Appoint Interim Trustee

The bankruptcy court may appoint an interim trustee to take possession of the debtor's property or operate the debtor's business "if necessary to preserve the property of the estate or to prevent loss to the estate," section 303(g). If an interim trustee is appointed, the debtor may regain possession by posting a bond.

b. If No Interim Trustee Appointed

Absent appointment of a trustee, the debtor may continue to buy, use, or sell property and to operate its business in the period after the bankruptcy filing and before the order of relief, section 303(f). Sections 502(f) and 507(a)(2) protect third parties who deal with a debtor after an involuntary petition has been filed.

5. Debtor's Remedies if Petition Dismissed

Notwithstanding the protection of section 303(f), the filing of an involuntary petition adversely affects the debtor's financial reputation and business operations. Section 303(i) attempts to protect debtors from ill-founded petitions by setting out the following remedies in cases in which an involuntary petition is dismissed after litigation:

1. The court may grant judgment for the debtor against the petitioning creditors for costs and a reasonable attorney's fee.

2. If an interim trustee took possession of the debtor's property, the court may grant judgment for "any damages proximately caused by the taking."

3.   If the petition was filed in "bad faith," the court may award "any damages proximately caused by such filing," such as loss of business, and also punitive damages.

C. Foreign Debtors

1. Commence a Regular Case

A foreign debtor can start its own United States bankruptcy case by filing a voluntary bankruptcy petition if it has a residence or domicile in the United States, a place of business in the United States, or assets in the United States. Section 109. Similarly, the creditors of such a foreign debtor may begin a bankruptcy case in the United States by filing an involuntary bankruptcy petition. Section 303(b). The Bankruptcy Code treats such foreign debtor filings no differently than filings by or against domestic debtors. Such foreign debtor cases will be independent of any foreign bankruptcy proceedings.

2. Commence an Ancillary Case

Chapter 15 of the Bankruptcy Code provides an alternative to commencing a full bankruptcy case in the United States. If a bankruptcy case is pending in a foreign country, a "foreign representative" of the debtor in such a case may file a "petition for recognition." Upon the issuance of an order for recognition under section 1517, the automatic stay and selected other provisions of the Bankruptcy Code become effective.

D. Conversion of Cases

Remember that there are five forms of bankruptcy relief: Chapter 7, Chapter 9, Chapter 11, Chapter 12 and Chapter 13. The party filing a petition elects one of these chapters: she files a petition for relief under Chapter 7 or 11 or 12 or 13. The petitioner's choice of a chapter is reversible; Chapter 7, Chapter 11, Chapter 12 and Chapter 13 have provisions governing conversion of a case under that chapter to another chapter. The grounds for conversion vary from chapter to chapter. The Code provides for both voluntary and involuntary conversion.

E. Dismissal

The bankruptcy court may dismiss or suspend a voluntary bankruptcy case even though it was filed by an eligible debtor. And, the bankruptcy court may dismiss or suspend an involuntary bankruptcy case even though all of the requirements are satisfied. Each bankruptcy relief chapter has its own dismissal provision.

1. Chapter 7 Cases

a. Section 707(a)—"For Cause"

Section 707 governs dismissal of Chapter 7 cases. Section 707(a) explains on of the standards a bankruptcy court is to apply in ruling on a motion to dismiss: "for cause." Section 707(a) gives two examples of cause in a voluntary case:

- Unreasonable delay by the debtor that is prejudicial to creditors; and

- Nonpayment of any bankruptcy fees or charges

This "cause" standard applies to motions to dismiss filed by the debtor as well as motions to dismiss filed by creditors. A debtor who files a Chapter 7 petition does not have an absolute right to have the bankruptcy case dismissed. Accordingly, a debtor might find it much easier to "get into" Chapter 7 than it is to "get out."

b. Section 707(b)—"Abuse"

Section 707(b) provides for dismissal of a Chapter 7, or conversion to Chapter 13 with the debtor's consent, upon a finding that the filing of the case amounts to an "abuse" of Chapter 7.

1) Three Alternative Tests

There are three alternative tests of "abuse:"

- **Bad faith**, 11 USCA § 707(b)(3);

- **Totality of the circumstances** of the debtor's financial situation (including whether the debtor seeks to reject a personal service contract and the financial need for such rejection as sought by the debtor), 11 USCA § 707(b)(3); or

- Presumptively, there is abuse if the debtor has sufficient income (i.e., has the financial means) to fund a Chapter 13 plan according to a congressional-formulated and formularized **"means test."** 707(b)(2)(A).

2) When the Means Test Does Not Apply

The **test does not apply** if the combined, current monthly income of the debtor and spouse is equal to or less than the median family income for the state. 11 USCA § 707(b)(7).

Current monthly income is a term of art. It basically means the average monthly income from all sources that the debtor receives during the previous six months, including any paid by any other person on a regular basis for debtor's household expenses. 101(10A).

In a case where the debtor's income equals or falls below the state median, the law presumes that, in terms of the congressional formula, the debtor lacks the means to fund a Chapter 13 plan; and nobody can move to dismiss for abuse under the means test.

In such a case, dismissal for abuse under the other tests of is possible but is triggered only upon motion of the judge or the U.S. Trustee (or administrator), not the Chapter 7 trustee or a party in interest. The issue then is what constitutes abuse absent the ability to pay under the statutory means test and, in such a case, what's the point of denying Chapter 7 relief. An example is In re O'Donohue (Bankr. E.D. Ark. 2004), which was decided before Congress added the means test to the Code but which likely remains good law even with the means test. In this case, Bankruptcy Judge Evans announced that "a debtor's inability to pay will not shield that debtor from Section 707(b) dismissal where bad faith is otherwise shown." The debtor's disposable income was a negative number, but the court dismissed the Chapter 7 case. The debtor's credit card debts increased from about $2,700 to $78,000 within 12 months before the bankruptcy, and $44,000 was accumulated within two months before the debtor filed. Plus, there was "evidence indicating the Debtor's dishonesty," and he "testified in a very limited and cagey manner. . . ."

3) When the Means Test Does Apply

The means test applies only when the current monthly income of the debtor and the debtor's spouse exceeds the state's median income.

Deciding that the test applies does not spell abuse. The test must be applied to the debtor's peculiar circumstances to reveal if the debtor has the formularized means to fund a Chapter 13 plan. To apply the test:

1. Take the debtor's monthly income, and

2. Subtract the debtor's monthly expenses (which are described and hugely detailed in section 707(b) and which are

largely keyed to national standards rather than actual expenses) but by reference to IRS collection standards).

3. If the net is

   a. Equal to or greater than $166.67, the debtor passes the means test and abuse is presumed;

   b. Less than $100, the debtor fails the means test and no abuse is presumed because of the test (though the there may be abuse on other grounds);

   c. Between $100 and $167.66, inclusive, more calculation is necessary. Multiply the monthly net income by 60 (five years) and compare this product to the total of the debtor's nonpriority, unsecured debts. The debtor passes the means test and abuse is presumed if the total, five-year income is sufficient to cover at least 25% of the total of the debts. Otherwise, the debtor fails the means test.

a) If the debtor fails the test

If the means test applies and the debtor fails the test, the court, the U.S. Trustee, the case trustee, or a creditor can seek to dismiss the debtor's case, or covert it to Chapter 13 with the debtor's consent, based on the alternative tests of abuse.

b) If the debtor passes the test

If the means test applies and the debtor passes the test so that a presumption of abuse arises under 707(b):

- "[T]he presumption of abuse may only be rebutted by demonstrating special circumstances, such as a serious medical condition or a call or order to active duty. . . to the extent that such special circumstances . . . justify additional expenses or adjustments of current monthly income for which there is no reasonable alternative;" 11 USCA § 707(b)((2)(B), and these expenses or adjustments cause the product of the debtor's current monthly income (reduced by the specified expenses) when multiplied by 60 to be less than the lessor of [25% of the debtor's nonpriority unsecured claims, or $6,000 (whichever is greater)] or [$10,000]. Plus, the proof requires detailed documentation and the debtor's affidavit that the expenses or adjustment to income is reasonable and necessary.

- Another, separate excuse from the means test—though not a special circumstance—is that "the debtor establishes by a preponderance of the evidence that the filing of a case under [Chapter 7] is necessary to satisfy a claim for a domestic support obligation." 11 USCA § 707(c)(3).

c. Section 707(c)(3)—Crime Victim

A separate, very specific basis for dismissal is: best interest of the victim of a crime of violence or drug trafficking, 11 USCA § 707(c)(2), on motion of the victim herself, except that the court cannot dismiss on this basis if the debtor proves that filing a Chapter 7 case is necessary to satisfy a claim for domestic violence. 11 USCA § 707(c)(3).

2. Chapter 11 Cases

In Chapter 11, like Chapter 7, the standard a bankruptcy court is to apply to a motion to dismiss is "for cause." Again, the statute sets out examples of cause. Section 1112(b). Again, the "cause" standard applies to both debtor and creditor motions.

3. Chapter 13 Cases

In Chapter 13, unlike Chapters 7 and 11, a debtor is given an absolute right to have his or her Chapter 13 case dismissed. Section 1307(b). Motions to dismiss filed by creditors in a Chapter 13 case are subject to the "for cause" standard. Section 1307(c) sets out examples of "cause."

4. Foreign Bankruptcy Cases

In Chapter 7, 11 and 13 cases, a debtor or creditors can also base a motion to dismiss on section 305. Section 305 empowers the bankruptcy court to dismiss or suspend a case if there is a foreign bankruptcy proceeding pending concerning the debtor or if "the interests of creditors and the debtor would be better served by such dismissal or suspension."

Example: D, Inc., is generally not paying its debts as they come due. D, Inc. is trying to negotiate a workout with its hundreds of creditors. Three of D, Inc.'s creditors are dissatisfied with the terms proposed in the workout and file an involuntary Chapter 11 petition against *D*, Inc. The bankruptcy court may decide to dismiss this petition if *D*, Inc. is making progress in negotiating a workout with its creditors.

A section 305 dismissal must be preceded by "notice and a hearing." The decision to dismiss (or not to dismiss) is not appealable. If an involuntary petition is dismissed under section 305, the petitioning creditors are not liable for costs, attorneys' fees or damages under section 303(i).

F. Review Questions

1. T or F   As a general rule, just about anybody can file a Chapter 7 case.

2. T or F   An "individual" can file a Chapter 13 case or a Chapter 11 case.

3. T or F   A corporation can file a Chapter 11 case or a Chapter 13 case.

4. T or F   A physician in solo practice can file a Chapter 13 case.

5. T or F   Insolvency is a requirement for filing any kind of bankruptcy case.

6. What is the global requirement that an individual must satisfy before she can file any kind of bankruptcy case?

7. When is a bankruptcy case commenced?

8. What are the usual, alternative bases for dismissing a Chapter 7 case?

9. When does the "means test" for dismissing a Chapter 7 case not apply?

10. Of the three principal kinds of bankruptcy cases (7, 11, and 13), in which kind of case is an involuntary petition not allowed?

VIII

Stay of Collection Actions and Acts

■ *ANALYSIS*

After the filing of a bankruptcy petition, a debtor needs immediate protection from the collection efforts of creditors. If the petition is a voluntary Chapter 7, the bankruptcy trustee needs time to collect the "property of the estate" and make pro rata distributions to creditors. If the petition is a voluntary Chapter 11 or Chapter 13, the debtor needs time to prepare a plan. And, if the petition is an involuntary Chapter 7 or Chapter 11, the debtor needs time to controvert the petition. Moreover, since creditors will receive payment through the bankruptcy process or the plan of rehabilitation and some claims will be discharged, continued creditor actions would interfere with orderly bankruptcy administration.

Accordingly, the filing of a voluntary petition under Chapter 7, Chapter 11 or Chapter 13, or the filing of an involuntary petition under Chapter 7 or Chapter 11, automatically "stays" (i.e., restrains or enjoins) creditors from taking further action against the debtor, the property of the debtor, or the property of the estate to collect their claims or enforce their liens. Section 362(a).

There are five questions about the stay that lawyers (and law students) most frequently ask:

1. When does the automatic stay become effective?

2. What is covered by the automatic stay?

3. When does the automatic stay end?

4. How can a creditor obtain relief from the stay?

5. What are the consequences of violating the stay?

A. Time Stay Arises

The automatic stay is triggered by the filing of a bankruptcy petition. It dates from the time of the filing, not from the time that a creditor receives notice of or learns of the bankruptcy. If D files a bankruptcy petition on April 5, the stay becomes effective April 5. The stay dates from April 5 even if creditors do not learn of the bankruptcy until much later. If C, not knowing of D's bankruptcy, obtains a default judgment against D on April 29, the default judgment violates the automatic stay and is invalid.

B. Scope of the Stay

1. Section 362

Paragraph (a) of section 362 defines the scope of the automatic stay by listing all of the acts and actions that are stayed by the commencement of a bankruptcy case. It is comprehensive and includes virtually all creditor collection activity.

a. Litigation

Subparagraphs (1) and (2) of section 362(a) cover most litigation efforts of creditors directed at collecting prebankruptcy debts. Section 362(a)(1) stays creditors from filing collection suits after the bankruptcy petition is filed or from continuing collection suits that were commenced prior to bankruptcy. Section 362(a)(2) bars creditors from enforcing judgments obtained prior to bankruptcy.

b. Informal Collection Efforts

Section 362(a)(6) stays "any act to collect . . . " and even bars informal collection actions such as telephone calls demanding payments and dunning letters.

c. Secured Creditors

Subparagraphs (3), (4), (5) and (7) of section 362(a) stay virtually all types of secured creditor action against the property of the estate or property of the debtor. Creditors are barred from obtaining liens, perfecting liens, or enforcing liens after the bankruptcy petition is filed.

d. Exceptions

While section 362(a) describes what is stayed, section 362(b) lists 18 kinds of actions that are not stayed. Most of the exceptions are very narrowly drawn; most of the exceptions apply in relatively few bankruptcy cases; but a few of them are more generally applicable and important, such as commencement or continuation of:

- a criminal action or proceeding against the debtor

- an action or proceeding for—(i) the establishment of paternity; or (ii) the establishment or modification of an order for alimony, maintenance, or support; or (B) of the collection of alimony, maintenance, or support from property that is not property of the estate; and

- an action or proceeding by a governmental unit to enforce such governmental unit's or organization's police and regulatory power, including the enforcement of a judgment other than a money judgment, obtained in an action or proceeding by the governmental unit to enforce such governmental unit's or organization's police or regulatory power.

e. Third Parties Not Protected

There is an important limitation on the scope of section 362 that is not dealt with in paragraph (b) of section 362. The automatic stay of section 362(a) only covers the debtor, property of the debtor, and property of the estate. It does not protect third parties.

Example: Assume that *D* borrows $3,000 from *C* and *G* guarantees repayment. If *D* files for bankruptcy, section 362(a) will stay *C* from attempting to collect from *D*. Section 362(a) will not, however, protect *G*.

2. Section 1301

While section 362(a) will not protect *G*, section 1301 might. When a Chapter 13 case is filed, section 362 applies and also section 1301. By reason of section 1301, the filing of a Chapter 13 petition automatically stays collection action against guarantors and other co-debtors if:

- The debt is a consumer debt, and

- The co-debtor is not in the credit business.

Section 1301's automatic stay of actions against co-debtors applies only in Chapter 13 cases.

3. Section 105

Section 105 grants to bankruptcy courts the power to issue orders "necessary or appropriate to carry out the provisions of this title." Courts have used this section 105 power to stay or restrain creditor action against third parties and stop other conduct not clearly covered by section 362(a) or perhaps even excepted from the stay by section 362(b).

a. Not Automatic

There is an important procedural difference between section 105 and sections 362 or 1301. An injunction or stay under section 105 will not be automatic. Rather, it will be granted according to the usual rules for injunctive relief.

b. Not Limited by Other Restrictions

There is also an important substantive difference between section 105 and sections 362 or 1301. In acting under section 105, the bankruptcy court is not expressly limited by the restrictions in section 362 or section 1301.

Example: If *D*, Inc. files for bankruptcy, a court cannot use section 362 to prevent creditors of *D*, Inc. from proceeding against *G*, who personally guaranteed *D*, Inc.'s debts. There are, however, numerous reported cases in which courts have invoked section 105 to protect *G* from *D*, Inc.'s creditors during the course of the bankruptcy. Courts that have so ruled have generally emphasized the importance of *G* to the success of *D*, Inc.'s bankruptcy—perhaps *G* is the chief executive officer who needs to devote all of her time and attention to *D*, Inc.'s bankruptcy, perhaps *G* is a possible source of the new funds that *D*, Inc. needs to reorganize.

C. Termination of the Stay

Section 362(c) describes three situations in which the automatic stay terminates automatically.

1. With Respect to Particular Property

Section 362(c)(1) provides that the automatic stay ends as to particular property when the property ceases to be property of the estate.

Example: Assume that *C* has a mortgage on *D* Corp.'s building. *D* Corp. files a bankruptcy petition. *C* is stayed from foreclosing its mortgage. The bankruptcy trustee sells *D* Corp.'s building to *X*. *C* is no longer stayed from foreclosing its lien.

Property also ceases to be property of the estate when it is abandoned to the debtor under section 554. Notwithstanding the language of section 362(c)(1), abandonment does not terminate the stay. The stay continues by reason of section 362(a)(5).

2. Otherwise and Generally

Section 362(c)(2) provides that the automatic stay ends when the bankruptcy case is closed or dismissed or the debtor receives a discharge. The typical Chapter 7 bankruptcy can be completed in a matter of months. In Chapter 11 cases and Chapter 13 cases, however, there can be a gap of several years between the filing of the petition and discharge. Accordingly, unless some action is taken, the stay can last several years.

3. Frequent Filings

The automatic stay is sometimes automatically terminated because the debtor had earlier filed another bankruptcy case. Section 362(c)(3) provides that if the debtor had been the debtor in an earlier bankruptcy case that was dismissed within one year of this bankruptcy case filing, then the automatic stay automatically terminates 30 days after the filing unless the debtor or some other party in interest can show that the second case was filed in good faith. If the debtor had two or more bankruptcy cases dismissed within the past year, the stay does not go into effect in the third or later case. Section 362(c)(4).

D. Relief From the Stay

A bankruptcy court may grant relief from the automatic stay on request of a "party in interest." Section 362(d). The relief will not always take the form of termination of the stay. Section 362(d) provides for "relief" "such as by terminating, annulling, modifying, or conditioning such stay." The Rules provide that the "request" in section 362 takes the form of a motion. Rules 4001(a), 9014. The facts of the reported cases make clear that the "party in interest" in section 362 is usually a secured creditor.

What must a creditor allege in its motion and establish in its proof in order to obtain relief from the stay? The grounds for relief from stay are set out in section 362(d).

1. Section 362(d)(1)

The most general statutory ground for relief from the stay is "for cause," section 362(d)(1).

a. "Cause" In General

There is very little reported case law on what constitutes "cause" for purposes of section 362(d)(1). Bankruptcy courts routinely find "cause" to lift the stay to allow tort suits against the debtor to go forward in state court to determine liability where the plaintiff agrees that any judgment will be collected only from the liability insurance carrier or some other third party.

b. "Lack of Adequate Protection" in Particular

Most of the reported section 362(d)(1) cases involve the specific example of cause set out in the statute—"lack of adequate protection of an interest in property of such party in interest."

1) Party in Interest

The party in interest is the person seeking relief from the stay. Again, typically, the party in interest under section 362(d)(1) will be a secured creditor.

2) What Is Protected

What must be protected is the secured creditor's interest in property, not the secured party's claim.

Example: If D owes C $1,000,000 and C has a security interest on equipment worth $600,000, section 362(d)(1) contemplates adequate protection of C's $600,000 lien position, rather than C's right to the payment of $1,000,000.

a) Loss in Value Through Depreciation

The questions of what interest in property is protected and how much protection is adequate protection are closely related. These questions (and the answers to the questions) are relatively easy in a situation where the collateral is losing value through use, obsolescence, or depreciation.

Example: Consider again the above example in which D owes C $1,000,000, and the debt is secured by equipment with a value of $600,000. Assume that the value of the equipment is declining by $5,000 a month. Section 362(d) contemplates that C will in some way be protected from a $5,000 a month loss due to decline in value of the collateral.

b) Not Lost Opportunity

A more difficult question is whether section 362(d) also contemplates that a partially secured creditor such as C would be protected from a loss due solely to delay in realization of the value of the collateral. The Supreme Court finally resolved this issue in United Savings Association of Texas v. Timbers of Inwood Forest Associates, Ltd. (1988).

In *Timbers*, a Chapter 11 debtor, an apartment complex limited partnership, owed more than $4.3 million to C, a creditor that had a deed of trust on the apartment complex. The collateral was worth at most $4.25 million and was not depreciating in value. C moved for relief from the stay contending that "adequate protection" under section 362(d) included payment to it of "lost opportunity costs." More specifically, C argued:

- Part of its "interest in property" is the right to seize and sell its collateral when the debtor defaults;

- If the debtor had not filed for bankruptcy, C could have sold the apartment complex for $4.25 million;

- C could have then lent this $4.25 million to another debtor and received interest on this new $4.25 million loan;

- Accordingly, in order to provide "adequate protection" of C's "interest in the property" as contemplated by section 362(d), the automatic stay should be conditioned on the debtor's making monthly payments to C equal to the amount that C would be receiving in interest payments on a new loan of $4.25 million. In sum, C's argument was that "adequate protection" means that a debtor is compelled to pay a secured creditor for its "lost opportunity costs."

Looking to both legislative history and statutory language such as section 506, the Supreme Court in *Timbers* rejected this argument.

3) How Is It Protected

Section 361 does not define "adequate protection"; rather, section 361 specifies three nonexclusive methods of providing adequate protection.

a) Payments

The first method of adequate protection specified is periodic cash payments to the lien creditor equal to the decrease in value of the creditors interest in the collateral. If C has a security interest in D's car and D files a bankruptcy petition, D can meet the adequate protection burden of section 362 by making cash payments equal to the depreciation on the car. Section 361(1).

b) Liens

Section 361(2) indicates that adequate protection may take the form of an additional lien or substitute lien on other property.

Example: Assume that *D* files a Chapter 11 petition. *C* has a perfected security in *D*'s equipment. *D* needs to use the encumbered equipment to continue operation of its business, to accomplish a successful Chapter 11 reorganization. Such use will, however, decrease the value of the equipment and *C*'s lien in the equipment.

Under section 361(2) adequate protection may take the form of a lien on other property owned by *D*; the new collateral does not necessarily have to be equipment.

c) "Indubitable Equivalent"

Section 361(3) grants the debtor in possession or trustee considerable flexibility in providing adequate protection. Section 361(3) recognizes such other protection, other than providing an administrative expense claim, that will result in the secured party's realizing the "indubitable equivalent" of the value of its interest in the collateral. The term "indubitable equivalent" is not statutorily defined. Even though sections 361 and 362(d) have remained unchanged since 1978, uncertainty remains as to (1) the importance of the "indubitable equivalent" language in section 361, and 361(2) the requirements of the "adequate protection" language in section 362(d). This uncertainty is attributable in part to the practice of negotiating rather than litigating section 362(d)(1) issues and in part to what is decided in section 362(d)(1) litigation. Section 362(d)(1) does not contemplate that the bankruptcy judge will decide what is adequate protection and mandate that it be provided. Rather, in section 362(d)(1) litigation, the bankruptcy judge merely decides whether what the bankruptcy trustee or debtor in protection has offered is adequate protection.

4) When Adequate Protection Is Inadequate

What if (i) there is section 362(d)(1) litigation, (ii) the bankruptcy judge decides that the debtor is providing adequate protection and (iii) the "adequate protection" proves to be inadequate?

Example: *X* has a perfected security interest in the inventory of *D*. *D* files a Chapter 11 petition. At the time of the petition, *D* owes *X* $100,000, and the encumbered inventory has a value of $60,000. *X* requests relief from the stay. The court concludes that *D*'s offer of a personal guarantee by *G* was "adequate protection," was an "indubitable equivalent." This conclusion turns out to be wrong. When *D*'s Chapter 11 reorganization fails, *G* is insolvent. The value of the inventory now securing *D*'s $100,000 claim is worth only $20,000. Obviously, *X* cannot sue the bankruptcy judge. What can *X* do?

Section 507(b) applies when "adequate protection" proves to be inadequate. It grants an administrative expense priority for the losses. In the above hypo, *X* would have a $40,000 administrative expense priority claim. The significance of an administrative expense priority is considered infra.

2. Section 362(d)(2)

Under section 362(d)(2) a lien creditor can obtain relief from the stay if

- The debtor does not have any equity in the encumbered property, AND

- The encumbered property is not necessary to an effective reorganization.

a. No Equity

The application of section 362(d)(2)(A) would not seem to present any difficult legal issues: generally equity is measured by the difference between the value of the property and the encumbrances against it. If, for example, property has a value of $100,000 and is subject to a $120,000 lien, "the debtor does not have any equity in such property."

b. Property Not Necessary to Effective Reorganization

A creditor cannot obtain relief from the stay under section 362(d)(2) merely by establishing no equity for purposes of section 362(d)(2)(A). Note the conjunction "and" connecting the no equity test of section 362(d)(2)(A) and section 362(d)(2)(B). A creditor relying on section 362(d)(2) then must satisfy both (A) and (B).

The language of paragraph (B) of section 362(d)(2) sets out two separate standards, provides two different opportunities for a creditor.

1) Not Necessary

The first possible creditor section 362(d)(2)(B) argument is that the encumbered property is not "necessary." Does the individual debtor need the car in order to get to her job so she can make the payments under her Chapter 13 plan? Does the business debtor need the equipment so that it can manufacture goods to make its Chapter 11 payments? The courts have been much more aggressive in deciding that an individual Chapter 13 debtor does not need a car or house than in deciding that a business debtor does not need equipment or a building.

2) Effective Reorganization

Even if the collateral is necessary for the Chapter 11 or 13 debtor's reorganization efforts, the phrase "effective reorganization" in section 362(d)(2)(B) enables a creditor who invokes section 362(d)(2)(B) to question whether the debtor can reorganize. Some financial problems can be solved only by an Act of God, not by a mere Congressional bankruptcy act. Does this debtor have a realistic possibility of an "effective reorganization"? Dicta in the Supreme Court decision in United Savings Association of Texas v. Timbers of Inwood Forest Associates, Ltd. (1988), suggests that this should be a meaningful test. "What this requires is not merely a showing that if there is conceivably to be an effective reorganization, the property will be needed for it, but that the property is essential for an effective reorganization *that is in prospect.*"

2. Section 362(d)(3)

Section 362(d)(3) is available only to a creditor with a lien on "single asset real estate," a phrase defined in section 101. The definition looks not only to the nature of the real estate but also to the nature of its use.

a. Meaning of Debt Limit "Single Asset Real Estate"

"[S]ingle asset real estate" means real property constituting a single property or project, other than residential real property with fewer than 4 residential units, which generates substantially all of the gross income of a debtor and on which no substantial business is being conducted by a debtor other than the business of operating the real property and activities incidental thereto. Section 101 (51B).

b. Basis for Relief

Under section 362(d)(3), a creditor with a lien on single asset real estate has a right to relief from stay unless the debtor, within 90 days after the order for relief, has either (A) filed a reorganization plan or (B) started monthly payments. If the debtor selects alternative A, the plan must be one that has "reasonable possibility of being confirmed within a reasonable time." If the debtor selects alternative B, the amount of the payment must equal interest at "the then applicable nondefault contract rate of interest" on the value of the creditor's interest in the real estate. Alternative B, in essence, partly reverses *Timbers* by giving an undersecured creditor has a right to interest—or at least a right to monthly equal in amount to interest. Section 362(d)(3)(B).

4. Relationship of Section 362(d) Subsections

Note that sections 362(d)(1), 362(d)(2), and section 362(d)(3) are connected by the conjunction "or." A creditor is entitled to relief from the stay if it is able to establish grounds for relief under either section 362(d)(1), section 362(d)(2), or section 362(d)(3). If, for example, a creditor is able to establish the lack of adequate protection, it is entitled to relief from the stay even though the property is necessary to an effective reorganization.

5. Burden of Proof in Section 362(d) Litigation

Section 362(g) allocates the burden of proof in stay litigation. The creditor or other party requesting the relief has the burden on the issue of whether the debtor has an equity in the property. The debtor or bankruptcy trustee has the burden on all other issues.

E. Consequences of Violating the Stay

1. Legal Effect of Conduct in Violation of the Stay: Void Ab Initio

The most significant effect of conduct violating the stay is that any legal result of the conduct is void. The dominant, general rule is that any act or occurrence that violates the stay is *void ab initio*. The rule means that to the extent that the stay is violated by anyone, including government, the act or occurrence itself lacks any legal effect against the debtor and other people whom the rule protects, as if the act or occurrence never happened. As against them, anyone who claims through the act or occurrence takes nothing because it is null and void ab initio and has no validity for any purpose.

The ineffectiveness of acts or occurrences violating the stay is not a temporary condition but is permanent. They are legally empty—not just suppressed or dormant—and thus remain void and ineffective even after the stay and the bankruptcy case end.

This rule is self-effective and carries no conditions, least of all knowledge of the stay or lack of innocence. It applies by its own force in every instance against anyone who violates the stay, including people acting completely in good faith and in complete ignorance of the bankruptcy.

2. Damages for Violating the Stay

Conduct that violates the stay is void against the stay's beneficiaries. This effect always occurs and is the primary consequences of violating the stay. A secondary consequence which sometimes occurs is damages prescribed by section 362(k).

a. Section 362(k)

"[A]n individual injured by any willful violation of a stay. . . shall recover actual damages, including costs and attorneys' fees, and, in appropriate circumstances, may recover punitive damages." Section 362(k)(1).

1) Who is the Plaintiff?

The meaning of "individual," who can recover damages under section 362(k), includes the debtor and, maybe, creditors who are harmed. The larger debate about the meaning of "individual" is whether the term is limited to natural persons or also includes corporations and other legal entities. The courts have disagreed.

2) Who is the Defendant?

With some exceptions, damages are recoverable from any entity responsible for the violation, including the person whose actions violated the stay and sometimes people (such as lawyers) who counseled or aided the actions.

3) What is the Wrong?

The wrong that triggers section 362(k) is a "willful violation" of the stay. No damages of any kind are recoverable under section 362(k) without it. A violation is most clearly willful when a creditor acts deliberately with knowledge of the stay or, more generally, the bankruptcy. A specific intent to violate the stay is not required, or even an awareness by the creditor that her conduct violates the stay. It is sufficient that the creditor knows of the bankruptcy and engages in deliberate conduct that, it so happens, is a violation of the stay.

4) What are the Damages?

The damages recoverable under 362(k) are actual damages, including costs and attorneys' fees, and punitive damages in appropriate circumstances. Actual damages must be based on losses actually suffered as a result of the violation of the stay. Punitive damages require more than a mere willful violation: an additional finding of maliciousness or bad faith.

b. Immunity from Liability for Damages

1) Creditors Without Proper Notice

Generally, lack of notice of the stay is not a defense to liability and damages under section 362(k). However, at least in a Chapter 7 or 13 case of a debtor who is an individual, the Bankruptcy Code prohibits any "monetary penalty" against a creditor for violation of the stay, or for failing to comply with provisions (section 542 or 543), based on conduct that occurs before the creditor receives section 342 notice of the case. 342(g)(2). There is no such notice unless the notice is sent to an address filed with the court or an address the creditor supplied to the debtor, within 90 days before filing, giving the debtor's account number and an address to which the creditors requests the debtor to send correspondence. Also, a notice sent to creditor is not effective, at least for purposes of section 342, unless the notice is brought to the creditor's attention. 11 USCA § 342(g)(1).

2) Sovereign Immunity

Government is traditionally shielded from liability by the decisional doctrine of sovereign immunity. The states are further protected by the Eleventh Amendment immunity from suit in federal court. Congress can waive the immunity of the federal government and, to some extent, does so in section 106. On its face and by its own terms, section 106 applies to any governmental unit, including the states. However, the effect of this provision on the states is affected by the limits of the Eleventh Amendment on the power of the Congress to abrogate or waive states' sovereign immunity. The Supreme Court has held that Article 1 of the Constitution does not always empower Congress to abrogate states' sovereign immunity under the Eleventh Amendment. See Seminole Tribe of Florida v. Florida (U.S. 1996). The extent to which *Seminole Tribe* applies to and limits the Congress' power to abrogate the states' immunity with respect to bankruptcy is not clear.

The Sixth Circuit decided that notwithstanding *Seminole Tribe*, the bankruptcy clause of the Constitution, Article I, section 8, gives

Congress the power to abrogate states' sovereign immunity. Hood v. Tennessee Student Assistance Corp. (6th Cir. 2003). The Supreme Court affirmed on other grounds. Tennessee Student Assistance Corp. v. Hood (USSC 2004).

So, the meaning of section 106 determines the extent to which the federal government can be held liable for damages for violating the stay and other provisions of the Code; and the meaning of section 106 and the meaning of the Eleventh Amendment determine the extent to which the states can be held liable. The issues are unsettled, complicated, and beyond the scope of this book. However, neither sovereign immunity nor the Eleventh Amendment blunts operation of the rule, even as against federal and state government, that actions or occurrences in violation of the stay are void. Also, the Eleventh Amendment does not prevent bankruptcy courts from exercising in rem jurisdiction to discharge debts owed to states because a discharge proceeding against a state is not a suit against the state for purposes of the Eleventh Amendment. Tennessee Student Assistance Corp. v. Hood (USSC 2004). The constitutional issue arises when a state is sued in personam for damages in bankruptcy, as under section 362(k).

F. Review Questions

1. D files a bankruptcy petition on January 15. C, a creditor of D, does not learn of the filing until January 22 and does not receive official notice of the filing until February 3. When is the stay effective against C?

2. C obtained a judgment against D and had the sheriff seize property of D. The sheriff's sale is scheduled for April 5. D files a bankruptcy petition of April 4. Does the automatic stay affect the scheduled sheriff's sale? What if C does not know of the filing and the sale is held?

3. D files a bankruptcy petition. After the bankruptcy, D is involved in an automobile accident with V. Does the bankruptcy filing prevent V from proceeding against D? Against D's insurance company?

4. D files a bankruptcy petition. Before the bankruptcy, D was involved in an automobile accident with V, and V had filed a tort suit against D. Does the bankruptcy filing prevent the suit from proceeding against D? Does the bankruptcy prevent V from going after D's insurance company?

5. D and C have a contract that D breached. The contract required settling disputes under the contract through binding arbitration. C initiated an

arbitration proceeding. D filed bankruptcy. Is the arbitration stayed.

6. D and C have a contract that D breached. D's obligations under the contract are guaranteed by D's Momma, who is a surety. D filed bankruptcy. C filed suit against Momma. Does this suit violate the stay?

7. D files a bankruptcy petition. D owes S $400,000. S has a security interest in equipment. The equipment is worth $300,000 and depreciating at a rate of $2,000 a month. Can S invoke section 362(d)(1) and recover its collateral?

8. T or F   An unsecured creditor cannot obtain relief from the automatic stay under section 362(d)(1).

9. What section of the Bankruptcy Code is sometimes used by the courts as a source of authority for enjoining conduct that is not automatically stayed under section 362?

10. T or F   Any debtor who is injured by a creditor's violation of the section 362 stay can recover damages under section 362(k).

IX

Property of the Estate

■ ANALYSIS

A. **Why Is Property of the Estate an Important Concept?**
   1. Chapter 7 Cases
   2. Reorganization Cases
B. **What Does Property of the Estate Include?**
   1. What Is Included in the Phrase "Interests of the Debtor in Property as of the Commencement of the Case"?
   2. What Else Is Included in Property of the Estate?
   3. What Is Excluded From Property of the Estate?
C. **Review Questions**

A. Why Is Property of the Estate an Important Concept?

"Property of the estate" is one of the most important, most basic bankruptcy concepts. The filing of any bankruptcy petition automatically creates an "estate" that includes the assets of the debtor as of the time of the bankruptcy filing. Section 541(a).

1. Chapter 7 Cases

In a Chapter 7 case, "property of the estate" is collected by the bankruptcy trustee and sold; the proceeds from the sale of the property of the estate are then distributed to creditors. Sections 704, 726. In other words, the loss of property of the estate is the primary cost of Chapter 7 bankruptcy to the debtor; the receipt of the proceeds from the sale of property of the estate is the primary benefit creditors derive from a Chapter 7 bankruptcy.

2. Reorganization Cases

In other kinds of bankruptcy cases, the importance of property of the estate is less obvious. Nonetheless, property of the estate is an important concept in cases filed under Chapter 11, 12 or 13.

a. Supervision of Property in Chapter 11 and 12 Cases

In most Chapter 11 and 12 cases, the debtor will remain in possession of "property of the estate" as "debtor-in-possession." However, the Chapter 11 or Chapter 12 debtor-in-possession's use of the property of the estate will be subject to bankruptcy court supervision.

Consider the example of Chapter 11 cases involving business debtors. Successful rehabilitation of a business generally requires continued operation of the business. Continued operation of the business generally requires continued possession and use of the business' property. A debtor will continue to operate its business in Chapter 11 as debtor-in-possession unless a request is made by a "party in interest" for the appointment of a trustee, and the bankruptcy court, after notice and hearing, grants the request. When a trustee is appointed in a Chapter 11 case, she takes possession of property of the estate. Even if a trustee is not appointed in a Chapter 11 case, the debtor-in-possession's use and sale of the property of the estate is subject to the supervision of the bankruptcy judge as provided in section 363.

Similarly, in Chapter 12 cases, the debtor will generally retain possession of the property and continue to operate the farm. As in Chapter 11, a "party in interest" can request that the debtor-in-possession be dispossessed and a trustee take over. And, again as in Chapter 11, if a trustee is not so installed, the Chapter 12 debtor in possession's use and sale of the property of the estate is subject to the supervision of the bankruptcy court as provided in sections 363 and 1206.

b. Supervision of Property in Chapter 13 Cases

While Chapter 13 contemplates that there will be a trustee in every case, a Chapter 13 trustee does not take possession of property of the estate. A debtor who files for Chapter 13 relief retains possession of his property. Again, however, the use and sale of "property of the estate" is subject to the supervision of the bankruptcy court as provided in section 363.

c. Basis for Determining Dividends in Chapters 11, 12, and 13

In both Chapter 12 and Chapter 13 cases, the value of the property of the estate determines the minimum amount that must be offered to holders of unsecured claims in the debtor's plan of repayment, sections 1225(a)(4), 1325(a)(4). Chapter 11 imposes a similar requirement as to non-assenting holders of unsecured claims, section 1129(a)(7)(A)(ii).

d. Other Importance of the Concept

A number of general provisions in Chapters 3 and 5 that are applicable in all bankruptcy cases use the phrase "property of the estate." For example, the automatic stay bars a creditor from collecting a claim from property of the estate, section 362(a)(3), (4).

B. What Does Property of the Estate Include?

Section 541 is the primary section to turn to in deciding "what does property of the estate include." With only minor exceptions, property of the estate includes all property of the debtor as of the time of the filing of the bankruptcy petition.

1. What Is Included in the Phrase "Interests of the Debtor in Property as of the Commencement of the Case"?

The seven numbered subparagraphs of section 541(a) specify what property becomes property of the estate. Paragraph one is by far the most comprehensive and significant.

a. Section 541(a)(1)

Section 541(a)(1) provides that property of the estate includes "all legal or equitable *interests of the debtor* in property *as of the commencement of the case*" (emphasis added).

NOTE: Third parties in possession of property in which the debtor has an interest are statutorily obligated to return such property to the trustee or debtor in possession, sections 542 and 543. When we consider these sections, we will consider the obligation of a secured creditor who has seized but not yet sold property that served as its collateral to return that property to the debtor.)

b. What "All. . . Interests" Includes

"All . . . interests of the debtor in property" is a very broad statement. Property of the estate thus includes both real property (such as a company's manufacturing facility or an individual's house) and personal property (such as a store's inventory or an individual's car), both tangible (the manufacturing facility, the car, etc.) and intangible property (such as an account receivable or a license), both property in the debtor's possession and property in which the debtor has an interest that is held by others.

1) Limited Interests

Note the phrase "interests of the debtor in property" in section 541(a)(1). If the debtor has a limited interest in some asset, it is that limited interest that is property of the estate. Consider the following two examples:

Example: Hugh Rodham and Roger Clinton own an island as tenants in common. If Rodham files a bankruptcy petition, only Rodham's limited interest in the island would be property of the estate. (While only Rodham's interest in the island is property of the estate, the entire island can be sold under section 363(h).)

Example: Neil Bush owns a new Chevrolet Silverado. He borrowed the money to buy the truck from a Colorado financial institution which retained a security interest in the truck. Under Article 9 of the Uniform Commercial Code, that security interest or lien is a property interest in the Silverado truck. Outside of bankruptcy then, both Bush and the Colorado bank have property interests in the Silverado. Accordingly, if Bush files a bankruptcy petition, under section 541 of the Bankruptcy Code, only Bush's property interest in the Silverado is property of the estate. (In the specific situations described in section 363(f), Bush's Silverado can be sold free and clear of the Colorado bank lien.)

2) Generally, Not Pre–Petition Interests

Second, consider the phrase "as of the commencement of the case" in section 541(a)(1). "Commencement of the case" is synonymous with the filing of a bankruptcy petition. Sections 301, 303. Thus, generally, assets that the debtor acquired prior to the petition become property of the estate; property acquired after the petition generally is not property of the estate.

Example: If Darva Conger files for bankruptcy on April 5, the money she earns from the personal appearances that she makes after April 5 is not property of the estate, section 541(a)(1), (6) ("earnings from services performed by an individual after the commencement of a case" excepted from property of the estate).

2. What Else Is Included in Property of the Estate?

While property of the estate is determined primarily by section 541(a)(1), i.e., "the interests of the debtor in property as of the commencement of the case," property of the estate also includes:

a. "Any interest in property that the trustee recovers," section 541(a)(3)

The bankruptcy trustee (and the debtor in possession in a Chapter 11 case) is empowered by the Bankruptcy Code to recover certain payments and other transfers of the debtor's interest in property. The trustee's use of these avoidance powers increases the property of the estate.

Example: Shawn Fanning pays $1,000,000 to one of his creditors, Recording Industry Association of America (RIAA) on January 10th, and Fanning then files for bankruptcy on January 15th. If the bankruptcy trustee is able use her avoidance powers under sections 547 and 550 to avoid that January 10th payment, then RIAA would have to return the $1,000,000, and that $1,000,000 would become property of the estate.

b. "Proceeds, product, offspring, rents or profits of or from property of the estate," Section 541(a)(6)

Assume that Homer and Marge Simpson file a bankruptcy petition and the next day their house is destroyed by an explosion of the Springfield nuclear power plant. Any insurance proceeds would be property of the estate.

Similarly, if Trump Realty Co. files for bankruptcy, both the buildings it owns as of the bankruptcy petition and the postpetition rents from the buildings would be property of the estate. And, if Trump Hotel and Casino Resorts, Inc., files for bankruptcy, property of the estate would include the corporation's postpetition earnings

Reconsider the last sentence. The postpetition earnings of a corporation or any other "person" other than an "individual" are property of the estate under section 541(a)(6). The postpetition earnings of an individual from the services that she performs after the bankruptcy are excluded from property of the estate—unless the debtor has filed a petition for relief under Chapter 11 or 13.

c. **"Earnings from services" and Other Property That the Debtor Acquires After the Filing of a Chapter 11 or Chapter 13 Petition, Sections 1115 and 1306**

If an individual debtor files a petition for relief under Chapter 11 or Chapter 13, property of the estate will be determined not only by section 541 but also by section 1115 or 1306. Under these provisions, postpetition earnings are property of the estate.

d. **Certain Other After–Acquired Property**

Despite the general rule that property acquired after filing bankruptcy is not property of the estate, the estate does include property that the debtor acquires or becomes entitled to within 180 days after the filing of the petition by (a) bequest, devise, or inheritance; (b) property settlement or a divorce decree; or (c) as beneficiary of a life insurance policy. Section 541(a)(5).

3. **What Is Excluded From Property of the Estate?**

There are some very specific exclusions from property of the estate in section 541(b) and (c). The most significant exclusions are these:

a. **Inalienable Trusts**

Section 541(c)(2) excludes from property of the estate the beneficial interest of the debtor in a trust that by federal or state law is inalienable, that is, cannot be reached by the debtor's creditors. This exclusion covers and keeps out of the estate traditional spend thrift trusts and an "ERISA-qualified pension plan." Patterson v. Shumate (U.S. 1992).

b. **Education Accounts**

Education IRAs and IRS-qualified state tuition credit accounts can generally be excluded from the bankruptcy estate if the designated beneficiary is the debtor's child, stepchild, grandchild or step-grandchild. However, deposits made within 365 days of the bankruptcy filing are not protected and those made between 366 and 720 days of filing are protected only up to $5,000 for any one beneficiary. Section 541(b)(5) & (6).

c. Exempt Property

Section 541 does not exclude from the estate property that an individual debtor can exempt from creditors' claims under state or other law. However, section 522 recognizes exemptions for individual debtors, and debtor that a debtor exempts under 522 is then excluded from the estate.

C. Review Questions

1. T or F   Property of the estate is an important concept only in Chapter 7 cases.

2. D Corp., files a bankruptcy petition. Does property of the estate include the assets of its principal shareholder, P?

3. D, an artist, files for Chapter 7 relief. Does property of the estate include everything stored in D's rent-a-garage storage unit?

4. D, an artist, files for Chapter 7 relief. Does property of the estate include the Picasso original she jointly owns with her Momma?

5. D, an artist, files for Chapter 7 relief. D is the beneficiary of a spendthrift trust established, for D's benefit, by her parents. Is the corpus of the trust part of the bankruptcy estate?

6. D, an artist, files for Chapter 7 relief. Are the earnings from work done after the Chapter 7 filing property of the estate?

7. D, an artist, files for Chapter 7 relief. Does the bankruptcy estate include the insurance proceeds she receives a month later as a beneficiary of a life insurance policy?

8. D, an artist, files for Chapter 13 relief. Are the earnings from work done after the Chapter 13 filing property of the estate?

9. D owns Blackacre. M has a mortgage on Blackacre. D files a Chapter 12 petition. Is Blackacre property of the estate?

10. Is property that a debtor can exempt from the claims of creditors in bankruptcy part of the bankruptcy estate?

X

Exemptions

■ ANALYSIS

A. **What Property Is Exempt?**
   1. Debtor's Choice
   2. Choice of Law
   3. Waivers of Exemptions
   4. Timely Objecting to Exemptions
   5. Pre–Petition Conversions of Property—Bankruptcy Estate "Planning"
B. **What Is the Significance in Bankruptcy of Exempt Property?**
   1. General
   2. Section 522(f)
   3. Section 722
C. **Review Questions**

Under the Bankruptcy Code, all of the interests in property that a debtor has when she files her bankruptcy petition is property of the estate. An individual debtor, however, is permitted to exempt certain property from property of the estate. In most respect, the law governing exempt property in bankruptcy is derived from nonbankruptcy law, usually state law.

A law student or lawyer need to be able to answer two general questions about exempt property in bankruptcy. First, what property is exempt? Second, what is the bankruptcy significance of property being exempt?

A. What Property Is Exempt?

1. Debtor's Choice

The Bankruptcy Code provides that "an individual debtor may exempt from property of the estate the property listed in either [section 522(b)(2)] or, in the alternative, [section 522(b)(3)]. . . ." Section 522(b)(1).

a. Section 522(b)(3)—Property Exempt Under State Law and Federal Law

Section 522(b)(3), which is available to every individual debtor, lists three four sets of property the debtor can exempt:

1) State-law exemptions

An individual debtor may assert the exemptions to which she is entitled under state law. Section 522(b)(3)(A). These exemptions are described in Chapter III, supra, and include certain personal property and also the real property where the debtor lives, i.e., her homestead. However, the homestead exemption, though based on state law, is limited in two ways by section 522:

- A state homestead exemption will be reduced by the amount that the homestead is attributable to the debtor's disposition of nonexempt property in the ten years prior to bankruptcy with the intent to hinder, delay, or defraud creditors, section 522(o); and

- Value added to the homestead within 1215 days before the bankruptcy is capped at $125,000. Section 522(p).

2) Tenancy-by-the-Entirety Property

The debtor can also exempt "any interest in property in which the debtor had, immediately before the commencement of the case, an interest as a tenant by the entirety or joint tenant to the extent that such interest . . . is exempt from process under applicable nonbankruptcy law. . . ." 522(b)(3)(B).

3) Non-Bankruptcy Federal Exemptions

The debtor can also exempt any property that is exempt under federal laws other than title 11, i.e., nonbankruptcy federal law. Section 522(b)(3)(A). Some of the items that may be exempted under federal laws other than title 11 include:

- Social security payments, 42 USCA § 407

- Civil service retirement benefits, 5 USCA §§ 729, 2265

- Veterans benefits, 45 USCA § 352(E).

4) Retirement Funds

Additionally, the debtor can exempt retirement funds in an IRS-qualified Individual Retirement Account (IRA) or a Simplified Employee Pension (SEP) (which is for a self-employed person with a few employees in a small business), section 522(b)(3)(C), though some such accounts may be subject to a $1,000,000 limit. Section 522(n).

b. Section 522(b)(2)—Property Exempt under Section 522(d)

Alternatively, instead of exempting the sets of property described in section 522(b)(3), individual debtors in a few states may claim the exemptions Congress described and set out in section 522(d). Section 522(d) is only available to individual debtors that reside in states that have not enacted "opt out" legislation pursuant to section 522(b)(1). Under section 522(b)(1), a state legislature can enact legislation precluding resident debtors from electing to utilize section 522(d). Most states have enacted such "opt out" legislation.

Even in states that have not "opted out" there are statutory limitations on the debtor's choice of exemption statutes:

- A debtor cannot select some exemptions from state law and some exemptions from section 522(d). He or she must choose either the nonbankruptcy exemptions or section 522(d).

- And, husbands and wives in joint cases filed under section 302 or in individual cases which are being jointly administered under Bankruptcy Rule 1015(b) must both elect either the nonbankruptcy exemptions or the section 522(d) exemptions. While under section 522(m) each spouse will be entitled to separate exemptions, it will not be possible for one to choose section 522(d) exemptions while the other chooses nonbankruptcy exemptions.

2. Choice of Law

The law that determines if the debtor can chose the 522(d) exemptions, and the law that determines the state exemptions available to the debtor, is the law of the state where the debtor was domiciled for two years (literally, "730 days") preceding bankruptcy. If the debtor was not domiciled in the same state for this two-year period, then the governing exemption law is the exemption law of the state where the debtor lived in the 180 days before the two-year period, i.e., where the debtor lived between two and two and one-half years before bankruptcy.

3. Waivers of Exemptions

The Bankruptcy Code expressly deals with the effect of a debtor's contracting away his or her exemptions. Such a contract has no effect. Whether an individual debtor elects to claim under nonbankruptcy exemption law or under section 522(d), waivers of exemption are not enforceable, section 522(e).

4. Timely Objecting to Exemptions

Together, the Bankruptcy Code and Rules deal with the situation in which the debtor claims too much property as exempt and no one makes a timely objection. Under section 522(l) and Rule 4003, an individual debtor files a list of the property she claims as exempt. In Taylor v. Freeland & Kronz (USSC 1992), the debtor's list of exempt property included the proceeds from a pending employment discrimination action. This asset was not exempt under relevant exemption laws. Nonetheless, the Supreme Court held that it was exempt in bankruptcy because of the absence of a timely objection.

Under relevant bankruptcy laws, there is a deadline for filing objections to the debtor's claimed exemptions, section 522(l) and Rule 4003. In the *Taylor* case, no objection was filed until long after that deadline. Looking to the "plain meaning" of section 522(l) and Rule 4003, the Supreme Court concluded that the debtor was entitled to keep the proceeds from the settlement of the employment discrimination action because there was no timely objection to his claim that it was exempt.

5. Pre–Petition Conversions of Property—Bankruptcy Estate "Planning"

The Bankruptcy Code does not expressly deal with the consequences of a debtor converting nonexempt property into exempt property on the eve of bankruptcy. What if, just before filing for bankruptcy, D takes funds from her bank account, nonexempt property under relevant law, and invests the money in a homestead? A number of different reported cases have answered this question—in a number of different ways. One common judicial approach is the "pig to hog analysis" in which the court compares the amount of property converted, the total amount of debt, and the total amount of other property still available to pay that debt and concludes that "when a pig becomes a hog, it is slaughtered."

Section 522(o) may implicitly deal with the issue with respect to homesteads. This provision reduces a state homestead exemption by the amount that the homestead is attributable to the debtor's disposition of nonexempt property in the ten years prior to bankruptcy with the intent to hinder, delay, or defraud creditors. Section 522(o), however, may not displace other, judge-made limits on converting non-exempt property to an exempt homestead and has no application to other kinds of exempt property.

Such "bankruptcy estate planning" raises other bankruptcy issues. There are reported cases that have withheld a discharge from a Chapter 7 debtor under section 727(a)(2) because of an eve-of-bankruptcy conversion of nonexempt property into exempt property, or worse, incurrence of a debt to purchase exempt property.

B. What Is the Significance in Bankruptcy of Exempt Property?

1. General

Generally, an individual debtor is able to retain his or her exempt property. Exempt property is not distributed to creditors in the bankruptcy case and is protected from the claims of *most* prepetition creditors after the bankruptcy case. (If the debtor chooses the set of exemptions set out in section 522(d), postpetition creditors will be able to reach items not exempted under relevant state law.)

Note the italicized qualifier "most." Section 522(c) identifies the prepetition claims that are, in essence, exempt from the exemptions. After bankruptcy, there are basically four groups of prepetition creditors who have recourse to property set aside as exempt in a bankruptcy case:

1. Creditors with tax claims excepted from discharge by section 523(a)(1);

2. Spouses, former spouses and children of the debtor with domestic claims excepted from discharge by section 523(a)(5);

3. Creditors whose claims arise from the debtor's fraud in obtaining funding for higher education;

4. Creditors with liens on exempt property that are neither avoided nor extinguished through redemption.

2. Section 522(f)

Some liens on exempt property that are valid and enforceable against exempt property outside of bankruptcy can be invalidated because of bankruptcy

The general invalidation provisions, discussed infra in Chapter XII, are applicable to liens on exempt property. And section 522(f) empowers the debtor to avoid judicial liens that impair exemptions and to avoid security interests that are both nonpurchase money and nonpossessory on certain household goods, tools of the trade, and health aids.

The most important thing for you to understand about section 522(f) is that it is not very important in the "real world." Again, it only affects (a) judicial liens and (b) certain kinds of consensual liens on certain kinds of exempt property.

a. Judicial Liens

Because of increases in the costs of obtaining a judicial lien and the increases in bankruptcy filing, creditors' use of judicial liens has decreased significantly. If a creditor does obtain a judicial lien on exempt property, the debtor can invoke section 522(f)(1)(A) to avoid that judicial lien "to the extent that such lien impairs an exemption."

Section 522(f)(2) explains the quoted phrase "to the extent that . . . . " The following examples "explain" section 522(f)(2).

Example: Assume *D*'s house is worth $100,000 and *F* has a $40,000 first mortgage on the house and *J* has a $50,000 judicial lien on the house and the relevant exemption lien permits *D* a $15,000 homestead. Add (a) the amount of the exemption—$15,000, plus (b) the amount of the judicial lien—$50,000, and (c) the amount of all other liens on the homestead—$40,000. The total in this hypothetical is $105,000. Subtract from that the value of the house—$100,000. Under these facts, the amount of impairment is $5,000 and so the debtor could use 522(f) to avoid $5,000 of *J*'s judicial lien—to reduce that lien from $50,000 to $45,000.

Example: Now increase the amount of *F*'s first mortgage by $50,000 to $90,000. This increases the amount of the impairment to $55,000 and so the debtor could use 522(f) to avoid all of *J*'s $50,000 judicial lien.

We used the example of a "judicial lien" to illustrate the application of section 522(f)(1)(A) because that is when you will use section 522(f)—if you ever use section 522(f).

b. Consensual Liens

Section 522(f)(1)(B) applies to certain kinds of consensual liens on certain kinds of exempt property. In particular, recall our limiting phrase "certain kinds of."

1) When 522(f)(1)(B) Applies to Such Liens

It only applies to a "nonpossessory, nonpurchase-money security interest in any—

1. household furnishings, household goods, wearing apparel, appliances, books, animals, crops, musical instruments, or jewelry that are held primarily for the personal, family, or household use of the debtor or a dependent of the debtor;

2. implements, professional books, or tools, of the trade of the debtor or the trade of a dependent of the debtor; or

3. professionally prescribed health aids for the debtor or a dependent of the debtor.

2) When 522(f)(1)(B) Does Not Apply

a) Does Not Apply to Purchase Money Liens

Section 522(f)(1)(B) does not apply to purchase money liens. It does not affect Circuit City's lien on the home entertainment center that it sold the debtor on credit; it does not apply to First Bank's lien on the dental equipment it financed.

b) Does Not Apply to Possessory Liens

Section 522(f)(1)(B) also is limited to consensual liens that are nonpossessory. "Nonpossessory" simply means that the creditor with a lien is not in possession of the property subject to his lien. Except for pawn shops, creditors with nonpurchase money liens on exempt personal property are rarely in possession of that property.

c) Does Not Apply to Usually Important Stuff

More limiting, section 522(f)(1)(B) does not apply to any consensual lien on houses and cars—the two most valuable exempt assets of most individuals. Section 522(f)(1)(B) only applies to nonpurchase money security interests in the kinds of exempt property described in section 522(f)(1)(B)(i), (ii) or (iii).

d) Further Limit—Section 522(f)(3)

The use of section 522(f)(1)(B) to avoid consensual liens on exemptions is further limited by section 522(f)(3). Even if the consensual lien is nonpurchase money and even if the exempt assets subject to the lien come within one of the categories described in section 522(f)(1)(B), the debtor may be precluded from avoiding the lien by section 522(f)(3). It is not clear when section 522(f)(3) applies or how section 522(f)(3) applies. In general, you will look at section 522(f)(3) only if the debtor has job-related or farm-related exempt property that is worth more than $5,000 and that exempt property is subject to nonpurchase money consensual liens.

3. Section 722

Possessory security interests in exempt personal property, purchase money security interests in exempt personal property, and any security interests on exempt personal property not covered by section 522(f) may be extinguished through "redemption." Section 722 authorizes an individual debtor to redeem or extinguish a lien on exempt personal property by paying the lienor the value of the property encumbered ("the amount of the allowed secured claim") in full at the time of redemption. Courts generally look to the liquidation value in determining the amount of the secured claim for purposes of section 722.

Example: Assume that D owes C $3,000. C has a security interest in D's Subaru. If D files a bankruptcy petition and the value of the Subaru is only $1,200, D can eliminate C's lien by paying C $1,200 in cash.

Section 722 applies to all liens on "tangible personal property intended for personal, family or household use" that secures a "dischargeable consumer debt." So, in theory, there is considerable overlap between section 522(f) and section 722. Is there any real overlap? If you understand what happens under section 522(f) and what happens under section 722, you understand that there is no practical overlap. A debtor will not invoke 722 to redeem property from liens by paying cash if she can invoke 522(f) to avoid such liens without paying.

C. Review Questions

1. T or F   Any debtor can exempt property from the bankruptcy estate.

2. Section 522(d) lists property that a debtor can exempt in bankruptcy, but this list almost never applies. Explain.

3. For most debtors in bankruptcy, what are the sources of law for exemptions?

4. D filed bankruptcy in Florida after having moved there 18 months earlier. Until then, she had lived all of her life in North Carolina. Which state's law is the source of law for her exemptions?

5. D filed bankruptcy in North Carolina where she and her husband have lived for 30 years. Their principal residence is in Charlotte, North Carolina; but she and her husband also jointly own a vacation home on Sunset Breach, North Carolina. The Charlotte house is the homestead and, for this reason, is exempt to some extent under North Carolina law and in bankruptcy. The vacation house is not exempt under North Carolina law but is owned by D and her husband as tenants by the entirety, which is a kind of property ownership recognized in North Carolina and some other states. Is the vacation home exempt in bankruptcy?

6. About a year before filing bankruptcy, when times were good, D paid off the mortgage on her home, added on a couple of rooms, and doubled the value from $250,000 to $500,000. The goods times did not last. Local law allows a debtor to exempt her homestead to the extent of her interest in the place not exceeding $500,000. In the bankruptcy case, can D exempt her $500,000 interest?

7. C loaned D money under a contract that included this clause: "In consideration herewith and therefore, D agrees to and hereby does waive any and all claims to exemptions of any kind under any law against efforts by C to collect this loan whether in bankruptcy or outside of bankruptcy." D files bankruptcy. Is the exemption waiver effective?

8. C loaned D money under a contract that created a consensual lien (i.e., an Article 9 security interest) on C's rights in a widget. A perfected the lien. A year later, D files bankruptcy without having repaid the loan. C makes a motion to lift the automatic stay to enforce C's lien. The collateral is exempt under applicable exemption laws. On these facts, can D resist C's motion and exempt the widget from C's lien?

9. Reconsider Question 8. Can D avoid the lien under section 522(f) and then exempt the widget from the bankruptcy estate?

10. D files Chapter 7 bankruptcy. She wants to keep her car, which is primarily for personal use and is exempt under local law. However, the car is subject to a purchase-money security interest, which is not affected by the exemption and cannot be avoided under section 522(f) or otherwise. It is likely that the secured party will make a motion to lift stay and that the court will grant the motion. Can the debtor "redeem" under section 722 and, if so, how?

XI

Avoidance of Prebankruptcy Transfers

■ *ANALYSIS*

In the absence of bankruptcy, some transfers of a debtor's property can be invalidated under state laws, such as state fraudulent conveyance laws. The Bankruptcy Code incorporates these state laws in section 544(b) so that a transfer of a debtor's property that can be invalidated under state law in the absence of bankruptcy can be invalidated under section 544(b) in the event of bankruptcy.

Chapter 5 of the Bankruptcy Code also contains several other "avoidance" provisions. Accordingly, some payments, sales, exchanges, judicial liens, security interests and other transfers that are valid under state law can be avoided in bankruptcy.

A. Basic Issues

1. Transfer Means Voluntary and Involuntary

The Bankruptcy Code's avoidance provisions reach both "voluntary" transfers such as a debtor's making a gift to a relative or granting a mortgage to a creditor and "involuntary" transfers such as a creditor's garnishing the debtor's bank account or subjecting the debtor's real property to a judgment lien. Note also that the Bankruptcy Code's avoidance provisions reach both "absolute" transfers such as gifts, payments and sales, and "security transfers" such as mortgages and judgment liens.

2. When Avoidance Is an Issue

In working with these avoidance provisions, law students and lawyers are called on to answer two basic questions: (1) what are the consequences of avoiding a transfer and (2) which transfers can be avoided. Law students are called on to answer these questions both in class and on exams. Lawyers are called upon to answer these questions not only in negotiating and litigating in bankruptcy cases but also in structuring transactions outside of bankruptcy.

Example: Assume that your client C buys a business from D for $2,000,000 and pays your firm $100,000 for your legal work on the transaction. If D later files for bankruptcy, you do not want to be in the awkward position of having to call C and tell her that D's bankruptcy trustee has been able to invoke the Bankruptcy's Code avoidance power to recover all of the assets that C purchased from D.

Understanding the Bankruptcy Code avoidance power provisions and the materials on these provisions set out below can be difficult. But not as hard as calling C.

3. Procedure

To understand the avoidance provisions, remember that avoidance does not occur by operation of law. Avoidance in bankruptcy of a prebankruptcy transfer requires litigation and raises all of the usual litigation questions:

1. Who can initiate avoidance litigation?

   The answer is the "Chapter 7 trustee, the Chapter 11 trustee, and the Chapter 12 and 13 trustee and. . . . " The avoidance provisions in Chapter 5 of the Bankruptcy Code generally use the phrase "the trustee may avoid." Accordingly, the trustee in a Chapter 7, 11, 12 or 13 case can initiate avoidance litigation.

   Recall that in Chapter 11 cases without a trustee, the debtor has the rights of a trustee. Thus the Chapter 11 debtor-in-possession, and in some instances a Chapter 11 creditors' committee, can initiate avoidance litigation. The cases are divided as to whether a Chapter 13 debtor can bring an avoidance action.

2. Where do I bring the action?

This question is answered in Chapter XX of this book dealing with allocation of judicial power over bankruptcy and bankruptcy-related litigation.

3. What are the time limitations on initiating an avoidance action?

Section 546 deals with the question of when an avoidance action must be brought: within two years after the order for relief except that if a trustee is appointed more than one year after the order for relief but within two years after the order for relief, then the trustee shall have one year.

4. Who can I sue and what can I recover?

Section 550 and the next part of this book cover the questions of who can be sued and what recovery can be had.

B. What Are the Consequences of Avoiding a Transfer?

1. Recovering Transferred Interest for the Estate

Think Robin Hood. Think of the Chapter 7 trustee (or the debtor in possession in a Chapter 11 case) as a guy in green tights who takes from the "rich" (i.e., the transferee) to give to the "poor" (i.e., all the holders of unsecured claims).

When the bankruptcy trustee avoids an absolute transfer of property, that property then becomes property of the estate.

Example: Assume that *D* owes *C* $25,000 on an unsecured debt. *D* repays *C* $12,000 of that debt. *D* later files for bankruptcy. At the time of *D*'s bankruptcy filing, the $12,000 paid to *C* is not property of the estate. If the bankruptcy trustee is able to invoke one of the Bankruptcy Code's avoidance provisions to avoid the $12,000 payment, the $12,000 will then become property of the estate, sections 541(a)(3), 550.

a. Affects Amount of Claim

The avoidance of an absolute transfer can also affect the amount of a creditor's claim. In the above hypothetical, *C* had a $13,000 claim at the time of *D*'s bankruptcy filing. Again, if the bankruptcy trustee is able to recover the $12,000 D paid C from C by avoiding the payment, then C will have a $25,000 claim against D, section 502(h). C will then have the same legal rights it had before the transfer. (If the trustee is able to establish that the $13,000 payment is avoidable under some section of the Bankruptcy Code but has not been able to recover the $13,000, then section 502(d) provides that the court shall "disallow" C's claim for the remaining $12,000 of debt. Disallowance of claims is covered in Chapter XV.)

b. Affect on Transfer of Interest for Security

The consequences of avoiding a security transfer are similar.

> Example: Assume, for example, that D borrows $77,000 from C and grants C a mortgage on Blackacre which is worth $120,000. D later files for bankruptcy. Absent the trustee's use of one of the avoidance powers, C has a $77,000 secured claim. Recall that under section 541, Blackacre itself is not property of the estate; rather the estate's interest in Blackacre is only D's limited equity and other rights in Blackacre. If, however, the bankruptcy trustee is able to avoid the grant of the mortgage on Blackacre, then C will have a $77,000 unsecured claim, and Blackacre without any encumbrance will be property of the estate.

2. Recovering Value

a. From Initial Transferee

In the two examples, the consequences of avoidance were the recovery of the property interest transferred from the party to whom it had been transferred. Under section 550, the consequences of avoidance are not limited to recovery of the property transferred, are not limited to the person to whom the transfer was made.

Under section 550(a), the court can order the recovery of the "value of the property" transferred, rather than the property.

> Example: Assume, for example, that the property transferred from D to T was worth $100,000 at the time of the transfer but is only worth $40,000 at the time of the avoidance litigation. The court can award the recovery of $100,000, instead of the recovery of the property.

b. From Later Transferees

And, under section 550(a), the recovery can be sought not only from the initial transferee but either (1) later transferees or (2) a person who benefited from the transfer.

Example: Assume, for example, that *D* is indebted to both *F* and *S* and that *F* has a $100,000 first mortgage and *S* has a $200,000 second mortgage on Greenacre which is worth $150,000. If *D* makes a payment of $80,000 to *F*, that transfer to *F* has the effect of providing a $50,000 benefit to *S*. Prior to transfer, there was only $50,000 of collateral available to satisfy *S*'s claim. After the transfer, there is $100,000 of collateral available to satisfy *S*'s claim.

C. Preferences

Common law does not condemn a preference. Under common law, a debtor or even an insolvent debtor may treat certain creditors more favorably than other similar creditors. Although *D* owes *X*, *Y* and *Z* $1,000 each, *D* may pay *X*'s claim in full before paying any part of *Y*'s claim or *Z*'s claim.

Some state statutes void certain transfers because of their preferential character. The trustee may take advantage of such statutes by virtue of his powers under section 544(b): if the state anti-preference provision protects any actual creditor of the debtor, it protects the bankruptcy trustee. Section 544(b) is considered infra.

Also, and much more importantly, bankruptcy law—section 547—condemns certain preferences. A House report that accompanied a draft of the Code explained the rationale for such a bankruptcy policy as follows:

"The purpose of the preference section is twofold. First, by permitting the trustee to avoid prebankruptcy transfers that occur within a short period before bankruptcy, creditors are discouraged from racing to the courthouse to dismember the debtor during his slide into bankruptcy. The protection thus afforded the debtor often enables him to work his way out of a difficult financial situation through cooperation with all of his creditors. Second, and more important, the preference provisions facilitate the prime bankruptcy policy of equality of distribution among creditors of the debtor. Any creditor that received a greater payment than others of his class is required to disgorge so that all may share equally." House Report 95–595 at 117–18.

1. Elements of a Preference

Section 547(b) sets out the elements of an avoidable preference; the bankruptcy trustee may void any transfer *of property of the debtor* if he or she can establish:

(1) The transfer was "to or for the benefit of a creditor"; and

(2) The transfer was made for or on account of an "antecedent debt," i.e., a debt owed prior to the time of the transfer; and

(3) The debtor was insolvent at the time of the transfer; and

(4) The transfer was made within 90 days before the date of the filing of the bankruptcy petition, or, was made between 90 days and 1 year before the date of the filing of the petition to an "insider" (which is defined in section 101 and includes relatives of an individual debtor and directors of a corporate debtor); and

(5) The transfer has the effect of increasing the amount that the transferee would receive in a Chapter 7 case.

a. "Transfer of an Interest of the Debtor in Property"

Don't miss the first element of a preference which comes before any of the numbered elements: "transfer of an interest of the debtor in property."

1) Transfers by Other People Not Preferences

Payments and other transfers by people other than the person who is later the debtor in the bankruptcy case are never section 547 preferences.

> Example: Assume for example, D owes $100 to A, B and C. M, D's momma, pays A but not B and C. D later files for bankruptcy. In a real sense, M's payment of A but not B or C treated A more favorably than B or C—preferred A over B or C. In a bankruptcy sense, M's payment is not a preference because it was not a "transfer of an interest of the debtor in property", not a diminution of property of D's estate. A of course benefited from being paid by M, but not to the detriment of D's other creditors.

2) Earmarking Doctrine

Now assume M gave the $100 to D who then used that $100 to pay A. Is D's payment to A a "transfer of interest an interest of the debtor in property"? In answering that question, most courts would look to the "earmarking doctrine." Under this court-created concept, if an insolvent debtor pays one of her creditors with funds from a third party that were clearly earmarked to pay a specific antecedent debt, there is no section 547 preference. Again, *A* benefited, but not to the detriment of other creditors. Generally, the pivotal questions in cases in which the earmarking doctrine is an issue is whether the debtor had any control over how the funds from the third party could be used.

b. "Transfer ... Made Within 90 Days Before ..."

1) And Perfection

In applying the fourth requirement of section 547(b), time of transfer, it may be necessary to look to section 547(e) and section 101. If under state law, a transfer is not fully effective against third parties until recordation or other public notice of the transfer has been timely given and the transfer was not timely recorded, then section 547(e) [considered later in this chapter] deems the transfer to have occurred at the time of recordation.

Example: Assume that on January 15, *D* borrows $100,000 from *S* and grants *S* a security interest on a piece of equipment. Under relevant nonbankruptcy state law, *S*'s security interest is not effective against other creditors who might claim a lien on that same equipment unless a financing statement was filed. *S* delays filing its financing statement until April 5. *D* then files for bankruptcy on July 1. By reason of section 547(e), the transfer from *D* to *S* creating *S*'s security interest is regarded as occurring on April 5, not January 15. And since the debt was incurred on January 15 and the transfer is not deemed to have occurred until April 5, the security interest was a transfer for an antecedent debt within 90 days of the July 1 bankruptcy.

2) And Insiders

Section 101's definition of "insider" becomes a part of the fourth requirement of section 547(b) in determining whether the transfer was made to an "insider" so that the relevant period is one year, rather than 90 days. Remember that the presumption of insolvency is limited to the 90 days immediately preceding the bankruptcy petition. Accordingly, in order to invalidate a transfer that occurred more than 90 days before the filing of the bankruptcy petition the trustee must establish that (i) the transferee was an "insider"; and (ii) the debtor was insolvent at the time of the transfer.

c. Preferential Effect

The fifth element essentially tests whether the transfer enabled the creditor/transferee to get *more* than she would have received if (a) the transfer had not taken place and (b) the case was a Chapter 7 case. This fifth element is satisfied unless:

1. The transferee has a claim secured by property worth more than the amount of its claim; or

2. The transferee has a secured claim and all that is transferred to her is part or all of the collateral that secured the claim; or

3. The estate is sufficiently large to pay all unsecured claims in full.

If any of these exceptions applies, a prebankruptcy transfer does not result in the creditor's receiving more than what she would receive in a Chapter 7 case if the transfer had not been made; she is simply receiving earlier all or part of what she would have ultimately received in the Chapter 7 case.

Section 547 is concerned with a creditor's receiving more, not a creditor's receiving earlier. And, except for the exceptions noted above, a transfer that satisfies sections 547(b)(1)-(4) will result in the creditor's receiving more, i.e., will also satisfy section 547(b)(5).

Example: Assume that D makes a $1,000 payment to C, a creditor with a $10,000 unsecured claim, on January 10. On February 20, D files a bankruptcy petition. The property of the estate is sufficient to pay each unsecured creditor 50% of its claim. An unsecured creditor with a $10,000 claim will thus receive $5,000. S, however, will receive a total of $5,500 from D and D's bankruptcy unless the January 10th transfer is avoided. ($1,000 + (50% × (10,000 − 1,000)) Accordingly, the bankruptcy trustee may avoid the January 10th transfer under section 547(b) to "facilitate the prime bankruptcy policy of equality of distribution among creditors."

2. Applying Section 547(b)

The following hypothetical problems illustrate the application of section 547(b).

Example: On February 2, *D* borrows $7,000 from *C* and promises to repay the $7,000 on March 2. *D* repays *C* on March 2 as promised. On May 24, *D* files a bankruptcy petition. The bankruptcy trustee can recover the $7,000 payment from *C*. See section 547(b); see also section 550.

Example: On February 2, *D* borrows $7,000 from *C*. *D* repays *C* on March 2. On June 6, *D* files a bankruptcy petition. The bankruptcy trustee *cannot* recover the $7,000 from *C* under section 547(b). Section 547(b)(4) is not satisfied—more than 90 days.

Example: On February 2, *D* borrows $7,000 from *C*. On March 2, *X*, a friend of *D's*, pays *C* the $7,000 *D* owed. On May 24, *D* files a bankruptcy petition. The bankruptcy trustee *cannot* recover the $7,000 from *C* under section 547(b). The payment was not a "transfer of an interest of the debtor in property."

Example: On January 10, *D* borrows $10,000 from *C* and grants *C* a security interest in its equipment. At all relevant times, the equipment has a value of $20,000. On March 3, *D* repays *C* $3,000 of the $10,000. On April 4, *D* files a bankruptcy petition. The bankruptcy trustee *cannot* avoid the March 3 payment under section 547(b). Section 547(b)(5) is not satisfied. Note that *C* had a security interest. Note also that the value of the collateral securing *C's* claim was greater than the amount of the claim. (See section 506. Under this provision, the amount of a secured claim is limited by the value of the collateral.) In a Chapter 7 case, the holder of a secured claim will receive either its collateral or its value up to the amount of the debt. Accordingly, even if the payment had not been made, *S* as a fully secured creditor would have been paid in full. A prebankruptcy payment to a fully secured creditor is not a preference.

Example: On February 2, *D* borrows $200,000 from *S* and *S* records a mortgage on Redacre, real property of *D's*. At all relevant times, Redacre has a value of $140,000. On April 5, *D* repays $40,000 of the loan. On May 6, *D* files a bankruptcy petition. The property of the estate is sufficient to pay each unsecured creditor 10% of its claim. The trustee may avoid the April 5 payment and recover the $40,000 for the estate. All of the elements of section 547(b) including section 547(b)(5) are satisfied. If the transfer had not been made, S would have received $146,000. If the transfer is not avoided, *S* will receive $182,000. [$140,000 secured claim + $40,000 payment + $2,000 on remaining $20,000 unsecured claim.]

Example: On March 3, *D* borrows $300,000 from *S*. On April 4, *S* demands security for the loan and *D* gives *S* a mortgage on Redacre. Redacre has a fair market value of $400,000. On May 5, *D* files a bankruptcy petition. The property of the estate is sufficient to pay each unsecured creditor 20% of its claim. The trustee may avoid the April 4 mortgage so that Redacre is property of the estate free and clear of *S*'s lien. Again all of the elements of section 547(b) are satisfied. The transfer would enable *S* to receive $300,000. If the transfer had not been made, *S* would receive only $60,000. [Section 547(b) invalidates liens to secure past debts.]

Example: On April 4, *D* borrows $40,000 from *S* and gives *S* a security interest in equipment. The equipment has a fair market value of $50,000. On June 6, *D* files a bankruptcy petition. The trustee may not avoid the April 4 security interest. The April 4 transfer was for present consideration, not "for or on account of an antecedent debt." Element #2 is not satisfied. [Section 547 does not invalidate liens to secure new debts.]

3. Indirect Preferences

All of the above preference illustrations involve two parties: the debtor transferor and the creditor transferee. The following language in section 547(b) contemplates three party transactions in which *D* makes a transfer to *C* that is preferential as to *X*: "to OR FOR THE BENEFIT OF a creditor," section 547(b)(1).

Example: Assume that *C* makes a loan to *D*, and *X* guarantees payment of the loan. It is obvious from reading the hypothetical that *C* is a creditor of *D*. And, it should be obvious from reading the definitions of "creditor" and "claim" in section 101 that *X* is also a creditor of *D* for purposes of section 547. What if *D* pays *C* on January 15 and then files for bankruptcy on January 17? *D*'s payment to *C* is a transfer "TO a creditor." The payment is also "FOR THE BENEFIT OF a creditor." As explained above, *X* is a creditor. *X* benefits from *D*'s payment to *C*: *D*'s payment to *C* frees *X* from her obligations under the guarantee. Accordingly, the payment to one creditor, *C*, can be an indirect preference to another creditor, *X*, if the other elements of section 547(b) are satisfied.

a. Important When Transferee Insolvent

Finding such an indirect preference can be important to D's bankruptcy trustee where the transferee, C, is also insolvent. Recovering from X is possible because section 550 allows the trustee to recover a preference from either the actual transferee or "the entity for whose benefit the transfer was made."

b. Important When Actual Transfer Not Avoidable

Finding such an indirect preference can also be important where the transfer is not avoidable as to the actual transferee.

Example: Assume that D pays C on January 15 and then files for bankruptcy on July 13. C is not an "insider," but X is. The payment to C is not a preference as to C. Since C is not an insider, the relevant section 547(b) time period is 90 days. The payment of C is a preference as to X. Since X (like most guarantors) is an insider, the relevant time period is one year. Obviously, the trustee could recover from X. Until the 1994 amendments, every circuit court that considered these facts held that the trustee could also recover from C.

1) *Levit* Case

Levit v. Ingersoll Rand Financial Corp. (7th Cir. 1989) (more commonly referred as the *Deprizio* case) was the first circuit court case to hold that a payment to a noninsider creditor where there was an insider guarantor could be recovered from that noninsider creditor even though it occurred more than 90 days before the bankruptcy filing. In so holding, the court relied primarily on the language of section 547 and 550.

The *Levit* decision and the several other circuit court decisions following it look at section 547 and 550 as independent, unrelated provisions. The methodology of these decisions can be outlined as follows. First, look at section 547(b) and determine if there has been a preference as to anyone. Second, if there is a preference as to anyone under section 547(b), look at section 550 and determine the possible responsible parties. The party responsible under section 550 does not have to be the same party as to whom the transfer was preferential. In application, even though the payment to C was only preferential as to X, the trustee can still recover from C since section 550 permits recovery from the actual transferee.

2) Amendment to Section 550 Overrules *Deprizio*

A 1994 amendment to section 550 changes the result in *Levit* (a/k/a *Deprizio*). The Congress added section 550(c) that precludes recovery from a creditor that is not an insider for preferences made more than 90 days before the bankruptcy filing.

While this amendment changes the *Levit* result, it does not change the *Levit* reasoning. The significance of the *Levit* approach to sections 547 and 550 is not limited to guaranteed loans.

Example: Assume that both F and S are creditors of D with a lien on Blackacre. F is owed $100,000 and has a first lien. S is owed $200,000 and has a second lien. The value of Blackacre is $150,000. Consider the consequences of D's paying F $30,000. If you remember what you have read, you will remember that a payment to a fully secured creditor is not preferential, section 547(b)(5). Accordingly, the payment to F cannot be a section 547 preference as to F. And, if you understand what you have read, you will understand that this payment to F is preferential as to S. By paying F $30,000 and reducing F's secured claim on Blackacre to $70,000, D has indirectly benefited S by increasing S's secured claim on Blackacre to $80,000. Accordingly, the payment to F can be a section 547 preference as to S. And, under *Levit* and its progeny, the trustee arguably can use section 550 to recover from either S or F.

3) Newer Amendment Finishes the Job

Section 550(c) only precludes recovering damages from the noninsider under section 550. It does not stop the trustee from avoiding the transfer to the noninsider under section 547(b). So, if the transfer was the creation of a lien in favor of the noninsider, the lien could still be avoided, leaving the noninsider without collateral. In 2005, Congress "fixed" this "problem" by adding this language to section 547: "If the trustee avoids [under 547(b)] a transfer made between 90 days and 1 year before the date of the filing of the petition, by the debtor to any entity that is not an insider for the benefit of a creditor that is an insider, such transfer shall be considered to be avoided under this section only with respect to the creditor that is an insider." 11 U.S.C.A. § 547(i).

4. Exceptions (Section 547(c))

Section 547(b) sets out the elements of a voidable preference. Section 547(c) excepts certain prepetition transfers from the operation of section 547(b). If a transfer comes within one of section 547(c)'s exceptions, the bankruptcy trustee will not be able to invalidate the transfer even though the trustee can establish all of the requirements of section 547(b).

a. Contemporaneous New Value

The first exception is for a transfer that

1. Was intended to be for new value, not an antecedent debt, and

2. Did in fact occur at a time "substantially contemporaneous" with the time that the debt arose, section 547(c)(1).

> Example:　D borrows $5,000 from C on April 5. Both parties then intend the loan to be a secured loan, secured by a pledge of D's X Corp. stock. On April 9, D pledges her X Corp. stock by delivering the certificates to C. On May 6, D files a bankruptcy petition. The bankruptcy trustee will not be able to void the April 9 pledge under section 547. The transfer for an antecedent debt is protected by section 547(c)(1).

Note that section 547(c)(1) requires both that the transfer actually be a "substantially contemporaneous exchange" and that the parties so intended. Assume that C makes a loan to D that both C and D intend to be a 180–day loan. Later that same day C first learns that D is in financial difficulty and so demands and obtains repayment. Section 547(c)(1) could not apply to the repayment. While the transfer actually was a "substantially contemporaneous exchange," it was not so intended. If bankruptcy occurs within 90 days, the trustee can avoid the payment under section 547(b).

b. Ordinary Course Payments

While section 547(c)(1) can apply to either an absolute or a security transfer, section 547(c)(2) protects only absolute transfers—payments. Section 547(c)(2) looks to both the nature of the debt in section 547(c)(2)(A) and the nature of the payment in section 547(c)(2)(B) and 547(c)(2)(C), in order to come under the protection of section 547(c)(2).

1. The *debt* must be in the ordinary course of business (business debtor) or financial affairs (nonbusiness debtor) of both the debtor and the creditor; and

2. The *payment* must be in the ordinary course of business or financial affairs of both the debtor and the creditor (subjective test); OR

3. The *payment* must be made according to ordinary business terms (objective test).

Example: *D* receives her water bill for January water use on February 2. *D* and most water customers regularly pay their water bills by check before the end of the month. *D* pays her water bill by check on February 14. Section 547(c)(2) applies.

Remember that section 547(c)(2) looks at both the nature of the debt and the nature of the payment. Section 547(c)(2)(A) focuses on the nature of the debt and must also be satisfied. Section 547(c)(2)(B) and 547(c)(2)(C) both focus on the nature of the payment but they are alternative tests and satisfying either of them, along with the other requirements of (c)(2), is sufficient. And, they are very different test: (c)(2)(B) makes the subjective inquiry of what was ordinary for this debtor and this creditor; (c)(2)(C) makes the objective inquiry of what is ordinary in the industry. So, when a debtor's late, prepetition payment to an unsecured creditor can be shielded by (c)(2) if the creditor can show that such a late payment was the norm as between this debtor and this creditor but not the norm in the industry.

c. Enabling Loans

The third exception protects "enabling loans." Section 547(c)(3) requires that:

1. The creditor gives the debtor "new value" to acquire certain real or personal property;

2. The debtor signs a security agreement giving the creditor a security interest in the property;

3. The debtor in fact uses the "new value" supplied by the creditor to acquire the property; and

4. The creditor perfects its security interest no later than 30 days after the debtor receives possession.

Example: On April 4, *F* borrows $34,000 from *S* to buy a new tractor and signs a security agreement that describes the tractor. *S* files a financing statement. On April 20, *F* uses *S*'s $34,000 to buy a new tractor. On May 5, *F* files a bankruptcy petition. *F*'s bankruptcy trustee may *not* avoid *S*'s security interest. All of the elements of section 547(b) are satisfied because: the creation of a lien is a transfer of property of the debtor. It was, of course, "to or for the benefit of a creditor." And, it was "for or on account of an antecedent debt." "For purposes of this section, a transfer is not made until the debtor has acquired rights in the property transferred," section 547(e)(3). However, all of the elements of section 547(c)(3) are also satisfied.

d. Subsequent Credit

Section 547(c)(4) provides a measure of protection for a creditor who receives a preference and "after such transfer" extends further unsecured credit.

Example: On June 6, *C* lends *D* $6,000. On July 7, *D* repays $4,000. On August 8, *C* lends *D* an additional $3,000. On September 9, *D* files a bankruptcy petition. The bankruptcy trustee can recover only $1,000. The July 7 payment of $4,000 was a preference under section 547(b). The trustee's recovery, however, is reduced by the amount of the August 8 unsecured advance of $3,000, section 547(c)(4).

Note that under section 547(c)(4), the sequence of events is of critical significance. The additional extension of credit must occur after the preferential transfer. If on June 6, *C* lends *D* $6,000; on July 7, *C* lends *D* an additional $3,000; on August 8, *D* repays $4,000, and on September 9, *D* files a bankruptcy petition, the trustee could recover $4,000 under section 547.

e. Floating Liens

Section 547(c)(5) creates a limited exception from preference attack for certain Article 9 floating liens. Article 9 provides a mechanism for establishing a "floating lien." Such liens are most commonly used in financing accounts or inventory which normally "turn-over" in the ordinary course of the debtor's business.

Example: On January 10 Credit Co., *C*, lends Department Store, *D*, $800,000 and takes a security interest in the store's inventory. Obviously, *C* wants *D* to sell its inventory so that it can repay the loan. It is equally obvious that as inventory is sold, the collateral securing *C* loan decreases unless *C*'s lien "floats" to cover the proceeds from the sale of the inventory and/or cover new inventory that *D* later acquires. Accordingly, the security agreement that *D* signs on January 10 will probably contain an after-acquired property clause—will probably grant *C* a security interest not only in the inventory that *D* now owns but also in the inventory that *D* later acquires.

1) How After–Acquired Interest Is a Preference

Even though *D* only signs this one security agreement, section 547 views *D* as making numerous different transfers of security interests. Under section 547(e)(3), "[f]or purposes of this section, a transfer is not made until the debtor has acquired rights in the property transferred." This means that every time *D* acquires additional inventory there is a new transfer for purposes of section 547. Thus, if *D* acquires new inventory on March 3 and files for bankruptcy within the next 90 days, it would *seem* that the trustee can invalidate *C*'s security interest in the March 3 inventory because there was

1. A transfer of property of the debtor to a creditor;

2. For an antecedent debt;

   [The debt was incurred on January 10. As noted above, section 547(e)(3) dates the transfer of the security interest in the March 3 inventory as March 3.]

3. Presumption of insolvency;

   [Remember section 547(f)]

4. Transfer made within 90 days of the bankruptcy petition; and

5. Transfer increased bankruptcy distribution to *C* (unless *C* was already fully secured.)

2) How 547(c)(5) Protects the After–Acquired Interest

Section 547(c)(5), however, will usually protect C. Under this provision, a creditor with a security interest in inventory or accounts receivable is subject to a preference attack only to the extent that it improves its position during the 90–day period before bankruptcy. The test is a two-point test and requires a comparison of the secured creditor's position 90 days before the petition and on the date of the petition. [If new value was first given after 90 days before the case, the date on which it was first given substitutes for the 90–day point.]

a) Two–Step Test

There are seven steps involved in applying section 547(c)(5)'s "two-step" test:

1. Determine the amount of debt on the date of the bankruptcy petition;

2. Determine the value of the debtor's accounts and/or inventory encumbered by the secured creditor's lien on the date of the petition;

3. Subtract #2 from #1;

4. Determine the amount of debt 90 days before the petition;

5. Determine the value of the debtor's accounts and/or inventory encumbered by the secured creditor's lien 90 days before the petition;

6. Subtract #5 from #4;

7. Subtract the answer in #3 from the answer in #6. This is the amount of the preference.

b) Applications of 547(c)(5)

The following examples illustrate the application of section 547(c)(5):

Example: At the time of its bankruptcy petition, D owes C $100,000 and has inventory with a value of $60,000. C has a security interest in all of D's inventory.

Ninety days before bankruptcy, *D* owed *C* $90,000 and had inventory with a value of $70,000. All of *D*'s inventory was acquired within the last 90 days. Under these facts, *C* has not improved its position. Under these facts, *C*'s security interest will be protected by section 547(c)(5).

Example: At the time of its bankruptcy petition, D owes C $100,000 and has inventory with a value of $75,000. C has a security interest in all of D's inventory. Ninety days before bankruptcy, D owed C $90,000 and had inventory with a value of $30,000. All of D's inventory was acquired within the last 90 days. Under these facts, the bankruptcy trustee may reduce C's secured claim from $75,000 to $40,000. There was a $35,000 reduction in the amount by which the claim exceeded the collateral: (90-30)-(100-75). The $75,000 secured claim is thus reduced by this $35,000 improvement in position.

Compare the facts of the above two examples. Which fact situation is more common? How often in the "real world" will a debtor in financial difficulty acquire additional inventory or generate an increased amount of accounts? In the usual situation, section 547(c)(5) completely protects a security interest in after-acquired inventory or accounts, that is, in the usual situation, the "except" language of section 547(c)(5) is inapplicable.

Example: *D* files a bankruptcy petition on April 22. At the time of the bankruptcy petition, *D* owes *S* $200,000. *S* has a security interest in *D*'s inventory of Oriental rugs which then have a value of $200,000. On January 22, 90 days before the bankruptcy petition was filed, *D* owed *S* $200,000, and the rugs had a fair market value of $150,000. *D* did not acquire any additional rugs after January 22; the value of *D*'s rugs increased because of market considerations. The trustee has no section 547 rights against *S*. There is no transfer to invalidate. *S*'s improvement in position was not "to the prejudice of other creditors holding an unsecured claim."

Example: *D* Manufacturing Co., *D*, files a bankruptcy petition on April 4. At the time of the filing of the
bankruptcy, *D* owes *C* Credit Corp., *C*, $40,000. *C*
has a valid in bankruptcy security interest in all of
D's equipment. The *D*-*C* security agreement has an
after-acquired property clause. On the date of the
filing of the petition, *D*'s equipment has a fair
market value of $31,000. On January 4, 90 days
before the filing of the bankruptcy petition, *D*
owed *C* $40,000 and *D*'s equipment had a fair
market value of $32,000. On February 2, *D* sold a
piece of equipment for $6,000. (*D* used the $6,000
to pay taxes.) On March 3, *D* bought other equipment for $5,000. The trustee can limit *C*'s security
interest to the equipment owned on January 4. The
March 3 "transfer" is a preference under section
547(b). (Remember, that March 3 is the date that
the transfer is deemed made for purposes of
section 547, section 547(e)(3).) The March 3 "transfer" of a security interest in equipment is not
protected by section 547(c)(5) because it only applies to security interests in inventory or accounts.

f. Statutory Liens

Section 547(c)(6) exempts "statutory liens" from the scope of section 547.
Statutory liens are covered by section 545; section 545 is covered infra.

"Statutory lien" is defined in section 101(45) as a lien "arising *solely* by
force of statute." Section 101(45) expressly provides that neither a
security interest nor a judicial lien is a "statutory lien." While there are
statutes providing for security interests and judicial liens, neither a
security interest nor a judicial lien arises "*solely* by force of statute." A
security interest will always require an agreement; a judicial lien will
always require court action.

The following hypothetical illustrates the operation of section 547(c)(6):

Example: *C* Construction Co. is building a warehouse for *D*. Under
relevant state statutes, a builder can obtain a mechanics lien.
C takes the steps required by the state law and obtains a
mechanics lien on the warehouse to secure payment for the

work that it has done. If *D* files for bankruptcy, the bankruptcy trustee will not be able to attack the mechanics lien under section 547.

g. Payment of Domestic Obligations

Section 547(c)(7) protects bona fide payment of a "domestic support obligation" from avoidance as a preference.

Example: *D* makes a $2,500 payment to cover five missed child support payments. Two weeks later *D* files a bankruptcy petition. Even though the $2,500 payment was for an antecedent debt, it cannot be recovered as a preference.

h. Payment of Consumer Debts

Section 547(c)(8) is also relevant only in cases in which the debtor is an individual. It applies only if

1. The debtor is an individual;

2. His or her debts are "primarily" consumer debts; and

3. The aggregate value of all property covered by the transfer is less than $600.

   Example: *D* owes *C* $1,200 and pays her $400 four days before filing for bankruptcy, the bankruptcy trustee will not be able to recover the $400 from *C* under section 547.

i. Payment of Debts by Non–Consumer

Similarly, section 547(c)(9) creates another de minimus exception which applies in a case filed by a debtor whose debts are NOT primarily consumer debts. In such a case, (c)(9) applies "if . . . the aggregate value of all property that constitutes or is affected by such transfer is less than $5,000." There are two important differences between section 547(c)(8) and (c)(9):

- First, the debtor: the latter applies to debtors who are not consumer debtors, and the former applies to consumer debtors.

- Second, the amount: the latter is less than $5,000, and the former is less than $600.

D. Setoffs

1. General Rules

a. Under State Law

At times, a person is both a debtor to and creditor of another person. Assume, for example, that *B* buys goods from *S* each month on credit. *B* owes *S* $100,000 on the December shipment, and *S* owes *B* $20,000 because of problems with the November shipment. *B* is both a debtor and a creditor of *S*, and *S* is both a debtor and a creditor of *B*.

The most common setoff situation involves a bank and its customer. Assume, for example, that *W* has a checking account at Bank *B*, *B*, with a $1,000 balance. *W* borrows $2,200 from *B*. *B* is in the position of a creditor of *W*'s on the loan; *B*, however, is in the position of a debtor of *W*'s on the checking account. *B* is thus both *W*'s creditor and *W*'s debtor.

In attempting to collect the $2,200 loan from *W*, *B* may assert its right of setoff. Professor Zubrow defines "setoff" as follows: "Set-off is the cancellation of cross demands between two parties. The term is commonly used to cover both judicially supervised set-offs and automatic extinction of cross demands." Zubrow, *Integration of Deposit Account Financing Into Article 9 of the Uniform Commercial Code: A Proposal for Legislative Reform*, 68 Minn.L.Rev. 899, 901 n.3 (1984).

To illustrate, if Bank *B* asserts its right of setoff against *W*, it will reduce *W*'s checking account balance from $1,000 to 0 and reduce the amount owed by *W* on the $2,200 loan to $1,200.

b. Right of Setoff Generally Preserved in Bankruptcy

What if W files a bankruptcy petition one day after the setoff? Can the bankruptcy trustee recover the $1,000 from B? If one day before the filing of a bankruptcy petition, W withdraws $1,000 from his savings account and uses that $1,000 to reduce his indebtedness to B, the trustee can recover the $1,000 under section 547. Is there any reason to treat B's setoff differently?

Yes. Two reasons:

1. First, section 506 expressly makes a right of setoff a secured claim. A secured claimant's taking its collateral is not a section 547 preference: it does not "enable such creditor to receive more.' Similarly, a secured claimant's exercising its right of set-off does receive more.

2. Second, section 553 expressly provides that section 547 does not apply to setoffs. Section 553 is the only provision of the Bankruptcy Code that limits prepetition setoffs.

So, except for the exceptions of 553, setoffs allowed under state law are generally protected and generally allowed in bankruptcy.

2. Exceptions

Section 553 contains a number of limitations on the right of setoff in bankruptcy:

a. "Mutual Debt"

The debts must be between the same parties in the same right or capacity. For example, a claim against a "bankrupt" as an administratrix cannot be set off against a debt owed to the "bankrupt" as an individual.

b. "Arose Before the Commencement of the Case"

Both the debt owed to the "bankrupt" and the claim against the "bankrupt" must have preceded the filing of the bankruptcy petition. A creditor cannot setoff its prepetition claim against a debtor against its postpetition obligation to the debtor.

c. "Disallowed," Section 553(a)(1)

Certain claims against a "bankrupt" are disallowed. See section 502 considered in Chapter XV. A claim that is disallowed under section 502 may not be used as the basis for a setoff.

Example: A owes B $4,000. B files a bankruptcy petition. The debt from A to B is property of the estate. The trustee attempts to collect the $4,000 from A. A only pays the trustee $3,000. A alleges that it had set off a $1,000 claim it had against B prior to the bankruptcy filing. If that $1,000 claim would be barred by the statute of limitations in a state collection action, it would be disallowed under section 502(b)(1) and the setoff would be disallowed under 553(a)(1).

d. "Acquired" Claims, Section 553(a)(2)

Certain acquired claims cannot be setoff. Assume for example, that B is insolvent; A owes B $4,000; B owes C $1,000. Because B is insolvent, C's $1,000 claim is of little value to C. C would be willing to sell its claim against B to A for less than $1,000. A would be willing to buy C's claim for less than $1,000 if it could then assert that claim as a setoff to reduce its debt to B from $4,000 to $3,000.

Under section 553(a)(2) claims against the "bankrupt" acquired from a third party may not be set off against a debt owed to the 'bankrupt' if:

1. The claim was acquired within 90 days before the bankruptcy petition or after the bankruptcy petition, *and*

2. The "bankrupt" was insolvent when the claim was acquired. [Section 553(c) creates a rebuttable presumption of insolvency.]

e. Build-ups, Section 553(a)(3)

Section 553(a)(3) precludes a setoff by a bank if:

1. Money was deposited by the "bankrupt" within 90 days of the bankruptcy petition; and

2. The "bankrupt" was insolvent at the time of the setoff (remember section 553(c)'s presumption of insolvency); and

3. The purpose of the deposit was to create or increase the right of setoff.

Example: *X* Bank makes a loan to *D* Corp. Payment of the loan is guaranteed by *P*, the president of *D* Corp. *D* Corp. suffers financial reverses. *X* Bank pressures *D* Corp. and *P* to increase the balance of the corporation's general bank account. *D* Corp. moves $100,000 from other banks to its *X* Bank account before filing its bankruptcy petition. Section 553(a)(3) would preclude *X* Bank from taking the $100,000 by way of setoff.

f. Improvement in Position, Section 553(b).

Section 553(b) is similar to section 547(c)(5), considered supra. Both are designed to prevent an improvement in position within 90 days of bankruptcy. Application of section 553(b) requires the following simple computations:

1. Determine amount of claim against the debtor 90 days before the date of the filing of the petition;

NOTE: If there is no "insufficiency" (as defined in section 553(b)(2)) 90 days before the petition, examine the 89th day, then the 88th day, etc. until a day is found that has an 'insufficiency.' Computations 1–3 will then focus on that day.

2. Determine the "mutual debt" owing to the "bankrupt" by the holder of such claim 90 days before the filing of the petition;

3. Subtract #2 from #1 to determine the "insufficiency."

4. Determine the amount of the debt on the date that the right of setoff was asserted;

5. Determine the amount of the setoff;

6. Subtract #5 from #4 to determine the insufficiency;

7. Subtract the answer in #6 from the answer in #3, to determine what part, if any, of the amount of setoff the trustee may recover.

1) Applications

The following problems illustrate the application of section 553(b):

Example: D files a Chapter 13 petition. 90 days before the petition, D owes B Bank $100,000 and has $40,000 on deposit. 10 days before the petition, B exercises its right of setoff. At that time, D owes B Bank $70,000 and the account has $60,000 balance. The trustee may recover $50,000 from B Bank. There was a $60,000 ($100,000–$40,000) "insufficiency" 90 days before the bankruptcy petition was filed. At the time of the setoff, the "insufficiency" was only $10,000 ($70,000–$60,000). There was a $50,000 improvement in position ($60,000–$10,000). The bankruptcy trustee may recover $50,000 of the amount of offset under section 553(b).

Example: D files a Chapter 7 petition. 90 days before the petition, D owes $200,000 to B Bank and has $200,000 on deposit at B Bank. 88 days before the petition, D withdraws $80,000 from the account; 5 days before the petition, B exercises its right of setoff. At that time, D owes B $70,000 and has $60,000 on deposit in B Bank. The trustee may recover $60,000 from B Bank. On the first date within the 90 day period that there was an "insufficiency," it was an insufficiency of $80,000. At the time of the setoff, the "insufficiency" was only

$10,000 ($70,000–$60,000). There was an improvement in position of $70,000 ($80,000–$10,000). Nevertheless, the trustee may recover only $60,000 under section 553(b). "The amount so offset" establishes the ceiling for recovery under section 553(b).

In summary, a bankruptcy trustee will apply the above six tests to any setoff that has occurred prior to the filing of the bankruptcy petition.

2) Postpetition Setoffs

Section 553(b) does not apply to postpetition setoffs.

3. Automatic Stay Applies to Setoffs

The filing of a bankruptcy petition automatically stays any further setoffs. Section 553 subjects the right of setoff to limitations provided in sections 362 and 363. Section 362(a)(7) stays setoffs. Thus, in order, to exercise a right of setoff after the filing of the bankruptcy petition it is necessary to obtain relief from the stay. Section 362(d), considered supra, governs relief from the stay. If a stay is terminated or modified to permit a postpetition setoff, the setoff will be limited by the section 553(a) requirements 1-5, discussed supra.

4. "Recoupment' Treated Differently

None of section 553 applies to recoupment. Recall from Chapter V that recoupment is like setoff, only different. In recoupment, the claim that each party has against the other must arise from the same transaction.

This difference is especially important in bankruptcy. Neither section 553 nor any other section of the Bankruptcy Code mentions recoupment.

Accordingly, according to most bankruptcy courts, a creditor's exercise of the right of recoupment is not affected by limitations of section 553 such as the requirement that the debts owing by and to the debtor both arose before the commencement of the case.

Example: Prepetition Medicare overpayments for nursing services made to the debtor in one fiscal year before bankruptcy and Medicare payment obligations for debtor's postpetition services made in a later fiscal year have been held to be part of the same "transaction' for purposes of equitable recoupment. Thus the government could, on grounds of equitable recoupment, deduct prepetition overpayments from the sums that the government owed to the debtor for postpetition services, without violating section 553 (or the automatic stay).

E. Fraudulent Transfers and Obligations

1. Section 548

a. Similar to State Law

The Bankruptcy Code, like nonbankruptcy law, invalidates transfers that are fraudulently made and obligations that are fraudulently incurred. Indeed, the Bankruptcy Code fraudulent conveyance provisions are very much like the nonbankruptcy fraudulent conveyance statutes considered supra. Section 548 is based on the Uniform Fraudulent Conveyances Act. [We know that today most states have moved from the Uniform Fraudulent Conveyance Act to the Uniform Fraudulent Transfers Act. In the 1970's, the drafters of the Bankruptcy Code did not yet know this.]

1. Section 548(a)(1)(A) corresponds to section 7 of the UFCA; it empowers the trustee to invalidate transfers made with actual intent to hinder, delay or defraud creditors.

2. Section 548(b) is similar to the partnership provisions of section 8(a) of the UFCA. Under section 548(b), the trustee of a bankrupt partnership may avoid a transfer of partnership property to a general partner if the partnership was or thereby became insolvent. The consideration given the partnership by the partner is irrelevant since a general partner is individually liable for the payment of the partnership's debts. Transfers by a partnership to a nonpartner are governed by section 548(a).

3. And section 548(a)(1)(B) resembles UFCA sections 4–7; it provides for avoidance of transfers where the debtor received less than a "reasonably equivalent value" and (i) was insolvent or became insolvent as a result of the transaction, or (ii) was engaged in business or was about to engage in a business transaction for which his remaining property was unreasonably small capital; or (iii) intended to incur or believed that he would incur debts beyond his ability to pay.

1) Actual Fraud

Like state fraudulent conveyance law, section 548(a) reaches transfers that are actually fraudulent, i.e., made by the debtor with the actual, subjective intention of defrauding creditors, section 548(a)(1)(A).

There is almost never any direct evidence of actual fraudulent intent. Establishing actual fraudulent intent is usually established through circumstantial evidence such as a close relationship between the transferor and the transferee. Reade v. Livingston (1818) involving a husband's gift to his wife of all of his real estate after a creditor won a judgment against him remains the classic example of a conveyance made with actual fraudulent intent, of a transfer that is actually fraudulent.

2) Constructive Fraud

Of far greater, current practical significance are conveyances that are constructively fraudulent. Section 548(a)(1)(B), like state fraudulent conveyance laws, also makes some transfers constructively fraudulent. Establishing a constructively fraudulent conveyance turns on the adequacy of consideration for the transfer and the financial position of the debtor, rather than the intention of the debtor. If the debtor is able to pay his debts, creditors (or at least the bankruptcy courts) are not concerned with what the debtor receives when he transfers property. On the other hand, if the debtor is in financial trouble as described by either section 548(a)(1)(B)(ii)(I) or (II) or (III), then bankruptcy courts are concerned with the adequacy of the consideration for the transfer.

b. Applied to Common Business Transactions

The easiest example of a transfer that is constructively fraudulent under section 548(a)(1)(B) is a gift by a person who is insolvent to a friend or relative. Increasingly, in bankruptcy courtrooms and law school classrooms, section 548(a)(1)(B) and the concept of constructively fraudulent conveyance are being applied to common business transactions such as foreclosure sales, intercorporate guarantees, and leveraged buyouts.

1) Foreclosure Sales

Assume, for example, that *D* borrowed $180,000 from *M*. The debt was secured by a deed of trust. *D* defaulted. *M* foreclosed on the realty and sold the property for $115,400, the amount of *D*'s outstanding debt. *M*'s foreclosure and sale completely complied with state law. A few days later, *D* filed for bankruptcy.

Do you see any possible fraudulent conveyance argument? What if *D* found an appraiser who was willing to testify that the value of the realty at the time of the foreclosure sale was $200,000? Can it be argued that the foreclosure sale was a fraudulent conveyance since it was a transfer for less than reasonably equivalent value while the debtor was insolvent? Such an argument was made in various cases with varying degrees of success until the Supreme Court decision in BFP v. RTC (1994). In a 5–4 decision, the Court held that "reasonably equivalent value" is the price received at the foreclosure sale so long as all the requirements of the state's foreclosure law have been complied with.

2) Intercorporate Guarantees

Intercorporate guarantees present even more challenging section 548(a)(1)(B) problems. In an intercorporate guarantee, the creditor generally is providing an appropriate amount of consideration but is providing the consideration to a person other than the guarantor.

Example: C lends $900,000 to X, Inc., D Corp., a subsidiary of X, Inc., guarantees repayment. A few months later D Corp. files for bankruptcy. The trustee can use section 548(a)(1)(B) to avoid D Corp.'s guarantee to C as a constructively fraudulent obligation.

Note that C provided a sufficient amount of consideration. C loaned $900,000. Note also that C provided that consideration to someone other than D Corp. It made the loan to X, Inc. Note that section 548(a)(1)(B) does not ask whether the creditor/transferee *gave* reasonably equivalent consideration to someone but rather whether the debtor *"received"* reasonably equivalent value. On these facts, the debtor—D Corp.—did not receive such value as value is defined under the law of fraudulent transfers.

Understand, however, that even though a bankruptcy trustee for the guarantor can challenge an intercorporate guarantee as a fraudulent obligation under section 548(a)(1)(B), such challenges will not always be successful. Recall that section 548(a)(1)(B) inquires not only into the adequacy of consideration to the debtor but also the financial condition of the debtor. What if D Corp. was clearly solvent at the time of the guarantee. Additionally, a loan to one corporation can benefit related entities. Conceivably, C's loan to X, Inc., D Corp.'s parent, did indirectly benefit D Corp. Accordingly, the appropriate inquiry is to compare what D Corp. gave and what D Corp. got from the loan to X, Inc. See Rubin v. Manufacturers Hanover Trust (1981).

3) Leveraged Buyouts

Leveraged buyouts can be approached similarly. In essence, a leveraged buyout (LBO) involves a person buying a business and then using the assets of that business to secure its financing.

Example: Assume that C makes a loan to X to enable her to buy all of the stock of D Corp. from its shareholders. Once X has all the D Corp. stock, X causes D Corp. to grant C a lien on the assets of D Corp., as collateral for the loan. Shortly after the LBO is completed, D Corp. files for bankruptcy.

Do you see the trustee's possible section 548(a)(1)(B) argument to avoid the lien on D Corp.'s assets? D Corp. made a security transfer of its assets to C. Was D Corp. solvent? If so, what consideration did D Corp. receive for the transfer? C gave value to someone; it made the loan to X that made the LBO possible. Was the change in ownership of value to D Corp.? Was it of a value reasonably equivalent to what D Corp. transferred?

c. Remember Insolvency

As the above LBO hypothetical reminds us, proof of a constructive fraudulent transfer under section 548(a)(1)(B) requires not only proof of the absence of reasonably equivalent value but also proof of the existence of insolvency or one of the other forms of financial distress described in section 548(a)(1)(B)(ii). Remember that.

d. Comparison of Fraudulent Transfers and Preferential Transfers

Assume that D has $100,000 of assets and owes $70,000 to A, $80,000 to B and $90,000 to C. D transfers $60,000 of assets.

If D transferred the $60,000 of assets to someone other than A, B or C and then files for bankruptcy, the transfer will be scrutinized as a fraudulent conveyance. The issue will be whether D received reasonably equivalent value for the transfer.

On the other hand, if D transferred the $60,000 to one of her creditors, then the transfer will be scrutinized as a preference. (Paying an antecedent debt is reasonably equivalent value under section 548. See section 548(d)(2).) And, the issue will be whether the creditor transferee was preferred.

e. Comparison of Section 548 and State Law

Section 548 differs from many states' fraudulent conveyance or transfer law in:

1) No Requirement of Actual Unpaid Creditors

Section 548 eliminates the requirement of actual unpaid creditors as to whom the transfer was fraudulent. Under the UFCA a transfer by an insolvent not for fair consideration may be set aside only by creditors who were creditors at the time of the transfer. Under section 548(a)(1)(B) such a transfer may be avoided even though all who were creditors at the time of the transfer have been paid.

2) One–Year Reach–Back Period

Under section 548, the bankruptcy trustee may only reach transfers made within two years of the filing of the bankruptcy petition. For purposes of section 548, a transfer will be deemed made when it becomes so far perfected that a bona fide purchaser from the debtor could not acquire an interest in the property transferred superior to the interest of the transferor, section 548(d). The problems of determining the date that a transfer will be deemed made are considered later in this chapter.

Example: Assume that in June of 2006, Marge Simpson gave her daughter Lisa a new piano as a birthday present. Mrs. Simpson was insolvent at the time of the gift. On August 1, 2008, Mrs. Simpson files a bankruptcy petition. By the date of bankruptcy, Mrs. Simpson has repaid all of her June, 2006 creditors except Mr. Burns whom she owed $10. Mrs. Simpson's bankruptcy trustee will not be able to recover the piano under section 548. The transfer was a fraudulent conveyance (a transfer for less than "reasonably equivalent value' while insolvent) but it was made more than a year prior to the bankruptcy petition.

The UFCA does not have its own statute of limitations. States generally have a three to six year limitations period for actions to invalidate fraudulent conveyances. The UFTA has a four-year limitations period the trustee can use state fraudulent conveyance law with its longer limitation period under section 544(b).

3) Exempt Property

Section 548 applies to transfers of both nonexempt and exempt property. The UFCA is limited to transfers of nonexempt property.

4)   No "Good Faith" Requirement

The test in section 548(a)(1)(B)(i) is "reasonably equivalent value." The test in sections 4–7 of the UFCA is "fair consideration." The "fair consideration" standard requires an inquiry into both the amount of consideration and the parties' good faith. Section 548's use of "reasonably equivalent value" eliminates a good faith requirement from value determination. However, the "good faith" of the transferee remains significant under section 548. Section 548(c) protects a transferee who takes "for value and in good faith." Accordingly, the practical significance of the use of "reasonably equivalent value" instead of "fair consideration" is the elimination of any inquiry into the good faith of the transferor in determining whether a trustee can recover property under section 548(a)(1)(B).

2.   Section 544(b)

Section 548's two-year reach back significantly limits the use of section 548. Section 548 is not, however, the only provision in the Bankruptcy Code that invalidates fraudulent conveyances. The trustee may also use section 544(b) to invalidate fraudulent conveyances.

a.   Incorporates State Law

Section 544(b) does not specifically provide for the invalidation of fraudulent conveyances. Rather it empowers the bankruptcy trustee to avoid any prebankruptcy transfer that is "voidable under applicable law by a creditor holding an unsecured claim that is allowable." (Section 502 governs allowance of claims. Section 502 is considered in Chapter XV.)

Section 544(b) incorporates state fraudulent conveyance law into the Bankruptcy Code. If, outside of bankruptcy, the transfer would be governed by a Statute of Elizabeth fraudulent conveyance statute, section 544(b) is a Statute of Elizabeth statute; if the state statute is the UFCA, then section 544(b) is UFCA; if UFTA, then UFTA. Section 544(b) reflects not only the state substantive law of fraudulent conveyances but also the state limitations period for fraudulent conveyances.

In the Simpson problem, the June gift of a piano would be a fraudulent conveyance under nonbankruptcy law, Statute of Elizabeth, UFCA, or UFTA as to Mr. Burns. Burns was a creditor holding an unsecured claim that is allowable. Accordingly, the bankruptcy trustee may use section 544(b) to recover the piano.

NOTE: The state limitations period determines which transfers may be challenged, not when the challenge must be made. Section

546 again gives the trustee time after his or her appointment to commence the action. To illustrate, D makes a fraudulent conveyance in January of 2000. State law imposes a five-year limitation period on fraudulent conveyance actions. If D files a bankruptcy petition in December of 2002 that satisfies or tolls the state law limitations period, D's bankruptcy trustee will have the additional section 546 period to commence a fraudulent conveyance action.

b. Effect of Avoidance Enhanced in Bankruptcy

While the existence of the trustee's section 544(b) avoiding powers depends upon the existence of an avoiding power held by an actual creditor, the extent of the trustee's section 544(b) avoidance powers is greater than the power of the actual creditor. In the Simpson problem, under state fraudulent conveyance law, if Lisa Simpson paid Mr. Burns $10, she could keep the piano. Under section 544(b), Lisa is not so fortunate. Legislative history clearly indicates that section 544(b) retains the rule of Moore v. Bay (U.S. 1931).

Under the rule of *Moore v. Bay*, the trustee is not limited in his recovery by the amount of the claim of the actual creditor. A transfer which is voidable by a single, actual creditor, may be avoided entirely by the trustee, regardless of the size of the actual creditor's claim. Thus Lisa may not keep the piano by simply paying the bankruptcy trustee $10.

3. Chart Comparing Sections 548 and 544(b)

The Simpson hypothetical points up the similarities and differences of sections 548 and 544(b).

These provisions are also compared by the following chart:

Section 548	Section 544(b)
1. Essentially UFCA	1. UFCA, UFTA or Statute of Elizabeth, which is the state law
2. Reaches transfers made within two years of bankruptcy petition [limitations period is measured from the time the transfer is deemed made]	2. Reaches all transfers made with state limitations period [limitations period is generally measured from the time the transfer was actually made]
3. Elements of fraudulent conveyance tested as of time that transfer was deemed made	3. Elements of fraudulent conveyance tested as of time that the fraudulent conveyance was actually made
4. Transferee that takes for value and in good faith protected	4. Transfer that takes for value and in good faith protected

5. No requirement of actual creditor as to whom conveyance is fraudulent	5. Voidable only if transfer is fraudulent as to an actual creditor with an unsecured allowable claim
6. Complete invalidation	6. Complete invalidation

F. Transfers Not Recorded or Otherwise Perfected

A bankruptcy trustee may avoid certain prepetition transfers that are not recorded or perfected. A failure to record can adversely affect other creditors. If creditor X does not record its lien on D's property, creditor Y might not know that D's property is encumbered. Relying on the mistaken belief that D holds his property free from liens, Y might extend credit, refrain from obtaining a lien, or forebear from instituting collection proceedings.

State law requires recordation or other public notice of a number of transfers. Real estate recording statutes require the recording of deeds and real property mortgages. And, Article 9 of the Uniform Commercial Code calls for public notice (perfection) of most security interests in personal property.

The Bankruptcy Code does not have its own public notice requirements. It does not simply invalidate all transfers not recorded within 10 days. Rather, the Bankruptcy Code makes use of the notoriety requirements of state law in the following invalidation provisions: sections 544, 545, 547 and 548.

Most recording statutes protect only bona fide purchasers or lien creditors—not creditors with unsecured claims. Accordingly, section 544(b) is *not* generally available to avoid a transfer because of delay in recordation. For examples:

Example: On January 10, D borrows $10,000 from M and gives M a mortgage on Redacre. On February 2, C lends D $10,000. On March 3, M records its mortgage. On July 7, D files a bankruptcy petition. On the date of the perfection, D still owes $10,000 to M and $10,000 to C. D's bankruptcy trustee will not be able to invalidate M's mortgage. The public notoriety requirements were not timely satisfied. M delayed in recording its mortgages. Most real property recording statutes only protect purchasers and/or lien creditors. C is not within the class of persons protected by the applicable recording statute. Section 544(b) empowers the trustee to invalidate transfers that are invalid as to actual creditors such as C. Since C cannot invalidate the transfer, the bankruptcy trustee cannot invalidate the transfer *under section* 544(b).

Example: On January 10, D borrows $10,000 from S and gives S a security interest in equipment. On February 2, C lends D $10,000. On March 3,

S perfects its security interest. On July 7, *D* files a bankruptcy petition. On the date of the petition, *D* still owes $10,000 to *S* and $10,000 to *C*. *D*'s bankruptcy trustee will *not* be able to invalidate *S*'s security interest. The public notoriety requirements of the UCC were not timely satisfied. *S* delayed in perfecting its security interest. Article 9's perfection requirements, however, protect only certain gap secured creditors and buyers. See section 9–201(a). Cf. section 9–317(2). *C* is not within the class of persons protected by the applicable recording statute. Section 544(b) empowers the bankruptcy trustee to avoid transfers that are invalid as to actual creditors. Since no actual creditor can invalidate the transfer, the bankruptcy trustee cannot invalidate the transfer.

1. Section 544(a) [a/k/a "Strong Arm Clause"]

a. Requirements

Section 544(a) focuses on the rights of hypothetical lien creditors and bona fide purchasers of real property. Section 544(a) empowers the bankruptcy trustee to invalidate any transfer that under nonbankruptcy law is voidable as to a creditor who extended credit and obtained a lien on the date of the filing of the bankruptcy petition or is voidable as to a bona fide purchaser of real property whether or not such a creditor or purchaser actually exists. In applying section 544(a), it is thus necessary to determine whether:

(1) Nonbankruptcy law public notice requirements have been satisfied as of date of the filing of the bankruptcy petition;

(2) A creditor who extended credit and obtained a lien on the date that the bankruptcy petition was filed or a bona fide purchaser of real property on the date of the bankruptcy petition comes within the class of persons protected by such state law.

b. Examples

The following examples illustrate the application of section 544(a):

Example: On January 10, *D* borrows $10,000 from *M* and gives *M* a mortgage on Redacre. On February 2, *D* files a bankruptcy petition. As of the date of the petition, *M* had not recorded its mortgage. The bankruptcy trustee may invalidate *M*'s mortgage under section 544(a).

The public notice requirements of the state real property recording statutes were not satisfied. Real property recording statutes typically protect bona fide purchasers. Since the mortgage was unrecorded on the date that the bankruptcy petition was filed, M's mortgage would be ineffective as against a bona fide purchaser of Redacre on the date that the petition was filed. Section 544(a) gives the bankruptcy trustee the same powers as a person who was a bona fide purchaser on the date that the bankruptcy petition was filed.

Example: On January 10, D borrows $10,000 from S and gives S a security interest in equipment. On February 22, D files a bankruptcy petition. S fails to perfect its security interest prior to February 22. The bankruptcy trustee will be able to invalidate S's security interest under section 544(a).

Again, the applicable public notice requirement was not satisfied. Article 9 of the Uniform Commercial Code requires that a security interest be perfected in order to be effective against a lien creditor, section 9–317(a)(2). Since the security interest was unperfected on the date that the bankruptcy petition was filed, S's security interest would be subordinate to the claim of a creditor who obtained a judicial lien on the date that the petition was filed. Section 544(a) gives S the same invalidation powers as a person who extended credit and obtained a judicial lien on the date that the bankruptcy petition was filed.

NOTE: Even though the Uniform Commercial Code uses the term "subordinate" instead of "voidable," a security that would be "subordinate" to a creditor that obtained a judicial lien on the date of the filing of the bankruptcy petition is "voidable" by the bankruptcy trustee.

Example: On January 10, D borrows $10,000 from S to buy equipment and gives S a purchase money security interest in the equipment. (S's security interest is "purchase money" since this extension of credit enabled D to obtain the property that is the collateral for the extension of credit. See section 9–103.) On January 28, D files a bankruptcy petition. On

January 29, S perfects its security interest. The bankruptcy trustee may not invalidate S's security interest.

Section 544(a) empowers the bankruptcy trustee to invalidate security interests that would be subordinate to the claims of a creditor who obtained a judicial lien on the date that the petition was filed, January 28. S did not perfect its security interest until January 29. Recall the general rule of section 9–317(a)(2), that an unperfected security interest is subordinate to a lien creditor. This general rule is subject to section 9–317(e)'s exception for purchase money security interests. Purchase money security interest perfected within 20 days prevails over a gap lien creditor. Section 9–317(e) applies. Section 9–317(e) provides: "[I]f a person files a financing statement with respect to a purchase money security interest before or within 20 days after the debtor receives delivery of the collateral, the security interest takes priority over the rights of a . . . lien creditor which arise between the time the security interest attaches and the time of filing." S's purchase money security interest perfected on January 28 (within the requisite 20 days) would be effective as against a creditor who obtained a lien on January 28, the date that the bankruptcy petition was filed. Accordingly, S's purchase money security interest is effective against the bankruptcy trustee.

Example: On January 10, Dudley Doright, D, borrows $10,000 from Snidely Whiplash, S, and gives S a security interest in equipment. On December 29, S properly files his financing statement. On December 30, D files a bankruptcy petition. The bankruptcy trustee may not invalidate S's security interest under section 544(a). (The bankruptcy trustee will probably be able to invalidate S's security interest under some other provision of the Bankruptcy Code. If D was insolvent on December 29, the bankruptcy trustee may invalidate S's security interest under section 547. The applicability of section 547 to transfers not timely perfected or recorded is considered later in this chapter.)

The public notice requirements of Article 9 were not timely satisfied; S delayed in perfecting its security interest for almost a year. Article 9's perfection requirements protect "gap" lien creditors and buyers. In this hypothetical, the bankruptcy trustee has the right of a lien creditor, but not a gap lien creditor. Section 544(a) gives the bankruptcy trustee the invalidation powers of a creditor who obtained a judicial lien as of the date of the bankruptcy petition. On the date of the bankruptcy petition, December 30, S's security interest was perfected. A perfected security interest is effective against lien creditors, cf. sections 9–201, 9–301. Accordingly, S's security interest may not be invalidated under section 544(a).

c. General Rules for Using 544(a)

These examples suggest three general rules for the use of section 544(a) in invalidating transfers:

1. If the transfer has been recorded or otherwise perfected prior to the date that the bankruptcy petition was filed, the trustee will not be able to invalidate the transfer under section 544(a).

2. Except as noted in (3) below, if the transfer was not recorded or otherwise perfected by the date that the bankruptcy petition was filed, the bankruptcy trustee will be able to invalidate the transfer under section 544(a).

3. The bankruptcy trustee will not be able to invalidate a purchase money security interest perfected within 10 days after the delivery of the collateral to the debtor even if the debtor files a bankruptcy petition in the gap between the creation of the security interest and perfection.

2. Section 545(2)

Section 545(2) invalidates statutory liens that are not perfected or enforceable on the date of the petition against a hypothetical bona fide purchaser. Section 546(b) recognizes any applicable state law "grace period." If under state law, the statutory lien may still be perfected and that perfection relates back to a prebankruptcy petition date, then the bankruptcy trustee will not be able to invalidate the lien.

Section 545(2) is of very limited practical significance because:

1. First, most statutory liens satisfy section 545(2)'s bona fide purchaser test regardless of whether there has been recordation or not.

2. Second, statutory liens are also subject to section 544(a) which can be used to invalidate any statutory lien on real property that is voidable by a hypothetical bona fide purchaser and any statutory lien on personal property that is voidable by a hypothetical lien creditor.

G. Transfers Not Timely Recorded or Otherwise Perfected

In the Dudley Doright/Snidely Whiplash hypothetical, *supra*, the bankruptcy trustee was not able to invalidate Snidely's security interest under section 544(a) notwithstanding Snidely's long delay in giving public notice of his lien. Should Doright's bankruptcy trustee be able to invalidate Snidely's lien?

1. Section 547(e)

As noted earlier, there are a number of reasons for invalidating such "secret liens." Creditors of Doright may have been misled by Snidely's failure to record or a delay in recording. Unaware of this "secret," unrecorded lien, Nell Fenwick might extend credit to Doright she would not extend if aware of the lien. Unaware of a "secret," unrecorded lien, Mr. Peabody might delay in collecting a delinquent debt from Doright he would try to collect if aware of the lien. The Bankruptcy Code should provide for invalidation of transfers that are not timely recorded. And it does. In section 547.

Although it is easy to see the reason for invalidating liens that are not timely perfected, it is difficult to understand why section 547 should be the mechanism for invalidating such liens. The easy way to invalidate such secret liens would be to add a section to the Bankruptcy Code to the effect that any lien that can be recorded or otherwise perfected under state law must be recorded within X number of days after it is obtained in order to be valid in bankruptcy. While that is the "easy way," it is not the way of the Bankruptcy Code.

a. "Deeming" Time of Perfection as Time of Transfer–Section 547(e)

Basically, the Bankruptcy Code's method for attacking delayed perfection is to "deem" that for purposes of applying the requirements of section 547(b), the date of transfers not timely recorded is the date of perfection, not the actual date of transfer.

NOTE: Section 547 does not specify the means of perfection. Rather, section 547(e)(1)provides that for purposes of section 547, transfers shall be perfected when effective under nonbankruptcy law against certain specified third parties. In a transfer of real property other than fixtures, the third parties are bona fide purchasers, i.e., the date of perfection is the date that the transfer is effective against bona fide purchasers. Nonbankruptcy law generally requires that transfers of interests in real property other than fixtures be recorded in order to be effective against bona fide purchasers.

The Doright/Whiplash example illustrates the practical significance of the statutory delay of the effective date of the transfer until public notice of the transfer has been given.

Example: Remember, Doright borrowed $10,000 from Snidely on January 10 and gave Snidely a security interest in equipment which Snidely perfected on December 29. Doright filed a bankruptcy petition on December 30. At first, it might seem that section 547 is not applicable—that the security transfer from Doright to Snidely was not for an antecedent indebtedness and did not occur within 90 days of the bankruptcy petition.

For purposes of section 547, however, the transfer will be deemed made on December 29, not January 10. [Under section 9–301, Snidely's security interest would not be effective as against subsequent judicial lien creditors until that date. Accordingly, by reason of section 547(e), the transfer will not be deemed made until that date.] Thus, the "December 29 transfer" would be within 90 days of the bankruptcy petition. Thus, the "December 29 transfer" would be for an antecedent indebtedness, i.e., the $10,000 loaned on January 10. Thus, the trustee would be able to invalidate S's security interest under section 547 if D was insolvent on December 29. [Remember section 547(f) creates a rebuttable presumption of insolvency.]

The above hypothetical illustrates that a delay in perfection can result in a security interest actually given for present consideration being deemed made for an antecedent indebtedness and thus a section 547 preference.

In the Dudley Doright hypothetical, over 11 months elapsed between the granting of the security interest and the perfecting of the security interest. What if the delay was eleven weeks? Eleven days? Eleven hours? Is there some sort of "grace period" in section 547?

b. Grace Period

Section 547(e) does not require immediate perfection; it provides a "grace period" for perfection.

Section 547(e)(2) describes three situations.

1. Section 547(e)(2)(A) deals with transfers perfected within 30 days. Such a transfer will be deemed made at the time of the transfer. A transfer deemed made at the time of the transfer is not vulnerable to attack by the bankruptcy trustee under section 547.

2. Section 547(e)(2)(B) deals with transfers not perfected within the grace period. Such a transfer will be deemed made at the time of perfection. A transfer deemed made at a point in time later than the time of the transfer is vulnerable to attack by the bankruptcy trustee under section 547.

3. Section 547(e)(2)(C) deals with the effect of filing a bankruptcy petition during the "grace period." Under such facts, the transfer will be deemed made at the time of the transfer if it is perfected within ten days of the transfer or will be deemed made at the time of the filing of the bankruptcy petition if it is not perfected within ten days.

c. Examples

The operation of section 547(e) is illustrated in the following five examples:

Example: On January 10, *S* lends *D* $10,000 and obtains a nonpurchase money security interest in *D*'s equipment. *S* perfects this security interest on January 19. For purposes of section 547, the security transfer will be deemed to have occurred on January 10, section 547(e)(2)(A). *S* perfected within 30 days after the transfer so the transfer is deemed made when it was actually made, January 10. Not a transfer for an antecedent debt—January 10 transfer for a January 10 debt. Not a preference.

Example: On January 10, *D* borrows $10,000 from *S* and grants *S* a security interest in its equipment. *S* perfects its security interest on February 22. *S* did not perfect within 30 days so that for purposes of the elements of section 547(b), the transfer will be deemed to have occurred when it was finally perfected, February 22. A transfer for an antecedent debt—a February 22 transfer for a January 10 debt. Possibly a preference.

Example: On January 10, *S* lends *D* $10,000 and obtains a purchase money security interest in equipment that *D* acquires that day. *S* perfects its security interest on January 25. The facts of this hypothetical are different from the facts of #2 in two important respects: (i) *S* has a purchase money security interest and (ii) *S* perfected within 20 days after the debtor received possession of the property. It is clear that a lawyer dealing with this problem would and should conclude that the trustee cannot avoid *S*'s security interest. It is less clear how a law student would explain this answer on a law school exam because of the statutory language. Section 547(e)(2)(A) establishes a 10–day grace period "except as provided in section 547(c)(3)(B)." A reading of section 547(e)(2)(A) together with section 547(a)(3)(B) can support the proposition that purchase money security interests perfected within 20 days relate back to the time that the debt and the security interest were created so that there is no transfer for an antecedent debt and no preference. Alternatively, the two provisions can support the proposition that there is a ten day grace period for all security interests but purchase money security interests perfected within the 20–day period are excepted from preference avoidance.

Example: On January 10, S lends D $10,000 and obtains a security interest in D's equipment. D files a bankruptcy petition on January 15. S perfects its security interest on January 19. For purposes of section 547, the security transfer will be deemed to have occurred on January 10, section 547(e)(2)(A), section 547(e)(2)(C)(ii). [Same facts as #1 except that D filed a bankruptcy petition before the security interest was perfected.]

NOTE: This hypothetical raises not only section 547(e) issues but also issues under section 544. Section 362(a)(4) bars the perfection of liens after the filing of a bankruptcy petition.

Section 362(b)(3), however, creates an exception for perfection "accomplished within the period provided under section 547(e)(2)(A)." Accordingly, it would seem that the perfection in problem #3 did not violate the automatic stay. Accordingly, it would seem that the bankruptcy trustee will not be able to avoid the security interest under section 547.

Example: On January 10, S lends D $10,000 and obtains a nonpurchase money security interest in D's equipment. D files a bankruptcy petition on January 15. S perfects its security interest on February 22. For purposes of section 547, the security transfer will be deemed to have occurred on January 15, section 547(e)(2)(C). Transfers not perfected within 30 days are deemed made at the date of the bankruptcy petition if the filing of the petition preceded perfection. [Same facts as (2) except that D filed a bankruptcy petition before the security interest was filed.]

2.   Section 548(d)

Section 548(d) is similar to section 547(e). Section 547(e) fixes the time when a transfer is deemed made for purposes of the preference invalidation provisions of section 547. Section 548(d) fixes the time when a transfer is deemed made for purposes of the fraudulent conveyance invalidation provisions of section 548: when the transfer is so far perfected that no subsequent bona fide purchaser of the property from the debtor can acquire rights in the property superior to those of the transferee.

The purpose of section 548(d) is to prevent a fraudulent conveyance from escaping invalidation by being kept secret.

Example: On January 10, 2006, D, who is insolvent, gives Redacre to X. X does not record the deed until November 11, 2008. On December 12, 2008, D files a bankruptcy petition. Remember, section 548 has a two-year reach-back period. The transfer of Redacre was actually made more than two years year before the bankruptcy petition was filed. The transfer, however, was not effective against a subsequent bona fide purchaser until it was recorded on November 11. Accordingly, under section 548(d), the transfer is deemed made on November 11, 2008. Without section 548(d), the bankruptcy trustee could not invalidate the gift by an insolvent under section 548.

The transfer from D to X in the preceding paragraph was a "true" fraudulent conveyance: a transfer by an insolvent without "reasonably equivalent value." Action 548(d), however, also may enable the bankruptcy trustee to invalidate some transfers that are not "true" fraudulent conveyances, i.e., transfers in which there has been merely a delay in recordation or perfection. Consider the following illustration.

Example: Wallace, W, gives Redacre to his brother Theodore, T, in December of 2005. W is solvent at that time. T, however, does not record the transfer until June of 2008. At that time, W is insolvent. In July of 2008, W files a bankruptcy petition. The bankruptcy trustee will be able to use section 548(a)(2) to invalidate the 2005 gift of Redacre because, for purposes of section 548, it will be treated as a 2008 gift.

Note that T's delay in recordation is crucial to the bankruptcy trustee's section 548 case. At the time that the gift is actually made, the donor, W, is solvent. There are no legal problems with people who are solvent making gifts. This happens every Chanukah and Christmas. Gifts are fraudulent conveyances when made by people who are insolvent.

While the donor, W, was solvent when the gift was actually made, he is insolvent when the gift is deemed made under section 548(d) the time the transfer is perfected against bona fide purchasers from the transferor. Section 547(e), enables the trustee to test all aspects of the transaction as of the time of recordation rather than as of the time of the actual transfer. Since W was insolvent when the transfer is deemed made at the time of recordation, the transfer was fraudulent as a transfer by an insolvent without reasonably equivalent value.

3. Section 544(b) [Not]

The most important thing for you to know about the application of section 544(b) to transfers that were not timely recorded is that section 544(b)'s application is *not* important.

Section 544(b) empowers the bankruptcy trustee to invalidate any transfer that under nonbankruptcy law is voidable as to any actual creditor of the debtor with an unsecured, allowable claim. In applying section 544(b), it is thus necessary to determine:

1. Whether nonbankruptcy law public notice requirements have been timely satisfied;

2. Which persons are protected by the nonbankruptcy requirement of public notice;

3. If any actual creditor of the debtor with an unsecured allowable claim comes within the class of persons protected by such state law.

The use of section 544(b) to invalidate prepetition transfers that were not timely recorded is severely limited. Section 544(b) gives the trustee the invalidation powers of any actual unsecured creditors. Most recording statutes protect lien creditors or bona fide purchasers, but not unsecured creditors.

H. Landlords' Liens

Sections 545(3) and 545(4) are the easiest invalidation provisions to read, understand and apply:

"The trustee may avoid the fixing of a statutory lien on the property of the debtor to the extent that such lien . . .

(3) is for rent

(4) is a lien of distress for rent."

Note that the provisions only invalidate *statutory* landlord liens, i.e., liens for rent arising "solely by force of a statute." If the lease agreement creates a security deposit or other Article 9 security interest in property of the lessee, this contractual lien is not affected by section 545.

Note, also, that when a landlord requires its tenant to sign a security agreement giving the landlord a security interest in property of the tenant to secure rental payments, the landlord has, of course, obtained a lien. This lien held by the landlord is not however, a "landlord's lien"; it is a security interest. Not all liens securing claims by landlords are A landlord's liens. Only Chuck Berry would be inclined to call a security interest obtained by Mabel "Mabelline." [We know that this "joke" is "dated," but then so are we.]

I. Disguised Priorities

Section 507 of the Bankruptcy Code is a priority provision; it sets out the order in which the various unsecured claims against the debtor are to be satisfied. It displaces any state priority statutes.

Section 545 protects this federal priority scheme from disruption by state priority provisions that are "disguised" as statutory liens. Section 545 reaches spurious statutory liens which are in reality merely priorities.

When is a statutory lien more like a priority than a lien? Recall that a priority does not arise until distribution of a debtor's assets on insolvency. Accordingly, section 545(1) provides for invalidation of a statutory lien which first become effective on the bankruptcy or insolvency of the debtor.

J. Seller's Reclamation and Return Rights

1. Rights Granted by State Law

When a buyer fails to pay for goods it accepts, the seller has a legal right to recover the contract price, UCC § 2–709. This legal right to be paid is of limited practical significance if the buyer is insolvent. Accordingly, the Uniform Commercial Code grants certain unpaid sellers a right to recover the goods. Section 2–702 of the Uniform Commercial Code empowers a seller to "reclaim" (recover) the goods if:

1. Credit sale, *and*

2. Buyer insolvent when goods received, *and*

3. Demand for reclamation is made within a reasonable time after the buyer's receipt of the goods.

Case law has created a similar right of reclamation for sellers paid with bad checks. This right of reclamation of a "cash" seller who has been paid by a check that is subsequently dishonored is based on Uniform Commercial Code sections 2–507 and 2–511.

2. Effect of Bankruptcy Law on State–Law Rights

What is the effect of the bankruptcy of the buyer on the seller's right of reclamation? Sections 546(c) and (d) deal with this question. Section 546 does not create a right of reclamation. Instead, it sets out the effect of bankruptcy on a right of reclamation created under nonbankruptcy law.

NOTE: Section 546(d) deals with the effect of bankruptcy on the nonbankruptcy reclamation rights of farmers who have sold grain to storage facilities and fishermen who have sold fish to processing facilities. Section 546(d) has the same general requirements as section 546(c). Accordingly, this Black Letter will discuss only section 546(c). Under section 546(d), the bankruptcy court may only deny reclamation if it secures the farmer or fisherman's reclamation claim by a lien.

Section 546(c) has five requirements:

1. The seller has a right of reclamation under nonbankruptcy law.

2. The buyer received the goods while insolvent.

3. The buyer received the goods within 45 days before the bankruptcy case was filed.

3. The sale was in the ordinary course of the seller's business.

4. The seller makes a written reclamation demand within 45 days after the buyer's receipt of the goods unless a bankruptcy petition is filed during that 45–day period. If there is a bankruptcy petition filed before the 45–day period has expired, the seller has 20 days from the buyer's bankruptcy filing to make the seller's written reclamation demand.

If a seller has complied with these four requirements, the bankruptcy trustee *cannot* invalidate the seller's right of reclamation under section 544(a), section 545, section 547, or section 549.

Section 546(c) does not protect the seller's right of reclamation from invalidation based on section 544(b). Section 544(b) is considered supra. If other unsecured creditors have rights superior to the seller's right of reclamation, the trustee may assert these rights under section 544(b) to defeat the seller's right of reclamation. If a secured creditor has rights superior to the seller's right of reclamation, the trustee may assert these rights only if the trustee is able to avoid the lien of the secured creditor and preserve it for the benefit of the estate.

3. Effect of Debtor's Transfer of Rights in Goods

Legally, the seller's right of reclamation turns on the seller's satisfaction of the various requirements in Uniform Commercial Code section 2–702 and Bankruptcy Code section 546. Practically, the seller's right of reclamation also turns on what the debtor has and has not done prior to the seller's reclamation demand. If the debtor has disposed of the goods prior to the seller's reclamation demand, then there is nothing to reclaim: under nonbankruptcy law, the reclamation remedy is limited to the goods that the seller delivered.

Similarly, if the debtor has granted another creditor a security interest that covers all of its inventory, there is nothing to reclaim: under nonbankruptcy law, a security interest has priority over a right of reclamation.

4. Priority Claim

Section 546(c) should be read together with section 503(b)(9). Even if an unpaid credit seller is unable to recover goods delivered on credit within 45 days before bankruptcy, the seller's claim—which is otherwise unsecured and equal to other, general unsecured claims—is given priority in payment—as an administrative expense of the bankruptcy case—to the extent of the value of any goods received by the debtor within 20 days before the date the bankruptcy case was filed. This priority applies even if the seller failed to provide the notice for reclamation under section 546(c)(1). 11 U.S.C.A. § 546(c)(2).

5. Bankruptcy Right of Return

Section 546(h) creates and adds a very limited right of return of goods to an unpaid seller for credit.

The express limitations on this right include:

1. Chapter 11 cases only,

2. Within 120 days after the case was commenced,

3. Consent of both the debtor and the seller,

4. Return for full credit of the purchase price, and

5. Court determination that the return is "in the best interests of the debtor."

This right of return is probably subject to an additional limitation: the rights of a secured party with a security interest on the debtor's inventory. Assume that X has a valid security interest in all of D's inventory, including after-acquired property. Y delivers goods to D on credit. Those goods would be subject to X's security interest, that is, would be a part of X's collateral. D later files for bankruptcy. D now taking a part of X's collateral and "returning" it to Y is "subject to the prior right of holders of security interests in such goods or the proceeds of such goods," section 546(h), i.e., is subject to X's secured claim.

K. Review Questions

1. T or F   The debtor can avoid pre-bankruptcy transfers under sections 544, 545, 547, and 548.

2. D Corp., owes C $20,000. P, the principal shareholder of D Corp., pays C the $20,000. D Corp., files a bankruptcy petition 89 days later. Is there a voidable preference?

3. D Corp., owes C $300,000. D Corp., pays C $90,000. Four months later, D Corp., files a bankruptcy petition. Is there a voidable preference?

4. Same facts as #3 except that P, the principal shareholder of D Corp., had guaranteed payment to C.

5. D owes C $500,000. C has a mortgage on Redacre. Redacre has a value of $550,000. Sixty days before filing for bankruptcy, D pays C $300,000. Is there a preference?

6. Same facts as #5 except that Redacre is only worth $300,000.

7. D, a lawyer, bought supplies from C on credit. C billed D at the end of the month and D paid by the 15th. Two months later, D filed a Chapter 11 petition. Was the payment to C a preference?

8. T or F   D owes B Bank $80,000. D has an account at B Bank with a $60,000 balance. B Bank exercises its right of setoff. D files a bankruptcy petition the next day. D can avoid the setoff under section 547.

9. S sold a building to T for a substantial discount but without any tacky intent. Eleven months after the sale, D filed a bankruptcy petition. T is not an insider. Can D's bankruptcy trustee cannot avoid the sale?

10. S obtained a security interest in D's farm equipment. Almost a year later, and only days before D filed bankruptcy, S finally perfected its security interest. Can D's trustee avoid the security interest under 547?

*

XII

Postpetition Transfers

■ *ANALYSIS*

A. When Do Postbankruptcy Transfers Happen?
B. How Does a Postbankruptcy Transfer Happen?
C. How Does Section 549 Affect Postbankruptcy Transfers of Property of the Estate by the Debtor?
   1. Authorized Transfers
   2. Gap Transfers
   3. Recorded Real Estate Transfers
D. How Does Section 542 Affect Postbankruptcy Transfers of Property of the Estate by Third Parties?
E. Review Questions

A. When Do Postbankruptcy Transfers Happen?

The prior chapter dealt with avoidance of transfers that occurred prior to the time that the bankruptcy petition was filed. Sections 544, 545, 547 and 548 apply only to prebankruptcy transfers. None of these provisions can be used to avoid an unauthorized transfer of property of the estate that occurs after the bankruptcy petition is filed. Section 549 applies to postbankruptcy transfers.

Postbankruptcy transfers of property of the estate present problems primarily in Chapter 7 cases. Only in Chapter 7 cases does the right of possession of property of the estate pass to the trustee; only in Chapter 7 cases are the proceeds from the trustee's liquidation of property of the estate what is distributed to creditors. In Chapter 11 and Chapter 13 cases, the debtor continues to possess property of the estate postpetition and creditors are paid under a plan that is generally based on the debtor's future earnings. And, in Chapter 11 and Chapter 13 cases, most postpetition transfers of property of the estate are permitted by section 363.

Accordingly, section 549 is much more important to Chapter 7 cases than to Chapter 11 cases or Chapter 13 cases. And, section 549 is much more important to Chapter 7 cases in law school than to Chapter 7 cases in the "real world." Most Chapter 7 debtors do not have significant assets to transfer postbankruptcy; and most Chapter 7 debtors do not make improper postbankruptcy transfers; and most Chapter 7 trustees are able to recover property of the estate that was transferred postbankruptcy without litigation.

B. How Does a Postbankruptcy Transfer Happen?

For most purposes, the date of the filing of the bankruptcy petition is the critical date in a Chapter 7 case. Subject to limited exceptions, only the property of the debtor as of the date of the filing of the petition becomes property of the estate. Generally, property acquired by the debtor after the bankruptcy petition has been filed remains property of the debtor.

The date of the filing of the petition is significant not only in determining what property becomes property of the estate but also in determining when the property becomes property of the estate. The filing of a bankruptcy petition—voluntary or involuntary—creates the estate.

The date of the filing of the bankruptcy petition is not, however, the date that the debtor loses possession of her property. Even in Chapter 7 cases. While section 701 provides for the appointment of an interim trustee in Chapter 7 cases "promptly after the order for relief," there will be some delay before the trustee takes possession of the property.

During the hiatus between the filing of the bankruptcy petition and the bankruptcy trustee's taking possession of the property of the estate, the debtor will usually have possession and control of the property of the estate. At times, the debtor will, after the filing of the petition, transfer property of the estate to some third party.

Example: Assume that *B* files a Chapter 7 petition on January 10. On January 12, *B* sells her summer home to *X*. On January 13, *B* sells her boat to *Y*.

Obviously, *B* should not have made these postbankruptcy transfers. Obviously, the trustee has a cause of action against *B* for conversion. Obviously, the trustee can claim any proceeds from the postbankruptcy transfers as property of the estate. And, obviously the claim against the debtor *B* and the right to remaining proceeds will usually be of limited practical significance. The significant inquiry is can the trustee recover the summer house from *X* and/or the boat from *Y*? Should the bankruptcy laws protect transferees *X* and/or *Y*?

C. How Does Section 549 Affect Postbankruptcy Transfers of Property of the Estate by the Debtor?

Section 549 protects *X* and *Y* in certain circumstances. Before considering these circumstances, remember that section 549 protects only the *transferee*, not the debtor-transferor.

Generally, section 549 protects the *transferee* if:

1. The transfer was authorized by the Bankruptcy Code or by the bankruptcy court; or

2. The transfer was after an involuntary petition for postbankruptcy consideration; or

3. The transfer was a real property transfer that was recorded before the bankruptcy was noted in the real property records.

1. Authorized Transfers

The first of the three situations in which a transferee is entitled to retain property of the estate transferred by the debtor after the bankruptcy filing is the easiest to understand and apply. Obviously, a postbankruptcy transfer will be effective against the bankruptcy trustee if the transfer was authorized by the Bankruptcy Code or the bankruptcy court. See section 549(a)(2)(B). Most of the postbankruptcy transfers by a Chapter 11 debtor will be authorized under section 363.

2. Gap Transfers

Second, section 549(b) validates transfers by the debtor that occur after the filing of an *involuntary* bankruptcy petition and before the order for relief to the extent that the transferee gave value to the debtor after the filing of the bankruptcy petition. To illustrate:

Example: On February 22, *D*'s creditors file an involuntary petition. On February 25, *D* sells her boat to *X* for $30,000. The trustee may *not* recover the boat from *X*. *X* is protected by section 549(b).

Example: Same facts, except that *X* knew of the involuntary petition. Same result. Section 549(b) protects postpetition transfers "notwithstanding any notice or knowledge of the case that the transferee has."

Example: On January 10, *C* lends *D* $30,000. On February 2, *D*'s creditors file an involuntary petition. On February 15, *D* transfers his boat to *C* in satisfaction of the January 10 debt. The trustee can recover the boat from *C*. The boat was transferred to satisfy a debt that arose before the petition. The transferee did not give value to the debtor after the filing of the bankruptcy petition. The transferee is not protected by section 549(b).

Example: On April 4, the creditors of *D* file an involuntary petition. On April 14, *D* sells Greenacre to *Y* for $40,000. The trustee may not recover Greenacre from *Y*. Section 549(b) protects transferees of both personalty and realty.

3. Recorded Real Estate Transfers

Third, section 549(c) protects postpetition transfers of *realty* from trustee avoidance. A transfer of real property by the debtor after the filing of a voluntary petition or after an order for relief in an involuntary case will be effective against the bankruptcy trustee if:

1. The transfer occurs and is properly recorded before a copy of the bankruptcy petition is filed in the real estate records for the county where the land is located, and

2. The transferee is a buyer or lienor for fair equivalent value without knowledge of the petition.

Consider the following hypothetical illustrating the operation of section 549(c):

Example: On February 2, *B* files a voluntary petition. On February 3, *B* sells land in White County to *Y* for $10,000, the "fair equivalent value" of the land. *Y* has no "knowledge of the commencement of the case." *Y* properly files the transfer in the White County real estate records on February 4. A copy of the bankruptcy petition is filed in the real estate records for White County on February 5. The trustee *cannot* avoid the transfer. *Y* is protected by section 549(c).

There is no personal property counterpart of section 549(c). Personal property of the debtor transferred by the debtor after the filing of a voluntary petition can be recovered from the transferee unless the transfer was authorized by the Bankruptcy Code or by the bankruptcy court.

D. How Does Section 542 Affect Postbankruptcy Transfers of Property of the Estate by Third Parties?

Some postpetition transfers of property of the estate are made by persons holding property of the debtor, not the debtor.

Example: For example, on January 15, *D* files a voluntary bankruptcy petition. As of that date, *D* has $30,000 in her checking account at *B* Bank. This checking account becomes property of the estate on January 15. On January 17, *B* Bank honors a $5,000 check issued by *D* to *X* on January 13 and charges *D*'s account. Can *D*'s bankruptcy trustee recover the $5,000 from *B* Bank? Bank of Marin v. England (1966) protected the bank under the Bankruptcy Act of 1898; section 542 protects the bank under the Bankruptcy Code.

Under section 542(c), a third party who in good faith transfers property of the estate after the filing of the petition is protected from the bankruptcy trustee if the third party had "neither notice nor actual knowledge of the commencement of the case." Accordingly, if *B* Bank has neither actual knowledge or notice of *D*'s petition, it will not be liable to the bankruptcy trustee.

Note that section 542(c) only protects *B* Bank, the party that transfers the property of the estate; it does not protect *X*, the transferee. The trustee has a right to recover the $5,000, property of the estate, from *X*. This is the point of the reference to section 542(c) in section 549(a)(2)(A). Even though section 542(c) protects the person who transfers property of the estate postpetition, section 549 empowers the trustee to recover the property from the transferee.

E. Review Questions

1. D files a Chapter 7 petition on January 5. D sells her boat to T on January 9 for $10,000. T knows of the bankruptcy filing. Can the trustee recover the $10,000 from D?

2. Same facts as Question 1. Can the trustee recover the boat from T even if T did not know of D's bankruptcy?

3. D Furniture Store, Inc., D, files a Chapter 11 petition on April 5. On April 6, D sells furniture to T in the ordinary course of its business. A trustee is later appointed. Can the bankruptcy trustee recover the furniture from T under section 549? What if T knew of D's bankruptcy filing?

4. D has a bank account at X Bank. D issues a check to Y. D files for Chapter 7 relief. After the bankruptcy filing, the check clears, i.e., is paid by X Bank. What are the rights, if any, of the trustee?

5. On February 2, B files a voluntary petition. On February 3, B sells land in White County to Y for $10,000, the "fair equivalent value" of the land. Y has no "knowledge of the commencement of the case." Y properly files the transfer in the White County real estate records on February 4. A copy of the bankruptcy petition is filed in the real estate records for White County on February 5. Can the trustee avoid the transfer?

XIII

Effect of Bankruptcy on Secured Claims

■ *ANALYSIS*

E. **Postponement of Tax Liens in Chapter 7 Cases**
   1. If No Valid Tax Lien, Then Section 507
   2. If Valid Lien in Chapter 7, Then Section 724

F. **Review Questions**

A. What Is a Secured Claim?

The Bankruptcy Code deals with "claims," not creditors. Accordingly, under the Bankruptcy Code there will be creditors with secured claims, not secured creditors.

1. Meaning

A creditor has a secured claim if it holds a lien on or has a right of setoff against "property of the estate." The claim is secured only to the extent of the value of "such creditor's interest in the estate's interest in such property," section 506(a). "Such creditor's interest" becomes important if more than one creditor has a lien on the same property. The phrase "estate's interest" becomes important if the debtor is a co-owner or has an otherwise limited interest in the encumbered property. To illustrate:

Example: *D* owes *X* $100,000 and *Y* $200,000. Both *X* and *Y* have mortgages on *D*'s building. *X*'s mortgage has priority over *Y*'s under state law. *D* files for bankruptcy. The building has a value of $160,000. Under these facts, *X* would have a $100,000 secured claim; *Y* would have a secured claim of $60,000 and an unsecured claim of $140,000.

Example: Same facts, except that *D* only has a 50% ownership interest in the $160,000 building. Under these facts, *X* would have an $80,000 secured claim and a $20,000 unsecured claim. *Y* would have a $200,000 unsecured claim.

Example: *J* obtains a $2,000 judgment against *D* and causes the sheriff to execute on personal property belonging to *D*. The personal property subject to *J*'s execution lien has a value of $800. *J* has a $800 secured claim and a $1,200 unsecured claim.

Example: *D* owes *B* Bank $30,000 on an unsecured loan. *D* has $9,000 on deposit in *B* Bank. *B* Bank has a $9,000 secured claim and a $21,000 unsecured claim.

The answer to the last example assumes that *B* Bank has a right of setoff under state law. The answers to the other three examples assume that the liens are valid in bankruptcy.

2. Valuation

All of the examples assume the value of the collateral. In law school hypothetical problems, the teacher gets to decide what the value of the collateral is. "Real lawyers" do not enjoy that luxury. The question of the value of the collateral is a difficult and important one. The Bankruptcy Code does not provide a method for valuing collateral. Section 506(a) states that value is to be determined by the court on a case by case basis in light of the purpose of the valuation and of the proposed disposition of the property.

a. The Rash Case—Replacement Value

The leading case on determining the value of a secured creditor's collateral for purposes of section 506(a) is the Supreme Court's decision in Associates Commercial Corp. v. Rash (1997). *Rash* is a Chapter 13 case in which the debtor wanted to retain his tractor truck and pay off the secured claim under the plan. In setting the amount of that secured claim, the debtor looked to the foreclosure value of the truck. The holder of the secured claim objected, contending that the replacement value of the truck should determine the amount of the secured claim.

The Court looked to the phrase "disposition or use" in section 506 and looked to the "disposition or use' in the debtor's Chapter 13 plan. Since the debtor's plan proposed that he retain the truck rather than the secured creditor foreclose on the truck, the Court concluded that the "value of the property retained * * * is the cost the debtor would incur to obtain a like asset.'

Note that *Rash* does not hold that replacement value is always the appropriate way of measuring the secured claim. The Rash opinion repeatedly emphasizes the section 506 phrase "disposition or use" and the Rash fact that the debtor was using a Chapter 13 "cramdown" to retain the tractor truck.

b. Foreclosure Value Sometimes Used

Section 506(a)(2), like *Rash*, looks to replacement value in determining the amount of the secured claim. Unlike *Rash*, section 506(a)(2) only applies if the following three factual requirements are met:

1. The debtor must be an individual; and

2. The encumbered property must be personal property; and

3. The case must be a Chapter 7 case or a Chapter 13 case.

While the *Rash* facts meet these three requirements, the *Rash* rule is not limited to cases with these three factual requirements.

B. Invalidation of Liens

Some liens that are valid outside of bankruptcy can be invalidated in a bankruptcy case. Section 522(f) considered supra, empowers the debtor to invalidate certain liens on certain exempt property. Sections 544, 545, 547, 548 and 549, considered supra, empower the bankruptcy trustee to invalidate certain transfers that create liens.

Example: Assume that S lends D $10,000 and obtains a security interest in D's inventory. S does not file a financing statement or otherwise perfect its security interest. Under section 9–201, this unperfected security interest is effective between S and D and is effective against most third parties. For example, S's right to D's inventory is superior to the rights of any of D's unsecured creditors. If, however, D files a bankruptcy petition, S's unperfected security interest may be invalidated by the trustee under section 544(a) so that S will simply have an unsecured claim for $10,000. (Section 544(a) gives the bankruptcy trustee the rights and powers of a creditor who obtains a judicial lien at the time the bankruptcy petition was filed. At the time the bankruptcy petition was filed, S's security interest was unperfected. An unperfected security interest is ineffective as against a creditor with a judicial lien, UCC § 9–317. Accordingly, S's unperfected security interest is ineffective as against the bankruptcy trustee.)

Note the effect of lien invalidation. All that is eliminated is the lien. The creditor's claim remains. Lien invalidation converts a secured claim into an unsecured claim.

C. What Can Happen to Secured Claims During Bankruptcy?

Most liens cannot be avoided under sections 522(f), 544, 545, 547, 548 or 549. What effect does bankruptcy have on a creditor that holds a valid in bankruptcy lien? This question is particularly important in Chapter 11 cases and Chapter 13 cases for two reasons:

1. A Chapter 11 or Chapter 13 case often lasts three years or more;

2. In Chapter 13 cases and in most Chapter 11 cases, the debtor remains in possession of encumbered property.

1. Delay in Realizing on Collateral

Recall that the automatic stay of section 362 prevents a creditor from enforcing its lien against property of the estate or property of the debtor. Accordingly, a creditor will not be able to sell or even seize encumbered property from a debtor who is in bankruptcy without obtaining relief from the automatic stay.

2. Debtor's Use, Lease or Sale of Collateral

Not only does the Bankruptcy Code bar the secured creditor from recovering its collateral, the Bankruptcy Code also empowers the debtor to continue using the collateral. More specifically, section 363 provides for continued use, lease, or sale of encumbered property during bankruptcy. The lien holder is protected by section 363's adequate protection requirements. Section 363 is considered infra.

3. Nonaccrual of Interest

Recall that generally the amount of a claim is fixed by the amount that is owed at the date of the filing of the petition. If D borrows $10,000 from C at 10% and then files for bankruptcy, section 502 limits the amount of C's claim in bankruptcy to the unpaid loan balance and the interest accrued "as of the date of the filing of the petition." Interest that has not accrued ("matured") as of the date of the filing of the petition is not allowable as part of C's claim in the bankruptcy case, section 502(b)(2).

The rule that the creditor does not earn interest after the bankruptcy petition is filed also applies to secured creditors with one exception. Section 506(b) provides for postpetition interest for oversecured creditors. If, and only if, the amount that is owed on a secured claim is less than the value of the collateral securing the claim, "to the holder of such claim, interest on such claim."

Test your understanding of the above two paragraphs with the two problems below:

Example: D borrows $10,000 from S at 10% interest. The note is secured by a first mortgage on Whiteacre. D files for bankruptcy. As of the time of the filing of the bankruptcy case, D owes S $10,000 plus $222 in accrued unpaid interest, and Whiteacre is worth $8,000. D will have a $8,000 secured claim and $222 unsecured claim. No additional claim for postpetition interest.

Example: Same facts, except that Whiteacre is worth $13,000. D will have a $10,222 secured claim that will increase as interest accrues.

While section 506(b) provides for interest on over-secured claims, it does not provide an interest rate. The reported cases are divided as to the appropriate rate of interest under section 506(b).

4. Loss of Priority

Section 364(d) empowers the bankruptcy court to approve the debtor's granting a postpetition creditor a lien on encumbered property that has priority over all prepetition liens.

Example: F makes a $600,000 construction loan to D and obtains and records a first mortgage on the project. D is unable to complete the building with the $600,000 provided by F. D is unable to obtain additional financing. D is able to file for Chapter 11. S is willing to loan D the $200,000 needed to finish the building if its mortgage has priority over F's. Under section 364(d), the bankruptcy court can authorize D's granting S, the later-in-time postpetition lender, a lien that has priority over F's.

Section 364(d) imposes three requirements on the granting of such a "super-priority":

1. There must be "notice and a hearing,"

2. The debtor in possession or trustee is unable to obtain credit otherwise, and

3. The holder of the prepetition lien is adequately protected.

Think about the third requirement. If you understand the third requirement, you will understand why prepetition creditors such as *F* are generally successful in opposing court approval of a section 364(d) priming lien for a postpetition creditor such as *S*. *F* can (and usually will) argue that if having a second mortgage is so damn adequate, why does *S* insists that it be given this extraordinary first mortgage.

5. Limitations on Floating Liens

a. Section 552(a) Sinks Floating Liens

In commercial credit transactions, security agreements usually provide that the collateral includes property that the debtor later acquires. Such after-acquired property clauses are expressly permitted by section 9–204 of the UCC; such after-acquired property clauses are expressly cut off in bankruptcy by section 552(a).

The following example illustrates the operation of section 552(a):

Example: On January 10, *S* extends credit to *D* and obtains and perfects a security interest in all of *D*'s inventory, now owned or later acquired. On March 3, *D* acquires additional inventory. On March 4, *D* files a Chapter 11 petition and continues operating its business. On April 7, *D* acquires additional inventory.

In bankruptcy, *S*'s claim would be secured by the January 10 inventory and by the March 3 inventory. It would not be secured by the April 7 inventory. (Section 552(a) thus needs to be read together with section 506. Section 552(a) has the effect of limiting a section 506 secured claim.) Section 552(a) states that a security agreement entered into before the commencement of the case does not reach property acquired after the commencement of the case except as provided in section 552(b).

b. Except for Proceeds

Section 552(b) generally permits a prepetition lien to reach proceeds and other specified forms of earnings from and product of prepetition collateral. If in the above example *D* sold inventory on March 5, the "proceeds" from this postpetition sale of prepetition collateral would be subject to *S*'s security interest. Similarly, if *X* had a prepetition lien on *Y*'s apartment buildings and the rents therefrom, *X*'s lien would reach the postpetition rents as "profits of such property."

While the Bankruptcy Code provides that the secured claim in bankruptcy includes postpetition proceeds, the Bankruptcy Code does not provide a definition of the term "proceeds." Obviously, the term "proceeds" in section 552(b) is a term in a federal statute and so its definition is a matter of federal law. Nonetheless, courts have generally looked to state law, more specifically to Article 9 of the Uniform Commercial Code, to determine what constitutes "proceeds." The 2001 revision of Article 9 expands significantly the definition of "proceeds" as used in section 9–609(b), section 9–102(64). This change in state law may effect a change in federal bankruptcy law, that is, may expand the definition of "proceeds" as used in section 552(b). (Or it may result in greater use of the qualifying language at the end of section 552(b): "except to the extent that the court * * * based on the equities of the case, orders otherwise.")

6. Return of Repossessed Property

Section 542(a) compels the holder of a secured claim that has taken possession of its collateral prior to bankruptcy to return it to the debtor when she files a bankruptcy petition. Assume, for example, that *S* extended credit to *D* and obtained and perfected a security interest in *D*'s inventory. *D* defaulted. S repossessed the inventory. *D* then filed for Chapter 11 relief. Reading section 362(a)(4) should leave you convinced that *S* cannot sell the inventory without obtaining relief from the stay. Reading section 542 should leave you confused.

a. Return What?

Section 542(a) compels the turnover of "property that the trustee may use, sell, or lease under section 363—unless such property is of inconsequential value or benefit to the estate." What is the antecedent of the pronoun "such"? If it is "property that the trustee may use, sell, or lease under section 363," then it is necessary to look at section 363. Section 363 provides for the use, sale, or lease of "property of the estate." (Section 363's use of the term "property of the estate" is probably misleading. Section 363 does more than just authorize the use, sale, or lease of property of the estate, i.e., the debtor's interest in property. Instead, section 363 authorizes the use, sale, or lease of property in which the debtor has an interest.) It is thus necessary to look at section 541 which describes property of the estate in terms of the "interest of the debtor in property." What is the interest of the debtor in inventory that has been repossessed? A right of redemption under section 9–506? A right to any surplus produced by a forced sale under 9–504? Are these rights of "inconsequential value" for purposes of section 542?

b. Whiting Pools Case

The Supreme Court worked through these questions in United States v. Whiting Pools, Inc. (1983), and concluded that section 542 requires that a creditor that seized its collateral prior to bankruptcy turn over the property to a Chapter 11 debtor. *Whiting Pools* involved a seizure by the IRS of property subject to a tax lien. It seems clear from dicta in *Whiting Pools* that the Court would reach a similar result if a private creditor seized property subject to its security interest, and most courts have so held.

7. Effect of Discharge on Secured Claims

Most individuals and many businesses that file voluntary bankruptcy petitions expect to receive a bankruptcy discharge. Discharge is considered in Chapter XVI supra.

A bankruptcy discharge simply relieves the debtor from any further personal liability for the debts covered by the discharge. A bankruptcy discharge does not wipe out the debts: the ability of creditors to look to other parties such as guarantors and insurers is unaffected. And, a bankruptcy discharge does not wipe out liens: the ability of secured creditors to look to their collateral is unaffected.

Example: Assume that *D* owes *M* $100,000 and *M* has a mortgage on *D's* house. *D* is in default on her mortgage obligations. *D* files for bankruptcy and receives a discharge. The discharge means that *M* is barred from attempting to collect the $100,000 from *D* personally. The discharge does not mean that *M* is barred from enforcing its lien by seizing and selling its collateral, *D's* house.

Example: What if the foreclosure sale of *D's* house only results in net proceeds of $70,000? The discharge would then preclude *M* from taking actions or acts to collect the $30,000 deficiency from *D*, section 524(a).

D.   Satisfaction of Secured Claims

1.   Recovery of Collateral

If the holder of a secured claim recovers its collateral, the secured claim is extinguished. Assume, for example, that D owes S $22,000 and S has a security interest on equipment worth $10,000. D files a Chapter 7 bankruptcy petition. If the trustee turns over the equipment to S, S no longer has a secured claim. S still has a $12,000 claim, but the claim is an unsecured claim.

Chapters 7, 11 and 13 all permit satisfaction of a secured claim by surrender of the collateral. Neither Chapter 7, nor Chapter 11, nor Chapter 13 requires the satisfaction of a secured claim by surrender of the collateral.

A holder of a secured claim can recover its collateral by obtaining relief from the stay under section 362(d) and foreclosing on its lien. A Chapter 7 trustee can voluntarily turn over encumbered property to a lien holder under section 725. Similarly, a plan of reorganization under Chapter 11, 12 or 13 can provide for the surrender of encumbered property to the lien holder.

A holder of a secured claim cannot recover its collateral by abandonment. Section 554 permits a bankruptcy trustee to abandon any property that is burdensome to the estate or of inconsequential value to the estate.

Example: Assume that James Kirk, *K*, files a Chapter 7 petition. Mr. Spock is appointed trustee. *K* owes Federation Bank, *F*, $100,000. *F* has a properly perfected security interest in *K*'s ship. The ship has a value of $80,000. Because the amount of *F*'s secured claim is greater than the value of the ship, the ship is of inconsequential value to the estate. Thus, Spock can abandon the ship to Kirk, the debtor.

Courts have looked to legislative history to hold that encumbered property must be abandoned to the debtor, not to a creditor with a lien on the property. If Spock abandons the ship to *K*, *K* can then release the ship to *F*.

2. Payment of Amount Equal to the Value of the Collateral in Chapter 7 and Chapter 11 Cases

If the holder of a secured claim does not recover its collateral, it should receive a payment equal to the value of the collateral.

a. Chapter 7

In a Chapter 7 case, this payment can come from the trustee's sale of the collateral, or this payment can come from the debtor.

1) Payment from Trustee's Sale

In certain limited situations, the trustee has the power to sell encumbered property free and clear of all liens and pay holders of secured claims with the proceeds from such sales. See section 363(f).

Example: Mr. Spock can sell *K*'s ship free and clear if the sale yields more than *F*'s $100,000 secured claim, section 363(f)(3). The proceeds of any such sale will first be used to cover the costs of the sale; the first $100,000 of net proceeds will be used to pay *F*.

2) Payment from Postpetition Money

And, in certain limited situations, the Chapter 7 debtor will want to pay holders of secured claims from postpetition borrowings and/or earnings. Recall that (i) most of the debtor's interests in property as of the date of the filing of the bankruptcy petition becomes property of the estate, (ii) the debtor can retain property that is either exempt under section 522 or abandoned to him, and (iii) if such property is encumbered by liens, the liens remain enforceable after a discharge. Accordingly, if Kirk's ship is exempt property, *K* keeps the $80,000 ship and *F* keeps its lien on the ship. Because *F* retains its lien notwithstanding the discharge, *K* may be willing to pay *F* from postpetition earnings or borrowings in order to retain the ship. If so, K should look to section 524 reaffirmation agreement and section 722 redemption.

a) Reaffirmation

Paragraphs (c) and (d) of section 524 deal with reaffirmation agreements. [This book deals with section 524(c) and 524(d) in Chapter XVII.] A reaffirmation agreement is a postbankruptcy agreement for the repayment of a prebankruptcy debt. For example, K and F might agree that K will pay F X dollars over Y months.

Note that section 524 does not require the payment of any particular amount. Note also that section 524 does require an agreement: the debtor and creditor must agree as to the amount that is to be paid and other terms.

b) Redemption

Section 722, on the other hand, does not require any agreement, but does require the payment of a particular amount. Section 722 empowers Chapter 7 debtors to extinguish liens on certain property by paying the holder of the secured claim an amount equal to the "amount of the allowed secured claim," i.e., an amount measured by the value of the collateral not the amount of the debt. If section 722 applies to the Kirk/Federation loan, K can extinguish F's lien by paying F $80,000 in cash. Note that section 722 would apply to the Federation lien only if (1) the ship was "intended for personal, family, or household use" (i.e., not an enterprise), (2) the debt was a "dischargeable consumer debt," and (3) the ship had been exempted or abandoned.

Think through the Kirk example again. Particularly the payment of $80,000 in cash.

Under the last clause of section 722, the amount of the section 722 redemption payment depends on the "amount of the allowed secured claim." Under the first sentence of section 506(a), the amount of the allowed secured claim depends on the value of the collateral. And, under 506(a)(2), added in 2005, that depends on the replacement price.

c) Comparison of Sections 524 and 722

The following chart compares the debtor's payment of a secured claim under section 524 with the debtor's payment of a secured claim under section 722.

	524	722
1. Reason for debtor's payment	Prevent holder of secured claim from selling property exempted by or abandoned to the debtor	Prevent holder of secured claim from selling property exempted by or abandoned to the debtor
2. Amount of payment	Determined by agreement between debtor and creditor	Determined by value of collateral, which is fixed at replacement value
3. Form of payment	Determined by agreement between debtor and creditor	Cash
4. Availability	a. Chapter 7, 11, 12 or 13	a. Chapter 7 only
	b. All kinds of collateral	b. Only collateral that is exempt or abandoned, only collateral that is tangible personal property, only collateral that is intended primarily for personal, family or household use

b. Chapters 11 and 13

What the holder of a secured claim receives in a Chapter 11 case (or a Chapter 13 case) depends on the provisions of the court approved plan; and the Bankruptcy Code sets some parameters on the plan provisions, as the follow example illustrates:

Example: *D* owes *S* $700,000, which is secured by a mortgage on Greenacre. The mortgage provides for a 10% interest rate and 36 equal monthly payments. *D's* Chapter 11 plan can modify *S's* contract rights. It can reduce the amount that *S* is to be paid, change the interest rate or the number of payments, and/or provide for payments in varying amounts.

1) Cram Down Explained

In some situations, the holder of the secured claim consents to these modifications. In other situations, the holder of the secured claim objects to the Chapter 11 plan's modifications of its rights. Notwithstanding such an objection, the court can still approve the plan. Lawyers, judges and law professors commonly call such court approval of a plan that changes a creditor's rights over that creditor's objection a "cram down" or a "cram down." And, so cram down (or cram down) needs to be a part of your bankruptcy vocabulary, even though the term does not appear in the Bankruptcy Code.

2) Limitations on Cram Down

Limitations on the cram down of a secured claim do appear in the Bankruptcy Code. And these limitations are so important that they appear three times in this book: (1) in the next few paragraphs of this chapter, (2) in the chapter on Chapter 11 and in the chapter on Chapter 13.

Section 1129(b)(2)(A)(i)(II) limits a bankruptcy court's confirmation of a cram down of a secured claim to a plan that provides for distributions to the holder of that claim that have a present value at least equal to the value of the collateral. By the way, the Bankruptcy Code provisions use the phrase "value as of the effective date of the plan" instead of the phrase "present value." And, the Bankruptcy Code uses the phrase "allowed amount of such claim" rather than the phrase "value of the collateral." The antecedent of the adjective "such" is "secured" claim; and, the amount of a secured claim is based on the "value of the collateral." Remember 506 and Rash earlier in this chapter.

Accordingly, a Chapter 11 cram down requires a court to answer two separate questions:

1. What is the amount of the value of the collateral?

2. How much more than that amount has to be paid if the amount is paid in installments over the life of the plan instead of in cash on the effective date of the plan, i.e., what is the cram down interest rate?

a) Value of the Collateral

The first question is answered in the second sentence of section 506(a), the Supreme Court's decision in *Rash* and an earlier part of this chapter. The Supreme Court later considered the second question in the *Till* case, which is discussed below.

Example: Assume again that *D* owes S $700,000, secured by a first mortgage on Greenacre. If, applying *Rash*, the court determines that the value of Greenacre is only $600,000, then $600,000 is the amount of S's secured claim. Or, as bankruptcy lawyers and judges put it, S's secured claim can be "stripped down' to $600,000. That $600,000 then becomes the amount by which the present value of the plan payments on the secured claim are to be measured.

b) Present Value of Plan Distributions

Obviously if D's Chapter 11 plan provides for a $600,000 cash payment to S on the effective date of the plan, that payment will meet the present value test. Obviously, most Chapter 11 plans provide for payments in installments. And, obviously, a plan provision for 60 monthly payments of $10,000 has a value significantly less than $600,000 in cash, right now. What is not obvious is how much more than $600,000 the debtor must pay under a plan that pays over 60 months, i.e., what is the cram down interest rate.

The Bankruptcy Code nowhere addresses this issue. The Supreme Court addressed the issue in Till v. SCS Credit Corp. (2004) and adopted a "formula approach": "The approach begins by looking at the national prime rate . . . . Because bankrupt debtors typically pose a greater risk of nonpayment than solvent commercial borrowers, the approach then requires the bankruptcy court to adjust the prime rate accordingly." The appropriate risk adjustment, of course, is an issue for litigation.

3) Distinguish Paying Interest on Over–Secured Claims

You can't confuse cram down "interest" under section 1129 (and section 1325) with interest on oversecured claims under section 506. The following hypothetical and then the chart should help you see the differences in the two.

Example: In January of 2005, D borrows $10,000 from C and offers to pay 10% interest on the debt until it is repaid. D grants C a mortgage on Blueacre. In February 2006, D files a Chapter 11 petition. At the time of the bankruptcy filing, D owes C $12,000 in principal and unpaid, accrued interest, and Blueacre has a value of $8,000. Accordingly, C has an $8,000 secured claim and a $4,000 unsecured claim, section 506(a).

D's Chapter 11 plan is confirmed in March 2007. C's $8,000 secured claim does not accrue interest from the date of bankruptcy filing in February 2006 until the time of confirmation in March 2007. Only a claim that is fully secured draws interest from the time of the filing of the petition to the date of confirmation of the plan, section 506(b). C's $8,000 secured claim will, however, draw interest from the time of confirmation of the plan until it is fully satisfied. It is not clear whether this interest will be 10% or some other rate.

To summarize, (1) only a claim that is fully secured will draw interest from the time of the bankruptcy filing until the confirmation of a plan; and (2) any claim that is paid in installments will draw interest from the time of the confirmation of the plan until the time of the last plan payment.

4) Comparison of Paying Interest on Over–Secured Claims and Calculating Cram Down Interest

	506(b)	1129(b)(2)(A)(i)(II) and 1325(a)(5)(B)(ii)
Which chapter?	Applies in all cases—Chapter 7, 11, 12, 13	Not Chapter 7
Which secured claims?	Applies only to over-secured claims, i.e., amount of debt is less than value of collateral	All secured claims
When?	Interest from the time of the petition to the time of the Chapter 7 distribution or the time of confirmation of the Chapter 11 or Chapter 13 plan	Interest from the time of the confirmation of the Chapter 11 or Chapter 13 plan through the entire period of plan payments

3. Payment of the Debt in Full in Chapter 13 Cases and Chapter 11 Cases With Individual Debtors

In Chapter 13 cases, like Chapter 11 cases, the payments on a secured claim are determined by a court-approved plan.

a. Chapter 13 Differences

In Chapter 13, unlike Chapter 11, the debtor's ability to cram down changes on secured claims is severely limited.

1. For claims secured by purchase money security interests in motor vehicles the debtor purchased within 910 days of bankruptcy, changes in number of payments, interest rate, and amount of each payment can be imposed (i.e., crammed down) on a creditor with a secured claim. The Chapter 13 plan cannot, however, change the total amount to be paid—cannot strip down the secured debt to the value of the collateral under section 506.

2. Similarly, for all secured debt incurred within one year of bankruptcy, changes in the number of payments, interest rate, and amount of each payment can be imposed (i.e., crammed down) on a creditor with a secured claim. The Chapter 13 plan cannot, however, change the total amount to be paid—cannot strip down the secured debt to the value of the collateral under section 506.

3. And for claims secured "only by a security interest in real property that is the debtor's principal residence" (i.e., home mortgages), no cram down at all is allowed—no court-approved changes in the number of payments, interest rate, or any other terms.

b. Chapter 11 Comparison

Chapter 11 cases involving individuals, in many respects, look more like Chapter 13 cases than like Chapter 11 cases. For example, an individual debtor cannot use Chapter 11 or Chapter 13 to cram down changes in her home mortgage obligations. Section 1123(b)(5).

Chapter 11 cases involving individuals are not, however, identical to Chapter 13 cases in all respects. For example, an individual debtor could use Chapter 11 but not Chapter 13 to cram down changes in a loan secured by her automobile. However, for reasons discussed later, it is highly unlikely that an individual debtor who meets the debt limits of Chapter 13 would choose to file Chapter 11 just to force changes in her car loan.

E. Postponement of Tax Liens in Chapter 7 Cases

1. If No Valid Tax Lien, Then Section 507

A government's claim for taxes is usually secured by a statutory lien. Such a statutory lien will not always be valid in bankruptcy. For example, an unfiled federal tax lien can be avoided by the trustee under section 544(a). An unfiled federal tax lien is not valid as against a creditor with a judicial lien, IRC 6323(a). Section 544(a) gives the bankruptcy trustee the rights and powers of a creditor that obtained a judicial lien as of the date of the bankruptcy filing. Accordingly, if the federal tax lien had not been filed prior to bankruptcy, the bankruptcy trustee can invalidate the tax lien under section 544(a). Section 544(a) is considered supra.

If the government has not obtained a tax lien prior to bankruptcy or if the tax lien has been avoided under section 544, the tax claim will be an unsecured claim. Such an unsecured claim is governed by section 507, not section 724.

2. If Valid Lien in Chapter 7, Then Section 724

Section 724 only applies if (1) the case is a Chapter 7n case, (2) the tax claim is a claim for taxes other than ad valorem property taxes, (3) the tax claim is secured by a valid in bankruptcy tax lien, and (4) the trustee has not been able to satisfy section 507(a)(1) to (7) propriety claims for assets of the estate not encumbered by the tax lien. When applicable, section 724 is an exception to the general rule that proceeds from the sale of encumbered property should be used to pay claims secured by that property before being used to pay section 507 priority claims. Section 724 postpones the payment of a secured tax claim until the complete payment of most section 507(a)(1) to (a)(7) priority claims.

F. Review Questions

1. D owes C $100,000. The debt is secured by a lien on property that D owns. D files bankruptcy. Does the bankruptcy filing cut off C's lien?

2. D owes C $100,000. The debt is secured by a lien on property that D owns. D files bankruptcy. C has a claim in the bankruptcy case. Is the claim a secured claim or an unsecured claim?

3. What is the test (e.g., replacement value, foreclosure value, etc.) for valuing collateral when calculating the amount of a secured claim?

4. T or F   D Corp. owes S $100,000. P, the president of D Corp., has guaranteed payment and has pledged her D Corp. stock to secure payment. D Corp. files a bankruptcy petition. If the pledged D Corp. stock is worth $65,000, S has a $65,000 secured claim.

5. D owed S $200,000 and had a security interest in D's equipment. On default, S repossessed the equipment and sold it to T. The sale completely complied

with the requirements of state law. One day after the sale, D filed a Chapter 11 petition. The debtor-in-possession needs the equipment to operate. Can the debtor-in-possession recover the equipment from T?

6. D owed S $200,000 and had a security interest in D's equipment, present and after-acquired. By terms of their security agreement, S's security interest would attach to any equipment that D in the future. This after-acquired property clause is effective under state law. D filed bankruptcy and acquired new equipment. Does S's security interest attach to the new equipment?

7. D owed S $200,000 and had a security interest in D's equipment. D filed bankruptcy and thereafter sold some of the equipment D owned before the bankruptcy case commenced. This equipment was subject to D's security interest before the filing and survived the filing. D used the money earned from selling the old equipment to buy new equipment. Does S have a security interest in the new equipment?

8. D owes C $20,000, which was secured by a security interest in D's widget. D filed bankruptcy. A discharge was granted. Can C sue D for the debt? Can C enforce her lien rights against D?

9. T or F   The trustee in bankruptcy can abandon encumbered property to the secured party.

10. T or F   The bankruptcy trustee can sell property free and clear of liens.

XIV

Claims

■ *ANALYSIS*

A. Why Is "Claim" an Important Bankruptcy Concept?
B. What Is a Claim? (and, Who Cares?)
C. What Is an Unsecured Claim?
D. Collection of Unsecured Claims From the Debtor
E. What Property Is Distributed to Holders of Unsecured Claims?
    1. What Property Is Distributed to Holders of Unsecured Claims in Chapter 7 Cases?
    2. What Property Is Distributed to Holders of Unsecured Claims in Chapter 12, Chapter 13, and Individual Chapter 11 Cases?
    3. What Property Is Distributed to Holders of Unsecured Claims in Other Chapter 11 Cases?
F. Which Holders of Unsecured Claims Are Eligible to Participate in the Bankruptcy Distribution?
    1. Proof of Claim
    2. Allowance
G. What Is the Order of Distribution?
    1. Treatment of Priority Claims in 7
    2. Treatment of Priority Claims in 11, 12, 13
    3. Section 507 Treatment of Priorities
    4. Section 510 Treatment of Subordination
    5. Classification of Claims
H. Review Questions

A. Why Is "Claim" an Important Bankruptcy Concept?

The word "claim" appears throughout the Bankruptcy Code, throughout a bankruptcy case. For example:

- An involuntary petition can be filed only by holders of claims;

- The automatic stay that is triggered by the filing of an involuntary or voluntary petition bars actions by holders of claims to collect on their claims from the debtor or property of the estate;

- A discharge bars further efforts by holders of claims to collect their claims from the debtor;

- Distributions in a Chapter 7 case are made to holders of claims;

- Payments under a Chapter 13 plan go to holders of claims; and

- Holders of claims vote on filed Chapter 11 plans and payments under an approved Chapter 11 plan go to holders of claims.

B. What Is a Claim? (and, Who Cares?)

The term "claim" is defined in section 101: "right to payment, whether or not such right is reduced to judgment, liquidated, unliquidated, fixed, contingent, matured, unmatured, disputed, undisputed, legal, equitable or unsecured." Both legislative history and case law describe the definition as an effort to be as comprehensive and inclusive as possible.

Example: *D*'s car runs into *C*. *C* contends that *D* was negligent and that her negligence caused *C* substantial damages. Before *C* files a law suit against *D*, *D* files for bankruptcy. Under these facts, *C* has a "claim" even though *D* disputes *C*'s allegations of negligence and even though the amount of any liability has not yet been liquidated.

Example: Similarly, on December 7, 2006, *D* borrows $666,666 from *C*. The loan provides for repayment on April 5, 2007. The loan also includes *X*'s guarantee of repayment if *D* fails to pay. *D* files for bankruptcy on January 15, 2007. Under these facts, *C* has a claim even though her right to payment had not yet matured. And *X* who would have a right of reimbursement from *D* if he has to pay the debt would also have a claim even though its right to payment was still contingent.

While the Bankruptcy Code concept of claim is comprehensive, there are two significant limitations on what is a claim. The first limitation is based on the language of section 101's definition of claim. "Claim" requires a right to payment. Obligations of the debtor that cannot be satisfied by payment are not within the definition of claim. This can be an issue in situations involving injunctions and specific performance.

Example: Assume that (i) *D* sells her business to *C* and, as part of the sale, contracts not to start a competing business for 5 years, (ii) under state law, *C* could enjoin *D* from opening a competing business, (iii) *D* files for bankruptcy a year later, and (iv) it appears that *D*'s creditors will only receive 25% on their claims. Under these facts, *C* might contend that her right to enforce the covenant to compete through injunction is not a "right to payment" and so is not a section 101(5) "claim" and so is not affected by the discharge which protects the debtor from any further personal liability on claims. Most courts have dealt with this contention by looking to state law to determine whether *C* could be compelled to take a money judgment instead of injunctive relief, that is, whether, in the language of section 101(5), *C* has a "right to payment."

The second limitation on what is a claim—timing—is not based on the language of section 101(5) but rather the language of various court decisions. In Epstein v. Official Committee of Unsecured Creditors of Piper Aircraft Corp. (1995), for example, the issue was whether a portion of the amount received from the sale of Piper Aircraft Corp. had to be held in trust for the people injured from plane crashes that occurred after the bankruptcy because of a defect in debtor's design or manufacture that occurred before the bankruptcy.

This timing issue has arisen with respect both to products liability matters and environmental cases. The cases differ as to whether future, unknown and unidentifiable victims of a prebankruptcy act of the debtor have section 101(5) claims. And, in different cases, lawyers for different parties are contending that these "future claimants" have a section 101(5) claim. If, for example, the debtor company is liquidating in Chapter 7 or is selling all of its assets in a Chapter 11 sale that provides protection for the purchaser from successor liability, then the lawyer representing the future claimants is likely to argue that her clients have section 101(5) claims and so should share in the sale proceeds. Epstein v. Official Committee of Unsecured Creditors of Piper Aircraft Corp. (1995). That same lawyer will make the different argument that her future claimant clients do not have a section 101(5) claim and so should not be subject to the discharge which only affects claims if the debtor company is reorganizing in Chapter 11 and that lawyer and her financial adviser are optimistic about the debtor company's ability to make meaningful payments from postbankruptcy earnings.

C. What Is an Unsecured Claim?

A claim is unsecured if the creditor has not obtained a consensual, judicial, or statutory lien or if the value of the property subject to the lien is less than the amount of the creditor's claim. Consider the following examples of unsecured claims:

Example: *D* buys her airline tickets using her American Express and *D* files a bankruptcy petition. At the time of the bankruptcy petition, *D* owes American Express $1,000 for airline tickets. American Express has an unsecured claim.

Example: *D* Corp. borrows $2,000,000 from *C* and grants *C* a mortgage on Redacre. At the time of *D* Corp.'s bankruptcy it still owes *C* $2,000,000 and the encumbered property has a value of $800,000. *S* is a creditor with a $1,200,000 unsecured claim. [*S* is also a creditor with a $800,000 secured claim.] (The rights of holders of secured claims are considered *supra* in Chapter XIII.)

D. Collection of Unsecured Claims From the Debtor

Under section 362, the filing of a Chapter 7 petition operates as a "stay." This automatic stay prevents a creditor from collecting its unsecured claim from the debtor until the bankruptcy case is closed. The automatic stay and relief therefrom are considered earlier.

Under section 727, the bankruptcy court generally grants the debtor a "discharge." This discharge prevents a creditor from collecting its claim from the debtor after the bankruptcy case is closed. The discharge and exceptions thereto are considered later.

The section 362 stay coupled with the section 727 discharge makes it necessary for most holders of unsecured claims to look to the "property of the estate" for the satisfaction of their claims.

Now that we know:

1. What an unsecured claim is, and that

2. The automatic stay generally precludes collection of unsecured claims from the debtor during the bankruptcy case, and that

3. The discharge generally bars collection of unsecured claims from the debtor after the bankruptcy case, we need to determine how to collect on unsecured claims in a Chapter 7 bankruptcy case.

It thus becomes necessary to learn:

1. What property is distributed to unsecured claims, and

2. Which holders of unsecured claims are eligible to participate in the distribution of this property, and

3. What is the order of distribution, i.e., which claims are paid first.

E. What Property Is Distributed to Holders of Unsecured Claims?

1. What Property Is Distributed to Holders of Unsecured Claims in Chapter 7 Cases?

The bankruptcy trustee has a statutory duty to sell the "property of the estate," section 704(1). The net proceeds received from the liquidation of the "property of the estate" are to be distributed to the holders of unsecured or general claims. Such claimants do not, however, receive the net proceeds from the sale of all of the "property of the estate":

- Some "property of the estate" will be turned over to the debtor as exempt property, section 522.

- Some "property of the estate" will be validly transferred after the filing of the bankruptcy petition to third parties, section 549.

- Some "property of the estate" will be subject to liens that are valid in bankruptcy. Encumbered property or the proceeds thereof must be first used to satisfy the holders of secured claims, cf. section 725.

- Some "property of the estate" must be used to satisfy the administrative expenses of the bankruptcy proceeding.

Subject to these four exceptions, holders of unsecured or general claims in Chapter 7 cases receive the net proceeds from the bankruptcy trustee's sale of the "property of the estate." The great majority of Chapter 7 cases are "no asset" cases, at least in the sense that there are no assets available to pay unsecured claims.

2. What Property Is Distributed to Holders of Unsecured Claims in Chapter 12, Chapter 13, and Individual Chapter 11 Cases?

In Chapter 12 cases and Chapter 13 cases, the plan controls the payment to holders of unsecured claims. Only the debtor can file the plan.

Section 1222 governs the contents of a Chapter 12 plan; section 1322 governs the contents of a chapter 13 plan. The two sections are markedly similar; in both sections, paragraph (a) governs what the plan *must* provide; paragraph (b) governs what the plan *may* provide.

In Chapter 12 cases and in Chapter 13 cases, creditors do not vote on the plan. Both chapters require the bankruptcy judge to confirm (approve) the plan, and creditors may object to the confirmation. Section 1225 and section 1325 set out the standards for confirmation of a plan. Please read sections 1225 and 1325. Especially 1225(b) and 1325(b). Note that in Chapters 12 and 13, the debtor must commit all "disposable income" to the repayment plan.

Since the 2005 amendments, there is a similar disposable income requirement commitment for individual debtors in Chapter 11 cases. Unless no holder of an unsecured claim objects, an individual debtor's Chapter 11 plan must have a minimum payment from the debtor measured by five years of disposable income. Section 1129(a)(15).

3. What Property Is Distributed to Holders of Unsecured Claims in Other Chapter 11 Cases?

In Chapter 11 cases, like Chapter 12 and 13 cases, the plan controls the payment to holders of unsecured claims. Chapter 11's treatment of holders of unsecured claims is significantly different from Chapter 12 or 13's in that

- Chapter 11 does *not* require that all of the debtor's "disposable income" be used to make payments under the plan.

- In Chapter 11, the holders of unsecured claims can file a plan, section 1121(c);

- In Chapter 11, holders of unsecured claims vote on the proposed plan. If the requisite majorities fail to vote for (accept) a plan, the standards for court approval (confirmation) are more onerous, cf. section 1129(a) and 1129(b).

The formulation, acceptance, and confirmation of Chapter 11 plans are considered later.

F. Which Holders of Unsecured Claims Are Eligible to Participate in the Bankruptcy Distribution?

1. Proof of Claim

The debtor will file a list of creditors, section 521. The court will then send notice of the bankruptcy case to the listed creditors, section 342. The creditors that wish to participate in the distribution of the proceeds of the liquidation of the "property of the estate" must file a proof of claim, sections 501, 726. In Chapter 11 cases, a creditor is required to file a proof of claim only if its claim is scheduled as disputed, contingent, or unliquidated, section 1111(a); Rule 3003(b)(1).

a. Bankruptcy Rules Govern Form

Most of the requirements as to form, content, and procedure for proofs of claim are found in the Bankruptcy Rules. For example, there is no statutory language governing the time for filing a proof of claim. Section 501 simply speaks of "timely filing." Rule 3002(c) governs the time for filing a proof of claim in a Chapter 7 case or a Chapter 13 case.

b. Debtor Filing for Creditors

Section 501(c) authorizes the debtor to file a proof of claim for a creditor who does not timely file. This provision is primarily intended to protect the debtor if the claim of the creditor is nondischargeable. When no proof of claim is filed, there will be no bankruptcy distribution to the holder of the claim. If no bankruptcy distribution is made to the holder of a claim excepted from discharge, the debtor will have to pay the claim in full after the bankruptcy case is closed. If, however, the debtor files a proof of claim, the holder of the nondischargeable claim will participate in the bankruptcy distribution and the postbankruptcy liability of the debtor to the creditor will be reduced by the amount of distribution.

Example: Assume that *D* files a Chapter 7 petition. He owes *C* $10,000. *C* made the loan to *D* because of a false financial statement; its claim against *D* is excepted from discharge. (Section 523(a)(2) excepts from discharge claims based on credit extended in reliance on a false financial statement. Section 523(a)(2) is considered infra.) If no proof of claim is filed by or for *C*, it will have a $10,000 claim against *D* after the close of the Chapter 7 case. If, however, *D* files a proof of claim for *C* Bank, its postbankruptcy claim against him will be reduced by the amount it receives in the bankruptcy distribution.

2. Allowance

In a Chapter 7 case, the proceeds of the liquidation of the property of the estate is not distributed to all holders of unsecured claims against the debtor. Rather, the distribution is only made to unsecured creditors whose claims are "allowed," section 502(a). The statute does not define "party in interest"; clearly, another creditor or the bankruptcy trustee is a "party in interest" for purposes of objections to allowance of a claim.

a.   Grounds for Disallowance in 502(b) and 502(d)

Section 502(b) sets out nine grounds for disallowing claims:

1.   If the claim is unenforceable against the debtor or the property of the debtor by reason of any agreement or applicable law, it will not be allowed, section 502(b)(1).

   [A nonrecourse loan is an example of an agreement which makes a claim unenforceable; UCC [00a7]2-302 is an example of a law which makes a claim unenforceable.]

2.   A claim for "unmatured" interest will be disallowed, section 502(b)(2).

   [Generally, interest stops accruing when a bankruptcy petition is filed. Only claims that are secured by collateral that has a value greater than the amount of the claim will accrue interest after the filing of a bankruptcy petition, section 506(b). Assume, for example, that D borrows $1,000 from C; the loan agreement provides for 14% interest. At the time of the bankruptcy filing, D owes $1,444. C's allowable claim will be $1,444; that amount will not continue to draw the 14% interest after the bankruptcy filing.]

3.   If a claim is for an ad valorem property tax, it will not be allowed to the extent that the claim exceeds the value of the estate's interest in the property, section 502(b)(3).

4.   If the claim is for services of debtor's attorney or an "insider," it will be disallowed to the extent the claim exceeds the reasonable value of such services, section 502(b)(4). 'Insider' is defined in section 101(28). 'Insider' includes the relatives of an individual debtor; the partners of a partnership debtor; and the officers, directors, and other control persons of a corporate debtor.

5.   If the claim is for postpetition alimony or child support, it will not be allowed, section 502(b)(5). These claims are excepted from discharge under section 523(a)(5). The following hypothetical illustrates the application of sections 502(b)(5) and 523(a)(5):

   Example: H and W are divorced in January 2005. The divorce decree orders H to pay alimony of $1,000 a month.

H files a bankruptcy petition on December 31, 2005. He owes W $2,000 for November and December alimony. W's claim for $2,000 of unpaid alimony is allowable. Section 502(b)(5) only disallows a claim for alimony that is "unmatured on the date of the filing of the petition." Accordingly, W's claim for postpetition alimony is disallowed.

If W's claim for $2,000 of unpaid 2005 alimony is not fully satisfied by the bankruptcy distribution, W may attempt to collect any deficiency from H personally. Section 523(a)(5) excepts alimony claims from the bankruptcy discharge. Accordingly, H's bankruptcy discharge will not affect W's right to collect postpetition alimony from H personally.

6. If the claim is that of a landlord for future rent, it will be limited to the greater of one year's payments or 15% of the payments for the balance of the lease, not to exceed three years' payments in total, section 502(b)(6).

Note that section 502(b)(6) only limits the allowance of claims for *future* rentals by a lessor of *real* property. It does not affect a claim for rentals due on or before the filing of the bankruptcy petition. It does not affect a claim for rentals under a lease of personal property. Also, section 502(b)(6) does not limit the amount of a claim for future rents of personal property. Section 547(e) suggests that the Bankruptcy Code considers "fixtures" to be real property. If so, section 502(b)(6) would apply to a claim by a lessor of equipment that was installed in such a manner as to become a fixture under state law.

Note also that section 502(b)(6) does not guarantee an allowable claim for back rent plus a minimum of one year's rent; rather, it places a ceiling on the allowance of rent claims.

Example: Assume, for example, that *D* rents a building from *C* and signs a 20–year lease at a monthly rental rate of $5,000. At the time that *D* files her bankruptcy petition, she owes *C* $10,000 in back rent. If *D* immediately rejects the lease and *C* then releases the building to *X* for $6,000 a month, *C*'s allowable claim will be limited to the $10,000 in back rent.

7.   Section 502(b)(7) imposes a similar limitation on the allowable claim for termination of an employment contract: no more than back wages due at the time of the bankruptcy filing and one year's future compensation.

8.   If the claim is a federal tax claim which arises because the state unemployment tax is paid late and so no federal tax credit is allowed, the federal claim will be treated the same as if the credit had been allowed in full in the federal return, which means the federal tax claim would be disallowed, section 502(b)(8).

9.   Section 502(b)(9) deals with disallowance of claims that are not timely filed. In reading and applying section 502(b)(9), law students and lawyers need to understand section 726 discussed later. Section 726 provides that late-filed claims will be paid in Chapter 7 but will be paid after claims that are timely filed. The reference to section 726 in section 502(b)(9) means that tardily filed claims will not be disallowed in a Chapter 7 case; instead their priority of distribution will be governed by section 726. Section 502(b)(9) will result in the disallowance of claims only in cases under Chapter 11, 12, or 13. Generally, the question of what constitutes a timely filing is left to the Rules; section 502(b)(9) does, however, give a governmental creditor at least 180 days from the order for relief for filing its claim.

Section 502(d) provides for the disallowance of a claim held by a creditor who received a voidable transfer and has not surrendered the property so transferred or its value.

Example: C's $100,000 claim can be disallowed under section 502(d) if the debtor had made a $2,000 fraudulent transfer to C that has not been turned over.

b.   Contingent Claims and 502(c) and 502(e)

With a limited exception, the fact that a claim is contingent or unliquidated at the time that the bankruptcy petition is filed does not affect its allowance. The court may either delay bankruptcy distribution until the claim is fixed in amount, or, if liquidation of the claim would "unduly delay the administration of the case," estimate the amount of the claim, section 502(c).

Example: V files a $100,000 tort suit against T. T immediately files a bankruptcy petition. V then files a proof of claim. V's claim is allowable. The court may either delay distribution to *T*'s creditors and the closing of *T*'s bankruptcy case until *V*'s tort claim has been litigated or estimate the amount of *V*'s claim. (28 USCA § 157(b)(2)(B) states that "estimation of contingent or unliquidated personal injury tort or wrongful death claims against the estate for the purposes of distribution" is not a "core proceeding.")

Section 502 does not dictate or even indicate how the bankruptcy court should estimate the claim. Most of the relatively few reported cases involve estimation of claims for the limited purpose of Chapter 11 plan voting. Cf. section 1126(c).

Section 502(e) provides for the disallowance of a claim for contribution or indemnity that is still contingent.

Example: Assume that D and X are both companies that "dumped waste' at the same site. The EPA investigates the site and notifies D and X that they are liable for cleanup costs. [Under the relevant law, CERCLA, the EPA can collect the cleanup costs from either or both. If the EPA collects the entire cleanup costs from X, then X has a right to contribution from D.] D immediately files for bankruptcy before the EPA takes any action. X's right of contribution, while contingent and unmatured, is a section 101(5) claim. But if X files a proof of claim, its claim will be disallowed under section 502(e). The rationale is that (i) since the EPA claim is allowable, then (ii) allowance of both the EPA claim and X's contingent contribution claim would result in the bankruptcy estate's paying twice for a single wrong.

c. Time of Claim

Generally, only claims that arise before the bankruptcy petition are allowable in Chapter 7 cases. If, for example, D files a voluntary bankruptcy petition on January 11, and C lends D $100 on February 2, C's claim is not allowable.

There are four exceptions to the rule that only claims that predate the bankruptcy petition are allowable in Chapter 7. (In Chapter 13 cases, certain postpetition taxes and consumer debts are allowable, section 1305(a).) The Chapter 7 exceptions are:

1. In an involuntary case, claims arising in the ordinary course of the debtor's business after the commencement of the case but before the

earlier of the appointment of a trustee or the order for relief will be allowed as if the claim had arisen before the bankruptcy petition, section 502(f).

2. Claims arising from the rejection of an executory contract or unexpired lease of the debtor are allowed as if the claim had arisen before the date of the filing of the petition, section 502(g).

3. A claim arising from the recovery of property because of a voidable transfer will be determined and allowed as though it were a prepetition claim, section 502(h).

   Example: Assume that on January 11, D repays C the $1,000 he owes her. On February 2, D files a bankruptcy petition. On May 5, D's bankruptcy trustee recovers the $1,000 from C as a section 547 preference. Under section 502(h), C has an allowable claim for $1,000.

4. A claim that does not arise until after the commencement of the case for a tax entitled to the seventh priority shall be treated as if the claim had arisen before the date of the filing of the petition, section 502(i).

Before a case is closed, a claim that has been allowed may be reconsidered for cause and reallowed or disallowed according to the equities of the case, section 502(j).

G.   What Is the Order of Distribution?

There are a number of statements in reported cases, law review articles, and legal texts praising the theme of equality of distribution to creditors in bankruptcy proceedings. Such statements must be using the term "equality" in the *Animal Farm* sense; in bankruptcy, some creditors are clearly "more equal" than others. Some unsecured claims must be fully satisfied before any distribution is made to other unsecured claims.

In a bankruptcy case, certain allowed unsecured claims are entitled to priority in distribution over other unsecured claims. Section 507(a) sets out the levels of priorities. In its proof of claim form, a creditor can assert a priority and state the amount and basis therefore. Most of the litigation over whether a claim is entitled to a priority involve assertions of section 507(a)(1) administrative expense status.

1.   Treatment of Priority Claims in 7

Chapter 7 requires that the various priority classes are paid in the order in which they are listed in section 507, section 726(a)(1). In other words, each first priority claim is to be paid in full before any second priority claim is paid at all. If there are not sufficient funds to pay all claims within a particular class, then generally all claims entitled to that priority are paid pro rata.

Section 726 establishes the rules for distribution in a Chapter 7 case to the holders of unsecured claims. Basically, the distribution is to be as follows:

1. Priorities under section 507 (section 507 is considered below)

2. Allowed unsecured claims which were either timely filed or tardily filed by a creditor who did not know of the bankruptcy

3. Allowed unsecured claims which were tardily filed by creditors with notice or actual knowledge of the bankruptcy

4. Fines and punitive damages

5. Postpetition interest on prepetition claims.

Each claim of each of the five categories must be paid in full before any claim in the next category receives any distribution. Each claim within a particular category shares pro rata if the proceeds from the liquidation of the property of the estate is insufficient to satisfy all claims in that category.

Example: Assume there is $20,000 available to pay to holders of unsecured claims and the following unsecured claims:

- $11,000 claims entitled to priority under section 507

- $4,800 claim by X that was timely filed

- $7,200 claim by Y that was timely filed

- $3,000 claim by Z that was not timely filed even though Z knew of the bankruptcy proceedings.

The distribution would be:

- $11,000 to holders of priority claims

- $3,600 to X [The first $11,000 must be used to pay priority claims. The remaining $9,000 ($20,000–$11,000) must be distributed pro rata to satisfy $12,000 ($4,800

+ $7,200) worth of timely filed claims. Accordingly, each timely filed claim will be paid at the rate of 75% on the dollar. ($9,000 / $12,000). Accordingly, X will receive $3,600 for its $4,800 claim.]

- $5,400 to *Y*.

In the very unlikely event that the sale of the "property of the estate" yields enough to satisfy each claim in each of the five "classes" listed above, the surplus is paid to the debtor.

2. Treatment of Priority Claims in 11, 12, 13

Chapter 11, Chapter 12 and Chapter 13 require the plan to provide for payment in full of all priority claims, although the payments of claims within certain priority classes may be stretched over a period of time, sections 1129(a)(9), 1322(a)(2).

3. Section 507 Treatment of Priorities

The task of distributing the proceeds from the sale of the property of the estate is complicated by the fact that claims do not come neatly labeled "claims entitled to priority under section 507." Instead, it is necessary to recognize which claims are entitled to priority under section 507.

The task of recognizing which claims are entitled to priority under section 507 is further complicated by the law which (1) requires that all section 507(a)(1) first priority claims be paid in full before section 507(a)(2) second priority claims are paid at all, that all second priority claims be paid in full before any third priority claims are paid at all, etc. and (2) looks to section 503 to determine which claims are entitled to a section 507(a)(1) first priority.

a. Domestic Support Obligations

The debtor's "domestic support obligations" as defined in section 101 have the first priority. And, then, there is a priority within this first priority. If proceeds from the trustee's sale of property of the estate are not sufficient to pay all "domestic support obligations," then support owed to children or former spouses is paid in full before any payment to a governmental unit on an assigned support obligation.

b. Administrative Expenses

After payment in full of all "domestic support obligations," distributions are made to the second priority: administrative expenses allowed under section 503(b). First priority claims—domestic support obligations—only arise in bankruptcy cases in which the debtor is an individual. Second priority claims—administrative expenses—arise in all bankruptcy cases.

Administrative expenses include the costs of maintaining, repairing, storing, and selling the property of the estate; taxes the trustee incurs in administering property of the estate; the trustee's fee; the debtor's at-torney's fees; the trustee's attorney's fee; and limited expenses of certain creditors.

Recall that as a result of the 2005 amendments, when a nonresidential real property lease is assumed and later rejected, then up to two years of post-rejection lease payments is an administrative expense. And, the 2005 amendments also create a new administrative expense priority for the value of goods sold on credit to the debtor in the ordinary course of the debtor's business and received by the debtor within 20 days before the commencement of the case.

c. Ordinary–Course Claims in Involuntary Cases

In an involuntary case, the third priority is accorded to claims arising in the ordinary course of the debtor's business after the commencement of the case but before the earlier of the appointment of a trustee or the order for relief. For example, the creditors of a restaurant, D, file an involuntary chapter 7 petition on January 11. On January 15, C makes his usual weekly delivery of vegetables to D. C's claim will be entitled to a third priority under section 507(a)(3).

d. Wage Claims

Section 507(a)(4) grants a fourth priority to wage claims. This priority includes claims for sales commissions, vacation pay, severance pay, and sick leave pay. It is subject to two limitations:

1. Timely: compensation earned within 90 days before the bankruptcy petition. (If the debtor's business ceased operations before the bankruptcy petition, the 90–day period is measured from the cessation of business operations.)

2. Amount: only $10,000 per employee.

e. Employee Benefit Plans

Claims for contributions to employee benefit plans receive a fifth priority under section 507(a)(5). This priority for fringe benefits is also subject to time and amount limitations:

(1) Time: only for services rendered within 180 days of the bankruptcy petition. (If the debtor's business ceased operations before the bankruptcy petition, the 180 days is measured from the cessation of business operation.)

(2) Amount: [$10,000 multiplied by the number of employees] minus [total payment to employees under section 507(a)(3)] plus [total payments to other employee benefit plans].

Note that payments under section 507(a)(5) will be made to the benefit plan, not directly to individual employees. Note also that section 507(a)(5) focuses on the aggregate of other payments to all employees covered by the plan, not the payments to an individual employee.

f.   Farmers and Fishermen

Section 507(a)(6) grants farmers a sixth priority for claims against grain storage facilities and fishermen a fifth priority against fish processing facilities. This priority is subject to a dollar limit.

g.   Consumer Deposits

Section 507(a)(7) grants a seventh priority to consumers who made a money deposit for property or services that were never provided, but this priority is also subject to a dollar limit.

h.   Tax Claims

Certain specified tax claims enjoy an eighth priority. Taxes entitled to this priority include:

(1) Income taxes for the three tax years immediately preceding the filing of the bankruptcy petition;

> NOTE: The three-year period is measured from the last date including extensions for filing a return to the date of the bankruptcy petition. If, for example, D files a bankruptcy petition on April 15, 2005, claims for taxes for 2004, 2003, and 2002 would be entitled to a priority. If, however, D files a bankruptcy petition on December 7, 2005, only claims for taxes for 2004 and 2003 would be entitled to a priority.

(2) Property taxes assessed before the filing of the bankruptcy petition and last payable without a penalty one year before that date; and

(3) If the debtor is an employer, taxes withheld from employees' paychecks.

Please remember that (1) section 507 affords priority to certain unsecured claims, (2) many tax claims are secured claims, and (3) section 724—discussed earlier—subordinates certain secured tax claims to certain priority claims.

i. Depository Institutions

The ninth priority is of limited application. It applies only in bankruptcies related to insured federal depository institutions and provides a priority for claims based upon a commitment to regulatory agencies to maintain the institution's capital.

j. DUI or FUI

The 2005 amendments add a tenth priority for claims for personal injuries or death caused by the debtor's operation of a motor vehicle, boat, or airplane while under the influence of alcohol or some other drug. There is no dollar cap on this priority.

4. Section 510 Treatment of Subordination

Section 507, the priority provision, has the effect of moving certain, specified claims to the head of the line. Section 510, the subordination provision, has the effect of moving some claims further back in the line.

Section 510 requires subordination in two instances:

1. Where there is a subordination agreement that would be enforceable under nonbankruptcy law, section 510(a);

2. When a seller or purchaser of equity securities seeks damages or rescission, section 510(b).

Additionally, the court has the discretion, after notice and hearing to subordinate any claim to other claims "under principles of equitable subordination," section 510(c).

The Bankruptcy Code does not define or even describe the principles by which equitable subordination is to be applied. The reported cases on equitable subordination emphasize facts, rather than specific rules or tests. The most significant fact is whether the holder of a claim is an insider or fiduciary. If a creditor is not in control of the debtor or otherwise an insider, courts are very reluctant to use equitable subordination.

5. Classification of Claims

In a Chapter 7 case, the debtor has no control over how the property of the estate is to be distributed. Section 726 prescribes the scheme of distribution to unsecured creditors in a Chapter 7 case. All allowed, unsecured nonpriority claims are treated alike: a pro rata distribution will be made to the holders of such claims after all priority claims are paid in full, section 726(a)(2).

Example: Assume that D owes $90,000 to X, $50,000 to Y and $60,000 to Z for total debts to X, Y and Z of $200,000. Assume further that X, Y and Z's claims are allowed, nonpriority, unsecured claims. If there is $100,000 available after satisfying secured claims and priority claims, then X, Y and Z will each receive 50 of its claim: $45,000 to X, $25,000 to Y and $30,000 to Z. [Total debts divided by total available funds equals percentage of each claim paid.]

In a Chapter 11 case, a Chapter 12 case or a Chapter 13 case, a debtor's plan can affect how the property of the estate is to be distributed. The plan can treat some unsecured claims differently than others: it can classify claims and provide for different treatment for each class, sections 1123(a)(1), 1222(b)(1), 1322(b)(1).

H. Review Questions

1. D owes S $100,000. If S has a security interest in D's equipment, S does not have an unsecured claim.

2. D owes S $100,000. The debt is unsecured. D files Chapter 7 bankruptcy. The automatic stay stops S from taking any steps to collect the debt outside of bankruptcy, but S has a $100,000 claim in the bankruptcy case. The stay ends when the bankruptcy case ends. So, when the case ends, can S sue to collect the debt?

3. What can S do in the Chapter 7 bankruptcy case to collect her debt?

4. D owes your client C $2,000. C learns that D has filed a Chapter 7 petition. Should C file a proof of claim?

5. T or F   When a proof of claim is filed, the claim is not allowed until the claimant proves the validity of her claim.

6. D owes S $100,000 on an unsecured, domestic support obligation. D files Chapter 7 bankruptcy. How is S's claim treated differently from other unsecured claims with respect to distribution of the bankruptcy estate?

7. D borrows $300,000 from C. The loan agreement provides that D will pay C—within one year—the principal plus $30,000 interest. The day before the loan was due, D files a Chapter 11 petition. What is the amount of C's claim?

8. D Mfg Co. manufactures snowmobiles. It gives a two year warranty. D Mfg Co. files a Chapter 7 petition. What are the rights of a person who bought a snowmobile within two years before the Chapter 7 filing?

9. On 1/15, D files a Chapter 7 petition. On 2/2, D injures C in an automobile accident. What is the effect of D's bankruptcy on C?

10. T or F   In Chapter 11 and 13 cases, the debtor's plan can divide unsecured claims into classes and provide for paying some classes more than other classes. Fair discrimination is allowed. The same is true in a Chapter 7 case in the sense that the debtor can decide to discriminate fairly in distributing proceeds of the estate to general, unsecured creditors.

*

XV

Leases and Executory Contracts

■ *ANALYSIS*

A. Overview

1. Hybrid Nature of Lease and Executory Contract

Bankruptcy involves both the assets and the obligations of the debtor. Bankruptcy deals with these assets and obligations through the creation of a fictional estate. The assets of the debtor become property of the estate. The estate is administered by a trustee or debtor in possession to satisfy the secured and unsecured obligations of the debtor. In the course of administration, the estate will incur its own obligations; these administrative expenses are given priority over the debtor's unsecured obligations.

Generally, the Bankruptcy Code's provisions dealing with the debtor's assets are separate from the Bankruptcy Code's provisions dealing with the debtor's obligations and the estate's obligations: property of the estate in section 541, allowable claims and administrative expenses in sections 502 and 503. A lease or executory contract involves potentially both property of the estate and a claim against the debtor or the estate.

This hybrid nature of a lease or executory contract is most apparent in lease situations in which the debtor is the lessee.

Example: Assume that *D* Store, Inc. (*D*) leases its store in the mall from *L*. *D* later files for bankruptcy. *D*'s rights to the use of the space in the mall is an asset of the estate. *D*'s lease, however, involves burdens as well as benefits. D has performance obligations under the lease such as paying rent. If these obligations are not performed, *L* will have a claim.

2. Bankruptcy Provisions

For almost 70 years, American bankruptcy statutes have had special sections for leases and executory contracts. In 1938, the Chandler Act Amendments added sections 70b and 63c. In 1978, the Bankruptcy Code replaced these provisions with sections 365 and 1110. And, later, section 1113. And, still later, section 1114. While there are now a few pages of bankruptcy statutes on leases and executory contracts instead of a couple of paragraphs, the core concepts from the Chandler Act have been retained.

3. Different Ways of Treating Lease or Executory Contract

The bankruptcy treatment of a lease or executory contract can take one of three possible forms:

1. Rejection;

2. Assumption;

3. Assignment.

In comparing rejection, assumption and assignment, it is important to keep in mind that the lease or contract involves potentially both property of the estate and a claim against the estate. The following chart provides a general view of the effect of rejection, assumption and assignment on property of the estate and claims against the estate.

	Rejection	Assumption	Assignment
Property of the estate	No property of the estate	Debtor's rights under contract or lease	Proceeds, if any, from assignment of debtor's rights under contract or lease
Claims	Unsecured claim for (i) prepetition defaults and (ii) breach resulting from rejection; administrative expense priority claim for postpetition obligations, if any.	Administrative expense priority claim for all obligations under contract or lease, postpetition or prepetition.	No claim against the estate. Nondebtor party to an assigned contract or lease looks solely to the assignee.

4. Debtor Limited in Changing Lease or Executory Contract

An understanding of the bankruptcy law of leases and executory contracts requires an understanding not only of rejection, assumption and assignment, the three different elections available to the debtor under the Bankruptcy Code, but also an understanding of the election that is not available to the debtor under the Bankruptcy Code. A debtor does not have a legal right to modify or change the terms of an unexpired lease or an executory contract.

Example: Assume that *D* Store, Inc. (*D*) leases space in a mall from *L* for $20,000 a year. *D* owes $600,000 to unsecured trade creditors and $3,000,000 to secured lenders. *D* files a Chapter 11 petition. *D* wants to continue operating in the mall, wants to retain the leasehold. *D* will have to assume the lease, will have to assume the lease payment as is: $20,000 a year, no change. In its Chapter 11 plan, *D* will be able to alter its payment obligations to lenders and trade creditors, secured and unsecured.

a. No Choice to Modify as of Right

D cannot, however, use bankruptcy to effect a modification in its obligations under its leases or executory contracts. Rejection, assumption or assignment. Not modification.

b. Power to Persuade

The previous statement in the text is both correct and misleading. There are only the three elections under the Bankruptcy Code. A debtor does not have a right under the Bankruptcy Code to change the terms of an unexpired lease or executory contract. Nonetheless, a debtor is often able to use its bargaining power and other legal rights under the Bankruptcy Code to "persuade" the other party to the lease or contract to "agree" to modifications in the lease or contract. For example, *D* is leasing a building from *L*. *D* files for bankruptcy. *D* wants *L* to reduce her rent. *D* presents *L* with the choice that either *D* will reject the lease which will leave *L* with an empty building and a general claim in *D*'s bankruptcy case or *L* will agree to modifications in the lease. *L* will often choose to "agree" to modify the lease.

5. Summary

To review, look primarily to section 365 to determine the effect of bankruptcy on a debtor's leases and executory contracts. Under section 365, a bankruptcy trustee can either:

1. Reject a lease or executory contract;

2. Assume a lease or executory contract;

3. Assign a lease or executory contract.

In order to understand section 365 and assess these three options, a law student or lawyer must be able to answer the following questions:

1. What is the effect of rejecting a lease or executory contract, of assuming a lease or executory contract?

2. What is the procedure for rejecting or assuming a lease or executory contract?

3. What are the limitations, if any, on rejecting a lease or executory contract?

4. What are the limitations, if any, on assuming or assigning a lease or executory contract?

5. What is an executory contract?

B. Effect of Rejection, Assumption, Assignment

Floyd Lawson, *L*, leases a building for his barbershop from Mayberry Realty Corp., *M*. The lease agreement provides for a ten-year term and monthly rentals of $250. *L* files a bankruptcy petition. What is the effect of the bankruptcy trustee or debtor in possession rejecting the lease? Assuming the lease? Assigning the lease?

1. If Lease Rejected

If the lease is rejected, *L* has no further right to use the building for his barbershop. If the lease is rejected, *L* has no further personal liability on the lease. The rejection of the lease is, of course, a breach of the lease, section 365(g). *M* will have an allowable unsecured claim against the bankrupt estate for back rent and future rentals, section 502(g), 502(a)(6). The amount that *M* will receive on this unsecured claim will depend on the property of the estate in a Chapter 7 case and will depend on the provisions of the plan in a Chapter 11 or Chapter 13 case.

2. If Lease Assumed

If the lease is assumed, the leasehold continues to be an asset of the estate. *L* can continue to operate his barbershop in the building. Assumption covers the burdens of the lease as well as the benefits. By assuming the lease, the trustee or debtor in possession is obligating the estate to make all payments under the lease. This obligation is a first priority administrative expense.

Example: *L*, a Haircutters franchisee, files for Chapter 11 relief owing suppliers, Haircutters and his landlords. If *D* assumes his leases and his Haircutters' licensing agreement, the landlords and Haircutters have an administrative expense priority and will be paid in full before the suppliers are paid at all.

Compare the Bankruptcy Code's treatment of the debtor's landlord with its treatment of the debtor's secured creditor. If a Chapter 11 or Chapter 13 debtor wants to retain a building that she is leasing, the debtor must continue to make all payments called for by the lease. Section 365 does not provide for the alteration or modification of leases; under section 365, the lease is either rejected or assumed, as is.

In contrast, if a Chapter 11 or Chapter 13 debtor wants to keep a building that is subject to a mortgage, the debtor can "impair or modify" the rights of the mortgagee in her plan, sections 1123(b)(1), 1322(b)(2).

Example: *D* Corp. files a Chapter 11 petition. *D* is using two buildings. It is leasing one of the buildings from *X* at a rental of $2,000 a month. *Y* is financing *D*'s purchase of the other building. The *D-Y* loan agreements grant *Y* a mortgage on the building and call for monthly payments of $3,000. *D* can keep the leased building only if it continues to pay *X* $2,000. *D* has greater flexibility with respect to retention of the building subject to *Y*'s mortgage.

3. If Lease Assigned

What if, in Floyd Lawson's bankruptcy, the trustee or debtor in possession sells the lease to Aunt Bea Taylor who wants to open an adult bookstore in the building? Such an assignment "relieves the trustee and the estate from any liability for any breach of such contract or lease occurring after such assignment," section 365(k). After the assignment, *M* can look only to Aunt Bea for the payment of the post-assignment obligations under the lease.

C. Procedure for Rejection or Assumption

Section 365(a) contemplates court approval of rejection or assumption. Rule 6006 provides that the assumption or rejection is a contested matter governed by Rule 9014. Neither the Code nor the Rules indicate what standard the court should apply in determining whether to grant or withhold its approval.

Most, but not all, cases seem to give great deference to the "business judgment" of the debtor in possession or trustee in approving a motion to reject an unexpired lease or executory contract. Because assumption of an unexpired lease or executory contract creates an administrative priority obligation that must be paid before other unsecured claims, courts give greater weight to creditors' objections to motions to assume.

1. Chapter 7 Cases (Other Than Nonresidential Real Property Leases)

In Chapter 7, there is a general rule that executory contracts and leases that are not assumed by the Chapter 7 trustee within 60 days after the order for relief are deemed rejected. Section 365(d)(1). You should know three exceptions to this general rule:

1. First, section 365(d)(1) provides that the court can extend the 60 days.

2. Second, section 365(d)(1) does not apply to nonresidential real property leases.

3. Third, section 365(p) provides a three-step process by which an individual debtor can herself assume a personal property leases.

   a) The first step is for the debtor to make a written request;

   b) The second step is for the lessor to notify the debtor of the lessor's willingness to have the lease assumed by the debtor; and

   c) The third step is for the debtor to notify the lessor that the lease is assumed.

   When a lease is assumed by the debtor under section 365(p), the debtor personally (and not the estate) has both the benefits and the burdens of the lease.

2. **Chapters 11 and 13 (Other Than Nonresidential Real Property Leases)**

   In cases under Chapter 11 or Chapter 13, the general rule is that executory contracts and leases can be assumed or rejected any time before the confirmation of the plan. Section 365(d)(2). Again, you should know two exceptions:

   1. First, section 365(d)(2) provides that the court can order an earlier determination of whether the contract or lease is to be assumed or rejected.

   2. Second, section 365(d)(2) does not apply to nonresidential real property leases.

3. **Nonresidential Real Property Leases in Chapter 7, 11, and 13 Cases**

   The general rule is that a lease of nonresidential real property is deemed rejected unless it has been assumed within 120 days after the order for relief. Section 365(d)(4). And, this general rule is also subject to two exceptions:

   1. First, if the plan is confirmed earlier, then the deadline becomes the date of the entry of the order confirming the plan.

2. Second, the court can extent the 120 day period by 90 days. The lessor must agree to any additional extension.

D. The Gap Period

There is going to be some gap period between the filing of a bankruptcy petition and action on a contract or lease. Accordingly, it would seem necessary to consider the rights and responsibilities of the debtor and nondebtor party during the interim between the commencement of the bankruptcy case and the assumption or rejection decision.

1. Nondebtor's Performance

Section 365 does not expressly deal with the performance obligations of the nondebtor party to a lease or executory during this gap period. The few cases that have expressly dealt with the question have held that the nondebtor party is obligated to perform. Most courts seem simply to assume that the nondebtor party is so obligated. If L is leasing a building or machinery to D, L's performance (providing the building or machinery) continues after D's bankruptcy filing.

2. Debtor's Performance

Section 365(d)(3) expressly deals with the performance obligations of the debtor party to a nonresidential real property lease: it requires a debtor/lessee to "timely perform" all obligations under a nonresidential real property lease.

Example: Assume that dentist D files for Chapter 13 relief. D leases her office from L; the unexpired lease provides for rent of $2,000 per month. While it is clear that section 365(d)(3) contemplates that within 60 days of the filing, D will be making all postpetition rent payments to L, it is not clear from the cases under section 365(d)(3) what happens if D is unable to perform during the gap period.

Section 365(d)(5) deals with the gap period performance obligations of the debtor on its equipment leases. Section 365(d)(5) needs to be read together with and compared to section 365(d)(3). While section 365(d)(3) contemplates that a debtor will make all postpetition rent payments on commercial real estate and will start making such payments within 60 days, section 365(d)(5) contemplates that the debtor will make equipment lease payments that first arise after 60 days. And, the court can excuse equipment payments that first arise after 60 days "based on the equities of the case."

Section 365(d)(5) also needs to be read together with section 363(e). Under section 363(e), a lessor of personal property can request that the court prohibit or restrict the debtor's use of its property. Unlike section 365(d)(5), section 363(e) applies to consumer leases.

E. Limitations on the Effect of Rejection of a Lease or Executory Contract

Nothing in section 365 limits the availability of rejection. Section 365 does, however, set out four situations in which the effect of rejection is limited:

1. Section 365(h) limits the effect of rejection of a lease of real property when the debtor is the landlord. A trustee for a debtor who owns rental real property may not use section 365 to evict tenants. Even, if the trustee decides to reject the debtor/lessor's leases, the tenant has a right to remain in possession. Assume, for example, that Epstein uses some of his Black Letter royalties to build an office building; your law firm rents an office in Epstein's building. If Epstein later files for bankruptcy and rejects the lease, your firm can still remain in possession of the leasehold.

    The trustee for the debtor/lessor may, however, use rejection to terminate some of the services required by the lease such as maintenance. The lessee may then offset any damages caused by such termination against its rent obligation.

2. Sections 365(h) and (i) provide similar limitations on a debtor/seller's rejection of a timeshare contract.

3. Section 365(i) provides similar limitations on the debtor/seller's rejection of an installment land sales contract.

4. Section 365(n) provides similar limitations on the debtor licensor's rejection of a lease of a patent, copyright or other "intellectual property." Under section 365(n), an intellectual property licensee, like a real property lessee, is granted an election with respect to the consequences of a debtor/licensor's rejection of the license agreement. The licensee may treat the rejection as a breach that terminates the lease and assert a claim for damages. Alternatively, the licensee may elect to retain its rights under license agreement as such rights existed immediately before the case commenced. Under section 101(35A) other intellectual property does not include trademarks and trade names.

1. Collective Bargaining Contracts

Congress added two sections to Chapter 11 to protect employee contracts. Section 1113 limits the rejection of collective bargaining contracts in Chapter 11 cases. Paragraph (f) of section 1113 prohibits a debtor/employer from unilaterally changing a prebankruptcy collective bargaining agreement. Paragraph (e) provides for court approval of interim changes pending court action on a request to reject a collective bargaining agreement. Paragraph (b) requires postpetition negotiations with and disclosures to the union as a condition precedent to rejection of the collective bargaining agreement. And, paragraph (c) sets out the standard the court is to apply in ruling on a motion to reject a collective bargaining agreement.

2. Employee Benefit Contracts

Section 1114 limits the rejection of employee benefits contracts in Chapter 11 cases. It (1) requires Chapter 11 debtors in possession or trustees to continue paying retiree medical and life insurance benefits at prebankruptcy levels until a modification is either agreed to by the retiree's "authorized representative" or authorized by the bankruptcy court and (2) provides that all preconfirmation retiree benefits are administrative expenses entitled to priority over other unsecured claims.

NOTE: Do you see that section 1114 encourages creditors to convert a case from Chapter 11 to Chapter 7? Section 1114 requires that retiree benefits claims be paid in full before other unsecured creditors are paid anything. Section 1114 only applies in Chapter 11 cases; it does not apply if a case has been converted to Chapter 7.

F.   Limitations on Assumption and Assignment

1.   Contract Limitations

Contract clauses that prohibit or limit the assumption and assignment of leases and executory contracts will not be effective in bankruptcy, section 365(e), (f). The trustee or debtor in possession can assume a lease even though the lease agreement provides in the lease for automatic termination or a right of termination because of bankruptcy or insolvency, section 365(e). Similarly, the trustee or debtor in possession can sell or otherwise assign a lease even though the lease agreement provides it is not assignable, section 365(f).

Example: In 2005, *D* leases a building from *L* for ten years. The lease provides that it can not be assigned without *L*'s written approval and that the lease terminates *ipso facto* on *D*'s bankruptcy. In 2007,

D files for bankruptcy. Her one valuable asset is the lease. Because of the desirability of the location and the favorable rental rate, third parties are willing to pay substantial sums to acquire the lease from *D*. Notwithstanding the language in the lease, *D*'s trustee can sell the lease by meeting the requirements for assignment set out in section 365(f).

2. Proceeds of Assignment of Lease

What happens to the "substantial sums" that the trustee receives when he sells the "nonassignable lease"? Recall that the debtor's interest in the lease was section 541(a)(1) property of the estate and that proceeds from the sale of property of the estate are property of the estate, section 541(a)(6). Accordingly, it would seem that the answer to this question is that the "substantial sums" from the sale of the "nonassignable lease" would, like the rest of the property of the estate, be available for distribution to unsecured creditors in a Chapter 7 case and be available for the debtor's plan performance in a Chapter 11 or 13 case.

By changing two facts, we can change this answer significantly. First, change the real property lease to a cable franchise contract and, second, add a security interest in the contract.

Example: Assume (1) that *D* has rights under a cable franchise contract that prohibits assignments and (2) notwithstanding this contractual prohibition, *D* has granted *S* a security interest in the cable franchise contract. If *D* files for bankruptcy, section 365(f) will still operate to make the contract prohibition against assignments ineffective. But now the practical effect of the operation of section 365(f) will be different; *S* will now get the "substantial sums" because:

1.   Section 9–408 of the 2001 version of Article 9 enables a creditor to obtain a security interest in a franchise contract or other "general intangible" even though the contract itself expressly prohibits such assignments. Section 9–408 only applies to promissory notes, healthcare insurance receivables and certain general intangibles. A real property lease is none of these. Indeed, Article 9 does not apply to a lien on a real estate lease. See 9–109(d)(11).

2.   Under section 552(b) of the Bankruptcy Code, *S*'s security interest would reach the proceeds from the sale of the franchise contract. See section 9–408, Official Comment 7.

3. Leases and Executory Contracts That Cannot Be Assumed or Assumed and Assigned

There are some leases and executory contracts that cannot be assumed and assigned.

a. Lease Terminated Before Bankruptcy

A lease or contract that has terminated before bankruptcy cannot be assumed.

Example: *D* leases Blackacre from *L*. *D* defaults. *L* takes the steps required by state law to evict *D* and terminate the lease. *D* later files for bankruptcy. *D* cannot assume the lease. Regardless of religious views, there is no such thing as a born-again lease.

b. Loan Commitment

A loan commitment or other financing arrangement cannot be assumed, section 365(c)(2).

Example: *C* agrees to provide *D* with a $250,000 line of credit. *D* files a bankruptcy petition before drawing on this line of credit. *D* cannot assume this executory contract and compel *C* to loan the $250,000.

c. Contracts Not Assignable Under Applicable Law

Contracts that are not assignable under "applicable law" are not assignable in bankruptcy, section 365(c)(1). "Applicable law" can be the common law of contracts.

Example: Under common law, for example, personal services contracts cannot be assigned and delegated. Batman contracts to patrol the streets of Gotham City. Batman later files a bankruptcy petition, Batman cannot assign this personal services contract to Madonna.

"Applicable law" for purposes of section 365(c) can also be a statute so long as it is a statute other than the Bankruptcy Code.

Example: Assume that state law prohibits the assignment of a car dealer franchise contract without the approval of the franchisor. *D* Ford dealer could not file for bankruptcy and then assign his franchise without the approval of the franchisor because of "applicable law."

4. Requirements for Assumption and Assignment

Paragraph (b) of section 365 sets out the requirements for assumption of a lease or executory contract.

a. Section 365(b) Applies if Default

Note that paragraph 365(b) only applies if there has been a default other than breach of a provision relating to bankruptcy filing or insolvency.

Example: Assume that D rents a building from L. D files a bankruptcy petition. At the time of the bankruptcy petition, D is current on all of its obligations under the lease. If D decides to assume the lease, section 365(b) does not apply.

b. Requirements

If there has been a default, section 365(b) imposes requirements with respect to the past failures to perform and requirements with respect to the future performance obligations. As to past defaults, section 365(b)(1) requires

1. Cure of past defaults or "adequate assurance" of prompt cure;

2. Compensation for "actual pecuniary loss" resulting from the default or "adequate assurance" of prompt compensation.

c. "Adequate Assurance"

As to future performance, section 365(b)(1)(C) requires "adequate assurance" of future performance. The term "adequate assurance" is not statutorily defined. Section 365(b)(3) indicates what constitutes "adequate assurance" if the lease covers real property that is a part of a "shopping center."

"Adequate assurance" is also a condition precedent to assignment of a lease or executory contract. Remember that after assignment, the other party to the lease or executory contract can look only to the assignee for the performance of the debtor's postassignment obligations under the lease or contract. To protect the nonbankrupt party, section 365(f)(2) requires that the assignee provide "adequate assurance" of future performance as a condition to any assignment.

Some prebankruptcy defaults cannot be cured. Assume, for example, that D Tavern's lease required that it not be closed for more than 72 consecutive hours and that in the week prior to its bankruptcy filing, D

Tavern was closed for 75 hours. In 2005, section 365(b) was amended to "clarify" that D Tavern can assume this lease even though it is impossible to cure an earlier nonmonetary default. (If your professor points out that section 365(b) is still not clear and makes a point of it, you might want to make a point of carefully comparing section 365(b)(1)(A) with section 365(b)(2)(D).)

G. Definition of Executory Contract

Section 365 applies to leases and executory contracts. The Bankruptcy Code does not define the term "lease." There is probably no need for a definition. When there is a problem as to whether a "lease" of personal property is a disguised credit sale, bankruptcy courts look to the definition of "security interest" in UCC § 1–201(37).

Similarly, the Bankruptcy Code does not define the phrase "executory contract." The most frequently cited and most thorough discussion of executory contracts in bankruptcy is a two-part, 142–page article written prior to the enactment of the Bankruptcy Code by Professor Vern Countryman. Professor Countryman concludes that an executory contract for purposes of bankruptcy is one that is so far unperformed on both sides that the failure of either party to complete her performance would be a material breach excusing further performance from the other party. See Countryman, *Executory Contracts In Bankruptcy*, 57 MINN.L.REV. 439 (1973); 58 MINN.L.REV. 479 (1974).

Most reported cases seem to follow the Countryman definition. There are, however, bankruptcy judges and law professors who use a different definition of "executory contract." Use whatever definition your professor uses.

H. Review Questions

1. T or F   A debtor's assumption, assignment, or rejection of a lease requires bankruptcy court approval.

2. T or F   D Corp files a Chapter 7 petition. If the Chapter 7 trustee neither assumes the lease nor obtains additional time from the court, D's Corp.'s lease of office space will be deemed rejected within 60 days after the order for relief.

3. T or F   If, after filing for bankruptcy, D rejects a lease or contract, the nondebtor party to the lease or contract will have an administrative expense priority claim,

4. T or F   If, after filing for bankruptcy, D assumes a lease or contract, the nondebtor party to the lease or contract will have an administrative expense priority claim.

5. D leases land from L. D files for bankruptcy. In February, after notice and hearing, D assigns its land lease to T. T fails to pay March rent. What are L's rights?

6. D, a Chapter 11 debtor, wants to assume an equipment lease. If D is not in default under the lease, what does it have to do in order to assume the lease?

7. D, a Chapter 11 debtor, leases a building from L. The lease provides that it can only be assigned with L's consent. D wants to assign the lease to T. What does D have to do?

8. T or F   A landlord who files for bankruptcy can assume its leases with its tenants.

9. T or F   D, a licensor of intellectual property files a bankruptcy petition. D's rejection of its intellectual property licenses would have no affect on the rights of the licensees.

10. T or F   D a licensor of intellectual property files a bankruptcy petition. D's rejection of its intellectual property licenses would have no affect on the payment obligations of its licensees who elect to retain their rights.

*

XVI

Discharge

■ *ANALYSIS*

Most debtors who file voluntary bankruptcy petitions expect that the bankruptcy case will wipe out all of their debts. These expectations are not always realized.

Bankruptcy *discharges certain* debtors from *certain* debts.

As the italicized words in the last sentence suggest, there are three major discharge questions:

1. Which debtors receive a discharge?

2. Which debts are discharged?

3. What is the effect of a discharge?

The answers to these three questions depend in substantial part on whether the bankruptcy case is a Chapter 7 case or a Chapter 11 case or a Chapter 13 case.

A. Which Debtors Receive a Discharge?

1. Chapter 7

In counseling a beleaguered debtor about Chapter 7, it is very important to ascertain her eligibility for discharge—to determine whether any of the grounds for withholding discharge can be established by the bankruptcy trustee or a creditor. If the debtor is denied a discharge, she loses two ways. The debtor will leave the bankruptcy case without her section 541 property yet owing the same debts that she owed at the time of the filing of the bankruptcy case less any distribution that creditors received from the trustee.

a. Substantive Grounds for Withholding a Chapter 7 Discharge

The grounds for withholding a discharge, i.e., objections to discharge, are set out in section 727(a). These 12 grounds are exclusive. Unless the bankruptcy trustee or a creditor is able to establish one of these ten objections, the debtor in a Chapter 7 case will receive a bankruptcy discharge.

1) Not an Individual

Only an individual is eligible to receive a discharge in a case under Chapter 7 of the Bankruptcy Code. A corporation may receive a discharge under Chapter 11, section 1141(d).

Section 727(a)(1) denies a discharge to corporations and partnerships. Section 727(a)(1) is intended to prevent "trafficking in corporate shells and partnerships." Generally, the owners of a bankrupt corporation do not need a bankruptcy discharge. Since the corporation is a separate legal entity, they are protected from personal liability for the corporation's debts.

2) Dishonesty

The next six grounds for withholding discharge have as their foundation some form of dishonesty or lack of cooperation by the individual debtor.

a) Fraudulent Transfers

Certain fraudulent transfers can be the basis for an objection to discharge. Section 727(a)(2) denies a discharge to a debtor who transfers property "with an intent to hinder, delay or defraud" within the twelve months immediately preceding the filing of the bankruptcy petition or after the filing of the bankruptcy petition.

b) Failing to Keep Records

An objection to discharge may be based on the unjustified failure to keep or preserve financial records, section 727(a)(3). A section 727(a)(3) objection raises the following issues of fact:

1. Has the debtor failed to keep financial records?

2. Is such failure "justified under all of the circumstances of the case"?

3. Is it still possible to ascertain the debtor's financial condition and business transactions?

The standards applied in resolving these fact questions will reflect the nature of the debtor's business and his assets and liabilities.

c) Withholding Information

Section 727(a)(4) lists four acts which tend to deprive the bankruptcy trustee of property of the estate or of information necessary to discover or collect property of the estate:

1. Making a false oath or account in connection with the bankruptcy case;

2. Presenting or using a false claim against the estate;

3. Receiving or giving consideration for action or inaction in the bankruptcy proceeding; or

4. Withholding books and records from the bankruptcy trustee.

Proof that the debtor "knowingly and fraudulently" committed one of these acts will bar discharge.

Proof that the debtor "knowingly and fraudulently" committed one of these acts will also subject the debtor to criminal sanctions: a fine of not more than $5,000 and/or imprisonment for not more than five years, 18 USCA § 152. The standard of proof under 18 USCA is beyond a reasonable doubt; section 727(a)(4) merely requires a preponderance of the evidence. Accordingly, section 727(a)(4) focuses on commission of the act, not conviction for the crime.

d) Failing to Explain Loss of Assets

The fifth ground for denial of discharge is the failure to explain "satisfactorily" any loss or deficiency of assets, section 727(a)(5). Section 727(a)(5) focuses on the truth of the debtor's explanation, not on the wisdom of his or her expenditures.

e) Refusing to Testify

Under section 727(a)(6), a debtor may be denied discharge if he refuses to testify after having been granted immunity or after improperly invoking the constitutional privilege against self-incrimination.

f) Conduct Relating to Another Bankruptcy Case

The seventh ground for withholding discharge is the debtor's commission of any act specified in section 727(a)(2)–(6) no more than a year before the filing of the bankruptcy petition in connection with another bankruptcy case concerning an "insider," section 727(a)(7). The term "insider" is defined in section 101(28). An individual's relatives, partners, partnership and corporation all come within the definition.

3) Earlier Discharge

Section 727(a)(8) and section 727(a)(9) limit the frequency of Chapter 7 discharge relief. If a debtor has received a discharge in a Chapter 7 or Chapter 11 case in the past eight years, she will be denied discharge, section 727(a)(8). If a debtor has received a discharge in a Chapter 13 case within the past six years she will be denied a discharge unless (a) payments under the plan totaled at least 100% of the allowed unsecured claims, or (b) payments under the plan totaled at least 70% of the allowed unsecured claims *and* the plan was proposed in good faith *and* was the debtor's "best effort," section 727(a)(9).

a) Measuring the Time Periods

The eight–year and six–year time periods are measured from filing date to filing date. Suppose X obtains a bankruptcy discharge on April 5, 2000, in a Chapter 7 case filed on January 15, 2000. In this case, section 727(a)(9) would not bar X's bankruptcy discharge in a Chapter 7 case filed in March 2008.

b) Limits on the Limit

Now that you understand what section 727(a)(8) and (9) do, be sure you understand what these provisions do not do. Section 727(a)(8) and section 727(a)(9) only limit the availability of a discharge in a Chapter 7 case. They do not affect the debtor's right to file a voluntary petition or creditors' right to file involuntary petitions under Chapter 7 or any other chapter. And, they do not affect the availability of a Chapter 13 discharge or a Chapter 11 debtor who "engages in business after consummation of the plan." Section 1141(d)(3)(B).

4) Waiver of Discharge

Section 727(a)(10) recognizes certain waivers of discharge. A debtor's waiver will bar discharge only if it is:

1. In writing, and

2. Executed after the filing of the bankruptcy petition, after the order for relief, and

3. Approved by the court.

5) New Grounds Added in 2005

The 2005 amendments added section 727(a)(11) which denies a discharge for failure to complete an approved "instructional course concerning personal financial management" and section 727(a)(12) which delays a discharge if there is a proceeding pending against the debtor and there is reasonable cause to believe that the debtor may be found guilty of a felony or liable for a debt arising from (1) violation of securities law, (2) RICO civil penalty, or (3) personal injury or death caused by the debtor's criminal act, intentional tort, or willful or reckless misconduct.

b. Procedure for Objecting to a Chapter 7 Discharge

Remember that section 727(a) is not self-executing. The bankruptcy trustee or a creditor must object to discharge, section 727(c)(1). The time for and form of objection are governed by Rules 4004 and 7001.

1) Complaint

Objections to discharge are initiated by complaints, filed with the bankruptcy court. Rule 4004 sets the time for filing complaints objecting to discharge. Any such complaint must be filed within 60 days of the first date set for the meeting of creditors. The court may "for cause" extend the time for filing a complaint objecting to discharge on motion of a party in interest. Such a motion, however, must be filed within the 60–day period.

2) Trial

If any creditor files an objection to discharge, the bankruptcy court tries the issue of the debtor's right to a discharge. Such a trial is an "adversary proceeding" governed by Part VII of the Bankruptcy Rules, Rule 4004(d). If no objection to discharge is filed, and the debtor has not waived his right to a discharge, has not failed to attend the meeting of creditors, and has paid the filing fees, the court shall grant the discharge, section 727(a), Rule 4004(c).

3) Post–Discharge Hearing

After the court has determined whether to grant a discharge, the court must hold a hearing and the debtor must appear in person, section 524(d). The hearing must be held within 30 days of the order granting or denying a discharge. Rule 4008. At the hearing, the court informs the debtor that a discharge has been granted, or why a discharge has not been granted.

2. Chapter 11 Cases: Business Entity Debtors

a. Confirmation Operates as Discharge

In Chapter 11 cases in which the debtor is a corporation, partnership, or some other business entity, the confirmation of the plan operates as a discharge, section 1141(d). The following hypothetical points out the practical significance of this rule:

Example: *D* Corp. owes *X* $100,000. *D* Corp.'s Chapter 11 plan proposes to pay *X* $70,000 over three years. On confirmation, *D*'s only obligation to *X* is to pay it $70,000 over three years as provided in the plan. The remainder of the debt has been discharged.

b. Grounds for Denying

The grounds for denying a discharge in a Chapter 11 case are different from the grounds for denying a discharge in a Chapter 7 case. A Chapter 11 debtor will be denied a discharge only if *all* of the following requirements are satisfied:

1. The plan provides for liquidation of all or substantially all of the property of the estate; AND

2. The debtor does not engage in business after consummation of the plan; AND

3. The debtor would be denied a discharge if the case were in Chapter 7, section 1141(d)(3).

c. Applying Section 1141(d)(3)

The following examples illustrate the application of section 1141(d)(3).

Example: *D* Corp. files a Chapter 11 petition. Its Chapter 11 plan provides for the sale of all of its assets, distribution of the proceeds from the sale to creditors, and termination of business operations. *D* Corp. would not receive a discharge.

Example: *D* Inc.'s Chapter 11 plan provides for the sale of six stores and continued operations of five stores. If its plan is confirmed, *D* Inc. will receive a discharge.

Example: *D*, an individual who owns and operates several small businesses as sole proprietorships, files a Chapter 11 petition. *D*'s Chapter 11 plan provides for the continued operation of these businesses. Because of her "bankruptcy history," *D* would be denied a Chapter 7 discharge under section 727(a)(9). If her Chapter 11 plan is confirmed, *D* will receive a discharge.

3. Chapter 13

a. Discharge Depends

In Chapter 13 cases, unlike Chapter 11 cases, the confirmation of the plan does not effect a discharge. In Chapter 13, the question of whether a debtor will receive a discharge cannot be resolved until the debtor either completes her payments under the plan or completes her efforts to make payments under the plan, section 1328.

1) Completing Plan

Section 1328(a) makes mandatory the discharge of a debtor who has completed all of the payments required by his Chapter 13 plan.

2) Experiencing Hardship

Section 1328(b) gives the court discretion to grant a "hardship" discharge to a debtor who has failed to make all of the payments required by his Chapter 13 plan. Section 1328(b) lists factors that the court should consider in exercising this discretion. However, a hardship discharge under section 1328(b) is not as comprehensive as a section 1328(a) discharge. In fact, most debts are excepted from a section 1328(b) hardship discharge.

b. Reasons for Denying Discharge

Section 727 provides for objections to discharge in Chapter 7 cases, as discussed earlier. Section 727 is not applicable in Chapter 13 cases. However, the 2005 amendments added three new requirements for a Chapter 13 discharge that are similar to the discharge objections in section 727.

1. First, in Chapter 13 cases, as in Chapter 7 cases, a debtor may be denied a discharge because of her bankruptcy history. New section 1328(f) denies a discharge because of what happened in another Chapter 13 case in the two-year period prior to the filing or another Chapter 7 or 11 case in the four-year period prior to the filing. [It is not clear from the language of section 1328(f) whether what happened during that time period has to be merely the granting of a discharge in a prior case during that period or both the filing of the prior case and the granting of discharge during that period.]

2. Second, section 1328(g), like section 727(a)(11), denies a discharge for failure to complete an approved "instructional course concerning personal financial management.

3. Third, section 1328(h), like section 727(a)(12), delays a discharge if there is a a proceeding pending against the debtor and there

is reasonable cause to believe that the debtor may be found guilty of a felony or liable for a debt arising from (1) violation of securities law, (2) RICO civil penalty, or (3) personal injury or death caused by the debtor's criminal act, intentional tort, or willful or reckless misconduct.

B. Which Obligations Are Affected by a Bankruptcy Discharge?

Even when the debtor receives a discharge, she is not necessarily freed from all of her obligations. Certain obligations are not affected by a discharge. In determining whether a discharge affects an obligation, it is necessary to consider the following three questions:

1. Is the obligation a "debt" as that term is defined in section 101?

2. Sections 727(b), 1141(d), and 1328 discharge the debtor from "debts." Remember that section 101 defines "debt" in terms of a "claim" and that section 101's definition of "claim" is very broad. Virtually all of a debtor's obligations will come within the term "debt."

3. If so, when did the obligation become a debt?

4. Subject to limited exceptions, a Chapter 7 discharge reaches only "debts that arose before the date of the order for relief," section 727(b). A Chapter 11 discharge covers debts that "arose before the date of such confirmation," section 1141(d)(1)(A). A Chapter 13 discharge reaches debts "provided for by the plan," section 1328(a), (c). This includes prepetition debts and postpetition debts that come under section 1305.

5. Is section 523 applicable?

6. Section 523 excepts certain debts from the operation of a discharge. Section 523 applies in all Chapter 7 cases, in Chapter 11 cases involving individual debtors, and in Chapter 13 cases in which the debtor receives a section 1328(b) "hardship discharge," section 727(b), 1141(d)(2), and 1328(c).

The next several pages cover section 523 and point out the extent to which Chapters 7, 11, and 13 differ with respect to debts affected by a discharge.

1. Chapter 7

In a Chapter 7 case, a discharge relieves a debtor from personal liability for debts that are both

1. Incurred prior to the time of the order for relief, and

2. Not within one of the exceptions to discharge set out in section 523.

It is very important to understand the difference between section 727(a) objections to discharge and section 523(a) exceptions to discharge. If an objection to discharge has been established, all creditors may attempt to collect the unpaid balance of their claims from the debtor. If a creditor establishes an exception to discharge, only that creditor may attempt to collect the unpaid portion of its claim from the debtor; all other prepetition claims remain discharged. Proof of an objection to discharge benefits all creditors; proof of an exception to discharge benefits only the creditor that establishes the exception.

Section 523(a) sets out 18 exceptions to discharge. Some exceptions are based on the nature of the debt. Other exceptions are based on the conduct of the debtor in connection with the debt.

a. Taxes

Bankruptcy affords very little relief to the delinquent taxpayer. Most taxes are not discharged in bankruptcy. Section 523(a)(1) excepts from the bankruptcy discharge all income and excise taxes for the three tax years immediately preceding bankruptcy. Taxes that are entitled to a priority are excepted from discharge, section 523(a)(1)(A). Section 507(a) provides a priority for taxes for a taxable year ending on or before the date of the filing of the petition for which a return, if required, is last due, including extensions, after three years before the date of the filing of the petition.

And, taxes more than three years old are nondischargeable if (a) a return was not filed, or (b) a return was filed within two years of the filing of the bankruptcy petition, or (c) a "fraudulent return" was filed.

Section 523(a)(1) needs to be read together with section 523(a)(14). A debt incurred to pay taxes that would have been nondischargeable is itself nondischargeable. If, for example, D uses her American Express card to pay such a federal tax, that portion of D's American Express bill would be excepted from discharge under section 523(a)(14).

b. Fraudulent Obligations

Section 523(a)(2), dealing with fraudulently incurred obligations, is the most frequently invoked exception to discharge. In subsections (A), (B) and (C), section 523(a)(2) describes several different fact patterns.

1) **False Statements and False Pretences—523(a)(2)(A) and (B)**

   a) **Comparison of Section 523(a)(2)(A) and (B)**

   Section 523(a)(2)(B) deals specifically with the fact pattern that includes the debtor's providing the creditor with a written false financial statement. Section 523(a)(2)(A) applies if the creditor alleges "false pretenses, a false representation, or actual fraud, other than a statement respecting the debtor's or an insider's financial condition." A close comparison of the language of section 523(a)(2)(A) with that of section 523(a)(2)(B) raises the question of whether a debtor's oral false representations about her financial condition falls between the two provisions.

   b) **Proof under 523(a)(2)(B)**

   A creditor faces difficult problems of proof under section 523(a)(2)(B). A creditor seeking an exception to discharge based on the debtor's providing false or incomplete financial information must establish:

   1. Materially false written statement respecting the financial condition of the debtor or an "insider";

   2. The creditor's reasonable reliance on the statement;

   3. The debtor's intent to deceive.

   Merely establishing the falsity of a written statement involving the debtor's financial condition will not suffice. The creditor will also have to establish its reliance, the reasonableness of the reliance, and, most difficult of all, the debtor's intent to deceive.

   c) **Reliance under 523(a)(2)(A)**

   A close comparison of the language of section 523(a)(2)(B) raises the more important question of whether the reasonable reliance and intent to deceive requirements that are expressed in section 523(a)(2)(B) should be implied under section 523(a)(2)(A). Courts, including the Supreme Court in Field v. Mans (1995), have held that section 523(a)(2)(A) does require proof of both the debtor's intent to deceive and the creditor's reasonable reliance.

2) **Luxuries—Section 523(a)(2)(C)**

   Section 523(a)(2)(A) must be read together not only with section 523(a)(2)(B) but also together with section 523(a)(2)(C), which deals with luxury goods and services and cash advances. More specifically, consumer debts incurred for luxury goods and services owed to a single creditor in excess of $500 incurred within 90 days of the bankruptcy filing as "presumed nondischargeable." Similarly, obligations to pay cash advances of $750 obtained within 70 days of the bankruptcy filing are "presumed to be nondischargeable."

Note section 523(a)(2)(C)'s use of the phrase "presumed to be nondischargeable." How can this presumption be rebutted? Section 523(a)(2)(C) begins with the phrase "for purposes of subparagraph (A) of this subsection." Section 523(a)(2)(A) deals with false representations. Arguably, when a person buys something on credit, he impliedly represents (1) an ability to pay and (2) an intent to repay. Section 523(a)(2)(C) seems to presume that with respect to the described luxury purchases and cash advances the debtor lacks that ability and/or intent. Accordingly, it would seem that the debtor can avoid section 523(a)(2)(C)'s exception from discharge by showing that he had both the ability and the intent to repay at the time of the transaction.

3) Risk of Asserting Section 523(a)(2) Objection

It is necessary to read section 523(a)(2) together with section 523(c) and section 523(d). Under section 523(c), discussed below, an exception to discharge based on section 523(a)(2) must be timely asserted during the bankruptcy case and adjudicated by the bankruptcy judge. See Bankruptcy Rule 4007. Under section 523(d), a creditor who unsuccessfully asserts a section 523(a)(2) exception to the discharge of a consumer debt may be required to pay the debtor's costs including an attorney's fee. Section 523(d)'s test is whether the creditor was "not substantially justified." Even if the position of the creditor was "not substantially justified," it can avoid section 523(d) liability if "special circumstances would make the award unjust."

c. Unscheduled Debts

Unscheduled debts are excepted from discharge by section 523(a)(3). A creditor needs to know that its debtor is involved in a bankruptcy case. Only a creditor that timely files a proof of claim shares in the distribution of the "property of the estate."

How does a creditor learn that its debtor is in bankruptcy? Section 521 requires the debtor to file a schedule of liabilities, and the bankruptcy court sends a notice to each creditor on the list. A creditor whose debt was not scheduled will not receive any notice; a creditor that does not receive the notice will not file a proof of claim unless it knows of the bankruptcy case; a creditor that does not file a proof of claim will not be paid from the property of the estate.

Accordingly, section 523(a)(3) excepts from discharge a debt not timely scheduled unless the creditor had notice or actual knowledge of the bankruptcy case.

d. Fraud as Fiduciary

Section 523(a)(4) excepts from bankruptcy discharge liabilities from "fraud or defalcation while acting in a fiduciary capacity." Proof of "fraud or defalcation" is not enough to establish the exception; section 523(a)(4) requires proof that it occurred while the debtor was a fiduciary. Section 523(a)(4) also makes nondischargeable all embezzlement and larceny liabilities, whether the debtor is a fiduciary or not.

e. Domestic Obligations

Section 523(a)(5) makes domestic support obligations nondischargeable. Section 523(a)(5) must be read together with section 101 that defines domestic support obligations and section 523(a)(15) which excepts nonsupport obligations owed to a spouse, former spouse, or child as a result of divorce or separation.

It can be important to understand the differences between what comes within the section 523(a)(5) exception and what comes within the section 523(a)(15) exception. Section 523(a)(5)–type obligations but not section 523(a)(15)–type obligations are afforded a first priority under section 507. Similarly, sections 362(b)(2) and 522(f)(1) and section 547(c)(7) apply only to section 523(a)(15) obligations.

f. Willful and Malicious Injury—Section 523(a)(6)

Section 523(a)(6) excepts from the operation of the bankruptcy discharge any debt arising from the debtor's "willful and malicious" injury of person or property. There had been considerable confusion as to the meaning of the limiting phrase "willful and malicious."

1) The *Kawaauhau* Case

In Kawaauhau v. Geiger (1998), the Supreme Court ended that confusion; it held that a malpractice claim based on a doctor's choice of a less than optimal course of treatment in order to keep costs down was *not* excepted from discharge under section 523(a)(6). The Court reasoned that "willful" modifies "injury" so that section 523(a)(6) requires proof of the debtor's intent to injure, not just proof that the debtor did an act intentionally which caused injury. Now there is confusion over how to pronounce and spell "Kawaauhau."

2) Relation to Other Provisions

Section 523(a)(6) needs to be read together with two other sections:

1. Personal injury and wrongful death claims based on a debtor's drunk driving are the subject of a separate exception from discharge, section 523(a)(9), which does not require proof of willfulness or maliciousness.

2. Under section 523(c), discussed below, an exception to discharge based on section 523(a)(6), but not an exception to discharge based on section 523(a)(9), must be timely asserted during the bankruptcy case and adjudicated by the bankruptcy judge. See Bankruptcy Rule 4007.

g. Fines Owed Government

Under section 523(a)(7), fines, penalties, or forfeitures that the debtor owes to a governmental entity are nondischargeable unless the debt is compensation for an actual pecuniary loss or a tax penalty on a dischargeable tax, section 523(a)(7). However, claims for fines, penalties and forfeitures have a very low priority in bankruptcy, section 726(a)(4).

h. Student Loans

Section 523(a)(8) excepts from discharge student loans and other obligations to repay "educational benefits." Earlier versions of section 523(a)(8) provided for the discharge of student loans if a certain time had elapsed. Under the present law, the debtor has to prove "undue hardship" to have her student loans discharged.

1) Test for Hardship

Most of the cases under section 523(a)(8) simply address the question of what is "undue hardship." These cases look to the totality of the circumstances.

2) Partial Discharge

There are, however, a number of section 523(a)(8) reported cases that address the legal question of whether the bankruptcy court can grant a partial discharge—it would be a hardship for the debtor to pay the $100,000 in college loans that she owes but she can pay $40,000 and so $60,000 is discharged and the remaining $40,000 is excepted from discharge under section 523(a)(8).

There is no language in section 523(a)(8) or anywhere else in the Bankruptcy Code that empowers a court to except a part of a debt from discharge. The courts that have granted partial discharge of student loans look to the policy objectives of section 523(a)(8) and the discretionary equitable powers reserved by the bankruptcy court by section 105.

i. Other Exceptions to Discharge

Exceptions to discharge based on section 523(a)(10)-(13) and (16)-(18) rarely arise in a bankruptcy case and never arise in a bankruptcy class.

2. Chapter 11

The answer to the question which debts are affected by a discharge is different in Chapter 11 than in Chapter 7 in two significant respects:

1. First, recall that generally a Chapter 7 discharge is limited to debts that arose before the date of the order for relief, section 727(b). A Chapter 11 discharge reaches debts that arose before the date of confirmation of the plan.

2. Second, every Chapter 7 discharge is subject to the exceptions to discharge of section 523. In Chapter 11, section 523 only applies if the debtor is an individual, section 1141(d)(2). Section 523 does not apply if the Chapter 11 debtor is a corporation or a partnership.

3. Chapter 13

In Chapter 13 cases, the answer to the question which debts are covered by the discharge depends on the nature of the Chapter 13 discharge. Recall that section 1328(a) governs the discharge of the Chapter 13 debtor who has made all plan payments, and section 1328(b) permits a hardship discharge even though the debtor was not able to complete payment payments.

a. Discharge Under 1328(b)

A section 1328(b) discharge is less comprehensive than a section 1328(a) discharge. If a debtor receives a discharge under section 1328(b), all of the exceptions to discharge in section 523 apply. Section 1328(c). A section 1328(b) discharge, therefore, is no more comprehensive than a section 727 discharge.

b. Discharge Under 1328(a)

The 2005 amendments diluted the section 1328(a) discharge but it is still more pervasive than a section 1328(b) discharge. Some debts that would be excepted from discharge in a Chapter 7 case are still dischargeable under section 1328(a):

1. Section 523(a)(6) debts for willful <u>and</u> malicious injury to <u>property;</u>

2. Section 523(a)(14) debts incurred to pay nondischargeable tax obligations; and

3. Section 523(a)(15) divorce or separation property settlement obligations.

4. Procedure for Asserting an Exception to Discharge

Most exceptions to discharge can be asserted after the bankruptcy case is over, in litigation in courts other than the bankruptcy court. Only exceptions to discharge based on section 523(a)(2), (4), or (6) must be asserted during the bankruptcy case in the bankruptcy court. If and only if the creditor's exception to discharge is based on one of the three statutory grounds for exception, the creditor must timely file a motion in the bankruptcy court.

When a creditor is relying on any other part of section 523(a), there is no requirement that the exception to discharge be asserted in the bankruptcy court during the bankruptcy case. In this event, the dischargeability issue is likely to arise in connection with the creditor's collection efforts in a nonbankruptcy forum.

Example: D owes C $1,000. D files a bankruptcy petition. D fails to list her debt to C on her schedule of liabilities. D receives a bankruptcy discharge. Six months later, C sues D in state court for the $1,000. If D asserts her bankruptcy discharge as a defense, C can counter by asserting a section 523(a)(3) exception to discharge.

C. Effect of a Discharge

1. What a Discharge Does

A discharge protects the debtor from any further personal liability on discharged debts. Section 524(a) provides that a discharge voids a judgment on discharged debts and enjoins any legal "action" to collect such a debt from the debtor or property of the debtor. A discharge also bars extrajudicial collection "acts" such as dunning letters or telephone calls to collect discharged debts.

2. What a Discharge Does Not Do

A discharge does not cancel or extinguish debts. It only protects the debtors from further personal liability on the debt.

a. No Protection of Co–Debtors

Section 524(e) limits the protection of the discharge to the debtor. A bankruptcy discharge does not automatically affect the liability of other parties such as co-debtors or guarantors. For example, the discharge of an insured tortfeasor does not affect the liability of the insurance company.

b. No Effect on Liens

A bankruptcy discharge has no effect on a lien. Remember, a discharge only eliminates a creditor's right to collect a debt from the debtor personally. It does not eliminate the debt; discharge does not eliminate liens securing payment of the debt.

Example: D owes C $10,000. The debt is secured in part by D's car which is worth $6,000. D files for relief under Chapter 7. The trustee abandons the car to the debtor under section 554. D receives a discharge. The discharge does not extinguish C's security interest. If D is in default, C can repossess the car. The discharge does, however, wipe out C's rights against D personally. If C repossesses and resells the car, C cannot obtain a deficiency judgment against D.

D. Reaffirmation

Law students and lawyers need to be able to answer three questions about reaffirmation agreements: (1) what is a reaffirmation agreement, (2) why would a debtor enter into a reaffirmation agreement and (3) what are the bankruptcy law issues related to reaffirmation agreements?

1. What Is a Reaffirmation Agreement?

First, a reaffirmation agreement is an agreement. It can't be done by the debtor alone; it can't be done by a creditor alone. It requires the assent of both the debtor and the creditor.

More specifically, a reaffirmation agreement is an agreement between a debtor and one of her creditors that the debtor will pay a debt she incurred before her bankruptcy filing that, but for the reaffirmation agreement, would have been dischargeable in the bankruptcy case. Under contract law, such an agreement is legally enforceable even though there is no bargained-for exchange, i.e., no consideration.

2. Why Make Such an Agreement?

Why would a debtor make such an agreement?

a. Keep Encumbered Property

The most common reason for a debtor's reaffirming a debt is to keep encumbered property.

Example: Assume that *D* owes GMAC $16,000 on her car loan at the time of her bankruptcy filing. *D*'s bankruptcy discharge will affect GMAC's contract rights against *D*—GMAC's ability to collect the $16,000 from *D* personally. The bankruptcy discharge will not, however, affect GMAC's property interest in the car—GMAC's ability to foreclose on its lien and take the car. Accordingly, *D* might enter into a reaffirmation agreement with GMAC to keep her car.

b. Protect Co–Debtors

A second common reason for reaffirmation is to protect co-debtors. What if *M*, *D*'s momma, guaranteed the car note? Neither the automatic stay in *D*'s Chapter 7 bankruptcy case nor any discharge that *D* might receive protects *M*. Accordingly, *D* might enter into a reaffirmation agreement with GMAC to keep GMAC from taking action against *M*.

c. Avoid Litigation About Discharge

Another common reason for reaffirmance is concern about dischargeability litigation. If, for example, *D* submitted a false financial statement to GMAC to get the car loan, she might enter into a reaffirmation agreement with GMAC to keep GMAC from filing a complaint under section 523(a)(2).

d. Preserve Relationship

And, debtors might reaffirm a debt to preserve a relationship with that creditor. At the time of his bankruptcy filing, *D* owed his proctologist *P* $666. If *D* needs to be examined by *P* again, he might decide that he needs to reaffirm that debt.

3. Bankruptcy Law Issues

Most of the bankruptcy law issues relating to reaffirmation relate to concern that a creditor might pressure a debtor into reaffirming its debt.

a. Effect of Stay

Can a creditor ever contact a debtor about reaffirming its debt without violating section 362(a)(6)? Isn't that contact "an act to collect a claim"?

Section 362(b) does not expressly except reaffirmation efforts from the operation of the automatic stay. Yet, as the Sixth Circuit noted in its decision in In re Duke (1996): "The option of reaffirming would be empty if creditors were forbidden to engage in any communication whatsoever with debtors who have pre-petition obligations." Case law has in essence created something of an exception to the automatic stay for some reaffirmation initiatives.

b. Limits on Enforceability

While the Bankruptcy Code has no provision as to what actions a creditor can take to obtain a reaffirmation agreement, section 524 has detailed provisions regarding the reaffirmation agreement. Section 524(c) and (d) limit the enforceability of reaffirmation agreements by

1. Requiring that the agreement be executed before the discharge is granted, section 524(c)(1);

2. Giving the debtor a right to rescind, section 524(c)(4);

3. Requiring that, before any reaffirmation is signed, the creditor provides the debtor with disclosures detailed in section 524(c)(3);

4. Requiring the agreement be filed with the court, section 524(c)(3);

5. Requiring a hearing if the debtor is an individual and not represented by an attorney in the reaffirmation negotiations, section 524(d), section 524(c)(6);

6. Requiring the attorney who represented the debtor in the reaffirmation to certify inter alia that the debtor was fully informed and that either the agreement does not impose an undue hardship on the debtor or the debtor has the ability to make the reaffirmation payments. Section 524(k)(5).

E. Protection From Discriminatory Treatment

Section 525 is entitled "Protection from Discriminatory Treatment." The title promises more than the section actually provides. The Boy Scouts could refuse to let someone serve as a scoutmaster because he filed for bankruptcy—even straight bankruptcy. More importantly, a store could refuse to extend credit or a bank could refuse to make a loan because of a person's bankruptcy history.

Notice that two of the three lettered subsections, 525(a) and 525(c), only apply to "governmental units." And, notice that two of the three subsections, 525(a) and 525(b), require proof that the adverse action occurred "solely" because of the bankruptcy history.

1. More specifically, subject to very limited exceptions, a governmental unit may not deny a debtor a license or a franchise or otherwise discriminate against a debtor *"solely because"* the debtor (i) filed for bankruptcy, (ii) was insolvent prior to and/or during bankruptcy, or (iii) refuses to pay debts *discharged* by his, her or its bankruptcy, section 525(a).

2. Similarly, a private employer cannot fire an employee or "discriminate with respect to employment" *"solely because"*:

   • the employee filed for bankruptcy,

   • was insolvent prior to or during the bankruptcy, or

   • refuses to pay debts *discharged* by his or her bankruptcy, section 525(b).

3. Section 525(c) prohibits a government unit operating a student loan program and any private lender making loans guaranteed under a student loan program from denying a loan because a person:

   • filed for bankruptcy,

   • was insolvent prior to or during the bankruptcy or

   • refuses to pay debts discharged by his or her bankruptcy.

As enacted in 1994, section 525(c), unlike section 525(a) and (b)) has a "because" and not a "solely because" standard.

F. Review Questions

1. T or F A partnership can never receive a Chapter 7 discharge.

2. T or F D filed for bankruptcy in 2004 and received a Chapter 7 discharge. D can not file another Chapter 7 petition for 8 years.

3. T or F   Either bankruptcy court judges or state court judges can hear and decide objections to discharge.

4. T or F   Either bankruptcy court judges or state court judges can hear and decide exceptions to discharge,

5. D files for bankruptcy. In the 90 days before bankruptcy, D incurred $5,000 of credit card debt. Will that debt be excepted from discharge?

6. T or F   Objections to discharge do not apply in a Chapter 11 case.

7. T or F   Objections to discharge do not apply in a Chapter 13 case.

8. T or F   D borrows $1000 from C. G guarantees payment of the debt. D files for bankruptcy and obtains a discharge. Notwithstanding the discharge, C can collect from G.

9. T or F   D files for bankruptcy and proposes to reaffirm its secured debt to C. The court can compel C to reaffirm if there is no "undue hardship."

10. T or F   After the 2005 amendments, a store can no longer refuse to extend credit to an individual if her current monthly income is less than the median annual income.

*

XVII

Chapter 13 Cases

■ ANALYSIS

A.   Commencement of the Case

1.   Eligibility

Chapter 13 of the Bankruptcy Code replaced Chapter XIII of the Bankruptcy Act of 1898. Chapter XIII was limited to a "wage earner," i.e., "an individual whose principal income is derived from wages, salary, or commissions."

Chapter 13 is open to more debtors. Subject to limited exceptions, the source of income is not an eligibility test. A debtor may file for Chapter 13 relief if she:

> 1.   Is *an individual, and*
>
> Chapter 13 is not available to corporations or partnerships. Also, neither a stockbroker nor a commodity broker—even if an individual— may file a petition under Chapter 13, section 109(e).

2. Ha*s a "regular income," and*

The phrase "individual with a regular income" is statutorily defined in section 101(30) as "an individual whose income is sufficiently stable and regular to enable such individual to make payments under a plan under Chapter 13 of this title."

3. Ha*s fixed unsecured debts of less than $307,675 and fixed secured debts of less than $922,975. Section 109(e).*

Note that the debt limitation only includes "fixed" debts. For example, Ally McBeal is sued for $25,000,000 for malpractice on April 4. She could still file a Chapter 13 petition on April 5.

Section 104 provides for periodic, automatic adjustments in dollar amounts to reflect changes in the Consumer Price Index.

2. Effects of 2005 Amendments to Code

a. Chapter 7 Means Testing

In 2005, Congress added the "means testing" requirements to section 707. Means testing can and will prevent some individuals from filing Chapter 7 relief, and in such a case the statute requires the court to dismiss the case or, if the debtor agrees, convert the case to Chapter 13. However, there is nothing in section 707 or section 109 or anywhere else in the Code that expressly requires anyone to file or convert to Chapter 13. On the other hand, the application of section 707 means testing will result in some debtors filing for Chapter 13 relief because they feel that they have no meaningful alternative: no protection from creditors under state law, no possibility of filing for Chapter 7 protection.

b. Changes Approach to Chapter 13

The 2005 amendments change the basic Congressional approach to debtors' choice under Chapter 13. Prior to 2005, the approach had been to include provisions in Chapter 13 that afford debtors greater rights than they would obtain in Chapter 7 so that debtors who could choose between Chapters 7 and 13 would choose Chapter 13. The 2005 amendments, in essence, take away the choice by means testing under Chapter 7 and takes away many of the advantages of Chapter 13. Sticks instead of carrots.

3. Filing Begins the Case

Chapter 13 is similar to Chapter 7 and Chapter 11 in that the case begins with the filing of a bankruptcy petition, section 301. Chapter 13 is different from

Chapter 7 and Chapter 11 in that only the debtor may file a Chapter 13 petition. There are no involuntary, i.e., creditor-initiated Chapter 13 cases.

4. Automatic Stay

The filing of a Chapter 13 petition also triggers the automatic stay of section 362 and the automatic co-debtor stay of section 1301, which stops civil collection activities directed against certain co-debtors of the individual who filed the petition. Section 1301.

B. Co-Debtor Stay

The automatic stay of section 362 applies in a Chapter 13 case. Also, section 1301, which applies only in a Chapter 13 case, restrains a creditor from attempting to collect a debt from the co-debtor of a Chapter 13 debtor.

Example: *D* borrows money from *C* to buy a pair of contact lenses. Her mother, *M*, signs the note as a co-maker. *D* later incurs financial problems and files a Chapter 13 petition. Section 362 stays *C* from attempting to collect from *D*; section 1301 stays *C* from attempting to collect from *M*.

1. Requirements of the Stay

Section 1301's stay of collection activities directed at co-debtors is applicable only if:

1.   The debt is a consumer debt, and

2.   The co-debtor is not in the credit business.

2. Termination of the Stay

This co-debtor stay automatically terminates when the case is closed, dismissed, or converted to Chapter 7 or 11.

3. Relief From the Stay

Section 1301(c) sets out three grounds for relief from the co-debtor stay. Section 1301(c) requires notice and hearing and requires the court to grant relief if any of the three grounds are established.

a. Co-Debtor Received the Consideration

First, the stay on collection from the co-debtor will be lifted if the co-debtor, not the Chapter 13 debtor, received the consideration for the claim, section 1301(c)(1).

Example: If in the above example, *M*, not *D*, filed for Chapter 13 relief, *C* could petition for relief under section 1301(c)(1) so that it could attempt to collect from *D*. Section 1301(c)(1) also covers the situation in which the Chapter 13 debtor is merely an accommodation endorser.

b. Plan Will Not Pay Claim

Second, when the Chapter 13 plan has been filed, a creditor may obtain relief from the co-debtor stay to the extent that "the plan filed by the debtor proposes not to pay such claim," section 1301(c)(2).

Example: Assume that *D* still owes *C* $200. *D*'s Chapter 13 plan proposes to pay each holder of an unsecured claim 70 cents on the dollar. *C* will thus be paid $140 under the plan. As soon as such a plan is filed, *C* can obtain relief from the stay so that it can obtain $60 from *M*, the other 30 cents on the dollar. A motion to lift the stay under section 1301(c)(2) is deemed granted unless the debtor or co-debtor files a written objection within 20 days, section 1301(d).

c. Irreparable Harm

Third, section 1301(c)(3) requires the court to grant relief from the co-debtor stay to the extent that "such creditor's interest would be irreparably harmed by continuation of such stay." The running of a state statute of limitations is not a basis for relief under section 1301(c)(3). Section 108(c) guarantees the creditor at least 30 days after the termination of the stay to file a state collection action against the co-debtor.

C. Trustees

There will be a trustee appointed in every Chapter 13 case, section 1302(a). In almost all districts, the United States trustee appoints a standing trustee who serves as trustee in every Chapter 13 case, section 1302(d).

1. Who Works as Trustee

Being a Chapter 13 standing trustee is a full-time job, but it is not a government job. The Chapter 13 trustee is not a government employee. Rather, she operates a private business. The Chapter 13 trustee does not receive a salary from the government. Rather, she receives a percentage of the funds disbursed to creditors under the Chapter 13 plans in her district.

2. Duties

The trustee in a Chapter 13 case is an active trustee. Section 1302 imposes a number of duties on a trustee in a Chapter 13 case.

a. Avoidance—Maybe, Maybe Not

Section 1302 does not clearly indicate whether a Chapter 13 trustee can assert the avoidance provisions. The statutory arguments for a Chapter 13 trustee being able to avoid preferences and other prebankruptcy transfers are

- Section 103—which indicates that provisions in chapter 5 such as section 547 are applicable in Chapters 7, 11, and 13;

- Use of the word "trustee" in section 547 and the other avoidance provisions.

The statutory argument for a Chapter 13 trustee *not* being able to avoid preferences and other prebankruptcy transfers focuses on section 1302(b)'s exclusion of section 704(1). If a Chapter 13 trustee is not empowered to "collect the property of the estate," she arguably should not be able to avoid prebankruptcy transfers.

b. Operating Business—Not

Operation of the debtor's business is *not* one of the trustee's duties listed in section 1302. If a debtor engaged in business files a Chapter 13 petition, section 1304(b) contemplates that the business will be operated by the debtor, not by the trustee, "unless the court orders otherwise."

c. Exact Role Varies

While a Chapter 13 trustee's duties are listed in section 1302, the exact role of a Chapter 13 trustee varies from district to district. And, while a Chapter 13 trustee does not collect property of the estate or bring avoidance actions or operate businesses, most Chapter 13 trustee's play the leading role in most Chapter 13 cases.

Think about Chapter 13 and the role of the trustee in terms of amounts.

1. First, the dollar amount of most claims. The amount owed by most Chapter 13 debtors to most of their creditors is too low for creditors to hire attorneys to represent them in the Chapter 13 case.

2. Second, the amount of cases. The amount of cases handled by the typical bankruptcy judge is too high for her to be able to spend significant time on Chapter 13 cases.

Accordingly, creditors and the bankruptcy judges generally rely on the Chapter 13 trustee to:

1. Review the debtor's Chapter 13 plan,

2. Raise plan issues, if any, with the debtor's attorney, and

3. Resolve those plan issues with the debtor's attorney.

d. Standard Roles With Respect to the Plan

Most Chapter 13 plans are presented to the judge without any objection. And, to the extent that there is a plan confirmation objection, the objection is generally raised by the Chapter 13 trustee. After the plan is confirmed by the court, it is the Chapter 13 trustee's office that distributes the plan payments.

D. Preparation of the Chapter 13 Plan

Only a debtor may file a Chapter 13 plan, section 1321. The court may dismiss a Chapter 13 case or convert it to Chapter 7 for "failure to file a plan *timely* under section 1321 of this title," section 1307(c)(3). The Code leaves the question of the meaning of "timely"—how many days the debtor has to file such a plan—to the Rules. It's within 15 days after filing the petition, Bankruptcy Rule 3015.

The two most important plan preparation questions are:

1. How much does the debtor have to pay under the plan?

2. How much do the various creditors get paid under the plan?

To answer these questions, look primarily to sections 1322 (which governs plan contents) and 1325 (which governs plan confirmation). Since plan confirmation (court approval) is the objective of a Chapter 13 debtor, she will look to both sections 1322 and 1325 in formulating her plan.

1. Contents of the Plan—Section 1322

Section 1322 governs the contents of a Chapter 13 plan. Subsection (a) of section 1322 specifies what the plan must provide; subsection (b) specifies what the plan may provide.

a. What the Plan *Must* Provide (Section 1322(a))

A Chapter 13 plan must provide for full payment in cash of all claims entitled to priority under section 507 unless the holder of the claim otherwise agrees, section 1322(a)(2), with a limited exception for as-signed domestic support obligations, section 1322(a)(4). A Chapter 13 plan may provide for less than full payment to other unsecured claims. It may not, however, arbitrarily pay some holders of unsecured claims less than others. Rather, the plan must either treat all unsecured claims the same or classify claims and provide for the same treatment of each unsecured claim within a particular class, sections 1322(a)(3), 1322(b)(4).

b. **What the Plan *May* Provide (Section 1322(b))**

A Chapter 13 plan may also modify the rights of most holders of secured claims. It may modify the rights of creditor A, who has a security interest on the Chapter 13 debtor's car. It may modify the rights of Creditor *B* who has a mortgage on the Chapter 13 debtor's store. It may not, however, modify the rights of Creditor *C* who has a mortgage *only* on the Chapter 13 debtor's principal residence, section 1322(b)(2).

Example: If before bankruptcy, *D*'s home mortgage provided for a principal balance of $100,000, interest at 10% and monthly payments of $625, the debtor has exactly the same home mortgage obligation in Chapter 13. No plan modification of home mortgages.

Note the word "only" in section 1322(b)(2). If C loaned D $100,000 and obtained a mortgage on both D's residence and D's store, the plan could modify D's rights.

Note, also that section 1322(b)(2) must be read together with the 2005 amendments to section 1325(a)(5) which, in essence, modify or limit the extent to which a Chapter 13 plan can modify the rights of holders of most secured claims, as you will read below in the discussion of how section 1325(a)(5) eliminates most Chapter 13 : "stripdowns."

2. **Home Mortgages**

While a Chapter 13 plan cannot modify a claim secured only by the debtor's principal residence, it can cure defaults with respect to such a claim, section 1322(a)(3), (5). If, for example, *D* missed four home mortgage payments of $625 each before filing for Chapter 13 relief, her Chapter 13 plan can provide for periodic payments over the duration of the plan to "cure" that $2,500 default. We will do more examples of curing defaults on secured claims and do examples of modifying secured claims when we do more with confirmation of Chapter 13 plan provisions relating to claims secured by houses and other secured claims later in this chapter.

3. Funding the Plan

In the typical Chapter 13 case, the source of the payments proposed by the plan will be the debtor's wages. This is not, however, a statutory requirement. Section 1322(a)(1) only requires that the plan provide for submission of "such portion of future earnings . . . of the debtor to the supervision and control of the trustee as is necessary for the execution of the plan." (Section 1322(a) needs to be read together with section 1325(b) ("disposable income").) Payments under the plan may also be funded by sale of property of the estate, section 1322(b)(8).

4. Length of Plan

The number of a debtor's monthly payments depends on the debtor's "current monthly income" and "median family income." Sections 1325(b)(2), 1325(b)(4), and section 1322(d). Generally, a debtor whose "current monthly income" multiplied by 12 for the state for a family of the same size will make plan payments for three years, and a debtor whose "current monthly income" multiplied by 12 is more than the "median family income" for the state for a family of the same size will make plan payments for five years.

E. Confirmation of the Chapter 13 Plan

In formulating a Chapter 13 plan, a lawyer or law student should look not only at section 1322 which deals with the contents of the plan but also section 1325 which covers confirmation of a plan. In Chapter 13, creditors do not vote on the plan. Chapter 13 requires only court approval. The standards for judicial confirmation of a Chapter 13 plan are set out in section 1325.

Section 1325(a)(1) requires that the plan satisfy the provisions of Chapter 13 and other applicable bankruptcy law requirements.

1. Filing Fee

Section 1325(a)(2) conditions confirmation on payment of the filing fee.

2. "Good Faith"

Section 1325(a)(3) sets out a "good faith" standard. Dicta in appellate court cases on section 1325(a)(3) (good faith) tend to list factors. Holdings in bankruptcy court cases on section 1325(a)(3) tend to focus on the facts.

Decisions under section 1325(a)(3) ("good faith") also often address the debtor's financial condition and the amount of payments proposed by the plan. The Eleventh Circuit in Kitchens v. Georgia R.R. Bank and Trust Co. (In re Kitchens) (1983), delineated 16 factors that courts should consider in determining a debtor's good faith under section 1325, including:

1. The amount of the debtor's income from all sources;

2. The living expenses of the debtor and his dependents;

3. The amount of attorney's fees;

4. The probable or expected duration of the debtor's Chapter 13 plan;

5. The motivations and sincerity of the debtor in seeking relief under the provisions of Chapter 13;

6. The debtor's degree of effort;

7. The debtor's ability to earn and the likelihood of fluctuation in earnings;

8. Special circumstances such as inordinate medical expenses;

9. The frequency with which the debtor has sought relief under the Bankruptcy Reform Act and its predecessors;

10. The circumstances under which the debtor has contracted debts and has demonstrated bona fides, or lack thereof, in dealings with creditors;

11. The burden which the plan's administration would place on the Trustee;

12. The extent to which claims are modified and the extent of preferential treatment among classes of creditors;

13. Substantiality of repayment to the unsecured creditors;

14. Consideration of the type of debt to be discharged and whether such debt would be nondischargeable under Chapter 7;

15. The accuracy of the plan's statements of debts and expenses and whether any inaccuracies are an attempt to mislead the court; and

16. Other factors or exceptional circumstances.

3. Adequacy of Plan Payments

Section 1325(a)(4) and section 1325(b) more directly address the adequacy of the plan payments.

a. "Best Interests of Creditors" Test

Section 1325(a)(4) protects the holders of unsecured claims by imposing a "best interests of creditors" test: the present value of the proposed payments to a holder of an unsecured claim must be at least equal to the amount that the creditor would have received in a Chapter 7 liquidation. The following hypothetical illustrates the practical significance of the "present value" language in section 1325(a)(4).

Example: Assume the following four facts:

1. D owes C $1,000;

2. D files a Chapter 13 petition;

3. If D had filed a Chapter 7 petition, the sale of the property of the estate would have yielded a sufficient sum to pay all priority creditors in full and pay unsecured creditors like C 36 cents on the dollar;

4. D's Chapter 13 petition proposes to pay C $10 a month for 36 months.

This plan does not satisfy the requirement of section 1325(a)(4). Payment of $360 over a 36–month period does not have a "present value" of $360.

This hypothetical is probably somewhat unrealistic. In the typical Chapter 7 case, an unsecured creditor would receive little if anything. Accordingly, in the typical Chapter 13 case, section 1325(a)(4) will be easily satisfied.

b. "Best Efforts"

Section 1325(a)(3) and (4) must be read together with section 1325(b). Section 1325(b) imposes a "best efforts" requirement. This requirement means that a Chapter 13 plan either provide for payment in full of all unsecured claims plus interest or commit all of the debtor's "disposable income" to such payments for the "applicable commitment period," as defined in section 1325(b)(4).

The phrase "disposable income" is defined in section 1325(b)(2). It means "current monthly income," other than child support income, that is not necessary to provide support for the debtor or the debtor's dependents. If (and only if) the Chapter 13 debtor's income is greater than the applicable "median family income," then it is necessary to read section 1325(b)(2) together with section 1325(b)(3) and necessary to limit the debtor's support needs by the Internal Revenue Service expense standards referenced in section 707(b)(2)(A)(ii)(I).

c. Secured Claims

Section 1325(a)(5) protects the holders of secured claims "provided for by the plan" by requiring one of the following:

1. Acceptance of the plan by such a creditor; or

2. Continuation of the lien and proposed payments to such a creditor of a present value that at least equals the value of the collateral. [This "cram down" provision is discussed below.]

3. Surrender of the collateral to the creditor.

d. Ability to Perform

Section 1325(a)(6) requires a determination of ability to perform; it requires that the debtor "will be able to make all payments under the plan and to comply with the plan."

e. Effects of Confirmation

A confirmed Chapter 13 plan is binding on the debtor and all of his creditors, section 1327(a). Unless the plan or the order confirming the plan otherwise provides, confirmation of a plan vests all of the "property of the estate" in the debtor free and clear of "any claim or interest of any creditor provided for by the plan," section 1327(c).

f. Performance of the Plan

After confirmation, the plan is put into effect with the debtor generally making the payments provided in the plan to a Chapter 13 trustee who acts as a disbursing agent.

g. Modification

A Chapter 13 plan can be modified after confirmation. Section 1329 expressly provides for postconfirmation modification on request of the debtor, the trustee, or the holder of an unsecured claim.

F. Cramdown (or Cram Down) of Secured Claims in Chapter 13

1. Alternatives to Cram Down

a. Agreed Upon Modifications

A Chapter 13 plan can propose modifications of a secured claim to which the holder of the claim consents. For example, the creditor might agree to wait longer for payment if the payment is increased. If the modification is acceptable to the holder of the secured claim, it will be acceptable to the court, section 1325(a)(5)(A). No secured claim plan confirmation issue.

b. Surrender

Alternatively, a Chapter 13 plan can propose to surrender the encumbered property to the holder of a secured claim.

Example: Assume that D owes S $200,000, secured by a first mortgage on Blackacre. If D's Chapter 13 plan surrenders Blackacre to S, then S no longer has a secured claim. If Blackacre's value is less than $200,000, S might still have a claim. Just not a secured claim.

Accordingly, a plan that "surrenders the property securing such claim" will be acceptable to the court, section 1325(a)(5)(C). Again, no secured claim plan confirmation issue.

2. Explaining Cram Down

Secured claim plan confirmation issues arise only if the plan proposes that (i) the debtor retain the encumbered property and (ii) the secured claim be modified and (iii) the holder of the secured claim does not accept the plan. These issues are called cram down issues (or cram down issues).

It's not the Bankruptcy Code that uses the phrase "cram down." Neither cram down nor cramdown appears anywhere in the Bankruptcy Code. Rather it is the bankruptcy lawyers, judges and law professors who have come to use the term cram down to describe court approval of a plan provision that effects changes in the payment of a claim that the claim holder objects to.

3. Requirements of Cram Down

In order to cram down a Chapter 13 modification of a secured claim, the bankruptcy court must apply section 1325(a)(5)(B). And, in order to apply section 1325(a)(5)(B), the court must determine the nature of the proposed modification.

a. Before 2005 Amendments

Prior to the 2005 amendments to the Bankruptcy Code, the most common form of secured debt modification was a "strip down," i.e., reducing the amount that was to be paid to the holder of the secured debt to the value of the collateral. And, prior to the 2005 amendments, in applying section 1325(a)(5)(B) to a "strip down," the bankruptcy court would make the following two determinations:

- What is the value of the collateral?

  The relevant language in section 1325(a)(5) is "allowed amount of SUCH CLAIM." The antecedent of "such claim" is "secured claim." Section 506 ties the amount of the secured claim to the value of the collateral.

- Is the present value of the plan payments at least equal to the value of the collateral?

  The relevant language in section 1325(a)(5) is "value, as of the effective date of the plan, of property to be distributed under the plan . . . ."

Example: D, an independent trucker, owes S $60,000. S has a security interest in D's tractor and trailer rig. D files a Chapter 13 plan that proposes to pay s $1,000 a month for 36 months. S does not consent.

1.   In applying section 1325(a)(5)(B) to this proposed strip down, the court would first have to determine the value of the collateral, that is, the value of the tractor and trailer rig. Looking to *Associates Commercial Corp. v. Rash*, discussed earlier, the court would determine the replacement value of the property.

2.   If the replacement value of the tractor and trailer rig was $36,000, then the proposed plan payments must have a present value of $36,000. Obviously, a Chapter 13 debtor's promise to pay $1,000 a month for 36 months has a present value significantly less than $36,000. The debtor would also have to pay cram down interest as measured by the formula approach of *Till v. SCS Credit Corp.*, also discussed earlier.

b. After the 2005 Amendments

The 2005 amendments to the Bankruptcy Code significantly limit a Chapter 13 debtor's ability to strip down secured loans. No strip down is allowed on any debt incurred within one year prior to the bankruptcy filing. And, no strip down is allowed on a purchase money loan incurred within 910 days before the bankruptcy filing if it is secured by a motor vehicle acquired by the debtor for her personal use.

Thank about what the 2005 amendments do and don't do. Think about what the typical Chapter 13 debtor can and cannot do with respect to the typical car loan.

Example: A Chapter 13 debtor owes $13,000 on a car that she wants to keep.

1. Now, she will have to make payments with a present value of $13,000. (Prior to the 2005 amendments, present value calculation would be pegged to the replacement value of the car, not the amount she owed on the car.)

2. On the other hand, while she cannot cram down a change in the principal top be paid, she can, consistent with *Till*, cram down a change in the interest rate; and she can, consistent with the requirements of section 1325(a)(5)(B)(iii) change the number of payments and the amount of each payment.

Remember that strip down is simply one form of cram down. A cram down is any change in the payment obligation approved by the court over the creditor's objection. The change can be changes in the interest rate, changes in the number of payments, changes in the amount of payments, etc. Or the change can be a change in the amount to be paid, i.e., a strip down.

Remember, too, that strip down is still possible in a case with the same facts as *Rash*. A strip down is still possible so long as (1) the debt was not incurred within a year of bankruptcy and (2) the collateral is not a personal use automobile and (3) the collateral is not the debtor's home.

G. Treatment of Home Mortgages in Chapter 13 Plans

Most home mortgages are protected from the cram down, protected from modification by a Chapter 13 plan. Section 1322(b) excepts claims "secured only by a security interest in real property that is the debtor's principal residence" from plan modification.

Reread the quoted language and identify the three "litigable" (i.e., "law school testable") issues. First, is the residence the only security for the loan, or did the creditor take a lien on some other collateral such as the debtor? What if the home loan is secured not only by a mortgage on the home but also a lien on the debtor's bank account? By a credit life insurance policy? By fixtures or furniture? Second, for Alabama students and lawyers, is the double-wide mobile home (pronounced mo-beal home) that the debtor lives in "real property"? Third, is a mixed use property such as a combination home/business office protected?

> Example: If D owes $100,000 on her home mortgage to M at the time that she files for Chapter 13 and her payments are $625 a month and the mortgage interest rate is 10%, D cannot use section 1322(b) to change her mortgage payment schedule or interest rate. Nor can D use section 1322 to reduce the amount of that secured claim, regardless of the value of the home. If, for example, the value of the home is only $70,000, D cannot use her Chapter 13 plan to "strip down" M's secured claim to $70,000. Nobelman v. American Saving Bank (1993).

1. Strip Down Versus Strip Off

Some courts have distinguished between a "strip down" and a "strip off."

> Example: Assume again that M has a $100,000 first mortgage on D's $70,000 home. Now also assume that S has a $25,000 second mortgage. As noted above, D cannot use section 1322(b)(2) to strip down M's secured claim to $70,000. How is S's claim different from M's? Under section 506, the amount of S's secured claim is zero—the value of SUCH creditor's interest (i.e., the second mortgage interest) in the house. If S has a "zero" secured claim in D's principal residence, some courts in essence reason that S gets "zero" protection from strip off from section 1322(b)(2). In sum, no "strip down," i.e., no reduction of a first or second mortgage where that mortgage has some value but possibly a "strip off," an elimination of a second or third mortgage where that mortgage has no value.

2. Allowed Modifications

Section 1322(b)(2)'s general prohibition against Chapter 13 plans "messing with home mortgages" is subject to two statutory exceptions.

a. Cure Default

First, section 1322(b)(5) permits a Chapter 13 plan to cure defaults on all home mortgages. Assume for example that *D* missed three home mortgage payments of $700 a month before she filed her Chapter 13 bankruptcy petition and under the terms of her mortgage her default in making these three payments triggered an acceleration which made the entire loan balance immediately due. *D* can use her Chapter 13 plan to cure these defaults "within a reasonable time" and maintain the mortgage by continuing to make her usual monthly payments, section 1322(b)(5).

It would seem reasonable to compare section 1322(b)(5)'s "reasonable time" standard for curing home mortgage defaults with section 365(b)'s "promptly" standard for curing lease defaults and conclude that the former is a less demanding standard. It would also seem reasonable to cross reference section 1322(b)(5) with section 1322(c)(1) which deals with a different but "time question" affecting curing home mortgage defaults: at what point in the foreclosure process is it too late to cure a default? Under section 1322(c)(1), read together with section 362, a debtor can cure home mortgage defaults so long as his Chapter 13 petition is filed before the "residence is sold at a foreclosure sale."

b. Short–Term Mortgages

Section 1322(c)(2) establishes a second exception to the "no Chapter 13 plan modification of home mortgages rule" of section 1322(b)(2): short-term mortgages. More specifically, section 1322(c)(2) permits a cram down of modifications in home mortgages if "the last payment on the original payment schedule" is due before the last payment under the plan.

Example: Assume that at the time *D* files her Chapter 13 petition, she owes 48 monthly payments under her second mortgage. By filing a plan with more than 48 monthly payments, *D* could invoke section 1322(c)(2) and modify that short-term second mortgage.

Demand notes and long-term mortgage notes that provide for acceleration raise issues under the "last payment on the original payment schedule" standard.

H. Preferring Some Claims

1. By Classifying Claims

A Chapter 13 debtor often wants to make certain that some creditors are paid in full by her Chapter 13 plan. Especially important are debts unaffected by the Chapter 13 discharge. For example:

- To get credit, the debtor may have had to get some willing, more creditworthy—a relative or close friend—to guarantee payment of the obligation. To the extent that the Chapter 13 plan does not pay that obligation, the creditor can and will collect from the co-debtor. Cf. section 1301(c)(2).

- And, some debts such as student loans are not covered by a Chapter 13 discharge. The debtor will, of course, want to pay all such nondischargeable debts in full in her Chapter 13 plan; otherwise the debtor will have to pay the balance after completing the Chapter 13 plan payments.

a. Using Claim Classification to Pay Some Debts in Full

A Chapter 13 debt can use claim classification to pay one or more of her creditors in full even though she does not have sufficient disposable income to pay all of her creditors in full. Under section 1322(b)(1), a Chapter 13 plan can divide unsecured claims into more than one class and treat the various classes differently.

b. Cannot "Discriminate Unfairly"

The primary limitation on this discrimination in the plan treatment of unsecured claims is that the classification may not "discriminate unfairly." The key word is, of course, "unfairly": any classification discriminates—what is required is that the discrimination not be unfair.

Most reported opinions under section 1322(b)(1) set out some sort of multi-factor test. The factor that seems most important is the difference in the amount of payment to the various classes. Obviously, it will be easier to get court approval of a plan that pays Class 2 100% and all other classes 90% than a plan that pays Class 2 100% and all other classes 10%.

Put Chapter 13 plan classification in context. All Chapter 13 plans must meet the "best interests" test of section 1325(a)(4). In other words, even the creditors in the classes receiving least favorable Chapter 13 plan treatment are still receiving at least as much as they would have received if the debtor had filed for Chapter 7 relief instead of Chapter 13.

2. By Paying Long–Debt Terms Beyond the Plan

A Chapter 13 debtor can also use section 1322(b)(5) to make preferential plan payments on long-term debts. Section 1322(b)(5) only applies if the last payment on the debt is due after the last plan payment. With respect to such debts, a Chapter 13 debtor can simply make payments according to the contractual terms. The advantage to this approach is that more of the debt can be paid during the Chapter 13 case. The disadvantage to this approach is that, even if the debt was otherwise dischargeable, the debtor will have to complete the payments under the contract notwithstanding any Chapter 13 discharge. Cf. section 1328(a).

I. Discharge

1. Requirements of Discharge

A Chapter 13 debtor does not receive a discharge until she:

1. completes all plan payments (section 1328(a)) and

2. certifies that she has paid all postpetition domestic support obligations (section 1328(a)) and

3. completes an instructional course concerning personal financial management (sections 111, 1328(g)).

2. Limits on Discharge

a. Debts Exceptions

A section 1328(a) discharge is subject to most but not all of the exceptions to discharge listed in section 523. For example, a section 1328(a) discharge, unlike a discharge in a Chapter 7 case, will cover debts for willful and malicious injury to property and debts for divorce or separation property settlements. Cf. section 1328(a)(2), (4).

b. Objection Based on Prior Bankruptcy

A Chapter 13 debtor will be denied a discharge from any and all debts because of her bankruptcy history. More specifically, a Chapter 13 debtor will be denied a discharge is she received a discharge in another Chapter 13 case in the two-year period preceding the filing of this Chapter 13 case. Section 1328(f)(2). Similarly, a Chapter 13 debtor will be denied a discharge if she received a discharge in a Chapter 7, 11, or 12 case in the four years preceding the filing of the Chapter 13 case. Section 1328(f)(1).

3. Hardship Discharge

Under section 1328(b), the bankruptcy court may grant a discharge (known as a "hardship" discharge) in a Chapter 13 case even though the debtor has not completed payments called for by the plan if:

1. the debtor's failure to complete the plan was due to circumstances for which she "should not justly be held accountable;" and

2. the value of the payments made under the plan to each creditor at least equals what that creditor would have received under Chapter 7; and

3. modification of the plan is not "practicable."

A section 1328(b) "hardship" discharge is not as comprehensive as a section 1328(a) discharge. A "hardship" discharge is limited by all of the section 523(a) exceptions to discharge. Section 1328(c)(2).

J. Dismissal and Conversion

Most Chapter 13 cases do *not* end in a discharge. Most bankruptcy cases filed as Chapter 13 cases are either dismissed or converted to Chapter 7 cases.

1. Dismissing or Converting to Chapter 7 Upon Debtor's Request

A debtor who files a Chapter 13 petition may change his mind. He may at any time request the bankruptcy court to dismiss the case or convert it to a case under Chapter 7, section 1307(a), (b).

2. Dismissing or Converting to Chapter 7 Upon Creditor's Request

The bankruptcy court may also dismiss a Chapter 13 case or convert it to a case under Chapter 7 on request of a creditor. The statutory standard for such creditor–requested conversion or dismissal is "for cause." Section 1307(c) sets out eight examples of "cause."

3. Converting to Chapter 11

Section 1307(d) gives a bankruptcy court the power to convert from Chapter 13 to Chapter 11 before confirmation of the plan on request of a party in interest and after notice and hearing. There is no statutory standard to guide the court in deciding whether to convert from 13 to 11. This is not a problem for most judges. Most judges have either (i) never seen a motion to convert from 13 to 11 or (ii) only seen a motion to convert from 13 to 11 based on the amount of the debtor's debts. Cf. section 109(e).

4. Treatment of Postpetition Claims and Property When Converting to Chapter 7

Converting a case from Chapter 13 to Chapter 7 raises questions about the treatment of postpetition claims and postpetition property.

Example: Assume that D files a Chapter 13 petition on January 15 and converts to Chapter 7 on April 5. What about the claims against D that arise from January 15 to April 5? According to sections 1305 and 348(d), claims arising in the period between filing of the Chapter 13 petition and conversion to Chapter 7 are allowable claims and cases have consistently so held.

What about property acquired between January 15 and April 5? Is it property of the estate?

Example: If D had filed a Chapter 7 petition, the property that D acquired after January 15 would not be property of the estate, section 541. However, property acquired after the filing of a Chapter 13 case is property of the estate under section 1306. Under section 348(f), property of the estate on conversion from 13 to 7 is limited to the property of the estate as of the January 15 initial filing that is still in the possession or control of D as of the April 5 conversion to 7.

K. Comparison of Chapters 7 and 13

Because the 2005 amendments eliminated many of the advantages of Chapter 13 and eliminated the possibility of filing for some individual debtors, real lawyers will rarely be asked by clients to compare Chapters 7 and 13. Nonetheless, law students will continue to be asked by law professors and so you might want to review the following chart:

	Chapter 7	Chapter 13
1. Automatic Stay	Automatic stay of section 362 protects the debtor from creditors' collection efforts	Automatic stay of section 362 protects the debtor from creditors' collection efforts. Automatic stay of section 1301 protects certain co-debtors
2. Loss of Property	"Property of the estate" as described in section 541 is distributed to creditors	Except as provided in the plan or in the order of confirmation, debtor keeps "property of the estate"
3. Availability of Discharge	Section 727(a) lists grounds for objection to discharge	Section 727 is inapplicable. Discharge depends on completing payments required by the plan, 1328(a). A "hardship" discharge to a debtor who makes some but not all payments required by the plan. 1328(b).
4. Debts Excepted from Discharge	Section 523(a) excepts 19 classes of claims from operation of the discharge	A section 1328(a) discharge is subject to most of the important section 523(a) discharge exceptions. A section 1328(b) discharge is subject to all of section 523(a)'s exceptions to discharge
5. Effect on Future Chapter 7 Relief	A debtor who receives a discharge in a Chapter 7 case may not obtain a discharge in another Chapter 7 case for eight years	A Chapter 13 discharge does not affect the availability of discharge in a future Chapter 7 case if the Chapter 13 plan was the debtor's "best effort" and paid 70% of all general claims, section 727(a)(9)
6. Whether Debtor's Postpetition Earnings are Property of the Estate	No, section 541(a)(6) ("earnings from services performed by an individual")	Yes, section 1306
7. Debtor's Ability to Terminate the Case	"Only for cause," section 707	"On request of the debtor at any time," section 1307(b)
8. Relief from Taxes	Ability to satisfy taxes not condition to discharge; most taxes unaffected by discharge	Subject to limited exceptions, plan must provide for full payment of all taxes, section 1322(a)(2); payment of taxes may be deferred over five year life of plan; no exception from discharge
9. Amount Required to be Distributed to Holders of Claims	Property of the estate, section 541	Plan controls, confirmation requires that holders of claims receive at least as much as they would in Chapter 7 and that plan commits all disposable income, sections 1325(a)(4); 1325(b)

L. Comparison of Chapters 11 and 13

The next chapter covers special provisions for individuals in Chapter 11 cases. Even if you read the next chapter casually and not carefully, you should see that a debtor who has a choice between Chapters 11 and 13 will almost always choose Chapter 13. Remember, though, that Chapter 13 is not available to all debtors.

Corporations and partnerships are not eligible for Chapter 13, and even individuals must meet the debt limits of section 109(e). Individuals who exceed the debt limits would file Chapter 11 if they want to reorganize under the Bankruptcy Code.

M. Review Questions

1. David is a lawyer—a sole practitioner. Is he eligible for Chapter 13 relief?

2. T or F   Only a debtor can file a Chapter 13 plan.

3. T or F   Creditors do not vote on Chapter 13 plans.

4. T or F   There is a trustee in every Chapter 13 case.

5. T or F   There is no property of the estate in a Chapter 13 case.

6. S has a mortgage on D's home. The mortgage payments are $600 a month. D missed two mortgage payments before filing her Chapter 13 petition. What is the effect of the Chapter 13 filing on S?

7. S sold D a car two years before D's bankruptcy filing. The car payments are $600 a month. D missed two car payments before filing her Chapter petition. What is the effect of the Chapter 13 filing on S?

8. T or F   "Strip down" is limited to holders of first liens and "strip off" applies only to holders of second liens.

9. T or F   A Chapter 13 debtor receives a discharge when her plan is confirmed.

10. D borrows money from to obtain a bar. D's brother B guarantees payment of the debt. If D files for Chapter 13 relief, will the automatic stay protect B?

*

XVIII

Chapter 11 Cases

■ *ANALYSIS*

F.   Special Forms of Chapter 11 Cases
1.   Prepackaged
2.   Small Business Cases
3.   Single Asset Real Estate Cases
4.   Individual Chapter 11 Cases
G.   Review Questions

The Bankruptcy Act of 1898 contained four separate chapters for the reorganization of businesses: Chapter VIII which dealt with railroad reorganizations; Chapter X which covered corporate reorganizations; Chapter XI for the arrangement of unsecured debts by corporations, partnerships and individuals; and Chapter XII which was available to noncorporate debtors who own encumbered real estate. Chapter 11 of the Bankruptcy Code replaced these four chapters. It contains some principles from each of the above chapters and some new concepts.

The use of Chapter 11 is not restricted to business debtors. In Toibb v. Radloff (1991), the United States Supreme Court held that an individual debtor not engaged in business is eligible to reorganize under Chapter 11. However, the typical Chapter 11 case involves a business debtor that is attempting to continue its business operations by restructuring its financial obligations. And, the typical Chapter 11 case involves disputes among creditors as to the order and the amount of payment and disputes between creditors generally and the stockholders or other owners of the debtor as to how much if anything the owners can retain.

Judge Goldberg of the United States Court of Appeals for the Fifth Circuit described these struggles in mystical terms:

> Bankruptcy serves a role in corporate life eerily similar to that of the doctrine of reincarnation in some eastern religions. Bankruptcy is the belief that the souls of a corporate entity, the equityholders, do not just vanish when their corporeal form dies. Rather, they learn from the mistakes of a previous incarnation and can once again live on the earth in corporate form. True, they may suffer for the sins of previous incarnations and have trouble raising venture capital, but such is the karmic burden. With luck, some day a corporation may achieve enlightenment and reach a plane of eternal bliss and nirvana—the Fortune 500.

> Though the relatives of a departed soul may receive intellectual comfort at the thought of reincarnation, they are often more touched by the pain and immediacy of their personal loss. Just as it is in life, so it is in bankruptcy. The close cousins of equityholders, the debtholders, take little spiritual comfort

from the knowledge that the equityholders may someday be reincorporated. Instead, they are more aware of the anguish of their personal loss, the money they loaned the deceased corporation. It is at this point that the black robed judge steps in as the saffron robed monk and comforter. Perhaps the corporation has left behind some small amount of worldly goods, some trinkets to remind the debtholders of their friendship with the departed. Ah, but how to divide the estate so that everyone can have some little item of memorabilia?

This is a question of great spiritual and temporal import. Fortunately, the sacred writings [of the Bankruptcy Code] can provide guidance and inspiration.

In re Gary Aircraft Corp. (1983). To be even more temporal, Chapter 11 is about money. More specifically, Chapter 11 is generally about deciding who gets the difference between the liquidation value of a business and its going concern value.

We know that in a Chapter 7 case, property of the estate is sold by the trustees and the net proceeds of the sale are distributed to creditors. In essence, in Chapter 7 cases, creditors' recovery is measured by the liquidation value.

And, we know from the overview in Chapter VI, supra, that Chapter 11 contemplates that a debtor keep its assets, continue its business and pay creditors from future business operations. The question in Chapter 11 is how much creditors get paid—or, to restate, how much of the difference between liquidation value and going concern value goes to creditors.

This question is answered by the debtor's plan. To get to the answer, we need to learn about the stages of a Chapter 11 case:

1. Commencement of the case

2. Operation of the business

3. Preparation of the plan

4. Creditor acceptance of the plan

5. Confirmation of the plan

A. Commencement of the Case

1. Filing the Petition
A case under Chapter 11 is commenced by the filing of a petition. The petition may be filed by either the debtor or creditors.

Insolvency is not a condition precedent to a voluntary Chapter 11 petition. With two exceptions, any "person" that is eligible to file a voluntary bankruptcy petition under Chapter 7 is also eligible to file a petition under Chapter 11. The first exception is stockbrokers and commodity brokers: they are eligible for Chapter 7, but not Chapter 11. The second exception is railroads: railroads are eligible for Chapter 11, but not Chapter 7.

If the Chapter 11 petition has been filed by an eligible debtor, no formal adjudication is necessary. The filing of the petition operates as an "order for relief," section 301.

The requirements for an involuntary, i.e., creditor-initiated, Chapter 11 case are the same as the requirements for an involuntary Chapter 7 case, section 303. These requirements are discussed earlier in Chapter VII.

2. Consequences of Commencing a Chapter 11 Case

As we have already seen, the filing of a Chapter 11 petition, like the filing of a Chapter 7 petition or a Chapter 13 petition, (i) triggers the section 362 automatic stay and section 541 property of the estate and (ii) is the "date of cleavage" for purposes of the avoiding powers and the treatment of claims. As we will now see, most Chapter 11 petitions are unlike Chapter 7 petitions or Chapter 13 petitions in that (i) the filing triggers business and legal issues that need to be resolved immediately and (ii) creditors have a statutory role in the resolution of those issues.

3. Notifying and Organizing the Creditors

a. Notice

How will creditors learn of a Chapter 11 filing? Sections 521 and 342 provide a partial answer.

Section 521 obligates the debtor to file a list of creditors. Section 342 requires giving creditors appropriate notice of the order for relief. Rule 2002 governs the content of and time for the notice.

b. Proof of Claim

Generally, a creditor whose claim is included on a Chapter 11 debtor's list of creditors is not required to file a proof of claim, unless the claim is scheduled as disputed, contingent or unliquidated, a proof of claim is "deemed" filed by section 1111(a).

Nonetheless, holders of unsecured claims often file proofs of claim in Chapter 11 cases. Reasons for filing a proof of claim include (1) disagreement with the amount of the claim shown on the debtor's schedule and (2) concern that the Chapter 11 case will be converted to Chapter 7.

c. Unsecured Creditors Committee

1) Trustee Appoints

In many Chapter 11 cases, the debtor has hundreds, if not thousands, of creditors. It would not be practical for the Chapter 11 debtor to attempt to negotiate with each creditor individually.

Accordingly, section 1102 directs the United States trustee to appoint a committee of unsecured creditors as soon as practicable after the order for relief. Note that it is the United States trustee and not the bankruptcy court who appoints committee members. And, note that section 1102 suggests, but does not require, that the committee have seven members, and that the seven have the largest claims.

2) Membership

Section 1102(b)(1) does require that the committee members be "representative of the different kinds of claims." If, for example, D owed significant amounts to lenders, vendors and tort claimants, the creditors' committee should have representatives from each "kind" of claim.

3) Functions

A creditors' committee performs a number of functions. It may:

1. Consult with the trustee or debtor in possession concerning the administration of the case

2. Investigate the debtor's acts and financial condition

3. Participate in the formulation of the plan

4. Request the appointment of a trustee

5. Perform such other services as are in the interest of those represented, section 1103(c).

The creditors' committee may also appear at various hearings as a party in interest, section 1109(b). And, the committee may file a plan in those situations where the debtor ceases to have the exclusive right to do so, section 1121.

To state the obvious, the creditors' committee acts on behalf of all unsecured creditors—members of the committee have a fiduciary duty to all holders of unsecured claims. Committees must provide their nonmember constituents with "access to information." Section 1102(b)(3).

The selection of a creditors' committee takes time. In many Chapter 11 cases, however, there are problems that need to be resolved immediately—on the first day of the case.

4. First Day Orders

The phrase "First Day Orders" does not appear in either the Bankruptcy Code or the Bankruptcy Rules. Nonetheless, "First Day Orders" appear in virtually every Chapter 11 case.

"First Day Orders" are court orders which the Chapter 11 debtor seeks to have entered by the bankruptcy judge immediately, on the same day as the filing of the petition or soon thereafter. Many First Day Orders deal with administrative matters such as notices and appointment of professionals are usually not controversial.

More problematic are First Day Orders dealing with business emergencies such as obtaining financing and making payments to employees for work they have done prepetition and other essential prepetition creditors for goods or services they provided prepetition. In dealing with these business emergencies in the first day of the case, bankruptcy courts have to balance the argument by the debtor that immediate action is required or the business will close against the argument by creditors that they have the right to be heard and need more time and the argument by the U.S. Trustee that this early payment of some prepetition claims is inconsistent with the provisions and policies of the Bankruptcy Code.

B. Operation of the Business

Successful rehabilitation of a business under Chapter 11 generally requires the continued operation of the business. No court order is necessary in order to operate the debtor's business after the filing of a Chapter 11 petition. Section 1108 provides: "Unless the court . . . orders otherwise, the trustee may operate the debtor's business."

1. Who Operates the Business?

a. Debtor in Possession (DIP)

Notwithstanding section 1108's use of the word "trustee," the debtor will remain in control of the business in most Chapter 11 cases. Prebankruptcy management will continue to operate the business as a "debtor in possession" unless a request is made for the appointment of a trustee and the court, after notice and a hearing, grants the request, section 1107.

b. Trustee

1) Statutory Grounds for Appointment

Section 1104 sets out the grounds for the appointment of a trustee. A trustee is to be appointed if there is cause (fraud, dishonesty, mismanagement, or incompetence) or if the appointment of a trustee is "in the interest of creditors, any equity security holders, and other interests of the estate." Section 1104 specifically instructs the court to disregard the number of shareholders or the amount of assets and liabilities of the debtor in deciding whether to appoint a trustee.

2) Statutory Procedures for Appointment of Trustee

Under section 1104 the court decides whether to appoint a trustee in a Chapter 11 case. The United States trustee then decides which person to appoint, subject to the court's approval, unless the creditors act to select the trustee themselves.

3) Statutory Duties

The duties of a trustee are enumerated in section 1106. Essentially, the trustee has responsibility for the operation of the business and formulation of the Chapter 11 plan.

4) Business Considerations

Who serves as trustee in Chapter 11 cases? Remember, the trustee has responsibility for operating the business. Are lawyers prepared to run a troubled business? What about appointing an outstanding, experienced business person as Chapter 11 trustee?

Even an outstanding, experienced business person is going to need time to familiarize herself with this particular business. And, if she is such an outstanding, experienced business person, why is she available to serve as trustee? Why isn't she already running some other business?

These business considerations caused Congress to decide to keep the debtor in possession unless a party in interest establishes cause, section 1104. And, in many cases, these business considerations cause the various parties in interest not to try to establish cause for the appointment of a Chapter 11 trustee.

c. Examiner

1) Requirements for Appointment

If a trustee is not appointed, the court can order the appointment of an "examiner." Again, the court decides whether to appoint and the United States trustee decides which person to appoint, with the court's approval.

Section 1104(c) sets out the requirements for the appointment of an examiner:

1. A trustee was not appointed, *and*

2. Appointment of an examiner was requested by a party in interest, *and*

3. The debtor's nontrade, nontax, unsecured debts exceed $5,000,000, or "such appointment is in the interests of creditors, any equity security holders, and other interests of the estate."

Read literally, section 1104(b)(2) compels the appointment of an examiner on request of a party in interest if the debtor has the requisite $5 million in debts. The cases, however, are divided.

2) Purpose

In theory, the role of an examiner is different from that of a trustee. An examiner does not run the debtor's business or run the debtor's Chapter 11 case. An examiner merely examines: she investigates the competency and honesty of the debtor and files a report of the investigation, sections 1104(b), 1106(b). In practice, the bright lines between the roles of an examiner and the roles of a trustee are sometimes blurred.

2. Use of Encumbered Property Including Cash Collateral

a. In Bankruptcy Most Property is Subject to Liens

In the typical Chapter 11 case, most of the property that the debtor owns at the time of the filing of the Chapter 11 petition is encumbered by liens.

1) Postpetition, After–Acquired Property

The property that the debtor acquires after the filing of the Chapter 11 petition is generally protected from prepetition liens. Property acquired by the debtor after it files a Chapter 11 petition will not be "subject to any lien resulting from any security agreement entered into by the debtor before the commencement of the case," section 552(a). After-acquired property clauses are not recognized in cases under the Bankruptcy Code.

Example: Assume that D files a Chapter 11 petition. If S contracted for a security interest in "all of D's inventory, now owned or hereafter acquired," section 552(a) will limit S's lien to D's inventory as of the time before the Chapter 11 petition was filed.

2) Proceeds

S's lien will probably also reach the accounts receivable and other identifiable proceeds from the sale of such prepetition inventory. The Bankruptcy Code does recognize a secured creditor's right to "proceeds, product, offspring, rents, or profits' from the disposition of prepetition collateral, section 552(b). Under section 552(b), a prepetition security interest reaches proceeds acquired after the bankruptcy petition was filed "except to any extent that the court, after notice and a hearing and based on the equities of the case, orders otherwise."

The "equities of the case" exception covers situations in which post-petition labor or property of the estate is used in converting the collateral into proceeds. Assume, for example, that S has a security interest in the raw materials of Charlie Dunn, D, a bootmaker. After filing for Chapter 11, D makes boots from the leather and sells the boots. A bankruptcy court could limit S's security interest in the proceeds from the sale of the boots.

b. But 362 Stay Stops Creditor From Repossessing

Section 362(a) stays a creditor with a lien on the property of a Chapter 11 debtor from repossessing the encumbered property. Section 362(d) provides for relief from the stay in limited situations.

c. And 363 Allows DIP to Use Collateral—With Conditions

Section 363 empowers the debtor in possession or trustee to continue using, selling, and leasing encumbered property.

1) Adequate Protection

The interest of the lien creditor is safeguarded against this continued use of the collateral by section 363's requirement of "adequate protection," section 363(e).

Section 361 is entitled "adequate protection." Note that section 361 provides for "adequate protection" of "an interest of an entity in property," not adequate protection of an entity in having its debt repaid. Note further that section 361 does not define "adequate protection." Rather, it provides examples of "adequate protection."

And, examples are the easiest way to understand "adequate protection."

Example: Assume that D files for bankruptcy owing S $1 million secured by equipment, which is worth $800,000. S has an interest in property that is worth $800,000. The purpose of adequate protection is to assure that at the end of the bankruptcy case S has (i) collateral worth $800,000; or (ii) payments of $800,000 or (iii) a combination of collateral and payments that total $800,000. Assume further that the court concludes that the value of the equipment is declining by $10,000 a month. Under sections 361 and 363, the bankruptcy court could require the debtor to make monthly payments to S of $10,000. If the bankruptcy lasts 14 months and the court was correct about the decline in the value of the equipment, then at the close of the bankruptcy case, S who had a lien on property worth $800,000 at the start of the bankruptcy case would have a lien on property worth $660,000 and $140,000 in adequate protection payments at the end of the bankruptcy case.

Example: D files for bankruptcy owing M $500,000 secured by a first mortgage on Greenacre which is worth $300,000. If the bankruptcy court concludes that the value of Greenacre will not decline during the course of the bankruptcy case, the bankruptcy court could conclude that Greenacre itself is adequate protection.

a) Inadequate Adequate Protection

Adequate protection works so long as the bankruptcy judge correctly foresees the future of the encumbered property. What if the value of the creditor's interest in property drops more significantly than the bankruptcy judge anticipated?

Under section 507(b), a creditor may seek an administrative expense claim for the amount by which the adequate protection ordered proves to be inadequate. Section 507(b) should always be read together with section 726(b). If the debtor's Chapter 11 efforts are not successful and the case is converted from Chapter 11 to Chapter 7, the administrative expenses from the 11 are not paid until the administrative expenses from the 7 are paid in full.

b) Raising the Issue

While a Chapter 11 debtor's use or sale of encumbered property is always subject to "adequate protection,' the rules as to who has the burden of raising the adequate protection issue depend on the nature of the encumbered property and the nature of the debtor's use.

2) Encumbered Property that is NOT "Cash Collateral'

Encumbered property that is not "cash collateral" as defined in section 363(a) may be used, sold, or leased in the ordinary course of business without a prior judicial determination of "adequate protection," section 363(c)(1). Section 363(c)(1) is applicable only if "the business of the debtor is authorized to be operated." In a Chapter 11 case, the trustee or debtor in possession is authorized to operate the business "unless the court orders otherwise," section 1108.

On "request" of the lien creditor, the court shall condition the use, sale, or lease of encumbered property so as to provide "adequate protection," section 363(e).

Example: If *D* Department Store, Inc., *D*, files a Chapter 11 petition and *C* Bank, *C*, has a perfected security interest in *D*'s inventory, *D* may continue to sell inventory in the ordinary course of business. *D* will not have to obtain court permission in order to make such sales; rather, *C* will have the burden of requesting the court to prohibit or condition such sales so as to provide "adequate protection" of *C*'s security interest.

Notice and a hearing on the issue of "adequate protection" is required before a Chapter 11 debtor uses, sells, or leases encumbered property in a manner that is not in the ordinary course of business, section 363(b).

Example: D, after filing its Chapter 11 petition, decides to discontinue its furniture department and wants to make a bulk sale of its furniture inventory, C must be first given notice and the opportunity for a hearing on the issue of "adequate protection."

Remember that "notice and hearing" means "such notice as is appropriate in the particular circumstances, and such opportunity for a hearing as is appropriate in the particular circumstances," section 102(1)(A).

3) "Cash Collateral" is Different

Use of cash collateral is treated different from the use of other collateral. Accordingly, it is necessary to understand (i) which collateral is "cash collateral" and (ii) when a debtor can use cash collateral.

a) What Is It?

"Cash collateral" is defined in section 363(a). There are three components to the definition. First, cash collateral must be collateral, i.e., property that a creditor has an interest in because its lien extends to the property. Second, cash collateral must be cash or cash equivalent. Third, cash collateral can be derived from other collateral, i.e., proceeds, rents, etc. from other collateral.

Example: In the above example of D Department Store, cash received by D from the postpetition sale of prepetition inventory would be C's cash collateral. Cash received from the sale of land or other property not subject to C's lien would not be cash collateral. And, accounts receivable generated by the postpetition sale of prepetition inventory would be C's cash collateral only when collected.

b) Use of Cash Collateral Only Upon Consent or Adequate Protection

Cash collateral may be used only if the lienholder C consents, or if the court, after notice and hearing, finds that C's collateral position is adequately protected and authorizes such use under section 363(c)(2). Until the use of cash collateral is authorized under section 363(c)(2), the debtor in possession must segregate and account for all cash collateral, section 363(c)(4).

To understand how section 363(c) typically works, it is necessary to understand (i) how the Uniform Commercial Code works, (ii) how the Bankruptcy Code works and (iii) how the real world works.

1. First, how the Uniform Commercial Code works. Under Article 9 of the UCC, a creditor who extends credit secured by inventory or accounts receivable can (and usually does) obtain a security interest in not only the accounts and inventory a debtor has at the time it extends credit but also the accounts and inventory that the debtor later acquires. Thus, in the *D* Department Store example, *C*'s collateral could be all of *D* Department Store's inventory, whenever acquired.

2. Now, how the Bankruptcy Code works. If *D* Department Store files for Chapter 11, section 552(a) limits the extent to which *C*'s lien can "float" to after-acquired property. More specifically, under section 552(a), *C*'s prepetition security interest does not cover inventory that *D* Department Store acquires after the date of the Chapter 11 filing. Accordingly, a Chapter 11 debtor such as *D* Department Store can offer its prepetition secured creditors a replacement lien in postpetition inventory and accounts receivable as "adequate protection" for *D* Department Store's use of cash collateral.

3. And, if you understand how the "real world' works you will understand that such an offer is generally the proverbial "offer he cannot refuse.'

Recall that a Chapter 11 debtor cannot use cash collateral unless the creditor with a lien on the cash collateral consents or the court approves the use, section 363(c). *D* Department Store is like most Chapter 11 debtors in that most of the cash it generates from business operations is cash collateral. Unless the business can use the cash collateral, the business will close.

Understandably, bankruptcy judges are sympathetic to the debtor's argument that unless it is permitted to use cash collateral, it will close and all of its employees will lose their jobs, their health insurance, their retirement benefits, etc. Understanding this, creditors generally agree to the debtor's use of cash collateral in exchange for some sort of replacement lien on postpetition inventory and receivables and some sort of administrative expense priority. Most court orders approving the use of cash collateral are consent orders.

While use of cash collateral is typically the debtor's initial source of credit, cash collateral alone is generally not a sufficient source of credit. Accordingly, one of the first problems confronting a debtor in possession or a Chapter 11 trustee is financing the operation of the business pending the formulation and approval of a plan of rehabilitation.

3. Basics of Funding a Debtor in Chapter 11 Bankruptcy Cases

In theory, issues of financing a debtor can arise after the filing of a Chapter 7, 11, 12 or 13 petition. In practice, these problems arise primarily in Chapter 11 cases.

a. Possible Sources of Funding

Recall, that in Chapter 11, the debtor generally continues to operate its business and is statutorily authorized to continue using and even selling its property. With court authorization, the debtor can even make sales that are not in the ordinary course of business and use the cash from ordinary course and ordinary course sales to continue business operations. These operations and sales are an important source of funds for the Chapter 11 debtor.

A Chapter 11 debtor, however, usually needs more funding than its business generates. Section 365(c)(2) prevents the Chapter 11 debtor from making use of prebankruptcy lines of credit. Debtor-in-possession financing pursuant to section 364 is the primary source of such additional financing. And, postpetition accounts and postpetition inventory are the primary sources of adequate protection for such financing.

Example: *D* Trucking Co. files a Chapter 11 petition. *C* has a perfected security interest in *D* Trucking Co.'s accounts; the security agreement contains the broadest possible after-acquired property language. *C's* security interest does not reach the postpetition accounts. (Again recall that section 552 significantly limits the postpetition float on a floating lien. Regardless of the language of the security agreement and the Uniform Commercial Code, section 552 limits a prepetition lender's security interest to property that the debtor has rights in as of the time of the filing of the petition and identifiable proceeds of such property.) *D* Trucking Co. may now offer *C* a security interest in the postpetition accounts as adequate protection for use of cash collateral under section 363 or as collateral for debtor-in-possession financing under section 364 from *C* or some other creditor.

b. Comparison of Use of Cash Collateral with Debtor-In-Possession Financing (a/k/a DIP Financing)

The creditor that does the debtor-in-possession financing—i.e., makes a loan to the debtor after its Chapter 11 filing—Is often the same lender who financed the debtor before bankruptcy. Most lenders consider financing the debtor under section 364 to be preferable to cash collateral usage under section 363. Some of the advantages of section 364 financing include (i) lender may have more control under a section 364 financing agreement than under a section 363 cash collateral usage order; and (ii) under section 364, the lender can get a higher priority and liens on additional collateral. Credit extended under the authority of section 364(c)(1) is superior to claims arising in favor of a creditor entitled to "adequate protection" for use of its cash collateral but whose adequate protection proves to be inadequate. Section 364(c)(1) provides inpertinent part: "with priority over . . . administrative expenses of the kind specified in . . . 507(b)."

c. Obtaining Additional Unsecured Credit From Vendors in the Ordinary Course of Business

To induce vendors to sell on credit to a Chapter 11 debtor, postpetition credit under section 364(a) is allowable as an expense of administration under section 503(b)(1). Section 364(a) has two requirements: (1) authority to operate the debtor's business and (2) extension of credit in the ordinary course of business. The first of the requirements is easy to satisfy in a Chapter 11 case. See section 1108. It is the ordinary course of business requirement that is the troublesome one. The phrase "ordinary course of business" is not defined in the Code. If in doubt as to whether an extension of credit is in the ordinary course of business, a creditor should look to section 364(b) not section 364(a).

d. Obtaining Unsecured Credit Not in the Ordinary Course of Business

Under section 364(b) the court may approve an extension of unsecured credit by a vendor or lender not in the ordinary course of business after a notice and hearing. The obligations so incurred are then allowable as an administrative expense priority under section 503(b)(1).

e. Obtaining Priority or Secured Credit

If the trustee or debtor-in-possession cannot obtain unsecured credit based upon such credit only being accorded administrative priority status under section 503(b)(1), the court, after notice and hearing, may authorize the trustee or debtor-in-possession to obtain credit with a special priority or with liens not interfering with existing liens, section 364(c).

f. Obtaining Priming Secured Credit

Under section 364(d), the court, after notice and hearing, may authorize the obtaining of postpetition credit secured by a senior lien on property of the estate that is already subject to a lien. Section 364(d) has two requirements: (1) the trustee is unable to obtain such credit otherwise and (2) the interest of a prepetition lienholders on the property whose liens are displaced by the borrowing are adequately protected. Section 364(d) is the "last resort" provision.

Court approval of a postpetition lien that primes prepetition liens is very uncommon. Most of the few reported cases granting a section 364(d) lien look to an equity cushion (i.e. value of collateral exceeds the amount of the prepetition secured debts) as the basis for adequate protection. If D owes C $2 million and C has a first lien on Greeancre, the strongest argument for P, a postpetition lender, seeking a section 364(d) priming lien for its proposed postpetition $1 million loan will be that Greenacre is worth more than $3 million. (C's obvious response is that if it is so clear that Greenacre is worth more than $3 million then there is no need for P, the postpetition lender, to seek a priming lien. In other words, if being second in line is so damn "adequate," why does the new lender insist on being first in line?)

g. Procedure for Obtaining Credit

Recall that court authorization after notice and hearing is required to obtain credit under paragraph (b), (c) and (d) of section 364. A proceeding to obtain this authorization is a core proceeding under 28 USCA 157(b)(2)(D). Bankruptcy Rules 4000(c) and 4000(d) govern the procedure for obtaining Bankruptcy Court authorization.

Rule 4001(c) provides that the proceeding is a contested matter under Rule 9014. It is initiated by filing and serving a motion under Rule 9013. Rule 4001(c)(2) empowers the court to conduct a preliminary emergency hearing and authorize interim credit to the extent necessary to avoid immediate and irreparable harm to estate pending a final hearing. If the court is convinced that the requirements of section 364 are satisfied, the court will enter an order approving the proposed financing.

h. Safe Harbor

A creditor who is extending credit pursuant to such an order is going to want to know that it can rely on the order. More specifically, the creditor does not want to lend the money to the debtor and later learn that some other judge has resolved an appeal of the financing order by deciding that the creditor is not entitled to the lien or priority provided for in the financing order. Accordingly, section 364(e) affords a "safe harbor"—provides that the reversal or modification on appeal of a "grant under this section [364] of a priority or a lien does not affect the validity of any debt so incurred, or any priority or lien so granted, to an entity that extended credit in good faith."

Note that the protection of section 364(e)'s "safe harbor" depends on the creditor's good faith in extending credit. Neither section 364(e) nor any other provision of the Bankruptcy Code defines "good faith."

i. Cross–Collateralization

Recall that frequently, postpetition credit is provided by prepetition lenders. A prepetition lender who is unsecured or undersecured may attempt to improve its position on its prepetition claim by agreeing to lend postpetition funds to the debtor with "cross-collateralization."

1) Meaning

The term "cross–collateralization" does not appear in the Bankruptcy Code. It is a creation and creature of the case law and commentary.

2) Forms

In theory, cross–collateralization can take two different forms. First, cross-collateralization results when a postpetition extension of credit is secured by both prepetition collateral and postpetition collateral. A second form of cross–collateralization involves securing prepetition claims with postpetition collateral as a condition for new credit. It is this second form of cross–collateralization that is controversial.

Effectively, this second form of cross–collateralization by which a creditor gets new postpetition collateral to secure an old prepetition debt is inconsistent with the priority scheme of the Bankruptcy Code. The debtor is dealing with the prepetition debt owed to its postpetition lender more favorably than the debtor's other prepetition debts.

3) Case Law on the Second Form of Cross Collateralization

The Bankruptcy Code nowhere deals with cross-collateralization. Relatively few reported cases deal with cross-collateralization.

The two "leading" reported cases on this second form of cross-collateralization are (1) the Second Circuit's decision in In re Texlon (1979), which was decided under the Bankruptcy Act of 1898 and is generally read as (i) holding that a court cannot approve cross-collateralization without notice and hearing and (ii) reserving the question of whether a court can approve cross-collateralization with proper notice and hearing, and (2) the Eleventh Circuit's decision in In re Saybrook Mfg. Co. (1992), which was decided under the Bankruptcy Code and held that cross-collateralization is not permitted.

C. Preparation of the Chapter 11 Plan

1. Who Prepares and Files

a. Debtor's Exclusivity

A Chapter 11 plan may be filed at the same time as the petition or any time thereof. Section 1121 answers the question who can file a Chapter 11 plan.

Section 1121 gives a Chapter 11 debtor a period of exclusivity in which only it can file a plan. Being the only party able to file a plan can be a very significant advantage to a debtor. So long as the debtor has exclusivity, creditors have the limited options of (i) accepting what the debtor proposes or (ii) moving to convert the case to Chapter 7 and liquidating all of the assets or (iii) moving to end the debtor's exclusivity.

Section 1121(b) grants the debtor exclusivity for the first 120 days of the case. If the debtor files its plan within that 120 day period, no other plan may be filed during the first 180 days of the case while the debtor tries to obtain creditor acceptance of its plan, section 1121(c)(3). Section 1121(d) empowers the bankruptcy court to extend or reduce the 120–day and 180–day periods. Note the relationship between the 120–day and the 180–day periods. Both begin running at the same time—the date of the order for relief. If, for example, the debtor files a plan 30 days after the order for relief, it will have 150 more days of exclusivity to obtain creditor acceptance.

It has been very unusual for courts to reduce the exclusivity periods. It has been very common for courts to extend the exclusivity period, especially in cases involving larger businesses.

The 2005 amendments to the Bankruptcy Code limit the power of the courts to extend the exclusivity periods. The 120–day period to file a plan and disclosure statement may not be extended beyond 18 months, and the 180–day period to obtain acceptance may not be extended beyond 20 months. Section 1122(d)(2).

b. Trustee

If a trustee is appointed, the trustee, the debtor, a creditor, the creditors' committee, and any other party in interest may file a plan, section 1121(c). More than one plan may be filed. Similarly, if the debtor fails to file a plan and obtain creditor acceptances within the specified exclusivity time periods, any party in interest may file a plan and more than one plan may be filed.

c. Creditors' Committee

Regardless of who files the plan, the Bankruptcy Code contemplates that the creditors' committee will play a role in formulating the plan, cf. section 1103(c)(3).

2. Contents of the Plan

A lawyer's questions about the contents of a plan are typically (i) what is my client getting under the plan and (ii) what are others getting under the plan. A law professor's question about the contents of a plan is typically does the plan comply with section 1123.

Section 1123 is entitled "Contents of Plan." Subparagraph (a) sets out the mandatory provisions of a Chapter 11 plan ("shall"); subparagraph (b) of section 1123 indicates the permissive provisions of a Chapter 11 plan ("may").

3. Funding for the Plan

Compliance with the requirements of section 1123 is not the difficult part of preparing a plan for the rehabilitation of a business under Chapter 11. Rather, the hard question is usually can this debtor satisfy its creditors?

If the plan provides for payments to creditors, how will the debtor fund the payments?

a. Possible Sources of Funding

Possible sources of such funding include

(1) New borrowing from creditors;

(2) New equity capital from investors;

(3) Sales of assets.

b. Using Securities

A Chapter 11 plan does not always provide for cash payments to creditors. A plan can offer creditors debt or equity securities rather than cash.

Generally, the issuance of a security requires expensive and time consuming federal and state registration. Section 1145(a)(1) exempts the issuance of the debtor's securities under a Chapter 11 plan from federal and state registration requirements. A creditor's resale of a security received under a Chapter 11 is also exempted from federal and state registration requirements, section 1145(b). Section 4(1) of the Securities Act of 1933 states in essence that transactions by any person who is not an "issuer, underwriter, or dealer" need not be registered. Section 1145(b)(2) provides an exemption to creditors who resell securities obtained under a Chapter 11 plan by indicating that such creditors are not "underwriters."

c. Selling Assets

While Chapter 11 is generally thought of as a reorganization rather than liquidation, a Chapter 11 plan may provide for the sale of all of the debtor's assets, section 1123(b)(4). A sale of everything is often called a "liquidating plan."

However, while assets may be sold as a part of the Chapter 11 plan process, asset sales more commonly occur in Chapter 11 earlier in the case pursuant to section 363.

Reread section 363(b)(1). Recall it provides for a "non-ordinary course" sale of assets after notice and hearing. Chapter 11 debtors in possession use this section 363 process to sell the business.

Debtors prefer to use section 363 sales instead of Chapter 7 sales because, in Chapter 11, the debtor in possession (i.e., usually existing management) can continue to operate the business until the sale and can negotiate the terms of the sale.

Both debtors and buyers prefer to use sales under section 363 instead of sales pursuant to a Chapter 11 plan because section 363 procedures are more time efficient and cost efficient than Chapter 11 plan procedures.

4. Classification of Claims

Classification of claims is important. It can affect not only who gets what under the plan but whether there is a plan.

Look at section 1123(a) and section 1122. Section 1123(a)(1) requires that the claims be classified, and section 1123(a)(4) requires the "same treatment" for all claims within a class. Section 1122 governs classification of claims in Chapter 11 plans.

a. Administrative Expense Class—Small Claims—1122(b)

Section 1122(b) is easy to deal with so let's start with that. Section 1122(b) says that the plan can segregate all small claims into a single class if "reasonable and necessary for administrative convenience." A plan proponent may use such an "administrative convenience class" to pay small claims in cash at the time of confirmation, instead of incurring the cost and inconvenience of processing and mailing monthly checks for dollars or even pennies over the course of the Chapter 11 plan.

b. Other Classes—"Substantially Similar'—1122(a)

Section 1122(a) is hard to deal with because of what it does not say. While section 1122(a) says that the test for whether claims can be included in the same class is "substantially similar,' it does not define "substantially similar.'

1) Grouping

In determining whether claims are "substantially similar" for purposes of section 1122(a), courts look primarily at legal rights. A claim with a section 507 priority has different legal rights from an unsecured claim and so priority claims and unsecured claims cannot be placed in the same class. Similarly, a secured claim has different legal rights than an unsecured claim or a priority claim and so secured claims cannot be placed in the same class with priority claims or unsecured claims. And, B's first mortgage on Blackacre has different legal rights from W's first mortgage on Whiteacre or S's second mortgage on both Blackacre and Whiteacre. Accordingly, each secured claim is placed in a separate class in most Chapter 11 plans. [If a debtor has issued public debt secured by its assets, the claims of the various debenture holders are "substantially similar" and can be placed in a single class.]

2) Excluding

And, section 1122(a) is hard to deal with because it does not say anything about claim exclusion—whether claims must be included in the same class. Section 1122(a) states that all claims in a class must be "substantially similar"; it does not state whether all claims that are "substantially similar" must be in the same class.

Example: Assume that X, Y and Z are unsecured creditors of Chapter 11 debtor, D. If D's plan places all three creditors' claims in the same class, section 1122(a) controls. It is clear from section 1122(a) that D cannot place the claims of X, Y and Z in a single class unless all three claims are "substantially similar." The limits on D's discretion in placing claims in a separate class are not clear from the Bankruptcy Code. Can C place X in a class different from Y and Z even though their claims are substantially similar?

3) Why Create Classes

There are both business reasons and a legal reason that a debtor might want to divide its unsecured debts into various classes.

a) Business Reason

First, a business reason. Some creditors such as long-term lenders or large vendors that are continuing to sell to the debtor might be willing to take long-term notes or even stock while other creditors such as short-term lenders or discontinued vendors might insist on short-term notes or even cash.

b) Legal Reason

And, there is also a legal reason for classification of claims. A plan proponent will sometimes place claims that will vote for the plan in a separate class so that at least one class of claims accepts the plan. As discussed below, the Chapter 11 plan approval process requires that (i) creditors vote on Chapter 11 plans, (ii) the creditor vote be tabulated by classes and by number of claims and amount of claims in that class, and (iii) at least one class of claims vote for the plan by the requisite majorities in number and amount.

c) Single–Asset Real Estate

This legal reason for classification and legal battles over classification often arise in cases in which the debtor's principal significant asset is a building. Assume, for example, that D is a limited partnership that owns an apartment complex valued at $12.2 million. M has a mortgage on the apartment complex to secure its $15 million claim. M thus has both a $12.2 million secured claim and a $2.8 million unsecured claim. M is not only D's only secured creditor; it is also D's largest unsecured creditor. M's $2.8 million unsecured, deficiency claim is larger than all other unsecured debts combined. Unless D can classify M's unsecured deficiency claim different from the claims of its other unsecured creditors, M can effectively veto any Chapter 11 plan.

The cases are divided on whether the deficiency claim of a single asset real estate debtor's secured creditor can be classified separately from other unsecured claims. That division and other single asset real estate issues are considered later in this chapter of the book.

D. Acceptance of the Plan

Chapter 11 contemplates a consensual restructuring of the debtor's financial obligations. While Chapter 11 does not require that every holder of a claim approve the plan (and indeed allows the cramming down of a plan opposed by most holders of claims), it does require that creditors receive adequate information about a plan and have an opportunity to vote on the plan.

1. Disclosure

"The premise underlying . . . Chapter 11 . . . is the same as the premise of the securities law. If adequate disclosure is provided to all creditors and stockholders whose rights are to be affected, then they should be able to make an informed judgment of their own, rather than having the court or the Securities and Exchange Commission inform them in advance whether the proposed plan is a good plan," H.R. 95–595, p. 226. Accordingly, the bankruptcy court does not review a Chapter 11 plan before it is submitted to creditors and shareholders for vote. Instead, the bankruptcy court reviews the information provided to creditors and shareholders to insure that their judgment is an "informed judgment."

Section 1125 requires full disclosure before postpetition solicitation of acceptances of a Chapter 11 plan. Creditors and shareholders must be provided:

1. A copy of the plan or a summary of the plan, and

2. "[A] written disclosure statement approved, after notice and a hearing, by the court as containing adequate information," section 1125(b).

"Adequate information" is defined in section 1125(a) as information which it is "reasonably practicable" for this debtor to provide to enable a "hypothetical reasonable investor" who is typical of the holders of the claims or interests to make an informed judgment on the plan. What constitutes "adequate information" thus depends on the circumstances of each case—or factors such as (1) the condition of the debtor's books or records, (2) the sophistication of the creditors and stockholders, and (3) the nature of the plan.

2. Who Votes?

Both creditors and shareholders vote on Chapter 11 plans. According to section 1126(a), creditors with claims "allowed under section 502" and shareholders with interests "allowed under section 502" vote on Chapter 11 plans.

a. Double Deeming

The statutory requirement of "allowed under section 502" is generally satisfied by the Bankruptcy Code's "double-deeming."

In a Chapter 11 case, section 1111 deems filed a claim or interest that is scheduled and is not shown as disputed, contingent, or unliquidated. And, section 502 deems allowed any claim or interest that is filed and not objected to by a party in interest.

Statutory "deeming" also eliminates voting by two classes of claims or interests. First, if a class is to receive nothing under the plan, it is deemed to have rejected the plan, and its vote need not be solicited, section 1126(g). Second, if a class is not "impaired" under the plan, the class is deemed to have accepted the plan and again its vote need not be solicited. Section 1126(f).

b. Impairment of Claims

The concept of "impairment" is unique to Chapter 11. Section 1124 is entitled "Impairment of Claims or Interests." Under section 1124 a class of claims or interests is impaired unless

(1) The legal, equitable, and contractual rights of the holder are left "unaltered"; [If the plan in any way changes the rights of the holder, it alters and thus impairs the holder. It is not necessary to determine whether the change adversely affects the holder.] *or*

(2) The only alteration of legal, equitable, or contractual rights is reversal of an acceleration on default by curing the default and reinstating the debt.

3. 1111(b) Elections

Section 1111(b), like section 1124, deals with a concept that is unique to Chapter 11. Generally, a creditor whose debt is only partially secured has two claims—a secured claim measured by the value of its collateral and an unsecured claim for the remainder, section 506(a).

Example: Assume that C's $100,000 claim against D is secured by real property owned by D that is valued at $70,000. Under section 506(a), C has a $70,000 secured claim and a $30,000 unsecured claim. Under section 1111(b), C can elect to have a $100,000 secured claim and no unsecured claim. [Note that section 1111(b) provides for election by classes of secured claims, not by individual holders of secured claims. Generally, each holder of a secured claim will be in a separate class. Note also that some classes of secured claims are not eligible to make a section 1111(b) election.]

Let's use the hypothetical in the previous paragraph to consider some of the advantages and the disadvantages of a section 1111(b) election:

a. Advantage of Section 1111(b) Election

If C makes the section 1111(b) election, section 1129(b), considered infra, requires that C be paid at least the full amount of its debt, $100,000, under the plan. Understand the difference between C's section 1129(b) right to be paid $100,000 under the plan and a right to be paid $100,000 in cash. The plan can and undoubtedly will delay the payment of a part or even all of the $100,000. Section 1129(b) requires that the payments under the plan to C total $100,000, not that the plan payments have a present value of $100,000. Section 1129(b) also requires that C's collateral secure the payment of the $100,000.

b. Disadvantages of Section 1111(b) Election

1. If C makes the section 1111(b) election, it will not be able to vote its $30,000 unsecured claim.

2. If C makes the section 1111(b) election, it will not participate in the distribution to holders of unsecured claims.

4. Needed Majorities

A class of claims has accepted a plan when more than one half in number and at least two thirds in amount of the allowed claims actually voting on the plan approve the plan, section 1126(c). The following hypothetical illustrates the application of section 1126(c):

Example: D files a Chapter 11 petition. D's schedule of creditors shows 222 different creditors and $1 million of debt. D's Chapter 11 plan divides creditors into four classes. Class 3 consists of 55 creditors, with claims totalling $650,000. Only 39 of the creditors in Class 3 vote on the plan. Their claims total $450,000. If at least 20 Class 3 creditors (more than 1/2 of 39) with claims totalling at least $300,000 (2/3 of $450,000) vote for D's plan, the plan has been accepted by Class 3. A class of interests has accepted a plan when at least two thirds in amount of the allowed interests actually voting on the plan approve the plan, section 1126(d).

E. Confirmation of the Plan

Approval of a Chapter 11 plan involves not only creditor acceptance but also court confirmation. A bankruptcy judge has the power to confirm a Chapter 11 plan that has not received the needed majorities; a bankruptcy judge has the power not to confirm a Chapter 11 plan that has been accepted by all holders of claims and interests.

Section 1128 requires that the bankruptcy court hold a hearing on confirmation and give parties in interest notice of the hearing so that they might raise objections to confirmation.

While it is possible for more than one plan to be filed and accepted, only one plan may be confirmed. If more than one plan meets the confirmation standards of section 1129, the court "shall consider the preferences of creditors and equity security holders in determining which plan to confirm," section 1129(c).

Subparagraphs (a), (b), and (d) of section 1129 contain the confirmation standards. Section 1129(d) prohibits confirmation of a plan whose "principal purpose" is the avoidance of taxes or the avoidance of registration of securities. Subparagraph (a) and (b) are discussed below.

1. Standards for Confirmation

a. Plans Accepted by Every Class

Section 1129(a) sets out 13 confirmation requirements for plans accepted by every class. Subject to the limited exception of sections 1129(c) and 1129(d), a plan that has been accepted by every class of claims and every class of interests must be confirmed by the bankruptcy court if the 13 enumerated requirements of section 1129(a) are satisfied. Section 1129(b) does not apply to plans that have been accepted by every class of claims and every class of interests.

Most of the requirements of section 1129(a) are easy to understand, easy to apply. Law school bankruptcy courses tend to cover only four of the requirements.

1) Best Interests of Creditors

First, section 1129(a)(7) creates a "best interests of creditors" test. [Section 1129(a)(7) does not use the term "best interest." Courts and commentators use the term "best interests" in applying section 1129(a)(7).] It requires that each dissenting member of a class—even dissenting members of classes that approve the plan—receive at least as much under the plan as it would have received in a Chapter 7 liquidation. [Section 1129(a)(7) looks to the value of the distribution under the plan as of the effective date of the plan. If for example the plan calls for payment to Creditor X of $100 a month for 20 months, the value of the payment to X "as of the effective date of the plan" is clearly less than $2,000.]

2) Priority Claims

Second, section 1129(a)(9) provides special treatment for priority claims. A holder of an administrative expense claim or a claim for

3. So far, Chapter 11 cram down of secured claims is identical to Chapter 13 cram down of secured claims. Now compare sections 1325(a)(5)(B) and section 1129(b)(2)(A)(II) more closely. Note that section 1129(a)(2)(A)(II) has an additional requirement that the amount of the plan payments must be at least equal to the amount of the secured claim.

In most Chapter 11 cases, this additional requirement is meaningless. Generally, a stream of payments that have a discounted present value equal to the value of the collateral will exceed the amount of the secured claim.

This additional Chapter 11 cram down requirement will only matter if a secured creditor made a section 1111(b) election. Recall that under Chapter 11 a secured creditor can elect to have its entire claim treated as secured, regardless of the value of its collateral.

Example: If D owes S $100,000 and the debt is secured by equipment with a value of $75,000, then under section 506, S has a $75,000 secured claim. But by making a section 1111(b) election, S can have a $100,000 secured claim. If S so elects, then a cram down of S's secured claim would require both that the stream of payments under the plan have a discounted present value of $75,000—"the value of such holder's interest in the estate's interest in such property"—and that the face amount of the plan payments total at least $100,000.

b) Unsecured Claims

Now, cram down of unsecured claims. Bankruptcy law professors, lawyers and judges (but not the Bankruptcy Code) use the phrase "absolute priority" to describe the standard for "fair and equitable" treatment of unsecured claims.

Section 1129(b)'s "fair and equitable" standard is satisfied with respect to a dissenting class of unsecured claims if "the holder of any claim or interest that is junior to the claims of such class will not receive or retain under the plan on account of such junior claim or interest any property." What does the quoted language mean? Who is "junior" to an unsecured creditor?

Under the Bankruptcy Code, as under corporate codes, stockholders are "junior" to unsecured creditors. Accordingly, the "absolute priority" rule of section 1129(b)(2)(B) requires payment in full to creditors before distributions to shareholders. [By "payment in full," we mean (or, more importantly, section 1129(b)(2)(B) requires) that the plan distributions to the dissenting class have a present value that at least equals the face amount of the claim.] Accordingly, a Chapter 11 plan can not be crammed down on unsecured creditors unless stockholders get nothing.

Example: *D* Corp. files for Chapter 11 relief. Its Chapter 11 plan provides for 70 cents on the dollar to a class of holders of unsecured claims and also provides for its shareholders to retain their *D* Corp. stock. Can the plan be confirmed? Yes, if accepted by the requisite majorities of all classes of claims. If *D* Corp.'s plan is accepted by all classes, then section 1129(b) does not apply. If, however, *D* Corp.'s plan is not accepted by all classes, section 1129(b) will apply and will preclude confirmation. This plan is not "fair and equitable" under section 1129(b)(2)(B): stockholders are junior to the dissenting class and are retaining property under the plan.

Reconsider the language of section 1129(b)(2)(B) set out above, particularly the phrase "on account of such junior claim or interest." Can shareholders retain their stock notwithstanding nonassenting classes and section 1129(b)(2)(B) by making a new capital contribution to the corporation? In Case v. Los Angeles Lumber Products Co. (1939), the Supreme Court, in dicta, recognized a "new value" exception to the absolute priority rule: shareholders of an insolvent debtor could retain an interest in a reorganized entity if their "participation [is] based on a contribution in money or money's worth, reasonably equivalent in view of all of the circumstances to the participation of the shareholder."

The Supreme Court in Norwest Bank Worthington v. Ahlers (1988), reversed an Eighth Circuit decision which had held that a farmer's efforts in managing his farm constituted "money or money's worth" and therefore could form the predicate for the *Case* "new value" exception to the absolute priority rule. The Solicitor General, in an amicus brief, argued that the Bankruptcy Code eliminated the *Case* exception to the absolute priority rule. The Court expressly declined to determine whether the *Case* exception is still good law.

In Bank of America v. 203 North LaSalle Street Partnership (1999), the Supreme Court again declined to rule whether the Bankruptcy Code eliminated the "new value" exception to the "absolute priority" rule. Instead, the Court limited its overruling of the Seventh Circuit's use of the new value exception to the specific facts of the case. More specifically, to the fact in the case that the debtor still enjoyed section 1121 exclusivity. The Supreme Court held that a debtor could not simultaneously retain the exclusive right to file a plan and then propose in its plan that its owners (and only its owners) could contribute new capital to obtain the ownership of the reorganized debtor. The Court reasoned that the exclusive opportunity to buy the ownership must be considered property received "on account of" old equity interests in the entity and so prohibited by 1129(a)(2)(B).

In sum, it is still not clear whether the Bankruptcy Code precludes use of a new value exception. All that is now clear is that the Supreme Court precludes use of both exclusivity and a new value exception.

c) Equity

Finally, cram down of equity under section 1129(b)(2)(C). Cram down of equity will not be covered in this basic student text because this (1) rarely arises in bankruptcy cases, and (2) even more rarely is covered in bankruptcy courses and (3) is well covered by Professor Ken Klee in *All You Ever Wanted to Know About Cram Down Under the New Bankruptcy Code*, 53 Am.Bankr.L.J. 133, 145–50 (1979) and (4) can be really hard stuff. [In its basic form, section 1129(b)(2)(C) is a form of absolute priority rule: While dissenting classes of claims must be paid in full before classes of equity interests receive anything, equity must receive what is left after dissenting classes of claims are paid in full. Cases rarely trigger the application of section 1129(b)(2)(C) in this basic form.]

2. Effect of Confirmation

a. Discharge

After confirmation of a Chapter 11 plan, the debtor's performance obligations are governed by the terms of the plan. The provisions of a confirmed Chapter 11 plan bind not only the debtor but also the debtor's creditors and shareholders "whether or not such creditor, equity security holder, or general partner has accepted the plan," section 1141(a). Subject to limitations noted below, confirmation of a Chapter 11 plan operates as a discharge, section 1141(d). The following hypothetical illustrates the possible application of section 1141(a) and section 1141(d).

Example: D's confirmed Chapter 11 plan provides for monthly payments to creditors. Each creditor in Class 2 is to receive 5% of its claim each month for 15 months. After making two payments under the plan, D defaults. At the time of the filing of the petition D owed C $10,000. C has received $1,000 under the plan. C's claim against D is now limited to $6,500. (75% × $10,000–1,000).

b. Limitations

Chapter 11 withholds discharge from some debtors and some debts. The plan may limit discharge, section 1141(d)(1). The order of confirmation may limit discharge, section 1141(d)(1). The exceptions to discharge in section 523 are applicable to individual debtors, section 1141(d)(2). The objections to discharge in section 727 are applicable only if (1) the plan provides for the sale of all or substantially all of the debtor's property, *and* (2) the debtor does not engage in business after the consummation of the plan, section 1141(d)(3).

Example: D Corp. owns and operates both motels and movie theaters. D Corp. files for Chapter 11. Its reorganization plan provides sale of the motels and continued ownership and operation of its movie theaters. On confirmation of the plan, D Corp. would receive a discharge. While section 727(a)(1) denies a corporation a discharge in Chapter 7 cases, that provision does not apply here because D Corp. will engage in business after consummation of its plan, section 1141(d)(3). And, since D Corp. is a corporate debtor and not an individual debtor, the section 523 exceptions do not apply to it, section 1141(d)(2).

c. Comparison of Discharge in Chapter 7 and 11 Cases

The following chart compares Chapter 11 discharge rules with those of Chapter 7.

	Chapter 7	Chapter 11
Corporations, partnerships	Not eligible for discharge	Eligible for discharge unless plan is a liquidating plan and the debtor terminates business
Section 523	Applicable to individuals	Applicable to individuals

Grounds for withholding discharge	Section 727	1. provision in plan
		2. provision in confirmation order
		3. Section 727 if
		   a. liquidating plan, and
		   b. termination of business operation

F. Special Forms of Chapter 11 Cases

1. Prepackaged

A prepackaged plan is a bankruptcy plan of reorganization which has been negotiated and accepted by the requisite number of creditors prior to the commencement of the bankruptcy case. A prepackaged Chapter 11 involves the same legal requirements as any other Chapter 11 case; a prepackaged differs only in the sequence in which the requirements are satisfied.

The prepackaged process contemplates that creditor committee selection, debtor-committee negotiations, disclosure statement preparation, and creditor acceptance all occur before a bankruptcy petition is filed. The statutory bases for a prepackaged plan include (i) section 1102 which recognizes prepetition creditors' committees, (ii) section 1121 which permits a debtor to file a plan of reorganization together with its petition, and (iii) section 1126(b) which provides for solicitation of acceptances prior to bankruptcy.

a. Good News

The benefits of a prepackaged Chapter 11 are obvious. Prepackaged plans minimize the amount of time that debtor operates in bankruptcy because the time-consuming negotiations occur prior to any bankruptcy filing. Less disruption to the debtor's business. Moreover, a debtor has more control over the process. A plan is finalized before the debtor submits to the bankruptcy court's jurisdiction.

b. Bad News

The disadvantages of a prepackaged Chapter 11 should be equally obvious. The debtor does not have any of the protections of Chapter 11 during the negotiations. No automatic stay, no ability to reject unfavorable contracts, no moratorium on the accrual of interest on unsecured debts, no ability to obtain needed funding by using the super-priority provision until the bankruptcy petition is filed. In general, prepackaged bankruptcy is better suited for a debtor looking for help with its highly leveraged capital structure rather than a debtor looking for help with its trade debt, a debtor with financial problems rather than operational problems.

2. Small Business Cases

Lawyers and law students need to be able to answer two questions about small business cases: (1) what is a small business Chapter 11 case and (2) how is a small business Chapter 11 case different from other Chapter 11 cases.

a. What Is a Small Business Case?

A small business Chapter 11 case is a Chapter 11 case involving a debtor that comes within the Bankruptcy Code's definition of "small business debtor." Section 101(51C).

The definition of "small business debtor" focuses primarily on the amount of unsecured debt and not the size of the business operations. More specifically, in order to be a "small business debtor" the debtor must meet three requirements:

1. The debtor's debt is not more than $2 million. [This includes both secured and unsecured debt. It does not include contingent or unliquidated debt.]

2. The debtor must be engaged in "commercial or business activities" other than simply "owning or operating real property."

3. Either the U.S. Trustee has not appointed a creditor's committee or the committee is "not sufficiently active and representative to provide effective oversight." [You see the importance of this requirement when you see how small business cases under Chapter 11 are different from other Chapter 11 cases and you see the expanded role of the U.S. Trustee designated to protect creditors in small business cases.]

Before the 2005 amendments, debtors that came within the definition could choose whether or not to be treated as "small business debtors." In other words, they could elect out of the definition and thus skip the special provisions of Chapter 11 that apply to small business debtors. Now, debtors that come within the definition cannot elect out of the definition or the special provisions. These provisions apply whether or not the small business debtor likes it.

b. How Is a Small Business Case Different?

A small business debtor Chapter 11 case is different from other Chapter 11 cases in that:

1. The U.S. Trustee has additional oversight duties, as described in section 1116 and 28 U.S.C.A. section 586,

2. A small business debtor has additional reporting requirements detailed in section 308 and other duties set out in section 1116,

3. The plan process can be simpler because section 1125(f) permits courts to:

   • Determine that a plan itself provides adequate information so that no disclosure statement is necessary;

   • Approve a standard form disclosure statement;

   • Combine approval of the disclosure statement with confirmation.

4. Time periods and deadlines are different:

   • 180 days of debtor exclusivity, section 1121(c);

   • 300–day deadline for filing plan and disclosure statement, section 1121(c);

   • 45 days after filing for confirmation of the plan, section 1129(e).

3. Single Asset Real Estate Cases

The phrase "single asset real estate case" is a part of the language of sections 101 and 362 and part of the language of bankruptcy judges and lawyers. The phrase "single asset real estate case" is not, however, a phrase that actually appears in Chapter 11.

a. **Meaning of Single Asset Real Estate Case**

It is a bankruptcy case involving "single asset real estate," which means real property constituting a single property or project and no substantial other business. Section 101(51B).

b. **Automatic Stay Works Differently**

The stay provision for single asset real estate cases in section 362(d) needs to be read together with section 1121. Even though section 1121 provides for an initial 120-day exclusivity period, the deadline in a single asset real estate case is sometimes 90 days, not 120 days. In such a case, lenders secured by the real property are entitled to relief from the stay 90 days after the bankruptcy filing unless the debtor has filed a plan and that plan has a reasonable possibility of being confirmed within a reasonable time or the debtor is making monthly payments to the lenders.

c. **Different Case Law**

Even though there is no statutory basis for treating Chapter 11 cases involving a real estate debtor differently than other Chapter 11 cases, a distinct body of Chapter 11 single asset real estate case law has developed. Facts common to these cases include:

1. Debtor's only asset is a piece of real estate, e.g., a shopping center, office building, apartment complex, undeveloped law.

2. The mortgage lender is seriously undersecured.

3. The amount of the lender's unsecured claim is substantially larger than the claims of all other unsecured creditors combined.

In sum, the typical single asset real estate case is really, almost completely a dispute between the debtor and one creditor over one asset. Not everybody believes—as a matter of policy—that bankruptcy should be used to resolve a dispute between a debtor and a single creditor.

4. **Individual Chapter 11 Cases**

Because of the 2005 amendments, a Chapter 11 case in which the debtor is an individual is now like a Chapter 13 case in most respects. More specifically:

1. Section 1115, like section 1306, includes property acquired by an individual debtor postpetition within property of the estate.

2. Sections 1123(a)(8) and 1129(a)(15), like section 1325(b), impose a "best efforts" kind of test, requiring commitment of "disposable income" to plan payments.

3. Section 1141(d)(5), like section 1328(a), defers discharge until completion of plan payments.

G. Review Questions

1. David, a bored but solvent law professor whose only income is his salary, wants to file for bankruptcy. Is he eligible for Chapter 11?

2. T or F   If an examiner is appointed, a trustee can not be appointed,

3. T or F   "First day order" describes the order for relief which is entered by the bankruptcy court on the day the petition is filed.

4. D Department Store Inc. (D) files for Chapter 11 bankruptcy on January 15th. What approval does D have to obtain in order to continue business operations?

5. T or F   Collateral that is not cash collateral on the date of bankruptcy can become cash collateral during the course of a Chapter 11 case.

6. T or F   A bankruptcy court can approve the debtor's use of cash collateral notwithstanding the lienholder's objection only if the debtor provides adequate protection of repayment of the lienholder's claim.

7. D Co. files a Chapter 11 plan two days after filing its Chapter 11 petition. When can creditors file competing plans?

8. T or F   P wants to purchase all of the assets of D Corp. To foster good relations with D Corp's customers and suppliers, P wants to the proceeds of the purchase to be used to pay claims against D Corp. D Corp. can file a Chapter 11 petition and plan that provides for the sale of all of its assets.

9. D, a Chapter 11 debtor, has 1000 different creditors.

10. Class 3 has 27 different creditors. How many of these creditors must vote for the plan in order for the plan to be accepted by Class 3?

11. T or F   In order to confirm a plan, a court must always determine whether the plan discriminates unfairly.

12. D, a Chapter 11 debtor, owes C $100,000. D's plan provides to pay C and other creditors in class 7 30% of the amount of their claim within two years

of plan confirmation. D's plan is confirmed. After making some of the plan payments to other classes but before making any plan payment to C and other class 7 creditors, D defaults. What are C's rights?

*

XIX

Allocation of Judicial Power Over Bankruptcy Matters

■ *ANALYSIS*

A. **History**
    1.   1898 Act
    2.   1978 Code
    3.   Marathon Pipeline Decision

B. **Operation of Present Law**
    1.   Bankruptcy Court as Part of the District Court, Section 151
    2.   Grants of Jurisdiction to the District Court, Section 1334(A) and 1334(B)
    3.   Role of the Bankruptcy Court, Section 157
    4.   Abstention Under Section 1334(C)

C. **Jury Trials**
    1.   When Is There a Right?
    2.   When Can a Bankruptcy Judge Hold a Jury Trial?

D. **Review Questions**

In the main, the substantive law of bankruptcy is in title 11 of the United States Code. Questions of judicial power over bankruptcy-related matters are, in the main, answered in title 28 of the United States Code.

The question of which court has the power to adjudicate the litigation that arises in bankruptcy can be an important one. Many attorneys that represent parties with claims against the bankrupt or parties against whom the bankrupt has claims prefer to litigate in some forum other than the bankruptcy court. Some believe that the bankruptcy judge has a pro-debtor bias; others are simply more comfortable or more familiar with state court procedures; others prefer state court for reasons of delay—a state court generally has a larger backlog of cases than a bankruptcy court so that filing in state court delays any litigation.

In considering the question of which court has the power to adjudicate the litigation that arises in bankruptcy, it is helpful to consider the kinds of matters that can arise in bankruptcy.

1. Some matters will involve only bankruptcy law. For example, *D* files a Chapter 7 petition. The Chapter 7 trustee alleges that *B*'s payment of $40,000 to *C* a month before bankruptcy is recoverable by the estate under section 550 as a section 547 voidable preference. *C* contends that the $40,000 payment is protected from avoidance as a section 547(c)(2) ordinary course of business payment.

2. Other matters will involve both bankruptcy law and nonbankruptcy law. For example, *D* files a Chapter 7 petition. *C* files a secured claim that describes its Article 9 security interest. The bankruptcy trustee takes the position that *C*'s security interest is invalid because it was not properly perfected. If this is litigated, it will probably involve both the Bankruptcy Code's invalidation provisions and the Uniform Commercial Code's perfection provisions.

3. And, still other matters will not involve substantive bankruptcy law. For example, *D*, Inc., a Chapter 11 debtor, files a breach of contract claim against *X*.

A. History

The allocation of judicial power over bankruptcy matters has been and still is one of the most controversial bankruptcy issues. A general familiarity with prior statutory schemes and prior controversies is helpful to understanding the present situation.

1. 1898 Act

Under the Bankruptcy Act of 1898, bankruptcy courts had limited jurisdiction. This jurisdiction was commonly referred to as "summary jurisdiction."

(The phrase "summary jurisdiction" is somewhat misleading. First, it incorrectly implies that under the Bankruptcy Act of 1898, bankruptcy courts had a second, non-summary form of jurisdiction. Summary jurisdiction is the only form of jurisdiction that a bankruptcy judge possessed under the Bankruptcy Act of 1898. Bankruptcy courts had only summary jurisdiction; other courts had plenary jurisdiction. Second, it incorrectly implies that in resolving controversies the bankruptcy judge always conducted summary proceedings.)

Summary jurisdiction extended to (1) *all* matters concerned with the administration of the bankruptcy estate and (2) *some* disputes between the bankruptcy trustee and third parties involving rights to money and other property in which the bankrupt estate claimed an interest. The tests for which disputes with third parties were within the bankruptcy judge's summary jurisdiction turned on issues such as whether (1) the property in question was in the actual possession of the bankrupt at the time of the commencement of the case, (2) the property in question was in the constructive possession of the bankrupt at the time of the commencement of the case, and (3) the third party actually or impliedly consented to bankruptcy court jurisdiction.

There was considerable uncertainty over which disputes were within the summary jurisdiction of the bankruptcy court. This uncertainty gave rise to considerable litigation.

2. 1978 Code

Apparently for the above reasons, Congress in 1978 decided to create a bankruptcy court with pervasive jurisdiction. Apparently for political reasons, Congress also decided that this bankruptcy court should *not* be an Article III court.

As you recall from your Constitutional Law course in law school or civics course in high school, Article III of the Constitution vests the judicial power of the United States in the United States Supreme Court and such inferior tribunals as Congress might create. To insure the independence of the judges appointed under Article III (the so-called constitutional courts), Article III provides them with certain protections. These include tenure for life, removal from office only by congressional impeachment, and assurance that their compensation will not be diminished. The constitutional courts created under Article III include the United States Supreme Court, the United States Courts of Appeal, and the United States District Courts. The United States Customs Court (now the Court of International Trade) is also an Article III court; its judges may be, and often are, assigned to hear cases in the district courts and the courts of appeal.

Congress, in the exercise of its legislative powers enumerated in Article I of the Constitution, may create other inferior federal tribunals—the so-called legislative courts. Judges of these legislative courts need not be granted tenure for life. In addition, they can be removed by mechanisms other than congressional impeachment, and their salaries are subject to congressional reduction. Historically, these Article I legislative courts and their judges have been granted jurisdiction over limited and narrowly defined subject matters, like the Tax Court. In other instances, jurisdiction has been limited to narrowly defined geographical territories, such as the territorial courts, the District of Columbia courts, etc.

In amending title 28 in 1978, Congress gave bankruptcy judges none of the protections found in Article III of the Constitution. Nevertheless, the 1978 amendments to title 28 gave bankruptcy judges much of the power and responsibilities of an Article III judge. Since bankruptcy debtors can be just about any kind of individual or business entity, this meant that litigation in the bankruptcy courts could deal with almost every facet of business and personal activity.

3. Marathon Pipeline Decision

The 1978 grant of pervasive jurisdiction to a non-Article III bankruptcy court was successfully challenged in the *Marathon* case.

Northern Pipeline, a Chapter 11 debtor, filed a breach of contract lawsuit against Marathon Pipeline in bankruptcy court. There was no question as to whether the bankruptcy court had jurisdiction over this lawsuit under 28 USCA 1471(c). Marathon Pipeline did, however, question whether section 1471(c) conferred Article III judicial power on non-Article III courts in violation of the separation of powers doctrine and filed a motion to dismiss. A divided Supreme Court sustained Marathon's challenge in Northern Pipeline Constr. Co. v. Marathon Pipeline Co. (1982).

The Court in *Marathon* was so divided that there was no majority opinion. Justice Brennan's opinion was joined by three other justices. Additionally, two justices concurred in the result. The holding of these six is perhaps best summarized in footnote 40 of Justice Brennan's plurality opinion which indicates that (1) the 1978 legislation does grant the bankruptcy court the power to hear Northern Pipeline's breach of contract claim, (2) the bankruptcy court, a non-Article III court, cannot constitutionally be vested with jurisdiction to decide such state law claims, and (3) this grant of authority to the bankruptcy court is not severable from the remaining grant of authority to the bankruptcy court.

After *Marathon*, Congress was urged to solve the constitutional dilemma by establishing bankruptcy courts as Article III courts. Congress rejected this solution. Instead, Congress in 1984 made the bankruptcy court a part of the federal district court, conferred jurisdiction in bankruptcy on the district court, and allocated judicial power in bankruptcy matters between the federal district judge and the bankruptcy judge. In the two-year gap between the 1982 Marathon decision and the 1984 legislation, the allocation of judicial power over bankruptcy was governed by an Emergency Rule adopted by all district courts.

It is easy for any lawyer or law student to criticize the provisions allocating judicial power over bankruptcy matters. It is more difficult (but probably more important) for a lawyer or law student to understand how these provisions operate.

B. Operation of Present Law

In understanding the present law allocating judicial powers over bankruptcy matters, it is necessary to understand three separate sections in title 28: (1) 151, (2) 1334 and (3) 157. By understanding these three provisions you will understand that (1) bankruptcy courts are a part of the United States District Court but bankruptcy judges are different from district court judges, (2) bankruptcy cases are different from bankruptcy proceedings, (3) bankruptcy cases can be handled by either bankruptcy judges or federal district judges (depending on withdrawal of the reference), but not by state court judges and (4) bankruptcy proceedings can be tried by bankruptcy judges or federal judges (depending on withdrawal of the reference) or even state court judges (depending on where the lawsuit was filed and removal and abstention). To understand even more, please read the following descriptions of the three key sections in title 28:

1. Bankruptcy Court as Part of the District Court, Section 151

Section 151 refers to a bankruptcy judge and a bankruptcy court as a "unit" of the district court. It is important to keep this reference in mind when reading other sections in title 28 dealing with the allocation of judicial power in bankruptcy matters. When the term "district court" appears in section 1334 or section 157, it could be referring to the United States district judge and/or the bankruptcy judge. After all, the bankruptcy judge is a part of the district court—a "unit" of the district court.

2. Grants of Jurisdiction to the District Court, Section 1334(A) and 1334(B)

a. Cases

Section 1334(a) vests original and exclusive jurisdiction in the district court over all cases arising under the Bankruptcy Code. "Case" is a term of art used in both the Bankruptcy Code and the Bankruptcy Rules. "Case" refers to the entire Chapter 7, 9, 11, 12 or 13—not just some controversy that arises in connection with it.

b. Proceedings

The term "case" is to be distinguished from the term "proceeding." A specific dispute that arises during the pendency of a case is referred to as a "proceeding." Section 1334(b) provides that the district courts have original but not exclusive jurisdiction over all civil proceedings, "arising under title 11, or arising in or related to cases under title 11."

"Proceedings" include "contested matters," motions brought in the main bankruptcy case and "adversary proceedings," lawsuits. Section 1334(b) grants the district court original but not exclusive jurisdiction over three types of "civil proceedings":

1) "Arising Under" Title 11

This involves adjudication of rights or obligations created by the Bankruptcy Code. For example, stay relief. For example, preference litigation.

2) "Arising in" a Case Under Title 11

This covers matters peculiar to bankruptcy but based on rights or obligations created by the Bankruptcy Code. For example, allowance or disallowance of claims. For example, assumption or rejection of executory contracts.

3) "Related to" a Case Under Title 11

This covers matters that impact on the bankruptcy case. Reported decisions on "related to" commonly quote from the Third Circuit's decision in Pacor, Inc. v. Higgins (1984): "The test for determining whether a civil proceeding is related to bankruptcy is whether the outcome of the proceeding could conceivably have any effect on the estate being administered in bankruptcy."

While it is not a "catch-all," it is certainly catches a lot. In Celotex Corp. v. Edwards (1995), the Supreme Court held that entry of an injunction prohibiting a judgment creditor from executing on a supersedeas bond of a third party surety of the debtor was "related to."

Example: If the Bada Bing Club, Inc. files a Chapter 11 petition, section 1334(a) gives the district court jurisdiction over the Bada Bing Chapter 7 case itself. And, section 1334(b) gives the district court jurisdiction over a complaint filed by Bada Bing's trustee alleging that payments to Tony Soprano were preferential or a complaint filed against Bada Bing by Epstein alleging unauthorized charges against his credit card.

3.   Role of the Bankruptcy Court, Section 157

Clearly, section 1334 confers jurisdiction over bankruptcy matters to the district court. It is equally clear that most federal district judges have neither the time nor the inclination to exercise this jurisdiction. Accordingly, section 157 empowers the district judge to refer bankruptcy matters to the bankruptcy judge.

a.   Procedural Role

Note the title of section 157, "Procedures." As this title suggests, section 157 is not a jurisdictional provision. It does not confer jurisdiction on the bankruptcy judge. Rather, it deals with procedure—the role that the bankruptcy judge, a unit of the district court under section 151, is to play in exercising the jurisdiction conferred by section 1334 on the district court.

b.   Core Versus "Noncore"

Section 157 differentiates between "core" and "noncore" proceedings. A nonexclusive list of core proceedings is set out in section 157(b)(2). [Bada Bing's section 547 action against Tony is an easy example of a core proceeding.] Generally, in core proceedings, the bankruptcy judge conducts the trial or hearing and enters a final judgment.

Obviously, if a matter is not a core proceeding, it is a "noncore proceeding." "Noncore proceeding" is neither defined nor illustrated in the statute. [Epstein's credit card abuse action against the Bada Bing Co. is an obvious example of a noncore proceeding.] In noncore proceedings, the bankruptcy judge still can hold the trial or hearing, but generally cannot issue a final judgment. She instead submits proposed findings of fact and law to the district court for review, section 157(c)(1). [The bankruptcy judge can enter a final order or judgment in a noncore matter only if the parties consent, 28 USCA § 157(c)(2).]

The bankruptcy judge is empowered to determine whether a matter is a core proceeding or a noncore proceeding, section 157(b)(3). Remember that a determination that a proceeding is noncore does not mean that the matter is withdrawn from the bankruptcy judge. Remember that a bankruptcy judge can hear noncore proceedings and prepare findings of facts and law.

c. **District Court Right of Withdrawal**

The district judge retains ultimate control over the role of the bankruptcy judge. Section 157(d) authorizes the district judge to withdraw a case or proceeding from a bankruptcy judge. The first sentence of section 157(d) provides for permissive withdrawal "for cause shown." Under the second sentence of section 157(d), withdrawal of the reference is mandatory if "resolution of the proceeding requires consideration of both Title 11 and other laws of the United States regulating . . . interstate commerce."

In applying this provision, most courts disregard the "plain language" quoted above. The plain language of section 157(d) indicates that withdrawal of the reference is mandatory only if both the Bankruptcy Code and another federal statute must be construed to resolve the proceeding. Under the statute's "plain language," a district court would be required to withdraw the reference only in actions involving both bankruptcy and nonbankruptcy law—not in matters involving nonbankruptcy law alone. And, under the statute's plain language, the bankruptcy court would have to abstain on all matters that involve both bankruptcy law and a nonfederal statute regulating interstate commerce, regardless of how simple and straight forward the application of the other statute.

Because the "plain language" of section 157(d)'s second sentence plainly does not work, most courts have ignored the literal language of section 157(d) for mandatory withdrawal. Instead, these courts require that the reference be withdrawn if an action involves a "substantial and material" consideration of a nonbankruptcy federal statute regulating interstate commerce, regardless of whether the action also involves consideration of the Bankruptcy Code.

Withdrawal of the reference from the district court to the bankruptcy judge is also mandatory for (1) claims for wrongful death or other personal injuries, section 157(a)(3)(5), or (2) matters in which a party has a right to a jury trial unless the district court has authorized the bankruptcy judge to conduct the jury trial and the parties have consented, section 157(e).

Remember that withdrawal under section 157(d) merely moves a matter from the bankruptcy judge to the federal district judge. Withdrawal under section 157(d) does not move a matter to a state court. That requires abstention.

4. Abstention Under Section 1334(C)

Abstention under section 1334(c) moves litigation from bankruptcy court to a state court. In considering and applying the abstention provisions of section 1334(c), it is important to recall the jurisdictional provisions of section 1334(b). As you learned from your readings in constitutional law and/or federal courts, a federal court with jurisdiction over a matter or controversy must exercise that jurisdiction except under unusual circumstances. And, as you learned from reading this book, Congress provided for broad, pervasive bankruptcy jurisdiction in section 1334(b) to eliminate the costly litigation over jurisdiction that occurred under the Bankruptcy Act of 1898. As a result, some of the matters covered by the jurisdictional grant in section 1334(b) are not really bankruptcy matters, are matters that would be better left to other courts. Section 1334(c) empowers the bankruptcy judge to leave such matters to other courts by abstaining.

Section 1334(c)(1) provides for permissive abstention. If the district court believes that abstention would be "in the interest of justice" or "in the interest of comity with State courts or respect for State law," it has the option of abstaining.

Section 1334(c)(2) provides for mandatory abstention. If the following six requirements of section 1334(c)(2) are satisfied, the district court must abstain:

1. A party to the proceeding must timely file a motion to abstain.

2. The proceeding is based on a state law claim or cause of action.

3. The matter is a "related to" proceeding, as contrasted with an "arising under" or "arising in" proceeding.

   [Section 1334(b) uses all three of these phrases. Section 1334(c)(2) limits mandatory abstention to its certain "related to" proceedings.

> There is no statutory definition of "arising under," "arising in" or "related to." Obviously, the Bada Bing Co.'s preference action against Tony is an example of "arising under"—it is a cause of action created by the Bankruptcy Code. Obviously, Epstein's credit card abuse action against the Bada Bing Co. is either "arising in" or "related to." It is not obvious from existing case law whether Epstein's action is "arising in" or "related to."]

4.   The action could not have been commenced in federal court in the absence of the jurisdiction conferred by section 1334. If there is any other basis for federal court jurisdiction, mandatory abstention is not available. This requirement means that mandatory abstention would not be available in the *Northern Pipeline* case because of the diversity of citizenship between the parties.

5.   An action is commenced in state court. There is a question as to whether this means that the state court action must be pending at the time of the bankruptcy filing.

6.   The state court action can be timely adjudicated.

C. Jury Trials

There are two questions about jury trials in bankruptcy proceedings. First, when is there a right to a jury trial? Second, can the bankruptcy judge conduct the jury trial?

1. When Is There a Right?

The Seventh Amendment to the Constitution governs the right to jury trials in federal courts—"suits at common law, where the value in controversy shall exceed twenty dollars." Note the phrase "at common law." The Seventh Amendment does not confer a right to jury trial to equitable actions or to those who seek equitable remedies. Which bankruptcy proceedings are "suits at common law"? When does a debtor or holder of a claim in a bankruptcy case seek an equitable remedy?

The Supreme Court addressed these questions (sort of) in Granfinanciera, S.A. v. Nordberg (1989), which found a right to jury trial in fraudulent conveyance litigation where (1) the trustee is seeking a money judgment and (2) the transferee has not filed a proof of claim. In so ruling, the Court compared "the statutory action to 18th-century actions brought in the courts of England prior to the merger of the courts of law and equity" and concluded that "actions to recover preferential or fraudulent transfers were often brought at law in late 18th-century England."

2. When Can a Bankruptcy Judge Hold a Jury Trial?

Section 157(e) answers the second question of whether a bankruptcy judge can hold a jury trial. Actually, the federal district judge and the parties to the proceeding answer the question of who holds the jury trial. Under section 157(e), the bankruptcy judge can conduct the jury trial only if she has been "specially designated" by the district judge and "all of the parties" consent.

D. Review Questions

1. T or F   Bankruptcy courts are Article I courts.

2. T or F   The district court has jurisdiction over bankruptcy cases.

3. T or F   The bankruptcy court has jurisdiction over bankruptcy cases.

4. T or F   The bankruptcy court can hear only core proceedings.

5. T or F   A Chapter 11 case is a core proceeding.

6. T or F   Litigation over an objection to a Chapter 7 discharge is a core proceeding.

7. T or F   The federal district court can withdraw a case but not a proceeding.

8. T or F   Withdrawal of a case moves the case from federal court to state court.

9. T or F   A state court can hear a noncore proceeding but not a core proceeding.

10. T or F   Abstention moves a case from state court to federal court.

*

APPENDIX A

Answers to Review Questions

CHAPTER I. EXTRAJUDICIAL COLLECTION DEVICES

1. None of them.

2. Lose. The creditor is not a debt collector.

3. A debt collector is any person who regularly collects debts owed to others. This includes attorneys who collect debts on a regular basis.

4. Personal, family, and household debts are covered under the Act.

5. A collector may contact you in person, by mail, telephone, telegram, or fax. However, a debt collector may not contact you at inconvenient times or places, such as before 8 a.m. or after 9 p.m., unless you agree. A debt collector also may not contact you at work if the collector knows that your employer disapproves of such contacts.

6. You can stop a debt collector from contacting you by writing a letter to the collector telling them to stop. Once the collector receives your letter, they may not contact you again except to say there will be no further contact or to notify you that the debt collector or the creditor intends to take some specific action. Please note, however, that sending such a letter to a collector does not make the debt go away if you actually owe it. You could still be sued by the debt collector or your original creditor.

7. If you have an attorney, the debt collector must contact the attorney, rather than you. If you do not have an attorney, a collector may contact other people,

but only to find out where you live, what your phone number is, and where you work. Collectors usually are prohibited from contacting such third parties more than once. In most cases, the collector may not tell anyone other than you and your attorney that you owe money.

8. A debtor collector cannot contact the debtor's employer except for the purpose of collecting information to locate the debtor.

9. Within five days after you are first contacted, the collector must send you a written notice telling you the amount of money you owe; the name of the creditor to whom you owe the money; and what action to take if you believe you do not owe the money.

10. A collector may not contact you if, within 30 days after you receive the written notice, you send the collection agency a letter stating you do not owe money. However, a collector can renew collection activities if you are sent proof of the debt, such as a copy of a bill for the amount owed.

CHAPTER II.   JUDICIAL DEBT COLLECTION

1. False.

2. True.

3. The two most important reasons are these: First, the state law may protect a larger part of her wages. Second, Title III provides no protection whatsoever once wages have been paid to an employee. State law ordinarily continues to shield exempt income received by a debtor even after she deposits it into a bank account.

4. No. For property to qualify as an exempt homestead, there must be a dwelling which the debtor occupies as her home.

5. No. The homestead exemption is available in most states only to a debtor who heads a "household" or a "family," which means that a person or people must reside with the debtor and depend on her partly or fully for support.

6. The answer is "false" for most states. Attachment ordinarily is limited to actions in which money damages are sought *and* in which certain extenuating circumstances, i.e., *grounds of attachment*, are present.

7. The usual procedural prerequisites to the issuance of a writ of attachment are: the plaintiff must commence suit; an affidavit of attachment must be

presented to the issuing officer; the plaintiff must post bond; and, in about half the states, the defendant must be notified that attachment is sought and be given a pre-seizure opportunity for a hearing.

8. Attached property ordinarily is not sold unless and until the attaching creditor wins judgment against the defendant. An exception is made when the property is perishable, threatens to decline speedily in value, or is unduly expensive to hold.

9. True. The determinative issue in a replevin action is whether the plaintiff has an immediate right to possession of the property as against the defendant. This issue does not necessarily turn on ownership.

10. False. In most states the replevin remedy is available in any replevin action when the plaintiff can demonstrate the probability that she is entitled to possession of the property as against the defendant.

11. *Mitchell* did not overrule *Sniadach.* Due process requires a constitutional accommodation of the interests of both debtor and creditor. These interests will vary from case to case, which means that the requirements of due process will vary. In *Sniadach,* the debtor's interests outweighed those of the creditor. In *Mitchell,* the creditor's interests were heavier. This difference in the facts, i.e., in the balancing of interests, not a difference in law, accounts for the different procedures required in the two cases.

12. In most states, a lien of judgment does not arise until the judgment is docketed or otherwise indexed or recorded as prescribed by statute.

13. The lien does not reach any of D's property in County Z unless and until C dockets her judgment there.

14. A writ of execution is issued by the clerk of the court that rendered the judgment or by the clerk of any court in which the judgment has been docketed.

15. Any of the debtor's nonexempt, tangible personal property and also most of her nonexempt interests in real estate can be seized and sold through execution.

16. False. Property seized through execution usually is held by the sheriff until such time as she sells it.

17. The sheriff returns the writ *nulla bona* if she is unable to locate any leviable property of the debtor.

18. In the majority of states, the lien of execution attaches and dates from the time the sheriff levies on property. In a minority of states, the lien dates from the time the writ of execution is delivered to the sheriff.

19. True. Federal law provides that district court judgments shall be enforced through execution process in accordance with the practice and procedure of the state in which the district court is held.

20. Garnishment typically begins with the judgment creditor, the garnishor, filing with the court an affidavit describing the judgment, complaining that the judgment is unsatisfied, and alleging that a third person, the garnishee, is indebted to, or holds property of, the judgment debtor. The judge or the court clerk then issues a garnishment summons that is served on the garnishee and the judgment debtor.

21. The jurisdictions differ with respect to the consequence of a garnishee failing to answer a garnishment summons. The garnishee risks liability for (1) the full amount of the garnishor's judgment against the debtor; (2) the amount or value of the debtor's property that the judgment creditor alleged was in the garnishee's hands; or (3) the actual damages suffered by the garnishor as a result of the garnishee's neglect in not answering the summons.

22. The garnishee is accountable for the amount of the garnishable wages paid to the debtor.

CHAPTER III. FRAUDULENT CONVEYANCES

1. Because of D's subjective intention to hinder or delay her creditors, the conveyance of the stock is actually fraudulent not only against existing creditors such as A, whose claim existed at the time of the conveyance, but also against future creditors such as B whose claim arose after the conveyance.

2. The answers are altogether different. The conveyance is neither actually nor constructively fraudulent against any of D's creditors. The conveyance is not actually fraudulent because there is no subjective intention to hinder, delay, or defraud creditors. Despite D's insolvency, there is no constructive fraud because fair consideration was given in exchange for the conveyance of the stock.

3. The conveyance is constructively fraudulent if D was insolvent at the time of the conveyance or, as a result of the conveyance, was rendered insolvent. Yet,

the conveyance is voidable only by creditors whose claims existed at the time of the conveyance. Future creditors are not protected against this kind of fraudulent conveyance.

4. The conveyance is not constructively fraudulent inasmuch as D was solvent at all times. Nevertheless, the lack of fair consideration and the familial relationship are badges of fraud indicating, and perhaps giving rise to a presumption of, actual fraudulent intention.

5. No. A creditor cannot attack a security transfer on the ground that the value of the property transferred is disproportionate to the debt secured because the mortgage or other lien only exists to the extent of the debt.

6. The answer is "no" under state law because of the traditional rule that a foreclosure sale of collateral conducted according to law cannot be attacked as a fraudulent conveyance solely on the basis of inadequacy of price. Same answer under federal bankruptcy law. The Supreme Court has decided that the price received at mortgage foreclosure sale conclusively established "reasonably equivalent value" of mortgage property, as long as requirements of state's foreclosure law were met. BFP v. Resolution Trust Corp., 511 U.S. 531 (1994).

7. There is no actual fraud, and the conveyance to A is not constructively fraudulent because there was fair consideration. Fair consideration is given when an antecedent debt is satisfied. The conveyance to A amounted to nothing more than a preference, which under traditional law is not subject to attack as a preference.

8. The answer is the same under traditional law. Mere preferences are not avoidable as fraudulent conveyances even if the preferred creditor is a relative. The answer might be different under the UFTA, which renders constructively fraudulent a preferential transfer to an insider, including a relative, if the insider had reasonable cause to believe that the debtor was insolvent. UFTA § 5(b).

9. The traditional rule is that a conversion of nonexempt property to exempt property is not vulnerable as a fraudulent conveyance regardless of the debtor's motive or financial condition.

10. The remedies generally available to protected creditors for curing a fraudulent conveyance are (1) restraining any further disposition of the property, appointing a receiver to take charge of it, or obtaining other judicial orders

designed to protect the property; (2) ignoring the conveyance and seizing the property through attachment or execution when such remedies are otherwise available; and (3) suing to set aside the conveyance.

11. R can defeat the action to set aside the conveyance by establishing that she was an innocent purchaser for fair consideration. R was not such a purchaser, however, if the real estate was worth only half the stock's value. Fair consideration requires the exchange of property having equivalent values. Nevertheless, if R made the exchange without actual fraudulent intent, she made retain the stock as security for return of the less than fair consideration she gave.

12. No. Only in exceptional cases does traditional law provide for the recovery of damages against the transferee of property which has been fraudulently conveyed. The answer may change under the new UFTA, which appears to allow the recovery of damages in any case where a fraudulent conveyance could be set aside by a creditor.

CHAPTER IV.   CREDITORS WITH SPECIAL RIGHTS

1. Security agreement; value; rights.

2. The creditor must be a secured party with a security interest in the property, and the debtor must have defaulted.

3. False. Perfection is important only in determining the priority of a security interest against third-party claims to the collateral.

4. Replevin.

5. Sue for a deficiency.

6. The answer is (a), (b) & (c). Filing a notice of tax lien is important for priority over third parties' claim, but filing is unimportant and totally unnecessary to the creation and enforcement of the tax lien against the taxpayer.

7. True and False. A federal tax lien cannot arise until the government has made a demand for payment of the assessed taxes and the taxpayer has refused to pay. Yet, once these conditions have been satisfied, the lien relates back to, and dates from, the time of the assessment.

8. False.

9. X takes the set free of the lien. See 26 U.S.C.A. § 6323(b)(3).

10. S's security interest is entitled to priority. See 26 U.S.C.A. '6323(a), which gives priority to a security interest that is perfected before the tax lien is filed.

11. The answer is different: the tax lien is entitled to priority.

12. S has priority as to the accounts arising on May 5 because of the 45–day rule of 26 U.S.C.A. § 6323(c), which protects perfected security interests in after-acquired commercial financing security including accounts. The IRS wins as to the accounts arising on June 6 because the security interest attaches more than 45 days after the tax lien was filed.

13. The IRS has priority as to all of the equipment. Security interests attaching to property after the filing of a tax lien notice ordinarily are subordinate to the tax lien. There is an exception in § 6323(c) for after-acquired commercial financing security, but equipment is not commercial financing security.

14. S's interest expands by $5000 when the additional loan is made. Ordinarily, this expansion would be subordinate to a previously filed tax lien. In this problem, however, the collateral is accounts which are commercial financing security, and thus the expansion is protected from the tax lien under the 45Bday rule of § 6323(c). S has priority as to both the original loan and the later advance for a total of $15,000. This answer assumes that S was ignorant of the federal tax lien when the future advance was made.

15. The future advance is protected by the 45–day rule of § 6323(d), which protects future advances that expand security interests in any kind of collateral. This answer assumes that S was ignorant of the federal tax lien when the future advance was made.

CHAPTER V. DEBTORS' STATE LAW REMEDIES a/k/a COLLECTIVE CREDITOR ACTION RIGHTS

1. The debtor voluntarily transfers her assets to another person in trust to liquidate the assets and distribute the proceeds to the debtor's creditors.

2. False.

3. False.

4. Chapter 7 liquidation.

5. A contract between the debtor and one or more of her creditors under which the creditors agree to take a specified partial payment in full satisfaction of the creditors' claims.

6. The creditors agree to extend the time for payment rather than to reduce the amount of payment.

7. A workout is a negotiated, nonbankruptcy modification of debtors between a debtor and one or more of her creditors and can involve either a composition or extension or combination of both.

8. False.

9. True.

10. Chapter 11 reorganization.

CHAPTER VI. BANKRUPTCY: AN OVERVIEW

1. True.

2. True.

3. Courts applying federal bankruptcy law look to state law to answer questions such as what are the property rights of debtors and what are the claims of creditors against the debtor and property of the debtor.

4. Liquidation and reorganization.

5. Chapter 7.

6. Chapters 11 and 13.

7. Liquidation involves taking all of the debtor's property, liquidating the property, and distributing the proceeds to creditors holding claims at the time of the bankruptcy. Reorganization mainly involves repaying claims from future earnings.

8. Federal district court.

9. The bankruptcy court is a "unit" of the federal district court.

10. Trustees are always appointed in Chapter 7 and 13 cases but only rarely, in the court's discretion, in Chapter 11 cases.

CHAPTER VII. COMMENCEMENT, CONVERSION, AND DISMISSAL OF A BANKRUPTCY CASE

1. True.

2. True.

3. False. Chapter 13 is limited to "individuals" with regular income and whose unsecured and secured debts don not exceed certain limited; and individual means a natural person.

4. True.

5. False.

6. "[A]n individual may not be a debtor under this title unless such individual has, during the 180–day period preceding the date of the filing of the petition by such individual, received from an approved nonprofit budget and credit counseling agency. . . .an individual or group briefing . . . that outlined the opportunities for available credit counseling and assisted such individual in performing a related budget analysis." 11 U.S.C.A. § 109(h)(1).

7. Filing the bankruptcy petition.

8. Bad faith; totality of circumstances; passing the means test (median income too high).

9. Currently monthly income of the debtor and spouse exceeds median family income.

10. Chapter 13.

CHAPTER VIII. STAY OF COLLECTION ACTIONS AND ACTS

1. The stay becomes effective as soon as the petition is filed. Knowledge or notice of the case is, for most purposes, irrelevant.

2. The automatic stay would bar the continuation of the collection process. If the sale is held in violation of the stay, it is void or voidable.

3. **No.** The automatic stay only affects efforts to collect prepetition claims from the debtor or property of the debtor, section 362(a)(1).

4. Yes; no.

5. Probably yes.

6. Only if D filed Chapter 13 and the contract debt is a consumer debt. See section 1301.

7. S can argue that its interest in the collateral is not being adequately protected, i.e., it is depreciating. That does not, however, mean that S will recover the collateral. Note the various forms of relief from the stay under section 362(d)(1). The debtor could propose that the stay be conditioned on making monthly payments measured by the amount of the depreciation.

8. False. An unsecured creditor can move for and receive relief under section 362(d)(1). Note that the general standard of section 362(d)(1) is cause. Typically, however, an unsecured creditor lacks sufficient cause and loses a motion to lift stay.

9. Section 105.

10. False. "[A]n individual injured by a willful violation" gets damages under section 362(k).

CHAPTER IX.   PROPERTY OF THE ESTATE

1. False. Property of the estate is an important concept in cases under Chapter 7, 11, 12, or 13. While generally a Chapter 11, 12, or 13 debtor retains possession of property of the estate, her sale and use of it is subject to court control under section 363. Moreover, property of the estate is a relevant consideration in plan confirmation.

2. No. Absent piercing the corporate veil.

3. Only the stuff in which D herself has an interest. The estate consists of the debtor's interests in property, not property of somebody else even if D is in possession of the property.

4. Only D's interest in the painting is property of her bankruptcy estate, not Momma's interest.

5. No. Section 541(c)(2).

6. An individual's earnings from post-petition services are not property of the estate in a Chapter 7 case. Section 541(a)(6).

7. Yes. Section 541(a)(5).

8. Yes. Section 1306.

9. Blackacre is not property of the estate. D's interest in Blackacre is property of the estate.

10. Exempt property is property of the estate when the debtor files bankruptcy, but the debtor can later exempt the property and thereby remove it from the estate.

CHAPTER X.   EXEMPTIONS

1. False. Only a debtor who is an individual.

2. This federal schedule of exemptions does not apply if the state has "opted out," which means the state legislature has enacted a state law providing that the section 522(d) list of exemptions is not available to its debtors. Almost all states have opted out.

3. State law; any nonbankruptcy federal law that establishes exemptions (which is uncommon); and section 522(n), which is a bankruptcy exemption for retirement funds that is available even to a debtor in an opt-out state.

4. North Carolina. Section 522(b)(3)(a).

5. Yes. Section 522(b)(3)(B).

6. No. Section 522(p) provides that "a debtor may not exempt any amount of interest [in a homestead] that was acquired by the debtor during the 1215–day period preceding the date of the filing of the petition that exceeds in the aggregate $125,000 in value. . . . " This provision applies even though the debtor lacked any tacky intent. Presumably, therefore, the debtor can exempt only $375,000 in value.

7. No.

8. No.

9. Only if C's lien is nonpossessory and nonpurchase money and only if the widget is a kind of property described in section 522(f)(1)(B).

10. Yes. D must pay in cash not the amount of the debt but only the value of the car, measured by its replacement value. Where does she get the cash? Momma is a real possibility.

CHAPTER XI. AVOIDANCE

1. False. These provisions set out the trustee's avoidance powers.

2. No. Section 547(b) deals with transfer of property of the debtor.

3. No. 90 days.

4. Preference period for insiders is one year. P is an insider. P is also a creditor of D; guarantee gives rise to a claim. While the transfer was to C, it was for the benefit of P.

5. Paying on a fully secured claim is not a preference, section 547(b)(5).

6. Paying on a partly secured claim can be a preference unless there is a release of collateral.

7. Yes, the payment was a preference. All of the requirements of section 547(b) are satisfied. The payments cannot be recovered, however, because of section 547(c)(2) and possibly section 547(c)(9).

8. Section 553 governs setoffs. If the trustee is going to challenge a pre-bankruptcy setoff, she must use section 553.

9. There is no preference here. However, the sale can be avoided under section 548, even absent actual intent to defraud, if the sale price was less than reasonably equivalent value and if S was insolvent or rendered insolvent because of the transfer. Whether or not T is an insider is irrelevant because the reach-back period under section 548 is universally two years.

10. At first blush, the likely answer is no because the security interest, i.e., the transfer, was well beyond the 90–day reach-back period of section 547. However, section 547 provides that a transfer in the form of a security interest is deemed to have occurred, for purposes of 547, when the security interest is perfected unless perfection occurs within 30 days of the actual transfer, i.e. actual attachment of the security interest. Section 547(e). So, in this case, the transfer occurred within the 90–day period and is avoidable if all of the other elements of 547(b) are satisfied and if none of the 547(c) exceptions applies.

CHAPTER XII. POSTPETITION TRANSFERS

1. Yes, but * * *. How likely is it that D still has the $10,000? That is why the section 549 rights against T are so important.

2. Yes. The general rule of section 549 is that the trustee can avoid post-bankruptcy transfers. None of the exceptions to this general rule are applicable to this transfer of personal property in a voluntary case.

3. Generally, in Chapter 11 cases, there is not a trustee. Assuming that a trustee was later appointed, she could not avoid this transfer. It was authorized under section 363 of the Bankruptcy Code.

4. Under state law, the issuance of a check does not effect a transfer of funds. The transfer occurs when the check was honored. Since the check was not honored prior to the bankruptcy filing, the funds in the account were property of the estate. Honoring the check was a post-petition transfer. Section 542(c) protects the bank if it did not have notice or knowledge. The trustee can pursue Y, the payee.

5. The trustee *cannot* avoid the transfer. Y is protected by section 549(c).

CHAPTER XIII. EFFECT OF BANKRUPTCY ON SECURED CLAIMS

1. No. Bankruptcy honors the principle of derivative title and, in theory, generally does not substantively affect liens or other interests of third parties. Therefore, liens survive the debtor's bankruptcy and are unaffected with a few exceptions such as: (1) the automatic stay will delay enforcing the liens, and (2) the trustee, under exceptional rules, can sometimes avoid liens.

2. The answer depends on the value of the collateral. The claim is a secured claim to the extent of the value of the collateral, not to exceed the amount of the debt. So, if the collateral is valued at $100,000 or more, C's claim is a fully secured claim. If the collateral is worth less than $100,000, C has a secured claim to the extent of the value of the collateral and an unsecured claim for the balance of the debt.

3. The *Rash* case holds that the test depends on the purpose of the valuation. You look to the disposition or use of the collateral at that point in the bankruptcy case. On the facts of the *Rash* case, the appropriate test was replacement value in light of the use of disposition in that case. Rash is a flexible, general rule that applies universally in every bankruptcy case, except when section 506(a)(2) applies. This section applies in a Chapter 7 or 13 case when the debtor is an individual and the collateral is personal property. In this event, Congress says that collateral is always valued using replacement value.

4. False. Section 506 looks to the value of the property of the debtor that secures the debt. Here the stock is property of a third party.

5. No. Section 542 deals with turnover of property of the estate, i.e., property in which the debtor has an interest. After the foreclosure sale, D has no interest in the property.

6. No. Section 552(a).

7. Yes. Section 522(b).

8. No; yes.

9. False. Property is abandoned to the debtor.

10. True.

CHAPTER XIV. CLAIMS

1. Maybe. If the value of the collateral is less than $100,000, S also has an unsecured claim.

2. No. Discharge.

3. File a claim and participate in the distribution of the estate.

4. Yes. Filing a proof of claim is a condition precedent to participating in the bankruptcy distribution. Filing a proof of claim has no effect on discharge or dischargeability.

5. False. A claim is deemed allowed unless a party in interest objects.

6. Priority claims are paid first from the estate, and a domestic support obligation is the first priority claim that is paid.

7. The loan agreement provides for interest; but interest stops running on unsecured claims as of the time of the bankruptcy filing.

8. The consumer's rights under the warranty comes within the Bankruptcy Code's definition of "claim." The Code provides for estimation of such claims but does not provide for the estimation mechanism.

9. The Chapter 7 bankruptcy only affects pre-petition claims. C is free to proceed against D outside of bankruptcy.

10. False.

CHAPTER XV.   LEASES AND EXECUTORY CONTRACTS

1. True.

2. False. Section 365(d)(1)'s general 60 day rule for Chapter 7 cases does not apply to nonresidential real property leases. Apply section 365(d)(4) instead.

3. False. Rejection creates general, unsecured claim.

4. True.

5. L has rights only against the assignee, T. Assignment relieves debtor and estate from liability for post-assignment breaches, section 365(k).

6. All that is required is court approval. Section 365(b)'s requirements do not apply since D was not in default.

7. Assignment always requires both court approval and satisfaction of the (1) cure, (2) compensate and (3) assure requirements of section 365(b). Contract provisions barring or limiting assignments are ineffective in bankruptcy, section 365(f)(1).

8. True.

9. False. While an intellectual property licensor can not use rejection to deprive licensees of use of licensee, licensor is freed from any obligations in license to update or upgrade. Note the phrase "as such rights existed immediately before the case commenced" in section 365(n)(1)(B).

10. True. Section 365(n)(2)(B), (C)(i).

CHAPTER XVI.   DISCHARGE

1. True.

2. False. Section 727(a)'s eight year ban affects the right to another Chapter 7 discharge, not the filing of another Chapter 7 petition by the debtor or by creditors.

3. False.

4. True (as limited by section 523(c)).

5. There is no special discharge exception for credit card debt, Litigation over the dischargeability of a credit card debt generally arises under section 523(a)(2)(A) and (C).

6. Under 523(a)(2)(C), it would be important to determine the nature of the credit card uses–"luxury goods or services" or "cash advances."

7. False. In the limited circumstances described by section 1141(c)(3), a liquidating plan by a business entity debtor would trigger section 727(a)(1).

8. True. There are grounds for withholding discharge from a Chapter 13 debtor—some of which are similar to objections to discharge—but section 727 does not apply in Chapter 13 cases.

9. True.

10. False.

11. False.

CHAPTER XVII. CHAPTER 13 CASES

1. Yes IF. Apply the definition of "individual with regular income" in section 101 and the debt limits in section 109.

2. True.

3. True.

4. True.

5. True.

6. D can cure the default. If the debt is secured ONLY by D's principal residence, D can not other change her payment obligations without S's agreement.

7. D can again cure the default. Again, D can not strip down the debt. D can, however, change the number of payments, the amount of each payment, and the interest rate (consistent with Till).

8. False.

9. False.

10. No. The co-debtor stay of Chapter 13 applies only to consumer debts.

CHAPTER XVIII. CHAPTER 11 CASES

1. Individuals can file for Chapter 11 but their Chapter 11 cases will, in many respects, be more like Chapter 13 cases than other Chapter 11 cases.

2. False. While the appointment of a trustee precludes the appointment of an examiner, the reverse is not true. At least on law school exams.

3. False.

4. D can continue ordinary course business operations—including selling inventory and paying its employees post-petition wages—without obtaining any approval. Nonordinary course actions require bankruptcy court approval, after notice and a hearing.

5. True.

6. False Adequate protection of an interest in property.

7. 180 days after the date of the bankruptcy petition BUT this time can be reduced by the court or can be increased to as long as 20 months after the date of the bankruptcy petition.

8. True.

9. We don't know. We need to know how many of the 27 Class 3 creditors voted—more than ½ majority is applied only to those voting.

10. F. That phrase appears in 1129(b) which applies only to a cram down.

11. C is limited to recovering from D personally the amount provided in the plan—30% of the $100,000. The balance of the original debt was discharged.

CHAPTER XIX. ALLOCATION OF JUDICIAL POWER OVER BANKRUPTCY MATTERS

1. True.

2. True.

3. True.

4. False.

5. False.

6. True.

7. False.

8. False.

9. False.

10. False.

APPENDIX B

Practice Examination

Three types of questions might appear on a final examination in a debtor-creditor course: (1) pure creditors' rights questions that involve only issues of state law and non-bankruptcy federal law; (2) pure or core bankruptcy questions; and (3) questions combining creditors' rights and bankruptcy issues. Teachers of debtor-creditor law tend to favor the third type because those kinds of questions are efficient testing tools (i.e., can kill two birds with one stone), and also because real-life bankruptcy problems typically involve mixed questions of bankruptcy and non-bankruptcy law. So be on guard: A problem set in bankruptcy may harbor important issues of state and federal creditors' rights law. Another warning: Debtor-creditor teachers especially like bankruptcy problems dealing with the trustee's avoiding powers, and can go absolutely nuts mixing avoiding powers with state creditors' rights law.

Here is a very straightforward, relatively simple, practice final examination which asks 15 questions totaling 100 points. As far as we know, this examination has never been given anywhere; but each of the questions has appeared on final examinations in one or more law schools. (That's right: law teachers share exam questions.) Some of the questions are objective; others are short essay. You should be prepared to explain fully all of your answers, including answers to the objective questions.

This examination, like any real law school final exam, is "comprehensive" only in the sense that it can potentially cover any issue in the course. As will be true of an actual debtor-creditor exam, however, this practice examination tests only a very narrow selection of issues that you will study in class or in reading this Black Letter or other secondary source. Be forewarned that the selection here might not mirror (or even be close) to your teacher's choice of issues on the final exam she prepares especially for you. Good luck!

Instructions: [Most teachers would give you three hours to take the examination, and would allow you to consult the Bankruptcy Code and other relevant federal statutes (such as the federal tax lien law). Some teachers (probably not most of them) would also allow you to consult state statutory law that was covered in the course.]

QUESTION 1

(10 points)

D owes the federal government $40,000 in back taxes; and in January, the IRS made a tax assessment against D.

In February, J obtained a $40,000 judgment against D, and in March docketed this judgment in Travis County.

The IRS filed a tax lien notice there in April.

In May, D bought land worth $50,000 in Travis County.

List the questions that should be considered in determining which lien, the tax lien or J's judgment lien, has priority to the Travis County land.

QUESTION 2

(5 points)

C won a $1.5 million judgment against Ace, Inc., and garnished First Bank where Ace maintained a deposit account containing $500,000. At the time, Ace owed the Bank $400,000. To what extent, if any, is the Bank, as garnishee, accountable to C? Explain you answer, and state any assumptions on which it is based.

QUESTION 3

(5 points)

D owned a townhouse in Hennepin County where she lived most of the time, and a lakeside vacation home in Clever County. J won a judgment against D and docketed it in Clever County. Thereafter, D changed her principal place of residence to Clever County and began living permanently in the vacation home. The townhouse had been destroyed in a bad storm. The loss was covered by insurance, but D decided to invest the insurance proceeds rather than replace the townhouse. Can J get the vacation home, or the insurance proceeds, or both? Explain.

QUESTION 4

(10 points)

A. With the actual intent to defraud her creditors, D sells everything she owns to various innocent buyers who pay substantial value for the property, and then D skips the country with the proceeds. Circle the best answer:

    a.   These sales can be set aside because of D's actual intent to defraud.

    b.   These sales cannot be set aside because they are not fraudulent conveyances.

    c.   These sales cannot be set aside due to the buyers' innocence.

B. D is insolvent. She needs cash. To get cash quickly, she makes a bargain-basement sale of her vacation home to a real estate company which paid less than fair market value for the property but did so in good faith. Circle the best answer:

    a.   The sale cannot be set aside because it is not fraudulent.

    b.   The sale cannot be set aside because the buyer acted in good faith.

    c.   The sale can be set aside as constructively fraudulent.

QUESTION 5

(10 points)

D owns and operates a pool service. D owes C $40,000. C has a timely and properly recorded security interest on D's equipment. D is behind on her payments to C and other creditors because of an illness from which D has now completely recovered. D has indicated to C that she is going to have to file for bankruptcy unless she is able to get some concessions from her creditors. D has proposed that she will make an immediate cash payment of $10,000 to C and will also agree in writing that she will not file a bankruptcy petition for five years if C will make the following concessions:

a. Decrease the amount owed so that after D makes the $10,000 payment she will only owe C $20,000;

b. Increase the time for paying off the note from 24 months to 36 months;

c. Reduce the amount of interest on the note form 12% to prime plus 1;

d. Reduce the amount of each monthly payment on the note to reflect the lower loan balance, lower interest rate and longer payout period.

C believes that it would recover $25,000 from repossessing the equipment. C also believes that it would cost D more than $35,000 to replace the equipment.

What are the bankruptcy law issues that might be relevant to C's decision on whether to accept D's proposal?

QUESTION 6
(5 points)

D, a long-time resident of Texas, was assaulted by T. D sues T in Texas state court. As a result of the assault, D is unable to work. While the suit is pending, D moves to Maine, to be nearer to his children who can help take care of him. Four months after moving to Maine, D files for Chapter 7 bankruptcy and the schedules accompanying D's petition claim the "pending law suit on an assault claim" as exempt property. While D's bankruptcy case is still pending, T wants to settle. With whom should T negotiate and to whom should T make a settlement payment?

QUESTION 7
(5 points)

The Winston–Salem Wildcats, Inc. (W) a professional lacrosse team that owns its own stadium, enters into a contract with Pig Pickens Barbecue (P) to rent its concession stand to P for ten years in exchange for 20% of P's gross receipts from the concession stand. Two years, later, W wants to get out of the contract with P Can W get out of the contract by filing for bankruptcy and not assuming the contract?

QUESTION 8
(10 points)

Dr. D is a dermatologist who privately practices medicine in the downstairs portion of her duplex. She lives upstairs. Because of bad investments, she is presently unable to pay all of her debts. She comes to you for legal advice.

A. If Dr. D files a Chapter 7 petition, why is it likely that her case will be dismissed?

B. If Dr. D files a Chapter 11 petition, will her post-petition earnings be property of the estate?

C. Assume that Dr. D files a Chapter 13 petition on August 18. On August 28, she pays $2,000 to C Medical Supplies, Inc. on a long-standing debt. On September 9, Dr. D converts her Chapter 13 case to a Chapter 7 case. Can the bankruptcy trustee recover the $2,000 from C Medical Supplies, Inc.?

QUESTION 9

(5 points)

X owes D a debt of $70,000 that is fully secured. D owes C $40,000 that is only partly secured. D and X agree that X will pay C the $40,000 that D owes C, and that the amount that X owes D will be reduced by $40,000. X makes the agreed upon $40,000 payment to C. A month later, D files a Chapter 7 petition. Can the bankruptcy trustee recover the $40,000 payment from C?

QUESTION 10

(5 points)

In December, D, a farmer, prepares a deed to 25 acres of her farm, puts the deed in a box which she wraps, and gives the package to S, D's daughter, as a Christmas present. The effect is to render S insolvent. S does not record the deed until the following January. D files a bankruptcy petition 91 days after the deed was recorded. Can D's gift of the land be avoided?

QUESTION 11

(10 points)

A. D and X are both in the chemical business. Each sells chemicals to the other on credit. D has just filed a Chapter 11 petition. Exactly 90 days before D's filing, D owed X $40,000, and X owed D $60,000. Exactly 70 days before D's filing, X paid D the $60,000 debt. Exactly 45 days before D's filing, D paid X the $40,000 debt. What are the effects, if any, of D's bankruptcy on the two payments between D and X?

B. D and X are both in the chemical business. Each sells chemicals to the other on credit. D has just filed a Chapter 7 petition. Exactly 90 days before D's filing, D owed X $40,000, and X owed D $60,000. Exactly 35 days before the filing, X exercised its right of setoff against D under state law and sent D a check for $20,000. What is the effect, if any, of D's bankruptcy?

QUESTION 12

(10 points)

A. D files a Chapter 11 petition on March 3. On March 5, D receives a bill from Dr. C for medical services rendered on February 20. D wants to pay the bill immediately. What are the possible bankruptcy law consequences, if any, of D paying the bill? Of Dr. C hounding D for payment if the bill is not paid?

B. You represent X Store and Bank. D is one of the suppliers for X Store. D has filed a Chapter 11 petition. Advise X Store as to the possible legal risks, if any, in continuing to buy goods from D. Advise Bank on how it can collect the loan made to D that is secured by D's inventory.

QUESTION 13

(5 points)

On January 10, D charged two round-trip, first-class tickets to Europe in March on Delta Airline. The tickets cost $3500, and their price was charged to D's Delta Airline credit card. D received the two tickets and a bill for $3500 payable within 25 days.

On February 2, before D had used the tickets or paid for them, she filed a Chapter 7 petition.

Discuss the significance of concluding that the tickets are executory contracts.

QUESTION 14

(5 points)

D asked Witte's Garage to repair her valuable sports car. Witte fixed it, but D failed to pay the repair charges. D filed Chapter 7. Must Witte surrender D's car to the trustee in bankruptcy? Does the answer depend on whether Witte has an artisan's or other lien on the car? Do the answers to the first and second questions determine whether Witte can sell the car and apply the proceeds in satisfaction of the repair bill?

APPENDIX C

Glossary*

A

Abandonment Conduct of a debtor that results in the loss of the homestead exemption and that usually involves moving away from the place with the present or subsequently formed intention never to occupy it again as a home. Also, a bankruptcy term that describes a trustee's release of property of the estate to the debtor.

Acceptance Vote of creditors in requisite number and amount for a Chapter 11 plan.

Adequate Assurance Standard applied in determining whether a debtor in default on a lease or other executory contract can assume under section 365.

Adequate Protection Phrase used in several sections of the Bankruptcy Code to describe protection afforded to holders of secured claims. More specifically, the lack of adequate protection of the creditor's interest in its collateral is a basis for relief from stay under section 362(d)(1); adequate protection is also the standard for creditor protection from sale or use or encumbrance of the collateral under sections 363 and 364. While adequate protection is not statutorily defined, section 361 sets out examples of adequate protection.

Affidavit A sworn statement of facts or allegations made to or before a person authorized by law to administer oaths.

Alias Writ of Execution A second writ of execution issued to enforce a judgment that was not fully satisfied by the sheriff acting under the first or original writ.

Artisans' Lien A lien that arises by law to secure payment of a person who cares for, repairs, or otherwise enhances the value of goods.

* For more terms and definitions, see the very helpful and reliable list compiled by the Administrative Office of the United States Courts: http://www. uscourts.gov/bankruptcycourts/bankruptcybasics/ glossary.html.

Attachment An extraordinary, prejudgment, statutory remedy which is ancillary to the main suit, has nothing to do with the merits of the action, and is a summary, anticipatory method of impounding defendant's assets to facilitate collection of the judgment against her, if and when a judgment is obtained.

Attachment Lien See Lien of Attachment.

Automatic Stay Bar on collection efforts, judicial and extrajudicial, directed to the debtor or the property of the debtor. The automatic stay becomes effective as soon as the bankruptcy petition is filed.

B

Badge of Fraud A circumstance or other fact accompanying a transfer of property that the courts recognize as an especially reliable indicator of the transferor's actual intention to hinder, delay, or defraud creditors in making the transfer.

Bankrupt No such person under the Bankruptcy Code. "Debtor" is the term used.

Bankruptcy Judge A judicial officer of the district court.

Bulk Sale A transfer out of the ordinary course of a major part of the inventory of the transferor whose business is the sale of goods from stock, which transfer is regulated by Uniform Commercial Code Article 6 so as to protect creditors of the transferor.

C

Cash Surrender Value The amount of money that the owner of an insurance policy can receive from the insurer in lieu of continued insurance coverage.

Choice of Law A contractual provision wherein the parties designate the state whose law will govern disputes arising out of their agreement.

Claim and Delivery See Replevin.

Cognovit A device, usually in the form of a contractual provision, by which a debtor consents in advance to the creditor's obtaining judgment on the debt without giving the debtor notice of the suit to enforce the debt or an opportunity for a hearing on the matter.

Confession of Judgment Often used as a synonym for cognvoit, but also can refer to a debtor's consent to entry of a judgment against her in any kind of proceeding, including a proceeding of which she was notified and in which she had a right to be heard.

Confirmation Judicial approval of a Chapter 11, 12, or 13 plan.

Construction Lien A lien that arises by law and attaches to real estate to secure payment of a person who improved the property through the rendering of labor or other services or the furnishing of materials or other supplies. Another name for this lien is mechanics' lien.

Core Proceeding Undefined term that covers the kind of cases that a bankruptcy judge can decide, absent withdrawal of the reference.

Cram Down Colloquial expression that describes court confirmation of a Chapter 11, 12 or 13 plan, notwithstanding creditor opposition.

Creditor's Bill A judge-made, equitable remedy, known also as a creditors' suit, that is a separate action following judgment against a debtor which is designed to uncover nonexempt assets of the debtor and to apply them in satisfaction of the judgment, including property fraudulently conveyed by the debtor.

Creditors' Committee Representatives of creditors in Chapter 11 cases.

Creditors' Suit See Creditor's Bill.

Current monthly income The average monthly income received by the debtor over the six calendar months before commencement of the bankruptcy case, including regular contributions to household expenses from nondebtors and income from the debtor's spouse if the petition is a joint petition, but not including social security income and certain other payments made because the debtor is the victim of certain crimes. 11 U.S.C.A. § 101(10A).

D

Debtor In bankruptcy law, person who files a voluntary petition or person against whom an involuntary petition is filed; in other words, the "bankrupt."

Debtor-in-Possession Debtor in a Chapter 11 or Chapter 12 case. To illustrate, in a Chapter 11 case either the debtor will remain in control of its business or assets or a trustee will be appointed to take control of the business or assets.

Delivery Bond A guaranteed undertaking by a defendant whose property has been seized through attachment promising that, in exchange for return of the property to her pending resolution of the main action, she will surrender the property or its value in satisfaction of judgment against her. Another name for this bond is "forthcoming bond."

Detinue Another name for replevin, although technically an ancestor of replevin describing in early common law a case in which goods had been delivered under a bailment and the bailee refused to redeliver after proper request.

Discharging Bond Same as a delivery bond except that not only does it permit defendant to regain possession of attached property, it also effects a release of the property from the lien of attachment. Another name for this bond is "dissolution bond."

Disclosure statement A written document prepared by the chapter 11 debtor or other plan proponent designed to provide "adequate information" to creditors to enable them to evaluate the chapter 11 plan of reorganization.

Dissolution Bond See Discharging Bond.

Distress Early common-law process which allowed a creditor to seize property of a debtor and hold the property as security for the debtor's obligation, as a landlord might do when a tenant defaulted in paying rent.

Docket A book or set of records in which a judge or clerk of court notes briefly all the proceedings in a case.

Dormancy Lapse in the executability of a judgment, and also in the effectiveness of the judgment lien, which is cured through revival of the judgment.

E

Elegit A judicial writ, which is no long used, that directed the satisfaction of a judgment through transfer of the debtor's personal property to the creditor at an appraised price, and, if this was insufficient, assignment of the use of one half of the debtor's land to the creditor as tenant by the *elegit* for a term based on an appraisal of its value.

Equitable Right of Setoff Self-help cancellation of cross demands. A remedy that is most often used by banks to unilaterally offset the general deposit accounts of a customer to satisfy matured debts the customer owes the bank.

Exceptions to Discharge Debts not affected by a bankruptcy discharge.

Execution Modern process whereby a state official (usually a sheriff) is directed by way of an appropriate judicial writ to seize and sell so much of the debtor's nonexempt property as is necessary to satisfy a judgment.

Execution Lien See Lien of Execution.

Executory Contracts Undefined term in bankruptcy law describing transactions subject to section 365. In bankruptcy, an executory contract can be assumed or rejected, but not modified.

Exemption or Exempt Property An item of, or interest in, property that is not subject to seizure and sale on process to secure or enforce a judgment against a debtor.

Ex Parte Refers to a proceeding in which a court takes action upon the application of only one side to a controversy without notifying the other side or giving the other side an opportunity to be heard with respect to the action.

F

Fair Consideration A term of fraudulent conveyance law describing whatever is given in exchange for a conveyance of debtor's property whenever the exchange involves property or other things having substantially equivalent values.

Fieri Facias (Fi. Fa.) Judicial writ directing sheriff to satisfy a judgment from the debtor's property; in its original form, the writ directed the seizure and sale of goods and chattels only, but eventually was enlarged to permit levy on real property, too; largely synonymously with modern writ of execution.

Foreign Attachment Refers to the use of the pre-judgment remedy of attachment against the property of a defendant who is not a resident of the jurisdiction where the main action is pending.

Forthcoming Bond See Delivery Bond.

Forum Non Conveniens Doctrine of civil procedure empowering a trial court to decline to exercise judicial jurisdiction if trying the case elsewhere would be more appropriate.

Forum-Selection Clause A contract provision through which the parties set the venue for litigation between them.

Full Faith and Credit Art. IV, '1 of the United State Constitution which mandates that valid civil judgments in one state or territory are entitled to enforcement in any other state or territory.

G

Garnishment A procedure, which sometimes is called "trustee process," for reaching obligations owed to the debtor or property of the debtor in a third party's possession.

Garnishment Lien See Lien of Garnishment.

Garnishee Third-party defendant in a garnishment proceeding who holds property of, or owes an obligation to, a debtor, which property or obligation the debtor's creditor seeks by way of the proceeding to reach and apply in satisfaction of her claim against the debtor.

Garnishor Creditor who initiates garnishment for the purpose of reaching property or credits of a debtor held or owed by a third person who is the garnishee.

Grounds for Attachment Certain extenuating circumstances that must be present before a plaintiff can have a defendant's property seized through the remedy of attachment, which grounds typically include the defendant threatening to remove her property from the jurisdiction or to dispose of her property.

H

Holder of Claim Creditor. If D owes C $300,000 and D files a bankruptcy petition, D will be a debtor and C will be the holder of a claim.

Holder of a Secured Claim Creditor with a lien on property of the debtor or a right of setoff against property of the debtor. The amount of a secured claim is limited by both the debt and the value of the collateral. If D owes C $300,000 and the debt is secured by inventory, the amount of C's secured claim will depend on the value of inventory. If inventory is valued at $200,000, then C's secured claim will only be $200,000. Under these facts, C will also have an unsecured claim for $100,000. A single credit transaction can be the basis for two claims: a secured claim and an unsecured claim.

Holder of an Unsecured Claim A creditor that does not have a lien or right of setoff against the debtor's property or a creditor that has a lien on or right of setoff against property of the debtor that has a value less than the amount of the debt.

Homestead or Homestead Exemption Generally refers to exempt real property which by statute is beyond the reach of creditors because the debtor resides there with a family which depends on her for support.

I

In Custodia Legis In custody of the law, as when a defendant's property is seized through the remedy of attachment and is held by the sheriff pending resolution of the main action between the parties.

In Personam Jurisdiction A type of judicial jurisdiction that supports a judgment binding the persons who are before the court.

In Rem Jurisdiction A type of judicial jurisdiction that supports a judgment determining the interests of all persons in property upon which the court acts.

Involuntary Case Bankruptcy case initiated by creditors' filing a petition.

J

Judicial Jurisdiction That which empowers a court to exercise judicial power and render valid and enforceable judgments.

Judgment Lien An encumbrance that arises by law when a judgment for the recovery of money is docketed and that attaches to the debtor's real estate located in the county where the judgment is docketed.

L

Levy The process whereby a sheriff or other state official empowered by writ or other judicial directive actually seizes, or otherwise brings within her control, a judgment debtor's property which is taken to secure or satisfy the judgment.

Lien of Attachment An encumbrance on property seized through the pre-judgment remedy of attachment that is inchoate when it first arises, usually upon the sheriff's levy of the property, and that becomes final and perfected upon judgment for the attaching creditor in the action who caused attachment to issue. For purposes of priority against third parties' claims to the property, a lien of attachment perfected by judgment dates from the time the lien first arose.

Lien of Execution An encumbrance that attaches by operation of law to a judgment debtor's real and personal property when the property is subjected to execution process and that gives the execution creditor a priority over subsequent transferees of the property and also over prior unrecorded conveyances of interests in the property.

Lien of Garnishment Encumbrance on property of a debtor held by a garnishee that attaches in favor of the garnishing creditor when garnishment summons is served upon the garnishee and that also impounds credits owed by the garnishee to the debtor so that they must be paid to the garnishing creditor.

Lis Pendens A common-law doctrine, now codified in many states so as to condition its effect on the filing of a notice, that binds a purchaser or encumbrancer of property to the results of any pending lawsuit which may affect the title to, any lien on, or possession of the property.

M

Means test Section 707(b)(2) of the Bankruptcy Code applies a "means test" to determine whether an individual debtor's chapter 7 filing is presumed to be an abuse of the Bankruptcy Code requiring dismissal or conversion of the case (generally to chapter 13). Abuse is presumed if the debtor's aggregate current monthly income (see definition above) over 5 years, net of certain statutorily allowed expenses is more than (i) $10,000, or (ii) 25% of the debtor's nonpriority unsecured debt, as long as that amount is at least $6,000. The debtor may rebut a presumption of abuse only by a showing of special circumstances that justify additional expenses or adjustments of current monthly income.

Mechanics' Lien See Construction Lien.

N

No-asset case A chapter 7 case where there are no assets available to satisfy any portion of the creditors' unsecured claims.

Nulla Bona Return A sheriff's return of a writ of execution indicating that she has been unable to find any leviable property of the judgment debtor to seize and sell in satisfaction of the judgment.

O

Objections to Discharge Grounds for withholding a discharge in a Chapter 7 case.

Order of Delivery Writ issued in furtherance of replevin remedy which directs sheriff to seize disputed property from person in possession of it. Other names include Writ of Possession and Writ of Replevin.

P

Pendente Lite During the lawsuit or litigation.

Pluries Writs of Execution Third and subsequent writs of execution issued to enforce a judgment that was not satisfied by the sheriff acting under the original and alias writs of execution.

Preference Except where defined more specifically by statute, a transfer of an insolvent debtor's property for or on account of an antecedent debt so that the preferred creditor receives more in satisfaction of her claim than other creditors with similar claims.

Priority Unsecured claims that by statute receive more favorable treatment in bankruptcy than other unsecured claims. In a Chapter 7 distribution, priority claims must be paid first. In a Chapter 11 plan, priority claims must be paid in full.

Probate Homestead Refers to the rights of a debtor's spouse and minor children to continue to possess and use a homestead after the debtor's death even though they have no interest in the property themselves notwithstanding the claims of heirs or devisees and free from the claims of the debtor's creditors.

Proof of Claim Filing required of creditors in cases under Chapters 7, 12, and 13.

Purchase Money (Encumbrance, Interest, Mortgage) A claim to property securing repayment of value given so as to enable acquisition of property.

Q

Quasi in Rem Jurisdiction A type of judicial jurisdiction that supports a judgment binding the interests of particular persons in property upon which the court acts.

R

Reaffirmation Post-petition agreement to pay pre-petition obligations. Court approval is required.

Receiver A person appointed by a court for the purpose of preserving property of a debtor pending an action against her, or applying the property in satisfaction of a creditor's claim, whenever there is danger that, in the absence of such an appointment, the property will be lost, removed or injured.

Reclaim or Reclamation A seller's very limited right under Uniform Commercial Code Article 2 to retrieve goods delivered to a buyer as when, in a cash transaction, the buyer pays with a worthless check or, in a credit transaction, the buyer is insolvent when she receives the goods.

Redemption The right of a debtor, and sometimes of a debtor's other creditors, to repurchase from a buyer at a forced sale property of the debtor that was seized and sold in satisfaction of a judgment or other claim against the debtor, which right usually is limited to forced sales of real property. Also, a bankruptcy term for extinguishing a lien on exempt property by making a cash payment equal to the value of the property.

Renewal of or Renewing a Judgment A judgment is a form of a debt. If this debt is not paid, the creditor can bring an action on it. This action sometimes is referred to as a renewal of a judgment. Renewal, however, is a new lawsuit, separate from the action that originally produced the judgment; the suit must be commenced before expiration of the statute of limitation governing the enforcement of judgments; and, if the creditor prevails, she obtains a new judgment and a fresh judgment lien. Moreover, the statute of limitation governing the enforcement of judgments begins running anew.

Replevin Refers to a civil action for possession of property wrongfully taken or detained by the defendant; refers also to a provisional remedy that is an incident of a replevin action which allows the plaintiff at any time before judgment to take the disputed property from the defendant and hold the property pendente lite. Other names for replevin include Claim and Delivery, Detinue, Revendication, and Sequestration.

Replevin in Cepit Replevin action in case where defendant has both wrongfully taken and wrongfully detained the property. Compare Replevin in Detinet.

Replevin in Detinet Replevin action in case where defendant rightfully obtained possession of property but wrongfully detains it. Compare Replevin in Cepit.

Return of Execution Writ The report of a sheriff to the court issuing a writ of execution on how successful the sheriff has been in enforcing the writ, which report typically must be made within 60 or 90 days following issuance of the writ.

Revendication The civil law equivalent of Replevin.

Revival of Judgment or Revivor A summary proceeding designed to substantiate and revitalize a dormant judgment. A revivor proceeding ordinarily is thought of as a continuation of the action that produced the judgment and not as a separate action producing its own judgment and judgment lien.

S

Scire Facias A judicial writ directing a debtor to appear and show cause why a dormant judgment against her should not be revived.

Sequestration In the law of creditors' rights, most often refers to an equitable form of attachment, although occasionally used (or misused) to identify a replevin-like process; very broad meaning implies any setting aside of a person's property to answer for the demands of another.

Set Off Refers generally to the right of any person to reduce the amount of her debt to another by any sum the other person owes her and includes the right of a bank to debit a customer's general deposit account in the amount of a debt which the customer owes the bank.

Small business case A special type of chapter 11 case in which there is no creditors' committee (or the creditors' committee is deemed inactive by the court) and in which the debtor is subject to more oversight by the U.S. trustee than other chapter 11 debtors. The Bankruptcy Code contains certain provisions designed to reduce the time a small business debtor is in bankruptcy.

Sovereign Immunity Common-law principle that forbids suit against a government without the government's consent.

Statute of 13 Elizabeth The source of modern fraudulent conveyance law that was enacted by Parliament in 1570 and condemned any conveyance of a debtor's property made with the actual intention to hinder, delay, or defraud the debtor's creditors.

Strip down The process of reducing the amount of a secured claim to the value of its interest in the collateral. For example, D owes F $100,000 and F has a first mortgage on Blackacre which is only worth $40,000. F's secured claim would be stripped down to $40,000. This becomes particularly useful in Chapter 11 cases and Chapter 13 cases which require that the secured claims be paid in full, unless the claim holder agrees to take less.

Strip off The process of reducing the amount of a secured claim to the value of its interest in the collateral where that interest has no value. For example, D owes F $100,00 and S $200,000 F has first mortgage on Blackacre and S has a second mortgage. Blackacre is only worth $40,000.

Summary Jurisdiction Phrase that describes the jurisdiction of bankruptcy courts under the Bankruptcy Act of 1898.

Supplemental or Supplementary Proceedings Post-judgment remedies provided by statute or procedural rules that allow discovery against persons who might have information on the whereabouts of nonexempt assets of the debtor (Supplemental Discovery) and that facilitate application of these assets in satisfaction of the judgment (Supplemental Relief).

T

Trustee Representative of the creditors, generally a private citizen, not an employee of the federal government. There will be a trustee in every Chapter 7, 12, and 13 case and some Chapter 11 cases. Her powers and duties vary from chapter to chapter. The trustee is generally appointed by the United States Trustee. Creditors can elect a trustee to replace an appointed trustee.

Trustee Process See Garnishment.

U

U.C.C. or UCC Uniform Commercial Code.

UFCA Uniform Fraudulent Conveyance Act (1919), which half the states have adopted.

UFTA Uniform Fraudulent Transfer Act (1984), which is the successor to the UFCA.

Underwater lien A lien on property of the debtor that is subordinate to other liens or other claims, and the property's value is equal to or less than the other claims leaving no value to secured the underwater lien. All of the value is absorbed or submerged by the other claims.

United States Trustee Federal government official that preforms appointing and other administrative tasks that a bankruptcy judge would otherwise have to perform. Chapter 15 of the Bankruptcy Code details the duties and powers of the United States Trustee.

V

Voluntary Case Bankruptcy case initiated by a debtor's filing a petition.

W

Writ A command or order from a court directing and empowering a sheriff or other officer to perform some act such as bringing a person before the court or seizing property against which further action may be required.

Writ of Execution Formal, written command of a court directing a sheriff or other state official to enforce a judgment through process of execution.

Writ of Possession See Order of Delivery.

APPENDIX D

Table of Cases

APPENDIX E

Table of Statutes

†